W9-AKE-136

HOW TO PREPARE FOR THE

CIVIL SERVICE EXAMINATIONS

SECOND EDITION

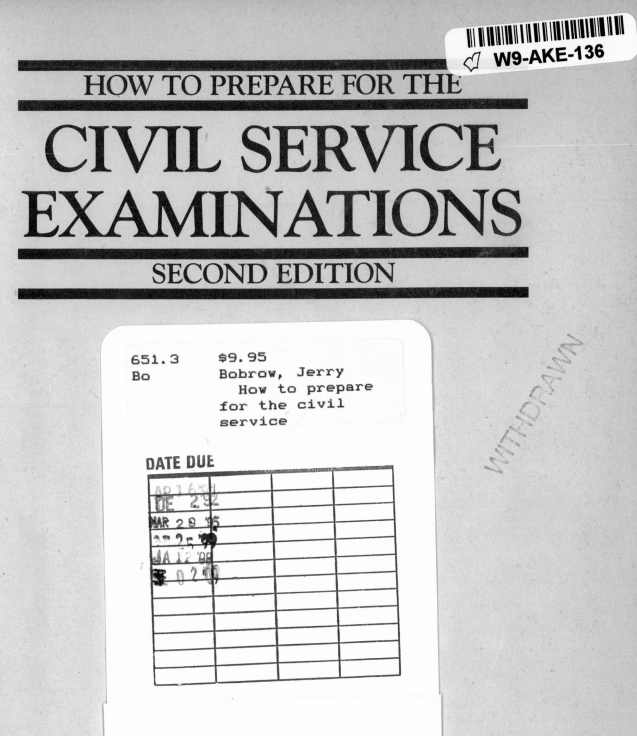

651.3 $9.95
Bo   Bobrow, Jerry
               How to prepare
        for the civil
        service

DATE DUE

AP 16'92			
DE 2'92			
MAR 29 '95			
AP 25'99			
JA 12'00			
FE 02'00			

EAU CLAIRE DISTRICT LIBRARY

DEMCO

Southeastern Book Co   7/5/90 $8.25

WITHDRAWN

HOW TO PREPARE FOR THE

CIVIL SERVICE EXAMINATIONS

SECOND EDITION

FOR
STENOGRAPHER, TYPIST, CLERK, AND
OFFICE MACHINE OPERATOR

BY

Jerry Bobrow, Ph.D.

Executive Director
Bobrow Test Preparation Services
Programs at major universities, colleges, and
law schools throughout California, Arizona, and Colorado
Lecturer, consultant, author of over eighteen nationally known test preparation books

IN COLLABORATION WITH

Peter Z Orton, M.Ed.

Author, lecturer, and developer
of test preparation programs at
universities, colleges, and law schools
Assistant Director
Bobrow Test Preparation Services

William Covino, Ph.D.

Associate Professor, Department of English
Author and Lecturer
University of Illinois at Chicago

BARRON'S EDUCATIONAL SERIES, INC.
New York • London • Toronto • Sydney

73303

© Copyright 1989 by Jerry Bobrow, Ph.D.
Prior edition © Copyright 1986 by Jerry Bobrow, Ph.D.

All rights reserved.
No part of this book may be reproduced
in any form, by photostat, microfilm,
xerography, or any other means, or
incorporated into any information retrieval
system, electronic or mechanical, without the
written permission of the copyright owner.

All inquiries should be addressed to
Barron's Educational Series, Inc.
250 Wireless Boulevard
Hauppauge, New York 11788

Library of Congress Catalog Card No. 88-29224
International Standard Book No. 0-8120-4160-7

Library of Congress Cataloging-in-Publication Data

Bobrow, Jerry.
   Barron's how to prepare for the Civil Service examinations
for stenographer, typist, clerk, and office machine operator /
by Jerry Bobrow, in collaboration with Peter Z Orton,
William Covino.
   p.   cm.
   Rev. ed. of: How to prepare for the Civil Service
examinations for stenographer, typist, clerk, and office
machine operator. c1986.
   ISBN 0-8120-4160-7
   1. Civil service—United States—Examinations.   2. Clerical
ability and aptitude tests.   I. Orton, Peter Z.   II. Covino,
William A.   III. Bobrow, Jerry. How to prepare for the Civil
Service examinations for stenographer, typist, clerk, and
office machine operator.   IV. Barron's Educational Series,
Inc.   V. Title. JK717.C54B63   1989
651.3'741'076—dc19   88-29224
                                                               CIP

PRINTED IN UNITED STATES OF AMERICA

901   100   987654

Contents

Will Studying Help Me?

The most common questions involving exams are "Will studying help me?" and, "If so, how should I study?"

Proper preparation *can* significantly improve your chances of doing your best on an exam. An exam gives you the opportunity to display your skills, knowledge, and ability to apply information. Your chances of doing your best and getting your best possible score will increase tremendously if you take the time to:

1. become aware of the types of questions on the exam;
2. understand the techniques and strategies that will help you on these questions; and
3. practice applying your skills by using the techniques and strategies at home before the exam.

Once you learn what is on your exam, you can focus your study on specific types of material. You can review the basic skills that you need in order to do well on the exam.

But how you study is also important. Make sure that your study time is "quality" study time. This time should be uninterrupted blocks of one to two hours, but usually not more than that. Many study periods of one to two hours are usually much more effective than fewer very long study periods. These study and practice times must be in a quiet, distraction-free setting that will make the study time more effective. This is important, as concentration is a key to good studying.

Make sure to have all the proper materials and supplies with you as you begin to study. It is easy to waste time and break concentration if you have to stop to find proper materials.

An effective study plan will help you review in an organized manner. Take some time to set up a study schedule. Then stick to it. Once you've completed your study regimen, you should go in to take the test with a positive attitude, because you've now prepared and are ready. Going in with this positive attitude will help you apply what you know and will help you to do your best.

Will studying help you? If you study properly, it can give you the opportunity and edge to do your best.

Why should you study? Because these exams are competitive and you want every advantage to do your best.

Acknowledgments

I would like to thank the following people for their contributions to this work:

Dianne Young, M.S., professor of Typing and Office Skills, Santa Monica Community College

Pam Mason, M.A., instructor, Los Angeles Unified School District

Bob Stoneham, M.A., reading/writing specialist, California State University, Northridge

Joy Mondragon, Stacey Plaskoff, Dana Lind—for organization and proofreading

My special thanks for permission to use excerpts from existing works to:

Gregg Publishing Division, McGraw-Hill Book Company, Inc., Student's Transcript of *Gregg Shorthand Simplified for Colleges,* Volume Two, Second Edition, pages 12, 19, 26–27, 34, 81. Authors Louis A. Leslie, Charles E. Zoubek, and Russell J. Hosler. Copyright 1958, for transcription material beginning on page 245.

South-Western Publishing Company, *College Typewriting,* Tenth Edition, pages 310, 312, 313, 315, 345, 368, 370, 371. Authors Wanous, Duncan, Warner, Langford. Copyright 1980, for typing passages beginning on page 224.

And finally, my appreciation to my wife, Susan, and my children, Jennifer Lynn, 10½, Adam Michael, 7½, and Jonathan Matthew, 3½, for their patience and moral support.

This book is designed to serve three purposes:

1. To provide information about the experience and training requirements for a variety of office occupations in the federal government, namely, stenographers, typists, clerks, and office machine operators.

2. To acquaint applicants with the step-by-step approach to getting a federal job and the tests required for these positions.

3. *To prepare applicants to do their best on the civil service exams.* This final purpose is the major emphasis of this book and includes
   —careful analysis of the test question types
   —important test-taking techniques
   —effective strategies for attacking each question type
   —basic skill review
   —extensive sample tests for practice and review

This introductory section (and Appendix B) will discuss How to Get a Federal Government Job, Career Opportunities, and Additional Information About the Civil Service Positions and Tests. The rest of the book focuses squarely on preparing for these important tests.

HOW TO GET A FEDERAL GOVERNMENT JOB

Step 1: Obtain an official Announcement and application form from the Federal Government Personnel Office, whose local address and phone number are listed in your telephone directory.

Step 2: Complete the application form, as instructed by the Announcement. Send it, along with the required fee, to the Office of Personnel Management, whose address should be printed on the application and/or announcement.

Step 3: Become familiar with the test, its required basic skills, and effective test-taking strategies. This information is contained in this book, Barron's *How to Prepare for the Civil Service Examinations,* and includes lots of practice tests to help you improve your basic skills as well as test-taking skills. Spend as much time as necessary for a thorough preparation.

Step 4: Meanwhile, you will receive by return mail an admission blank and instructions for taking a civil service test, if required. The instructions will list the location and time of the test, and the proper materials for you to bring to the exam (such as sharpened #2 pencils, a photo I.D., and more).

Step 5: Become familiar with the location of the test site so that . . .

Step 6: On the day of the exam, you arrive early and prepared to do your best.

Step 7: After your exam, the Office of Personnel Management evaluates your qualifications and places your application in its working files.

Step 8: The Federal Agency requests a list of names from the Office of Personnel Management of the best qualified candidates for its position openings.

Step 9: The Office of Personnel Management refers the best qualified candidates (hopefully *you*!).

Step 10: The Federal Agency interviews candidates and makes selections based upon candidate qualifications and interview.

At this point, you will either be chosen to go to work, or your name will be returned to the Office of Personnel Management for future referrals.

CAREER OPPORTUNITIES

CLERK-TYPIST AND CLERK-STENOGRAPHER

The positions filled from these examinations are paid under the General Schedule (see Appendix), in which there are a number of grades that indicate the difficulty and responsibility of the work and the necessary qualifications requirements. Normal entrance levels* are GS–2 for Clerk-Typist positions and GS–3 for Clerk-Stenographer positions. This difference in grade reflects the greater difficulty of the stenographic work and the additional skill required.

Where there are concentrations of federal employees, the opportunities for well-qualified typists and stenographers are very favorable. The demand for GS–3 Clerk-Stenographers and GS–2 Clerk-Typists continues to be steady. There is also a need for persons with extra qualifications required for GS–4 Clerk-Stenographer and GS–3 Clerk-Typist.

---

*For current entrance salary rates, consult the latest examination announcement or the Salary Supplement if the announcement does not show salaries. These forms are available at Federal Job Information Centers.

There are about 61,100 Clerk-Typist and 8,100 Clerk-Stenographer full-time positions in the federal government.** Vacancies are constantly occurring in these positions as employees are promoted to higher grade positions, transfer to other jobs, or leave for personal reasons. Career development and promotion programs make Clerk-Stenographer and Clerk-Typist positions a good training ground and an avenue of promotion to higher grade positions of these types and to Secretarial positions, of which there are about 91,500. There are also opportunities for promotion to other kinds of positions, such as Administrative Assistant and related occupations.

CLERK

The title "Clerk" covers many specialized fields. While some positions at the GS–2 and 3 levels call for specialized experience or training, most of the specialized work is at the GS–4 and higher levels. In the federal service, clerks have many opportunities to advance to higher-level clerical, supervisory, and administrative positions. Descriptions of some of the major groups of jobs follow.

In *accounting, payroll,* and *fiscal* work, there are about 49,000 clerical and clerical-administrative positions, exclusive of those in professional accounting. Accounts Maintenance Clerks perform accounting clerical work that requires ability to learn and to apply specific instructions, rules, regulations, and procedures, but does not require technical knowledge of bookkeeping or accounting. Other clerks in this area work in the general accounting field; some of these positions provide experience in almost the full range of accounting duties and, when supplemented by appropriate education, help prepare the employee for professional accounting careers. Related large occupational groups include Military Pay Clerks and Leave and Payroll Clerks.

A very important group comprises about 5,500 Voucher Examiners. These jobs begin at the GS–3 level, but most are at higher levels because of the responsible and difficult nature of the work.

A distinct job is Cash Processing Clerk. These clerks handle and watch for irregularities in cash items; they also learn and apply requirements for accepting documents that are the basis for the transactions of commercial, federal, and other financial institutions in processing cash items.

A very large group of clerical positions is in the *general clerical* and *administrative* field. This includes over 23,700 Mail and File Clerks, a much smaller group of Correspondence Clerks, and several thousand other clerical jobs of types too numerous to list here. Grades range from GS–1 through GS–6.

In the *personnel* field, clerks have an opportunity to advance to a variety of administrative and technical positions in support of professional personnel work.

The movement of people and material makes up a large part of the business of the federal government. In particular, the movement of military personnel and supplies and the movement of agricultural and other shipments offer additional opportunities for clerks. These clerical positions are in grades GS–2 through GS–5. Many of the positions provide opportunity for promotion to freight or passenger rate work or other higher-level assignments.

The huge problems of supply for the Department of Defense, Veterans Administration, and other agencies call for close to 39,400 clerks in *general supply, stock control,* and *storekeeping*. Most of these positions are in the two agencies just mentioned, but there are sizable numbers in the Treasury Department and in the General Services Administration, the agency in charge of procurement, supply, and maintenance of property for the federal government.

Finally, the extensive statistical programs of the federal government utilize about 2,300 skilled Statistical Assistants. Their work includes the collection and analysis of data from census and other surveys, crop prediction reports, work measurement studies, and many other functions. While the entry level into these jobs is usually at GS–3, many opportunities for advancement exist, and specialized training courses in statistics and in data processing are available to employees.

OFFICE MACHINE OPERATOR

Approximately 11,900 Data Transcribers operate numeric and alphabetic machines using skills similar to those required in typewriting. There is a considerably smaller number of Electric Accounting

---

**The federal government also hires many part-time and temporary workers.

Machine Operators, who operate a variety of tabulating equipment. In these groups most employees are at the GS–2, GS–3, and GS–4 levels.

These jobs provide an opportunity to work with and learn various data processing systems. With additional specialized training or experience, employees are able to prepare for careers in computer system operations, programming, and planning.

There are several thousand other Office Machine Operators, whose duties include the operation of one or more types of office imprinting (including embossing), duplicating, or reproducing machines, or the operation of miscellaneous office machines or equipment. Most of these positions are at the GS–2 level.

Bookkeeping Machine Operator and Calculating Machine Operator positions require special skills and training. Most of the positions in this group are GS–2 and GS–3.

THE TESTS

The tests required for the positions just described include

1. dictation
2. typing
3. verbal abilities
4. clerical skills

There are also some special tests for certain Office Machine Operator positions, including a simplified typing test for Teletypists and other operators of machines with alphabetic keyboards, and a test of abstract reasoning for Electric Accounting Machine Operators (Tabulating Machine Operators) and Cryptographic Equipment Operators.

With the diagnostic and model tests included in this book, candidates can determine if they have sufficient ability to meet the standards of the federal government, or if they need to build their skills, and, if so, to what degree. These tests can also help candidates in identifying their shortcomings while there is time to focus their training accordingly. Applicants can thus diagnose areas needing improvement and then practice to strengthen their weak areas.

ADDITIONAL INFORMATION ABOUT THESE CIVIL SERVICE POSITIONS AND TESTS

The following paragraphs summarize current information concerning office positions, including stenographer and typist positions. (For the sake of brevity, in this book positions are often referred to as stenographer and typist positions rather than by the official titles of Clerk-Stenographer and Clerk-Typist.)

SALARIES AND OTHER BENEFITS

Appointments to stenographer positions are usually made at GS–3 and GS–4.* For the latter grade, 1 year of appropriate experience or education above the high school level is required. Appointments to typist, dictating machine transcriber, clerk, and office machine operator positions are usually made at GS–2 and GS–3. Appointments are also made at GS–4 to specialized clerk positions. Always consult your local announcement for current salary rates.

Group life insurance is available at a cost to the employee of 27½ cents biweekly per thousand dollars of insurance; government pays the rest of the cost. The amount of insurance is $10,000 or the amount of the employee's salary (rounded to the next higher $1,000) plus $2,000, whichever is larger.

Group health insurance, partly paid for by the government as an employer, is also available. This voluntary program offers an employee a chance to join a group health benefits plan, with better rates and better protection than could be secured by an individual.

Paydays occur every 2 weeks. Deductions for federal income tax, as well as for retirement purposes, are withheld from the paycheck. Periodic increases of $250 to $425 a year, depending upon grade level, are provided for competent employees under salary schedules in effect in January 1985. Increases are at yearly intervals for the first 3 years of service in the grade, then at 2-year intervals for the next 6 years of service, and then at 3-year intervals until the maximum salary for that grade is reached. How-

---

*At the present time, a test is required for Clerk-Stenographer at the GS–4 level and for Secretary. For more information on the Secretary position, see "Occupational Duty Sheet, Secretary" in the Appendix.

ever, a promotion to higher levels, from an entry level grade, would raise an employee's salary by an amount equal to at least two periodic increases. Thus, a grade-level promotion from GS–2 would give at least $950 a year more in salary.

Vacation benefits range from 13 working days a year to 20 days a year for employees with from 3 to 15 years of service, and 26 days a year for those with more than 15 years of service.

All employees, regardless of length of service, earn 13 days of sick leave with pay each year. There is no restriction on the accumulation of unused sick leave.

TEST AND EXPERIENCE REQUIREMENTS

Tables 1 and 2 indicate the tests that are to be taken and the education and experience requirement for the positions.

Final numerical rating in the examination as a whole is based on the written tests of verbal and clerical abilities. Typing and dictation tests are qualifying only and are not added into the final rating. Higher scores are generally required for the higher grades.

Table 1
Clerk, Typist, and Stenographer

	Tests				Education/Experience**
	Verbal	Clerical	Typing*	Stenography*	
Clerk GS–2	Yes	Yes	No	No	High school graduate or 6 months of appropriate experience.
Typist GS–2	Yes	Yes	Yes	No	
Stenographer GS–3	Yes	Yes	Yes	Yes	
Clerk GS–3	Yes	Yes	No	No	1 year of appropriate experience or 1 academic year of post–high school education.
Typist GS–3	Yes	Yes	Yes	No	
Stenographer GS–4	Yes	Yes	Yes	Yes	

*An acceptable proficiency certificate can be substituted for these tests—see section "Proficiency Certificates."
**The appropriate experience for clerk is progressively responsible clerical or office work. Appropriate experience for typist and stenographer is either (1) experience that included, as a significant part of the work, application of the required skill (i.e., typing, dictating machine transcribing, or stenography); or (2) any type of clerical work that demonstrates the ability to perform the duties of the position to be filled, *provided* that the applicant demonstrates an adequate degree of proficiency in the required skill(s).

Table 2
Office Machine Operator

	Tests	Education/Experience*
GS–2	Verbal and clerical tests for all applicants. For additional tests for certain positions, see section "The Office Machine Operator Special Tests," page 245.	a) 6 months specialized experience, or b) specialized course of instruction in operation of appropriate machine and 3 months of experience, or c) successful completion of a federally financed course of instruction (e.g., Work Incentive Program, Job Corps, Comprehensive Employment Training Act Program, etc.) of appropriate content, intensity, and duration, or d) high school graduation. Education must have included training in operation of appropriate machine, unless a performance test is available for the particular occupation.
GS–3		a) 1 year of office-type experience of which at least 6 months is specialized, or b) 1 academic year of post–high school education, which included training in the operation of appropriate machine, unless a performance test is available for the particular occupation.

*Different requirements may be in effect in some localities. If so, these different requirements will be stated in the examination announcements for those localities.

PROFICIENCY CERTIFICATES

Arrangements have been made with many schools and other authorized training organizations to accept from the applicants a teacher's certificate of proficiency in typing and shorthand. Submission of such a certificate will excuse the applicant from taking the typing and/or shorthand tests. The certificate must be on the official form furnished by the Office of Personnel Management (OPM). On this form, a teacher may certify that the student has demonstrated proficiency in typing and/or shorthand on unfamiliar and continuous material at a standard at least high enough to meet the OPM's requirements. Certificates are valid for only a limited period and are usually issued only to those persons who are still in school. Applicants with satisfactory certificates will still have to take the verbal and clerical abilities tests. If you have any questions concerning the use of proficiency certificates, contact the area office of the U.S. Office of Personnel Management servicing your area.

PHYSICALLY HANDICAPPED APPLICANTS

Although applicants for federal employment must be able to perform the duties of a position, this does not prevent physically handicapped persons from being hired. Physically handicapped persons are encouraged to apply for positions in the federal government. Each area office of the Office of Personnel Management has a Selective Placement Specialist who is responsible for assuring that all handicapped applicants are able to take advantage of the available employment opportunities for which they apply. Federal agencies also have coordinators for Selective Placement to assist in job placements. In addition to regular competitive placements, severely handicapped persons may be able to secure excepted appointment in some positions.

Most clerical, typing, stenographer, and office machine operator jobs require good distant vision in one eye and the ability to read, without strain, material the size of typewritten characters. Glasses may be used. However, blind typists can fill many positions, such as dictating machine transcribers. Blind applicants should state on their application cards that they are blind, since special arrangements must be made for their examination.

Ability to hear the conversational voice is required for most positions; however, some positions are suitable for deaf applicants.

EQUIPMENT NEEDED FOR TESTS

In some localities, competitors taking the typing test must furnish a typewriter and a typing table for use in the examination. Applicants who wish to use an electric typewriter should ask the examining office, in advance of the examination date, whether there is an electric outlet in the examining room.

Stenographer applicants may use any system of taking and transcribing dictation provided it does not interfere with the dictation or with other competitors. Any system of manually written shorthand notes or any noiseless shorthand writing machine may be used provided the notes are given to the examiner after they have been transcribed. Blind persons may be required to furnish a transcribing machine for use in the examining room.

HOW AND WHERE TO APPLY

Civil Service examinations for typists and stenographers are usually announced together and given at the same time. Examinations for Clerk and for various types of Office Machine Operator, such as Data Transcriber, may be announced separately. However, some or all of these examinations may be combined in a single Office Assistant examination. There may also be some training positions in these occupations. Check with your local U.S. Office of Personnel Management for details on positions, locations, and grade levels for which the examination is being held, and specific instructions on how to apply. Applicants are usually provided with samples of the tests to be given in the examination.

Full information about applying for these and other federal jobs is provided by Federal Job Information Centers throughout the country. These offices are usually listed in local telephone directories under "U.S. Government." If there are none listed in your directory dial 800-555-1212 to obtain the toll free number for your state.

COMPLETION OF ANSWER SHEET

Most test answer sheets are machine scored. Therefore, it is very important that they be filled out properly. Most tests allow only one answer for each question; if there is more than one answer, the scoring machine is programmed to score the answer as incorrect. Therefore, an applicant must be careful to erase an answer completely if he or she changes it.

Great care must be taken to insure that his or her name and Social Security account number is recorded properly.

PART ONE

The Verbal Abilities Test

CHAPTER 1

General Strategies
A Diagnostic Test
with Answer Explanations
Analysis of Strengths and Weaknesses

THE VERBAL ABILITIES TEST

The Verbal Abilities Test includes questions that measure such language skills as knowledge of the meaning and relationship of words, ability to spell common words, and skill in recognizing sentences that are grammatically correct in contrast to others that are not acceptable. The test also includes questions that measure the ability to read and understand written material. There are 85 questions on the test, *with a time limit of 25 minutes.**

Word meaning	25 questions
Analogy	20 questions
Grammar	10 questions
Spelling	20 questions
Reading	10 questions

The question types are "scrambled" throughout the test; that is, you will have 5 word meaning, then 4 analogy, then 2 grammar, then 4 spelling, then 2 reading questions. This series will repeat four more times for a total of 85 questions. Each question has equal value toward your final score. Your score on the Verbal Abilities Test is the number of questions you answer correctly. There is no penalty for an incorrect answer.

PROCEDURE

You will have 3 minutes to study the directions and sample questions on the front of your test booklet and to mark the answers to these sample questions in the space provided. You will then be told when to begin the actual test, for which you will have 35 minutes.

GENERAL STRATEGIES

Since there is a limited amount of time (35 minutes) to answer 85 questions, some very important considerations regarding speed, marking, eliminating choices, and guessing come into play. We recommend you become familiar with the following strategies:

Marking in the Test Booklet

Many test takers don't take full advantage of opportunities to mark key words and cross out wrong choices *in the test booklet*. Remember that writing in your test booklet (as explained later) can significantly help you stay focused, as well as help you isolate the correct answer choices. It will also enable you to successfully use the following strategy.

The One-Check, Two-Check System

Many people score lower than they should on the Verbal Abilities Test simply because they do not get to many of the easier problems. They puzzle over difficult questions and use up the time that could be spent answering easy ones. In fact, the difficult questions are worth exactly the same as the easy ones, so it makes sense not to do the hard problems until you have answered all the easy ones.

To maximize your correct answers by focusing on the easier problems, use the following system:

1. Attempt the first question. If it is answerable quickly and easily, work the problem, circle the answer in the question booklet, and then

---

*The U.S. Office of Personnel Management currently plans to drop the analogies portion of this test in late 1986. When this is done, the number of questions in the other sections will be increased to retain an 85-question test.

mark that answer on the answer sheet. The mark on the answer sheet should be a complete mark, not merely a dot, because you may not be given time at the end of the test to darken marks.

2. If a question seems impossible, place two checks (✔✔) on or next to the question number in the question booklet and mark the answer you guess on the answer sheet. (*There is no penalty for a wrong guess.*) The mark on the answer sheet should be a complete mark, not merely a dot, because you may not be given time at the end of the test to darken marks.

3. If you're in the midst of a question that seems to be taking too much time, or if you immediately spot that a question is answerable but time-consuming (that is, it will require a minute or more to answer), place one check (✔) next to the question number, mark an answer you guess on the answer sheet, and continue with the next question.

NOTE THAT NO QUESTIONS ARE LEFT BLANK. AN ANSWER CHOICE IS *ALWAYS* FILLED IN BEFORE LEAVING THAT QUESTION, SINCE THERE IS NO PENALTY FOR GUESSING.

4. When all the problems in a section have been attempted in this manner, there may still be time left. If so, return to the single-check (✔) questions, working as many as possible, changing each guessed answer to a worked-out answer, if necessary.

5. If time remains after all the single-check (✔) questions are completed, you can choose between
   a. attempting those "impossible" double-check (✔✔) questions (sometimes a question later on in the test may trigger your memory to allow once-impossible questions to be solved);
                        or
   b. spending time checking and reworking the easier questions to eliminate any careless errors.

6. You should try to use *all* the allotted time as effectively as possible.

Use this system as you work through the Verbal Ability diagnostic and model tests in this book; such practice will allow you to make "one-check, two-check" judgments quickly when you actually take your exam. As our extensive research has shown, use of this system results in less wasted time.

The Elimination Strategy

Faced with four or five answer choices, you will work more efficiently and effectively if you immediately *eliminate* unreasonable or obviously wrong choices. In many cases, several of the choices will immediately appear to be incorrect, and these should be crossed out *on your test booklet* immediately. Then, if a guess is necessary among the remaining choices, you will not reconsider these obvious wrong choices, but will choose from the remaining choices.

Consider the following reading question:

> According to the theory of aerodynamics, the bumblebee is unable to fly. This is because the size, weight, and shape of his body in relationship to his total wingspan make flying impossible. The bumblebee, being ignorant of this "scientific truth," flies anyway.

> *The paragraph best supports the statement that* bumblebees
> A) cannot fly in strong winds
> B) are ignorant of other things but can't do all of them
> C) do not actually fly but glide instead
> D) may contradict the theory of aerodynamics

Test takers who do not immediately eliminate the unreasonable choices here, and instead try to analyze every choice, will find themselves becoming confused and anxious as they try to decide how even unreasonable choices might be correct. Their thinking might go something like this:

> "Hmmmm, I've never seen a bumblebee in a strong wind. I'm not sure what (B) means. I wonder if bumblebees do glide;
> I've never looked at them *that* closely. Hmmmm, (D) could be right, but what about the other three? I had better look at them again in case I missed something."

On and on they go, sometimes rereading choices three or four times. In a test of this nature—only 35 minutes allotted for 85 questions—they cannot afford to spend so much time on one question!

Using the elimination strategy, a confident test taker proceeds as follows:

> "A)? Ridiculous and irrelevant. Cross it out.
> B)? I don't understand this. Put a question mark after it.
> C)? That sounds ridiculous. Cross it out.
> D)? That's possible. In fact, that's a much better choice than (B), which I'm not sure I even understand. The answer I'll mark is (D)."

This test taker, aware that most answer choices can be easily eliminated, does so without complicating the process by considering unreasonable possibilities.

To summarize this strategy:

—Look for incorrect answer choices. Cross them out in the test booklet.
—Put question marks after choices that chould be possible.
—Never reconsider choices you have eliminated.

Eliminating incorrect choices will lead you to correct choices more quickly and will increase your chances when you make a guess.

Guessing

As previously mentioned, there is no penalty for an incorrect answer, even if it is a guess. So *never* leave a blank on the Verbal Abilities Test. (This rule does not apply to the other tests, however.)

Whenever you are faced with a difficult, seemingly impossible, or time-consuming question, never leave it until you have *at least registered a guess on the answer sheet.*

Changing Answers and Stray Marks

If you find it necessary to change an answer on your answer sheet, make sure to erase the incorrect answer *completely*. Any partial marks in the answer spaces may be picked up by the scoring machine as a "second answer choice marked" on one question, and that question will be marked incorrect. Therefore take great care to erase completely and not to make stray marks on your answer sheet.

A DIAGNOSTIC TEST WITH ANSWER EXPLANATIONS

The purpose of this diagnostic test is to familiarize you with the Verbal Abilities Test. It is designed to introduce you to the testing areas and to assist you in evaluating your strengths and weaknesses. This will help you focus your review. Chapter 2 will give you a more complete range of problem types and specific strategies for each section. After correcting the diagnostic test and assessing your strengths and weaknesses, you should start your area reviews and practice in the next chapter.

The diagnostic test should be taken under strict test conditions.

First take 3 minutes to review the sample questions given here before starting the exam. (NOTE: Sample questions are usually distributed with the announcement and if so may not be given in the official examination.) Now tear out your answer sheet from this book, turn to the next page, and begin the exam.

REVIEWING THE KEY STRATEGIES

Remember to:

1. Answer easy questions first.

2. Skip "impossible" questions, marking them with the double check (✔✔).

3. Skip "time-consuming" questions, marking them with the single check (✔), coming back to these later, if possible.

4. Answer every question. Fill in a guess, if necessary.

5. Use *all* the allotted time.

ANSWER SHEET

SIGNATURE: _____
(Please Sign)

EXAMINATION TITLE: _____

PLACE OF EXAMINATION: _____
City _____ State _____

TODAY'S DATE: _____

SAMPLE Ⓐ ● Ⓒ Ⓓ Ⓔ

DIRECTIONS FOR MARKING ANSWER SHEET

Use only a **No. 2 (or softer) lead pencil.** Darken completely the circle corresponding to your answer. You **must** keep your mark within the circle. Stray marks may be counted as errors. Erase **completely** all marks except your answer.

1. In the boxes below, **PRINT** your name. Print only as many letters as will fit within the areas for the last name, first initial (F.I.), and middle initial (M.I.) Below each box, darken the circle containing the same letter. SEE SAMPLE NAME GRID

SAMPLE NAME GRID

LAST NAME | F.I. | M.I.

M C C A B E | C | A

2. In the boxes below, enter your 9-digit Social Security Number. Below each box, darken the circle in each column corresponding to the number you have entered.

SOCIAL SECURITY NUMBER

3. OCCUPATIONAL GROUP NUMBER

LAST NAME | F.I. | M.I.

SECTION 1

PART

TEST SERIES

TEST NUMBER

Make no marks or entries in the columns to the right until you receive instructions from the administrator.

1 Ⓐ Ⓑ Ⓒ Ⓓ Ⓔ	11 Ⓐ Ⓑ Ⓒ Ⓓ Ⓔ	31 Ⓐ Ⓑ Ⓒ Ⓓ Ⓔ	51 Ⓐ Ⓑ Ⓒ Ⓓ Ⓔ	71 Ⓐ Ⓑ Ⓒ Ⓓ Ⓔ	91 Ⓐ Ⓑ Ⓒ Ⓓ Ⓔ 111 Ⓐ Ⓑ Ⓒ Ⓓ Ⓔ
2 Ⓐ Ⓑ Ⓒ Ⓓ Ⓔ	12 Ⓐ Ⓑ Ⓒ Ⓓ Ⓔ	32 Ⓐ Ⓑ Ⓒ Ⓓ Ⓔ	52 Ⓐ Ⓑ Ⓒ Ⓓ Ⓔ	72 Ⓐ Ⓑ Ⓒ Ⓓ Ⓔ	92 Ⓐ Ⓑ Ⓒ Ⓓ Ⓔ 112 Ⓐ Ⓑ Ⓒ Ⓓ Ⓔ
3 Ⓐ Ⓑ Ⓒ Ⓓ Ⓔ	13 Ⓐ Ⓑ Ⓒ Ⓓ Ⓔ	33 Ⓐ Ⓑ Ⓒ Ⓓ Ⓔ	53 Ⓐ Ⓑ Ⓒ Ⓓ Ⓔ	73 Ⓐ Ⓑ Ⓒ Ⓓ Ⓔ	93 Ⓐ Ⓑ Ⓒ Ⓓ Ⓔ 113 Ⓐ Ⓑ Ⓒ Ⓓ Ⓔ
4 Ⓐ Ⓑ Ⓒ Ⓓ Ⓔ	14 Ⓐ Ⓑ Ⓒ Ⓓ Ⓔ	34 Ⓐ Ⓑ Ⓒ Ⓓ Ⓔ	54 Ⓐ Ⓑ Ⓒ Ⓓ Ⓔ	74 Ⓐ Ⓑ Ⓒ Ⓓ Ⓔ	94 Ⓐ Ⓑ Ⓒ Ⓓ Ⓔ 114 Ⓐ Ⓑ Ⓒ Ⓓ Ⓔ
5 Ⓐ Ⓑ Ⓒ Ⓓ Ⓔ	15 Ⓐ Ⓑ Ⓒ Ⓓ Ⓔ	35 Ⓐ Ⓑ Ⓒ Ⓓ Ⓔ	55 Ⓐ Ⓑ Ⓒ Ⓓ Ⓔ	75 Ⓐ Ⓑ Ⓒ Ⓓ Ⓔ	95 Ⓐ Ⓑ Ⓒ Ⓓ Ⓔ 115 Ⓐ Ⓑ Ⓒ Ⓓ Ⓔ
6 Ⓐ Ⓑ Ⓒ Ⓓ Ⓔ	16 Ⓐ Ⓑ Ⓒ Ⓓ Ⓔ	36 Ⓐ Ⓑ Ⓒ Ⓓ Ⓔ	56 Ⓐ Ⓑ Ⓒ Ⓓ Ⓔ	76 Ⓐ Ⓑ Ⓒ Ⓓ Ⓔ	96 Ⓐ Ⓑ Ⓒ Ⓓ Ⓔ 116 Ⓐ Ⓑ Ⓒ Ⓓ Ⓔ
7 Ⓐ Ⓑ Ⓒ Ⓓ Ⓔ	17 Ⓐ Ⓑ Ⓒ Ⓓ Ⓔ	37 Ⓐ Ⓑ Ⓒ Ⓓ Ⓔ	57 Ⓐ Ⓑ Ⓒ Ⓓ Ⓔ	77 Ⓐ Ⓑ Ⓒ Ⓓ Ⓔ	97 Ⓐ Ⓑ Ⓒ Ⓓ Ⓔ 117 Ⓐ Ⓑ Ⓒ Ⓓ Ⓔ
8 Ⓐ Ⓑ Ⓒ Ⓓ Ⓔ	18 Ⓐ Ⓑ Ⓒ Ⓓ Ⓔ	38 Ⓐ Ⓑ Ⓒ Ⓓ Ⓔ	58 Ⓐ Ⓑ Ⓒ Ⓓ Ⓔ	78 Ⓐ Ⓑ Ⓒ Ⓓ Ⓔ	98 Ⓐ Ⓑ Ⓒ Ⓓ Ⓔ 118 Ⓐ Ⓑ Ⓒ Ⓓ Ⓔ
9 Ⓐ Ⓑ Ⓒ Ⓓ Ⓔ	19 Ⓐ Ⓑ Ⓒ Ⓓ Ⓔ	39 Ⓐ Ⓑ Ⓒ Ⓓ Ⓔ	59 Ⓐ Ⓑ Ⓒ Ⓓ Ⓔ	79 Ⓐ Ⓑ Ⓒ Ⓓ Ⓔ	99 Ⓐ Ⓑ Ⓒ Ⓓ Ⓔ 119 Ⓐ Ⓑ Ⓒ Ⓓ Ⓔ
10 Ⓐ Ⓑ Ⓒ Ⓓ Ⓔ	20 Ⓐ Ⓑ Ⓒ Ⓓ Ⓔ	40 Ⓐ Ⓑ Ⓒ Ⓓ Ⓔ	60 Ⓐ Ⓑ Ⓒ Ⓓ Ⓔ	80 Ⓐ Ⓑ Ⓒ Ⓓ Ⓔ	100 Ⓐ Ⓑ Ⓒ Ⓓ Ⓔ 120 Ⓐ Ⓑ Ⓒ Ⓓ Ⓔ
21 Ⓐ Ⓑ Ⓒ Ⓓ Ⓔ	41 Ⓐ Ⓑ Ⓒ Ⓓ Ⓔ	61 Ⓐ Ⓑ Ⓒ Ⓓ Ⓔ	81 Ⓐ Ⓑ Ⓒ Ⓓ Ⓔ	101 Ⓐ Ⓑ Ⓒ Ⓓ Ⓔ	121 Ⓐ Ⓑ Ⓒ Ⓓ Ⓔ
22 Ⓐ Ⓑ Ⓒ Ⓓ Ⓔ	42 Ⓐ Ⓑ Ⓒ Ⓓ Ⓔ	62 Ⓐ Ⓑ Ⓒ Ⓓ Ⓔ	82 Ⓐ Ⓑ Ⓒ Ⓓ Ⓔ	102 Ⓐ Ⓑ Ⓒ Ⓓ Ⓔ	122 Ⓐ Ⓑ Ⓒ Ⓓ Ⓔ
23 Ⓐ Ⓑ Ⓒ Ⓓ Ⓔ	43 Ⓐ Ⓑ Ⓒ Ⓓ Ⓔ	63 Ⓐ Ⓑ Ⓒ Ⓓ Ⓔ	83 Ⓐ Ⓑ Ⓒ Ⓓ Ⓔ	103 Ⓐ Ⓑ Ⓒ Ⓓ Ⓔ	123 Ⓐ Ⓑ Ⓒ Ⓓ Ⓔ
24 Ⓐ Ⓑ Ⓒ Ⓓ Ⓔ	44 Ⓐ Ⓑ Ⓒ Ⓓ Ⓔ	64 Ⓐ Ⓑ Ⓒ Ⓓ Ⓔ	84 Ⓐ Ⓑ Ⓒ Ⓓ Ⓔ	104 Ⓐ Ⓑ Ⓒ Ⓓ Ⓔ	124 Ⓐ Ⓑ Ⓒ Ⓓ Ⓔ
25 Ⓐ Ⓑ Ⓒ Ⓓ Ⓔ	45 Ⓐ Ⓑ Ⓒ Ⓓ Ⓔ	65 Ⓐ Ⓑ Ⓒ Ⓓ Ⓔ	85 Ⓐ Ⓑ Ⓒ Ⓓ Ⓔ	105 Ⓐ Ⓑ Ⓒ Ⓓ Ⓔ	125 Ⓐ Ⓑ Ⓒ Ⓓ Ⓔ
26 Ⓐ Ⓑ Ⓒ Ⓓ Ⓔ	46 Ⓐ Ⓑ Ⓒ Ⓓ Ⓔ	66 Ⓐ Ⓑ Ⓒ Ⓓ Ⓔ	86 Ⓐ Ⓑ Ⓒ Ⓓ Ⓔ	106 Ⓐ Ⓑ Ⓒ Ⓓ Ⓔ	126 Ⓐ Ⓑ Ⓒ Ⓓ Ⓔ
27 Ⓐ Ⓑ Ⓒ Ⓓ Ⓔ	47 Ⓐ Ⓑ Ⓒ Ⓓ Ⓔ	67 Ⓐ Ⓑ Ⓒ Ⓓ Ⓔ	87 Ⓐ Ⓑ Ⓒ Ⓓ Ⓔ	107 Ⓐ Ⓑ Ⓒ Ⓓ Ⓔ	127 Ⓐ Ⓑ Ⓒ Ⓓ Ⓔ
28 Ⓐ Ⓑ Ⓒ Ⓓ Ⓔ	48 Ⓐ Ⓑ Ⓒ Ⓓ Ⓔ	68 Ⓐ Ⓑ Ⓒ Ⓓ Ⓔ	88 Ⓐ Ⓑ Ⓒ Ⓓ Ⓔ	108 Ⓐ Ⓑ Ⓒ Ⓓ Ⓔ	128 Ⓐ Ⓑ Ⓒ Ⓓ Ⓔ
29 Ⓐ Ⓑ Ⓒ Ⓓ Ⓔ	49 Ⓐ Ⓑ Ⓒ Ⓓ Ⓔ	69 Ⓐ Ⓑ Ⓒ Ⓓ Ⓔ	89 Ⓐ Ⓑ Ⓒ Ⓓ Ⓔ	109 Ⓐ Ⓑ Ⓒ Ⓓ Ⓔ	129 Ⓐ Ⓑ Ⓒ Ⓓ Ⓔ
30 Ⓐ Ⓑ Ⓒ Ⓓ Ⓔ	50 Ⓐ Ⓑ Ⓒ Ⓓ Ⓔ	70 Ⓐ Ⓑ Ⓒ Ⓓ Ⓔ	90 Ⓐ Ⓑ Ⓒ Ⓓ Ⓔ	110 Ⓐ Ⓑ Ⓒ Ⓓ Ⓔ	130 Ⓐ Ⓑ Ⓒ Ⓓ Ⓔ

VERBAL ABILITIES DIAGNOSTIC TEST

Time allotted—35 minutes

Directions and Sample Questions

Study the sample questions carefully. Each question has four suggested answers. Decide which one is the best answer. Find the question number on the Sample Answer Sheet. Show your answer to the question by darkening completely the space corresponding to the letter that is the same as the letter of your answer. Keep your mark within the space. If you have to erase a mark, be sure to erase it completely. Mark only one answer for each question. Do NOT mark space E for any question.

Sample Questions

I. *Previous* means most nearly
   A) abandoned   C) timely
   B) former   D) younger

II. Just as the procedure of a collection department must be clear cut and definite, the steps being taken with the sureness of a skilled chess player, so the various paragraphs of a collection letter must show clear organization, giving evidence of a mind that, from the beginning, has had a specific end in view.

   The paragraph best supports the statement that a collection letter should always
   A) show a spirit of sportsmanship
   B) be divided into several paragraphs
   C) be brief, but courteous
   D) be carefully planned

Decide which sentence is preferable with respect to grammar and usage suitable for a formal letter or report.

III. A) They do not ordinarily present these kind of reports in detail like this.
    B) A report of this kind is not hardly ever given in such detail as this one.
    C) This report is more detailed than what such reports ordinarily are.
    D) A report of this kind is not ordinarily presented in as mush detail as this one is.

Find the correct spelling of the word and darken the proper answer space. If no suggested spelling is correct, darken space D.

V. A) athalete   C) athlete
   B) athelete   D) none of these

V. SPEEDOMETER is related to POINTER as WATCH is related to
   A) case   C) dial
   B) hands   D) numerals

Answer Explanations for Sample Questions

I.   **(B)** *Previous* means came before, or *former*.
II. **(D)** "A specific end in view" indicates a careful plan in mind.
III. **(D)** In (A), "these kind" is incorrect; it should be "this kind." In (B), "not hardly ever" is incorrect; it should be "hardly ever." In (C), "than what such reports" is incorrect; the "what" should be deleted.
IV. **(C)** The correct spelling is *athlete*.
V.   **(B)** The second word is the "indicator" on the first word.

THE TEST

Read each question carefully. Select the best answer and darken the proper space on the answer sheet.

Word Meaning

1. *Flexible* means most nearly
   - A) breakable
   - B) flammable
   - C) pliable
   - D) weak

2. *Option* means most nearly
   - A) use
   - B) choice
   - C) value
   - D) blame

3. To *verify* means most nearly to
   - A) examine
   - B) explain
   - C) confirm
   - D) guarantee

4. *Indolent* means most nearly
   - A) moderate
   - B) hopeless
   - C) selfish
   - D) lazy

5. *Respiration* means most nearly
   - A) recovery
   - B) breathing
   - C) pulsation
   - D) sweating

Analogies

6. PLUMBER is related to WRENCH as PAINTER is related to
   - A) brush
   - B) pipe
   - C) shop
   - D) hammer

7. LETTER is related to MESSAGE as PACKAGE is related to
   - A) sender
   - B) merchandise
   - C) insurance
   - D) business

8. FOOD is related to HUNGER as SLEEP is related to
   - A) night
   - B) dream
   - C) weariness
   - D) rest

9. KEY is related to TYPEWRITER as DIAL is related to
   - A) sun
   - B) number
   - C) circle
   - D) telephone

Grammar

10. A) I think that they will promote whoever has the best record.
    B) The firm would have liked to have promoted all employees with good records.
    C) Such of them that have the best records have excellent prospects of promotion.
    D) I feel sure they will give the promotion to whomever has the best record.

11. A) The receptionist must answer courteously the questions of all them callers.
    B) The receptionist must answer courteously the questions what are asked by the callers.
    C) There would have been no trouble if the receptionist had have always answered courteously.
    D) The receptionist should answer courteously the questions of all callers.

Spelling

12. A) collapsible
    B) collapseable
    C) collapseble
    D) none of these

13. A) ambigeuous
    B) ambigeous
    C) ambiguous
    D) none of these

14. A) predesessor
    B) predecesar
    C) predecesser
    D) none of these

15. A) sanctioned
    B) sancktioned
    C) sanctionned
    D) none of these

Reading

16. The secretarial profession is a very old one and has increased in importance with the passage of time. In modern times, the vast expansion of business and industry has greatly increased the need and opportunities for secretaries, and for the first time in history their number has become large.

    The paragraph best supports the statement that the secretarial profession
    - A) is older than business and industry
    - B) did not exist in ancient times
    - C) has greatly increased in size
    - D) demands higher training than it did formerly

17. Civilization started to move ahead more rapidly when people freed themselves of the shackles that restricted their search for the truth.

The paragraph best supports the statement that the progress of civilization
- A) came as a result of people's dislike for obstacles
- B) did not begin until restrictions on learning were removed
- C) has been aided by people's efforts to find the truth
- D) is based on continually increasing efforts

18. *Vigilant* means most nearly
- A) sensible
- B) watchful
- C) suspicious
- D) restless

19. *Incidental* means most nearly
- A) independent
- B) needless
- C) infrequent
- D) casual

20. *Conciliatory* means most nearly
- A) pacific
- B) contentious
- C) obligatory
- D) offensive

21. *Altercation* means most nearly
- A) defeat
- B) concurrence
- C) controversy
- D) vexation

22. *Irresolute* means most nearly
- A) wavering
- B) insubordinate
- C) impudent
- D) unobservant

23. DARKNESS is related to SUNLIGHT as STILL-NESS is related to
- A) quiet
- B) moonlight
- C) sound
- D) dark

24. DESIGNED is related to INTENTION as ACCI-DENTAL is related to
- A) purpose
- B) caution
- C) damage
- D) chance

25. ERROR is related to PRACTICE as SOUND is related to
- A) deafness
- B) noise
- C) muffler
- D) horn

26. RESEARCH is related to FINDINGS as TRAIN-ING is related to
- A) skill
- B) tests
- C) supervision
- D) teaching

27. A) If properly addressed, the letter will reach my mother and I.
- B) The letter had been addressed to myself and my mother.
- C) I believe the letter was addressed to either my mother or I.
- D) My mother's name, as well as mine, was on the letter.

28. A) The supervisors reprimanded the typists, whom she believed had made careless errors.
- B) The typists would have corrected the errors had they of known that the supervisor would see the report
- C) The errors in the typed reports were so numerous that they could hardly be overlooked.
- D) Many errors were found in the reports which they typed and could not disregard them.

29. A) minieture
- B) minneature
- C) mineature
- D) none of these

30. A) extemporaneous
- B) extempuraneus
- C) extemperaneous
- D) none of these

31. A) problemmatical
- B) problematical
- C) problematicle
- D) none of these

32. A) descendant
- B) decendant
- C) desendant
- D) none of these

33. The likelihood of America's exhausting her natural resources seems to be growing less. All kinds of waste are being reworked and new uses are constantly being found for almost everything. We are getting more use out of our goods and are making many new byproducts out of what was formerly thrown away.

The paragraph best supports the statement that we seem to be in less danger of exhausting our resources because
- A) economy is found to lie in the use of substitutes
- B) more service is obtained from a given amount of material
- C) we are allowing time for nature to restore them
- D) supply and demand are better controlled

34. Telegrams should be clear, concise, and brief. Omit all unnecessary words. The parts of speech most often used in telegrams are nouns, verbs, adjectives, and adverbs. If possible, do without pronouns, prepositions, articles, and

copulative verbs. Use simple sentences rather than complex or compound ones.

The paragraph best supports the statement that in writing telegrams one should always use
A) common and simple words
B) only nouns, verbs, adjectives, and adverbs
C) incomplete sentences
D) only the words essential to the meaning

35. To *counteract* means most nearly to
A) undermine   C) preserve
B) censure   D) neutralize

36. *Deferred* means most nearly
A) reversed   C) considered
B) delayed   D) forbidden

37. *Feasible* means most nearly
A) capable   C) practicable
B) justifiable   D) beneficial

38. To *encounter* means most nearly to
A) meet   C) overcome
B) recall   D) retreat

39. *Innate* means most nearly
A) eternal   C) native
B) well-developed   D) prospective

40. STUDENT is related to TEACHER as DISCIPLE is related to
A) follower   C) principal
B) master   D) pupil

41. LECTURE is related to AUDITORIUM as EXPERIMENT is related to
A) scientist   C) laboratory
B) chemistry   D) discovery

42. BODY is related to FOOD as ENGINE is related to
A) wheels   C) motion
B) fuel   D) smoke

43. SCHOOL is related to EDUCATION as THEATER is related to
A) management   C) recreation
B) stage   D) preparation

44. A) Most all these statements have been supported by persons who are reliable and can be depended upon.
B) The persons which have guaranteed these statements are reliable.

C) Reliable persons guarantee the facts with regards to the truth of these statements
D) These statements can be depended on, for their truth has been guaranteed by reliable persons.

45. A) The success of the book pleased both the publisher and authors.
B) Both the publisher and they was pleased with the success of the book.
C) Neither they or their publisher was disappointed with the success of the book.
D) Their publisher was as pleased as they with the success of the book.

46. A) extercate   C) extricate
B) extracate   D) none of these

47. A) hereditory   C) hereditairy
B) hereditary   D) none of these

48. A) auspiceous   C) auspicious
B) auspiseous   D) none of these

49. A) sequance   C) sequense
B) sequence   D) none of these

50. The prevention of accidents makes it necessary not only that safety devices be used to guard exposed machinery but also that mechanics be instructed in safety rules which they must follow for their own protection, and that the lighting in the plant be adequate.

The paragraph best supports the statement that industrial accidents
A) may be due to ignorance
B) are always avoidable
C) usually result from inadequate machinery
D) cannot be entirely overcome

51. The English language is peculiarly rich in synonyms, and there is scarcely a language spoken that has not some representative in English speech. The spirit of the Anglo-Saxon race has subjugated these various elements to one idiom, making not a patchwork, but a composite language.

The paragraph best supports the statement that the English language
A) has few idiomatic expressions
B) is difficult to translate
C) is used universally
D) has absorbed words from other languages

52. To *acquiesce* means most nearly to
    A) assent   C) complete
    B) acquire   D) participate

53. *Unanimity* means most nearly
    A) emphasis   C) harmony
    B) namelessness   D) impartiality

54. *Precedent* means most nearly
    A) example   C) law
    B) theory   D) conformity

55. *Versatile* means most nearly
    A) broad-minded   C) up-to-date
    B) well-known   D) many-sided

56. *Authentic* means most nearly
    A) detailed   C) valuable
    B) reliable   D) practical

57. BIOGRAPHY is related to FACT as NOVEL is related to
    A) fiction   C) narration
    B) literature   D) book

58. COPY is related to CARBON PAPER as MOTION PICTURE is related to
    A) theater   C) duplicate
    B) film   D) television

59. EFFICIENCY is related to REWARD as CARELESSNESS is related to
    A) improvement   C) reprimand
    B) disobedience   D) repetition

60. ABUNDANT is related to CHEAP as SCARCE is related to
    A) ample   C) inexpensive
    B) costly   D) unobtainable

61. A) Brown's & Company employees have recently received increases in salary.
    B) Brown & Company recently increased the salaries of all its employees.
    C) Recently Brown & Company has increased their employees' salaries.
    D) Brown & Company have recently increased the salaries of all its employees.

62. A) In reviewing the typists' work reports, the job analyst found records of unusual typing speeds.
    B) It says in the job analyst's report that some employees type with great speed.
    C) The job analyst found that, in reviewing the typists' work reports, that some unusual typing speeds had been made.
    D) In the reports of typists' speeds, the job analyst found some records that are kind of unusual.

63. A) oblitorate   C) obbliterate
    B) oblitterat   D) none of these

64. A) diagnoesis   C) diagnosis
    B) diagnossis   D) none of these

65. A) contenance   C) countinance
    B) countenance   D) none of these

66. A) conceivably   C) conceiveably
    B) concieveably   D) none of these

67. Through advertising, manufacturers exercise a high degree of control over consumers' desires. However, the manufacturer assumes enormous risks in attempting to predict what consumers will want and in producing goods in quantity and distributing them in advance of final selection by the consumers.

    The paragraph best supports the statement that manufacturers
    A) can eliminate the risk of overproduction by advertising
    B) distribute goods directly to the consumers
    C) must depend upon the final consumers for the success of their undertakings
    D) can predict with great accuracy the success of any product they put on the market

68. In the relations of humans to nature, the procuring of food and shelter is fundamental. With the migration of humans to various climates, ever new adjustments to the food supply and to the climate became necessary.

    The paragraph best supports the statement that the means by which humans supply their material needs are
    A) accidental
    B) varied
    C) limited
    D) inadequate

69. *Strident* means most nearly
    A) swaggering   C) angry
    B) domineering   D) harsh

70. To *confine* means most nearly to
    A) hide   C) eliminate
    B) restrict   D) punish

71. To *accentuate* means most nearly to
    A) modify   C) sustain
    B) hasten   D) intensify

72. *Banal* means most nearly
    A) commonplace   C) tranquil
    B) forceful   D) indifferent

73. *Incorrigible* means most nearly
    A) intolerable   C) irreformable
    B) retarded   D) brazen

74. POLICEMAN is related to ORDER as DOCTOR is related to
    A) physician   C) sickness
    B) hospital   D) health

75. ARTIST is related to EASEL as WEAVER is related to
    A) loom   C) threads
    B) cloth   D) spinner

76. CROWD is related to PERSONS as FLEET is related to
    A) expedition   C) navy
    B) officers   D) ships

77. CALENDAR is related to DATE as MAP is related to
    A) geography   C) mileage
    B) trip   D) vacation

78. A) Since the report lacked the needed information, it was of no use to them.
    B) This report was useless to them because there were no needed information in it.
    C) Since the report did not contain the needed information, it was not real useful to them.
    D) Being that the report lacked the needed information, they could not use it.

79. A) The company had hardly declared the dividend till the notices were prepared for mailing.
    B) They had no sooner declared the dividend when they sent the notices to the stockholders.

C) No sooner had the dividend been declared than the notices were prepared for mailing.
D) Scarcely had the dividend been declared than the notices were sent out.

80. A) compitition   C) competetion
    B) competition   D) none of these

81. A) occassion   C) ocassion
    B) occasion   D) none of these

82. A) knowlege   C) knowledge
    B) knolledge   D) none of these

83. A) deliborate   C) delibrate
    B) deliberate   D) none of these

84. What constitutes skill in any line of work is not always easy to determine; economy of time must be carefully distinguished from economy of energy, as the quickest method may require the greatest expenditure of muscular effort, and may not be essential or at all desirable.

The paragraph best supports the statement that
A) the most efficiently executed task is not always the one done in the shortest time
B) energy and time cannot both be conserved in performing a single task
C) a task is well done when it is performed in the shortest time
D) skill in performing a task should not be acquired at the expense of time

85. It is difficult to distinguish between bookkeeping and accounting. In attempts to do so, bookkeeping is called the art, and accounting the science, of recording business transactions. Bookkeeping gives the history of the business in a systematic manner; and accounting classifies, analyzes, and interprets the facts thus recorded.

The paragraph best supports the statement that
A) accounting is less systematic than bookkeeping
B) accounting and bookkeeping are closely related
C) bookkeeping and accounting cannot be distinguished from one another
D) bookkeeping has been superseded by accounting

ANSWER KEY

Word Meaning

1. C	18. B	35. D	52. A	69. D
2. B	19. D	36. B	53. C	70. B
3. C	20. A	37. C	54. A	71. D
4. D	21. C	38. A	55. D	72. A
5. B	22. A	39. C	56. B	73. C

Analogies

6. A	23. C	40. B	57. A	74. D
7. B	24. D	41. C	58. B	75. A
8. C	25. C	42. B	59. C	76. D
9. D	26. A	43. C	60. B	77. C

Grammar

10. A	27. D	44. D	61. B	78. A
11. D	28. C	45. D	62. A	79. C

Spelling

12. A	29. D	46. C	63. D	80. B
13. C	30. A	47. B	64. C	81. B
14. D	31. B	48. C	65. B	82. C
15. A	32. A	49. B	66. A	83. B

Reading

16. C	33. B	50. A	67. C	84. A
17. C	34. D	51. D	68. B	85. B

ANALYSIS CHART

Now that you've corrected your exam, use the following chart to analyze your results and spot your strengths and weaknesses. This analysis should help you focus your study and review efforts.

Section	Total Number of Questions	Number Correct	Number Incorrect	Number Unanswered*
Word Meaning	25			
Analogies	20			
Grammar	10			
Spelling	20			
Reading Comprehension	10			
TOTAL	85			

*Since there is no penalty for incorrect answers on the Verbal Abilities Test, you should have left no question unanswered. Even if you didn't have time to answer a question, at least you should have filled in the answer space with a guess.

ANSWER EXPLANATIONS

1. (C) *Flexible* means bendable, or *pliable*. *Flex* means bend.
2. (B) *Option* means selection or alternative, or *choice*.
3. (C) *To verify* means to prove, or to *confirm*.
4. (D) *Indolent* means not inclined to work, or *lazy*.
5. (B) *Respiration* means inhaling and exhaling, or *breathing*.
6. (A) The second word is a tool of the first word.
7. (B) The second word is sent or delivered in the first word.
8. (C) The first word eliminates the second word.
9. (D) The first word is the operative mechanism on the second word.
10. (A) In (B), the verb tenses should be "would like to have promoted." "Such of them" in (C) is incorrect. (D) should read: "whoever has the best record."
11. (D) In (A), "all them callers" is incorrect; it should be "all callers." In (B), "what are asked" is incorrect; it should be "asked." In (C), "had have" should be "had."
12. (A) collapsible
13. (C) ambiguous
14. (D) Correct spelling: predecessor.
15. (A) sanctioned
16. (C) "Their number has become large" indicates that the number of secretaries has greatly increased in size.
17. (C) "When people freed themselves of the shackles that restricted their search for the truth," civilization moved ahead. This indicates that civilization's progress was aided by people's efforts to find the truth.
18. (B) *Vigilant* means on guard, or *watchful*. Note the root word, *vigil*.
19. (D) *Incidental* means of minor event or circumstance, or *casual*.
20. (A) *Conciliatory* means to bring together or make peaceful. *Pacific* is the best synonym. Note the root word, *pacify*.
21. (C) *Altercation* is a quarrel, or *controversy*.
22. (A) *Resolute* means firm; *irresolute* means *wavering*.
23. (C) The first word is the absence of the second word.
24. (D) *Designed* means *by intention*. *Accidental* means *by chance*. The first word occurs through the action of the second word.

25. (C) The second word eliminates or lessens the first word.
26. (A) The second word is the intended result of the first word.
27. (D) In (A), (B), and (C), the phrase should be "my mother and me."
28. (C) In (A), "Whom" should be "who." In (B), "of known" is incorrect; it should be simply "known." In (D), "they" is vague, and "and could not disregard them" is awkward.
29. (D) Correct spelling: miniature
30. (A) extemporaneous
31. (B) problematical
32. (A) descendant
33. (B) "Getting more use out of our goods" indicates that more service is obtained from a given amount of material.
34. (D) "Concise" and "brief" indicate that, in telegrams, one should use only words essential to the meaning.
35. (D) To *counteract* means to check the effects of an action, or to *neutralize*. Note the prefix, *counter*, meaning against, and the root word, *act*.
36. (B) *Deferred* means put off, or *delayed*.
37. (C) *Feasible* means possible, able to be done, or *practicable*.
38. (A) To *encounter* means to come in contact with, or to *meet*.
39. (C) *Innate* means inborn, or *native*.
40. (B) The first word learns from the second word.
41. (C) The first word takes place in the second word.
42. (B) The first word consumes the second word for energy.
43. (C) The first word is a place for the purpose of the second word.
44. (D) In (A), "reliable and can be depended upon" is repetitious. In (B), "which" should be "who." In (C), "the facts with regards to the truth" is repetitious and awkward.
45. (D) In (A), "both" indicates two people, whereas "publisher and authors" must mean a minimum of three people. In (B), "was" should be "were," among other errors. (C) should be "Neither they *nor* . . ."
46. (C) extricate
47. (B) hereditary
48. (C) auspicious
49. (B) sequence
50. (A) The necessity that "mechanics be instructed in safety rules" indicates that accidents may be due to ignorance.

51. (D) "There is scarcely a language spoken that has not some representative in English speech" indicates that the English language has absorbed words from other languages.
52. (A) To *acquiesce* means to give in, or to *assent*.
53. (C) *Unanimity* means total agreement, or *harmony*. Notice the root, *unanimous*.
54. (A) *Precedent* means a standard, or *example*.
55. (D) *Versatile* means multiskilled, or *many-sided*.
56. (B) *Authentic* means worthy of trust or reliance, or *reliable*.
57. (A) The first word is a book using the second word.
58. (B) The first word is made by means of the second word.
59. (C) The first word results in the second word.
60. (B) The second word is the price of the first word.
61. (B) In (A), the *'s* should be on *Company*, not *Brown*. In (C), "has" and "their" must agree; the correct form is "its employees." In (D), "have" should be "has" to agree with "its."
62. (A) The error in (B) is the vague use of "it." The error in (C) is awkward sentence structure, not as direct or clear as it could be. The error in (D) is the informal phrase "kind of" unusual.
63. (D) Correct spelling: obliterate
64. (C) diagnosis
65. (B) countenance
66. (A) conceivably
67. (C) That "the manufacturer assumes enormous risks in attempting to predict what consumers will want" indicates that manufacturers must depend upon the final consumers for the success of their undertakings.
68. (B) "*New adjustments* to the food supply and to the climate" indicates that the means by which humans supply their material needs are varied.
69. (D) *Strident* means grating, or *harsh*.
70. (B) To *confine* means to keep within bounds, or to *restrict*.
71. (D) To *accentuate* means to increase, or to *intensify*.
72. (A) *Banal* means worn-out and predictable, or *commonplace*.
73. (C) *Incorrigible* means uncorrectable, or *irreformable*.
74. (D) The first word is the person who restores the second word.

75. (A) The second word is a tool of the first word.

76. (D) The first word is a collection or group of the second word.

77. (C) The second word is a unit comprising the first word.

78. (A) The main error in (B) is "were"; it should be "was." The main error in (C) is "real useful"; it should be "really useful," or simply "useful." The main error in (D) is a nonstandard phrase, "being that"; it should be "because."

79. (C) Each of the incorrect choices here is unclear about the relationship between declaring the dividend and sending the notices.

80. (B) competition

81. (B) occasion

82. (C) knowledge

83. (B) deliberate

84. (A) That "economy of time must be carefully distinguished from economy of energy" indicates that the most efficiently executed task is not always the one done in the shortest time.

85. (B) "It is difficult to distinguish between bookkeeping and accounting," as they are closely related.

CHAPTER 2

Understanding the Sections
Key Strategies
Practice, Practice, Practice

WORD MEANING

This question type tests your vocabulary. You are given words and must decide which choice means the same or most nearly the same as the given word. For example:

To *terminate* means most nearly
A) schedule   C) finish
B) begin   D) disallow

Since to *terminate* means to *cease* or to *put an end to*, the best choice is (C) *finish*.

HELPFUL TECHNIQUES AND STRATEGIES

1. Choose the most nearly correct word from among the choices given. Sometimes the best choice may not be perfect or convey exactly the same meaning you would use yourself, but if it is the *best* of the choices, it is the correct answer.
2. Work as quickly as you can. Scan the possible answers and decide immediately on the correct one. Take time out to study each individual choice only if the words are unfamiliar or especially difficult for you.
3. Although the words used should not be technical or obscure, they may be long and/or dif-ficult. Break these words up into prefixes, suffixes, and roots to help in understanding the meaning. Item 6 contains a list of prefixes, suffixes, and roots.
4. If possible, use the given word in a short, clear sentence. This may help give you a context to work from and increase your understanding of the word's meaning. Then substitute the choices into your sentence to see if the sentence retains the same meaning.
5. Many words carry a strong connotation. If, for example, a word sounds "positive" or "good," then choose a word that has a positive connotation. If a word sounds "negative" or "bad," then your choice should reflect this negative connotation. Sometimes you may not know the exact meaning of a certain word, but it will just sound "positive" or "negative" to you. Trust your instincts and select the answer choice that reflects this connotation. Example:

Noxious means most nearly
A) clean   C) famous
B) luminous   D) poisonous

Since *noxious* has a strong negative connotation, you can eliminate all choices except (D) *poisonous*, which also is negative, and is the correct answer.

6. Review the list that follows.

SOME COMMON PREFIXES, SUFFIXES, AND ROOTS

Prefix	Meaning	Examples
ad-	to; at; near	*adhere* stick to
anti-	in opposition; against	*antislavery* against slavery
auto-	self; by self; of one's self	*automatic* self-acting
bene-	good; well	*benevolence* disposed to do good
bi-	two; twice; double	*bisect* cut into two equal parts
circum-	around; all around	*circumnavigate* sail around (the globe)
co-		*cooperate* perform together
com-; con-	with; together; altogether	*combine* merge with *connect* join together
contra-	against; contrary	*contradict* assert the contrary of
de-	down; from; away	*descend* travel down
dia-	through; between; across	*diagonal* across a figure
dis-	not; apart	*disapprove* not approve
ex-	out of; out; from	*expel* drive out
extra-	beyond; without	*extraordinary* beyond the ordinary
fer-	wild; untamed	*ferocity* wildness
fore-	beforehand; in front	*foresee* see beforehand
geo-	earth	*geography* the study of the earth and its inhabitants
hemi-	half	*hemisphere* one-half a sphere or globe
hyper-	too much; beyond; over	*hypersensitive* oversensitive
hypo-	beneath; too little	*hypodermic* beneath the skin
inter-	between; among	*interfere* enter between or among others
intro-	within; in; into	*introduce* bring or lead in
mal-, male-	bad; ill; badly	*malfunction* function badly
mis-	wrongly; badly	*misinformed* badly informed
mon-, mono-	single; having only one	*monomania* obsessed by one idea
non-	not	*nonprofessional* not belonging to a profession
omni-	all; everywhere	*omnipotent* all-powerful
per-	through; throughout; thoroughly	*perforate* pierce through
poly-	many	*polygamy* having many husbands or wives at one time
post-	after; behind	*postnatal* after birth
pre-	before; prior to	*preview* see beforehand
pro-	before; forth; forward	*produce* bring forth
re-	back; again	*recall* call back
sal-	health	*salutory* healthful
semi-	half	*semicircle* half circle
sub-	under; beneath; inferior	*subordinate* inferior in rank
super-	above; greater; more than	*superhuman* greater than human
trans-	across; through; beyond	*transport* carry across
un-	not	*uncommon* not common

Suffix	Meaning	Examples
-able	able to; capable of being	*lovable* capable of being loved
-acity	character; quality	*veracity* the quality of truth
-ence, -ance	a state of being	*abundance* the state of being abundant
-ful	full of	*grateful* full of gratitude
-fy	to make	*beautify* to make beautiful
-ion, -sion, -tion	the act or condition of	*reaction* the act of reacting
-ism	belief in; practice of; condition of	*activism* the practice of being actively involved
-less	free from; without	*penniless* without mercy
-logy	doctrine or science; the study of	*geology* the study of the earth
-ness	state of being	*emptiness* state of being empty
-some	abounding in; full of	*troublesome* full of trouble
-wise	in the manner of; in the direction of	*lengthwise* in the direction of length

Root	Meaning	Examples
acr	sharp; bitter	*acrimonious* bitter
ag, act	to do; to act	*agent* doer *retroactive* having a reverse action
agog	leader	*demagogue* false leader
agri, agrari	fields	*agrarian* farmer; one who works on fields
ali	another	*alias* another name
alt	high	*altitude* height
anim	mind; soul	*unanimous* of one mind
ann	year	*annuity* yearly payment *biennial* every two years
arch	ruler, government	*anarchy* no government
aqua	water	*aquatic* living in water
aud	to hear	*audible* can be heard
belli	war	*belligerent* carrying on war or aggression
ben, bene	good; well	*benefactor* one who does good
biblio	book	*bibliography* list of books
bio	life	*biography* story of a person's life
breve	short	*brevity* briefness; shortness
cap	head; to take	*captain* chief; headwaiter *capture* seize; to take captive
cede, cess	to go; to yield	*precede* to go before *concession* the act of yielding
chron, chrono	time	*chronicle* a register of events arranged in order of time *chronology* the time order of events

Root	Meaning	Examples
cid, cis	to kill; to cut	*homicide* killing of a person by another *incision* a cut
civi	citizen	*civil* relating to citizens
clos, clud	to close; to shut	*enclose* to close in *exclude* to shut out
dic, dict	to say; to speak	*diction* speech
domin	to rule	*dominate* to rule or have power over
duc	to lead	*induce* to lead or bring on
ego	I; self	*egocentric* self-centered
gam	marriage	*bigamy* marriage to two people at once
gen, gener	class; race; kind	*general* applying to a whole class or race
geo	earth	*geochemistry* the chemical study of the earth
greg	flock; herd; group	*gregarious* grouping together
jac, jact, ject	to throw	*projectile* something thrown forward
labor, laborat	to work	*laboratory* workplace
liber	book; free	*library* collection of books *liberty* freedom
man, mani, manu	hand	*manufacture* create; make by hand
mar	sea	*submarine* under the sea
mit, miss	to send	*transmit* send across *dismiss* to send away
mov, mot, mob	to move	*remove* to move away *emotion* "moving" feelings *mobile* movable
nav	ship	*navigate* sail a ship
pac	peace	*pacific* peaceful
port, portat	carry	*portable* able to be carried
put, putat	to calculate; to cut	*compute* to calculate *amputate* to cut off
quer, quisit	to ask	*query* to ask a question *inquisitive* questioning
quies	quiet	*acquiesce* to agree quietly, without protest
radi	ray	*irradiate* to shine light on
rap, rapt	to seize	*rapine* the act of seizing others' property by force *rapture* the state of being seized or carried away by emotion
rid, ris	to laugh	*deride* to laugh at scornfully *risible* capable of laughing
rog, rogate	to ask	*interrogate* to ask questions of
rupt	break	*rupture* a break
sag	wisdom	*sage* a wise person *sagacity* wisdom
sat, satis	enough	*satiate* to provide with enough or more than enough *satisfy* to meet the need of
schis, schiz	to cut; to split	*schism* a split or division *schizophrenia* a mental disorder characterized by separation of the thoughts and emotions

Root	Meaning	Examples
sci	to know	*science*　knowledge
scop	to watch; to view	*telescope*　an instrument for viewing things from a distance
scrib, script	to write	*prescribe*　to write a medical prescription *transcript*　a written copy
sec, sect	to cut	*section*　to cut into parts *bisect*　to cut in two
sed, sess, sid	to sit	*sedentary*　doing much sitting *session*　a meeting *preside*　to sit in position of authority
sent, sens	to feel; to perceive	*resent*　to feel annoyance *sensible*　perceiving through the senses
sequ, secu, secut	to follow	*sequel*　that which follows *consecutive*　one following another
solv, solut	to loosen; to solve	*absolve*　to free (loosen) from guilt *solution*　act of solving a problem
soph	wise; wisdom	*sophisticate*　a wordly-wise person
spec, spect, spic	to watch; to look; to appear	*spectator*　observer *inspect*　to look over *perspicacious*　having sharp judgment
spir, spirit	to breathe	*expire*　to exhale; to die *spirit*　life
sta, stat	to stand	*stable*　steady *stationary*　fixed; unmoving
stru, struct	to build	*construe*　to explain or deduce the meaning *structure*　a building
suas, suad	to urge; to advise	*persuasive*　having the power to cause something to change *dissuade*　to advise someone against something
sum, sumpt	to take	*assume*　to take on *resumption*　taking up again
tact, tang	to touch	*tactile*　perceptible through touch *intangible*　unable to be touched
tempor	time	*contemporary*　at the same time
ten, tent, tain	to hold	*tenure*　holding of office *retentive*　capable of holding *retain*　to hold onto
tend, tens	to stretch	*extend*　to stretch out or draw out *tense*　to stretch tight
terr	land; earth	*terrestrial*　pertaining to the earth
the, theo	god	*atheist*　one who believes there is no God *theocracy*　rule by God or by persons claiming to represent Him
thermo	heat	*thermal*　relating to heat
tract	to draw	*attract*　to draw
trud, trus	to thrust; to push	*protrude*　to stick out *intrusive*　pushing into or upon something
tum, tumid	to swell	*tumor*　a swelling *tumify*　to cause to swell
un, uni	one	*unanimous*　of one opinion *uniform*　of one form

Root	Meaning	Examples
urb	city	*suburban* outside the city
ut, util	to use; useful	*utility* the quality of being useful
vac	empty	*vacuum* empty space
ven, vent	to come	*intervene* come between *advent* an arrival
ver	true	*verify* to prove to be true
verb	words	*verbalize* using words *verbatim* word for word
verd	green	*verdant* green
vert, vers	to turn	*avert* to turn away
vi, via	way	*deviate* to turn from the prescribed way *via* by way of
vid, vis	to see	*evident* easily seen *invisible* unable to be seen
vinc, vict	to conquer; to win	*invincible* unconquerable *victorious* winning
vit, viv	to live	*vital* alive *vivacious* lively
voc, voke, vocat	to call	*revocable* capable of being called back *invoke* to call on *vocation* a calling
void	empty	*devoid* empty of (feeling)
volv, volut	to roll or turn around	*evolve* to develop by stages; to unfold *revolution* movement around
vol	to fly	*volatile* vaporizing quickly

PRACTICE SET 1

Select the best answer to each question and write the letter of your choice in the space provided.

1. To *amend* means most nearly to _____
   A) pass
   B) correct
   C) legislate
   D) finish

2. *Respite* means most nearly _____
   A) rest
   B) dine
   C) despite
   D) few

3. *Mammoth* means most nearly _____
   A) mammal
   B) extinct
   C) gigantic
   D) dead

4. *Iota* means most nearly _____
   A) tiny bit
   B) group
   C) speedster
   D) friend

5. *Latitude* means most nearly _____
   A) freedom
   B) style
   C) emotion
   D) worth

6. *Jargon* means most nearly _____
   A) puzzle
   B) lizard
   C) language
   D) container

7. *Knoll* means most nearly _____
   A) bell
   B) instrument
   C) hill
   D) harmony

8. *Liaison* means most nearly _____
   A) go-between
   B) foreigner
   C) rifle
   D) gallop

9. *Proximity* means most nearly _____
   A) closeness
   B) cleanliness
   C) prurient
   D) fitness

10. To *saturate* means most nearly to _____
    A) enjoy
    B) soak
    C) construct
    D) disturb

11. *Stamina* means most nearly _____
    A) strength
    B) root
    C) dye
    D) limb

12. To *tantalize* means most nearly to _____
    A) please
    B) seize
    C) tease
    D) freeze

13. *Toxic* means most nearly _____
    A) waste
    B) smelly
    C) poisonous
    D) growing

14. *Lesion* means most nearly _____
    A) league
    B) injury
    C) army
    D) ridicule

15. *Clandestine* means most nearly _____
    A) friendly
    B) remorseful
    C) secret
    D) pensive

16. *Combustible* means most nearly _____
    A) eatable
    B) breakable
    C) burnable
    D) thinkable

17. To *condone* means most nearly to _____
    A) condemn
    B) require
    C) forgive
    D) praise

18. *Frailty* means most nearly _____
    A) weakness
    B) frenzy
    C) real estate
    D) purpose

19. *Mandatory* means most nearly _____
    A) required
    B) able
    C) masculine
    D) separate

20. *Medley* means most nearly _____
    A) half-note
    B) interruption
    C) mixture
    D) snoop

21. *Lustrous* means most nearly _____
    A) lawsuit
    B) shining
    C) willowy
    D) fortunate

22. *Benevolent* means most nearly _____
    A) warlike
    B) generous
    C) angry
    D) rebellious

23. *Emaciated* means most nearly _____
    A) content
    B) strong
    C) wasted
    D) lofty

24. *Glossy* means most nearly _____
    A) free
    B) shiny
    C) stealthy
    D) refurbished

25. To *maim* means most nearly to _____
    A) defoliate
    B) beg
    C) issue
    D) injure

ANSWERS FOR PRACTICE SET 1

1. **(B)** correct
2. **(A)** rest
3. **(C)** gigantic
4. **(A)** tiny bit
5. **(A)** freedom
6. **(C)** language
7. **(C)** hill
8. **(A)** go-between
9. **(A)** closeness
10. **(B)** soak

11.	**(A)** strength	19.	**(A)** required
12.	**(C)** tease	20.	**(C)** mixture
13.	**(C)** poisonous	21.	**(B)** shining
14.	**(B)** injury	22.	**(B)** generous
15.	**(C)** secret	23.	**(C)** wasted
16.	**(C)** burnable	24.	**(B)** shiny
17.	**(C)** forgive	25.	**(D)** injure
18.	**(A)** weakness		

PRACTICE SET 2

Select the best answer to each question and write the letter of your choice in the space provided.

1. *Plagiarism* means most nearly _____
   A) theft   C) illness
   B) anarchism   D) evilness

2. To *reiterate* means most nearly to _____
   A) compound   C) affect
   B) repeat   D) retreat

3. *Monotonous* means most nearly _____
   A) large   C) uninteresting
   B) growing   D) jagged

4. *Futile* means most nearly _____
   A) engine   C) useless
   B) missile   D) decorative

5. *Pensive* means most nearly _____
   A) wealthy   C) thoughtful
   B) tense   D) idle

6. *Utilitarian* means most nearly _____
   A) useful   C) rich
   B) despondent   D) indolent

7. *Trepidation* means most nearly _____
   A) tearfulness   C) hard work
   B) anxiety   D) cleverness

8. *Labyrinth* means most nearly _____
   A) infantile   C) maze
   B) hardship   D) welcome

9. *Defection* means most nearly _____
   A) sickness   C) bad temper
   B) problem   D) desertion

10. *Cumbersome* means most nearly _____
    A) clumsy   C) vegetation
    B) remarkable   D) encompass

11. *Intimidation* means most nearly _____
    A) memory   C) fear
    B) secret   D) expectation

12. *Dais* means most nearly _____
    A) platform   C) prejudice
    B) waste   D) dress

13. *Candid* means most nearly _____
    A) hidden   C) frank
    B) peeping   D) funny

14. *Ambiguous* means most nearly _____
    A) long   C) reliable
    B) uncertain   D) aloof

15. *Chassis* means most nearly _____
    A) engine   C) framework
    B) classic   D) reliable

16. *Carmine* means most nearly _____
    A) model   C) sweet
    B) red   D) speedy

17. *Complacent* means most nearly _____
    A) self-satisfied   C) quiet
    B) ordered   D) natural

18. *Audible* means most nearly _____
    A) profitable   C) hearable
    B) knowledgeable   D) greedy

19. *Affluent* means most nearly _____
    A) proud   C) wealthy
    B) keen   D) understanding

20. To *loathe* means most nearly to _____
    A) bake   C) clean
    B) detest   D) limp

21. *Levity* means most nearly _____
    A) air   C) gaiety
    B) measurement   D) judgment

22. *Lethal* means most nearly _____
    A) ancient   C) deadly
    B) gas   D) formal

23. To *ferret* means most nearly to _____
    A) search out   C) wander
    B) cut   D) whip

24. *Genial* means most nearly _____
    A) scientific   C) kindly
    B) wizardly   D) superficial

25. *Vacuum* means most nearly _____
    A) utensil   C) blower
    B) cleaning   D) empty

ANSWERS FOR PRACTICE SET 2

1.	(A) theft	14.	(B) uncertain
2.	(B) repeat	15.	(C) framework
3.	(C) uninteresting	16.	(B) red
4.	(C) useless	17.	(A) self-satisfied
5.	(C) thoughtful	18.	(C) hearable
6.	(A) useful	19.	(C) wealthy
7.	(B) anxiety	20.	(B) detest
8.	(C) maze	21.	(C) gaiety
9.	(D) desertion	22.	(C) deadly
10.	(A) clumsy	23.	(A) search out
11.	(C) fear	24.	(C) kindly
12.	(A) platform	25.	(D) empty
13.	(C) frank		

PRACTICE SET 3

Select the best answer to each question and write the letter of your choice in the space provided.

1. *Oaf* means most nearly _____
    A) tree   C) stupid person
    B) rest   D) model

2. *Mobile* means most nearly _____
    A) fixed   C) movable
    B) gasoline   D) car

3. *Migratory* means most nearly _____
    A) protected   C) unhappy
    B) wandering   D) fickle

4. *Gusty* means most nearly _____
    A) enjoyable   C) windy
    B) throaty   D) happy

5. *Hapless* means most nearly _____
    A) unfortunate   C) disappointed
    B) sad   D) reliant

6. *Arcade* means most nearly _____
    A) passageway   C) games
    B) shipwreck   D) curvature

7. *Fraudulent* means most nearly _____
    A) perfect   C) deceitful
    B) friction   D) dangerous

8. To *goad* means most nearly to _____
    A) urge   C) bark
    B) punish   D) gather

9. *Homogenous* means most nearly _____
    A) pasteurized   C) similar
    B) blended   D) healthy

10. *Hubbub* means most nearly _____
    A) uproar   C) comedy
    B) friend   D) sidekick

11. *Omnipotent* means most nearly _____
    A) odorous   C) all-powerful
    B) obsolete   D) homesick

12. *Placid* means most nearly _____
    A) peaceful   C) perfunctory
    B) straight   D) foremost

13. *Tirade* means most nearly _____
    A) carnival   C) scolding
    B) fuselage   D) parade

14. *Stagnant* means most nearly _____
    A) smelling   C) playful
    B) motionless   D) ancient

15. *Succinct* means most nearly _____
    A) brief   C) loving
    B) achieving   D) tarnished

16. *Disgruntled* means most nearly _____
    A) belittled   C) discontent
    B) prudent   D) injured

17. To *amputate* means most nearly to _____
    A) hospitalize   C) prune
    B) dissolve   D) electrocute

18. *Apothecary* means most nearly _____
    A) talisman   C) curse
    B) druggist   D) opening

19. *Intermittent* means most nearly _____
    A) periodic   C) winterized
    B) settled   D) joking

20. To *aspire* means most nearly to _____
    A) sweat   C) seek
    B) hurry   D) allow

21. *Tenacious* means most nearly _____
    A) sportsmanlike   C) steadfast
    B) boring   D) angry

22. *Haphazard* means most nearly _____
    A) deliberate   C) unfortunate
    B) accidental   D) hairy

23. *Infamous* means most nearly _____
    A) notorious   C) expensive
    B) heroic   D) unknown

24. *Inept* means most nearly _____
   A) worrisome   C) incompetent
   B) relentless   D) lazy

25. *Increment* means most nearly _____
   A) increase   C) infirmity
   B) prohibition   D) insufficient

ANSWERS FOR PRACTICE SET 3

1. (C) stupid person
2. (C) movable
3. (B) wandering
4. (C) windy
5. (A) unfortunate
6. (A) passageway
7. (C) deceitful
8. (A) urge
9. (C) similar
10. (A) uproar
11. (C) all-powerful
12. (A) peaceful
13. (C) scolding
14. (B) motionless
15. (A) brief
16. (C) discontent
17. (C) prune
18. (B) druggist
19. (A) periodic
20. (C) seek
21. (C) steadfast
22. (B) accidental
23. (A) notorious
24. (C) incompetent
25. (A) increase

PRACTICE SET 4

Select the best answer to each question and write the letter of your choice in the space provided.

1. *Murkiness* means most nearly _____
   A) mud   C) gloom
   B) cheer   D) accident

2. *Perimeter* means most nearly _____
   A) area   C) boundary
   B) machine   D) yardstick

3. *Haughty* means most nearly _____
   A) dour   C) flabby
   B) proud   D) quick

4. *Forte* means most nearly _____
   A) strength C) score
   B) battalion D) barracks

5. To *engross* means most nearly to _____
   A) outnumber C) absorb
   B) revile   D) dislike

6. To *deduce* means most nearly to _____
   A) reason   C) remain
   B) subtract D) forbid

7. *Contorted* means most nearly _____
   A) aborted   C) twisted
   B) playful   D) harbored

8. To *cauterize* means most nearly to _____
   A) mix   C) burn
   B) count   D) dissuade

9. *Berserk* means most nearly _____
   A) frenzied C) friend
   B) ornate   D) sheltered

10. To *rectify* means most nearly to _____
   A) make right C) destruct
   B) turn away   D) build

11. *Pugnacious* means most nearly _____
   A) small   C) quarrelsome
   B) queasy   D) foreboding

12. *Mediocre* means most nearly _____
   A) brownish C) ordinary
   B) healthful D) small-minded

13. To *hone* means most nearly to _____
   A) sharpen   C) return
   B) possess   D) rank

14. To *reminisce* means most nearly to _____
   A) publish   C) answer
   B) remember D) lessen

15. *Frivolous* means most nearly _____
   A) obstinate C) trivial
   B) patient   D) ornate

16. To *flaunt* means most nearly to _____
   A) bury   C) praise
   B) allow   D) display

17. *Precarious* means most nearly _____
   A) not reckless C) risky
   B) prepared   D) formidable

18. *Mishap* means most nearly _____
   A) sadness   C) strange looking
   B) accident D) beggar

19. *Fiasco* means most nearly _____
   A) celebration C) failure
   B) pottery   D) artwork

20. *Crony* means most nearly _____
   A) companion C) retiree
   B) money   D) polish

21. *Scrutiny* means most nearly _____
   A) deceit   C) inspection
   B) wicked   D) fear

22. *Robust* means most nearly _____
   A) automaton C) healthy
   B) decaying D) stealing

23. To *relinquish* means most nearly to _____
   A) tie up   C) give up
   B) sum up   D) pick up

24. *Gnarled* means most nearly _____
   A) eaten   C) twisted
   B) fused   D) flabby

25. To *debilitate* means most nearly to _____
   A) ease   C) weaken
   B) pay back   D) show off

ANSWERS FOR PRACTICE SET 4

1. (C) gloom   14. (B) remember
2. (C) boundary   15. (C) trivial
3. (B) proud   16. (D) display
4. (A) strength   17. (C) risky
5. (C) absorb   18. (B) accident
6. (A) reason   19. (C) failure
7. (C) twisted   20. (A) companion
8. (C) burn   21. (C) inspection
9. (A) frenzied   22. (C) healthy
10. (A) make right   23. (C) give up
11. (C) quarrelsome   24. (C) twisted
12. (C) ordinary   25. (C) weaken
13. (A) sharpen

PRACTICE SET 5

Select the best answer to each question and write the letter of your choice in the space provided.

1. *Benediction* means most nearly _____
   A) argument   C) blessing
   B) retirement   D) treason

2. To *acquiesce* means most nearly to _____
   A) yield   C) understand
   B) familiarize   D) resolve

3. To *abhor* means most nearly to _____
   A) yell   C) dissolve
   B) force   D) detest

4. *Unwitting* means most nearly _____
   A) unconscious   C) droll
   B) ill-humored   D) stupid

5. To *recant* means most nearly to _____
   A) take back   C) allow
   B) deceive   D) forbid

6. *Morbid* means most nearly _____
   A) gruesome   C) allowable
   B) stiff   D) enthusiastic

7. *Occult* means most nearly _____
   A) mysterious   C) cold
   B) silent   D) oily

8. *Preposterous* means most nearly _____
   A) commonplace   C) profound
   B) skilled   D) absurd

9. To *resuscitate* means most nearly to _____
   A) revive   C) remind
   B) reneg   D) reproach

10. *Subtle* means most nearly _____
   A) soft   C) not obvious
   B) dirty   D) careless

11. *Uncanny* means most nearly _____
   A) pure   C) moldy
   B) strange   D) open

12. *Vigilant* means most nearly _____
   A) angry   C) forceful
   B) watchful   D) unknowledgeable

13. *Environs* means most nearly _____
   A) vicinity   C) chains
   B) forest   D) prison

14. *Entrepreneur* means most nearly _____
   A) roughneck   C) foreigner
   B) businessman   D) deceiver

15. To *poach* means most nearly to _____
   A) trespass   C) instruct
   B) model   D) hang

16. *Revelry* means most nearly _____
   A) merrymaking   C) anger
   B) reminder   D) overthrow

17. *Shoddy* means most nearly _____
   A) doubting   C) cheap
   B) intermittent D) ghostly

18. *Virile* means most nearly _____
   A) sick   C) manly
   B) deadly   D) watchful

19. *Mutinous* means most nearly _____
   A) silent   C) ponderous
   B) rebellious   D) changeable

20. *Profound* means most nearly _____
   A) discovered   C) very deep
   B) receptive   D) absurd

21. To *fabricate* means most nearly to _____
   A) enhance   C) lie
   B) free   D) urge

22. To *falter* means most nearly to _____
   A) blame   C) stumble
   B) draw out   D) decree

23. *Coy* means most nearly _____
   A) bashful   C) cowardly
   B) brief   D) aware

24. *Bland* means most nearly _____
   A) musical   C) mild
   B) friendly   D) happy

25. *Calligraphy* means most nearly _____
   A) measurement   C) penmanship
   B) profession   D) communication

ANSWERS FOR PRACTICE SET 5

1.	(C) blessing	14.	(B) businessman
2.	(A) yield	15.	(A) trespass
3.	(D) detest	16.	(A) merrymaking
4.	(A) unconscious	17.	(C) cheap
5.	(A) take back	18.	(C) manly
6.	(A) gruesome	19.	(B) rebellious
7.	(A) mysterious	20.	(C) very deep
8.	(D) absurd	21.	(C) lie
9.	(A) revive	22.	(C) stumble
10.	(C) not obvious	23.	(A) bashful
11.	(B) strange	24.	(C) mild
12.	(B) watchful	25.	(C) penmanship
13.	(A) vicinity		

PRACTICE SET 6

Select the best answer to each question and write the letter of your choice in the space provided.

1. To *haggle* means most nearly to _____
   A) show off   C) bargain
   B) rob   D) raid

2. *Boisterous* means most nearly _____
   A) masculine   C) sentimental
   B) rowdy   D) trite

3. *Molten* means most nearly _____
   A) melted   C) lost
   B) furry   D) evil

4. *Mentor* means most nearly _____
   A) teacher   C) temperature
   B) salesperson   D) adage

5. To *avow* means most nearly to _____
   A) marry   C) acknowledge
   B) adapt   D) help

6. *Mercenary* means most nearly _____
   A) greedy   C) murderous
   B) quick   D) reliable

7. To *reimburse* means most nearly to _____
   A) profit   C) pay back
   B) require   D) foretell

8. *Paltry* means most nearly _____
   A) chicken   C) insignificant
   B) friendship   D) white

9. *Mandatory* means most nearly _____
   A) masculine   C) required
   B) foolish   D) perceptive

10. To *petrify* means most nearly to _____
   A) harden   C) frighten
   B) kiss   D) embezzle

11. *Interim* means most nearly _____
   A) upset   C) meantime
   B) boundary   D) subject

12. To *desist* means most nearly to _____
   A) punish   C) stop
   B) forgive   D) allow

13. *Component* means most nearly _____
   A) part   C) circle
   B) conduct   D) conspiracy

14. *Avocation* means most nearly _____
   A) job   C) hobby
   B) trip   D) decoration

15. *Apathetic* means most nearly _____
   A) important   C) calm
   B) horrified   D) indifferent

16. *Compliant* means most nearly _____
   A) submissive   C) argument
   B) unhappy   D) restrictive

17. *Soothsayer* means most nearly _____
   A) dentist   C) predictor
   B) sleepwalker   D) debater

18. *Sinister* means most nearly _____
   A) winding   C) evil
   B) smiling   D) truthful

19. *Redundant* means most nearly _____
   A) bouncing   C) self-reliant
   B) repetitious   D) hardy

20. To *mimic* means most nearly to _____
   A) pander   C) imitate
   B) mumble   D) threaten

21. *Impeccable* means most nearly _____
    A) faultless   C) encouraging
    B) hairy   D) religious

22. *Idiosyncrasy* means most nearly _____
    A) peculiarity   C) rhythm
    B) weirdness   D) reliability

23. *Furtive* means most nearly _____
    A) sneaky   C) powerful
    B) sterile   D) limited

24. To *gorge* means most nearly to _____
    A) blast   C) cut short
    B) stuff   D) corrupt

25. *Dank* means most nearly _____
    A) dark   C) damp
    B) dim   D) dear

ANSWERS FOR PRACTICE SET 6

1. (C) bargain
2. (B) rowdy
3. (A) melted
4. (A) teacher
5. (C) acknowledge
6. (A) greedy
7. (C) pay back
8. (C) insignificant
9. (C) required
10. (A) harden
11. (C) meantime
12. (C) stop
13. (A) part
14. (C) hobby
15. (D) indifferent
16. (A) submissive
17. (C) predictor
18. (C) evil
19. (B) repetitious
20. (C) imitate
21. (A) faultless
22. (A) peculiarity
23. (A) sneaky
24. (B) stuff
25. (C) damp

REVIEWING THE KEY STRATEGIES

Remember to:

1. Look for the best, or closest, meaning.

2. Work as quickly as possible.

3. Use prefixes, suffixes, and roots.

4. Try the word in a clear sentence.

5. Look for positive or negative connotations.

ANALOGIES

This question type tests your vocabulary and your ability to understand relationships. Each question gives you one pair of related words, and one word from a second pair. You are given four choices for completing the second pair, so that it expresses a relationship similar to the first.

For example:

HEN is related to CHICK as HORSE is related to
A) bull   C) colt
B) milk   D) kitten

Notice the first pair, "HEN is related to CHICK." In this pair, the second word is a "young version" of the first word. Now look at the first word of the second pair: HORSE is related to . . . To complete this pair you must express the same relationship as in the first pair, so that the second word is a "young version" of the first word. The answer choice (second word) that best expresses that relationship is COLT. A COLT (second word) is a young version of a HORSE (first word). (C) is the correct answer.

HELPFUL TECHNIQUES AND STRATEGIES

1. Always try to determine the relationship expressed in the first pair of words. Is the relationship "cause to effect" or "part to whole," or what? Then look at the first word of the next pair.
2. It may help to read this question type by thinking to yourself, "A is related to B *in the same way* as C is related to (D)." The (D) word is the one you are looking for in your answer choices.
3. Remember that *order* must be the same in both pairs. For example,

   STREAM is related to RIVER as LAKE is related to
   A) pond   C) fish
   B) ocean   D) water

   Notice the relationship in the first pair: SMALL is to LARGE. Therefore the second pair should say that LAKE (small) is related to OCEAN (large). If you made the mistake of reversing the order in the second pair, you would have chosen (A) POND, which is incorrect.
4. The parts of speech in each pair should be consistent. Look at the question below:

SKYSCRAPER is related to TALL as FREIGHT TRAIN is related to
A) track   C) quickly
B) engine   D) long

Notice that the first word in each pair is a noun (person, place, or thing) and the second word in the first pair, TALL, is an adjective. Therefore the second word in the second pair must also be an adjective. Notice that answer choice (D), LONG, is an adjective, whereas the other choices are not: SKYSCRAPER (noun) is related to TALL (adjective) as FREIGHT TRAIN (noun) is related to LONG (adjective).

5. Remember that the second pair of words does not have to concern the same "subject" as the first. Look at the following question:

   PUPPY is related to DOG as SAPLING is related to
   A) house   C) leaf
   B) tree   D) syrup

   Notice that the "subject" of the first pair is animals and the "subject" of the second pair is plants. However, it is the *relationship* between words that is important. The relationship in the first pair is "younger" to "older." With this relationship in mind, you should conclude that SAPLING (younger) is related to TREE (older).

6. Look at all the choices before deciding on an answer, but don't spend too much time on any one question.

7. Usually you will be able to eliminate one or two choices immediately. Those that remain may all seem like good answers, but remember that you are looking for the *best* answer, one that best expresses the same relationship.

8. Analogies can be classified into specific categories. You will find it helpful to be able to recognize some of these categories and the common relationships immediately. Do not try to memorize these categories or to classify the analogies you are given on the exam. Instead, reason out the relationships shown in the first pair of analogies and then carefully choose a second pair that has a corresponding relationship.

   Following are some BASIC TYPES of analogies:

   a. CLASSIFICATIONS—sorts, kinds, general to specific, specific to general, thing to quality or characteristic, opposites, degree, etc.

A broad category is compared to a narrower category:

RODENT	:	SQUIRREL	::	fish	:	flounder
(broad category)		*(narrower category)*		*(broad category)*		*(narrower category)*

A person is compared to a characteristic:

SPRINTER	:	FAST	::	jockey	:	small
(person)		*(characteristic)*		*(person)*		*(characteristic)*

The general is compared to the specific:

SPORT	:	HOCKEY	::	machine	:	typewriter
(general)		*(specific)*		*(general)*		*(specific)*

A word is compared to a synonym of itself:

ENORMOUS	:	HUGE	::	quick	:	speedy
(word)		*(synonym)*		*(word)*		*(synonym)*

A word is compared to an antonym of itself:

SERVANT	:	MASTER	::	sad	:	happy
(word)		*(antonym)*		*(word)*		*(antonym)*

A word is compared to a definition of itself:

REGULATE	:	CONTROL	::	segregate	:	separate
(word)		*(definition)*		*(word)*		*(definition)*

A male is compared to a female:

ROOSTER	:	CHICKEN	::	buck	:	doe
(male)		*(female)*		*(male)*		*(female)*

A family relationship is compared to a similar family relationship:

AUNT	:	NIECE	::	uncle	:	nephew
(family relationship)				*(family relationship)*		

A virtue is compared to a failing:

RESPONSIBILITY	:	CARELESSNESS	::	honesty	:	dishonesty
(virtue)		*(failing)*		*(virtue)*		*(failing)*

An element is compared to an extreme of itself:

DRY SPELL	:	DROUGHT	::	water	:	flood
(element)		*(extreme)*		*(element)*		*(extreme)*

A lesser degree is compared to a greater degree:

HAPPY	:	ECSTATIC	::	hot	:	scorching
(lesser degree)		*(greater degree)*		*(lesser degree)*		*(greater degree)*

The plural is compared to the singular:

CHILDREN	:	CHILD	::	they	:	he
(plural)		*(singular)*		*(plural)*		*(singular)*

b. STRUCTURALS—part to whole, whole to part, part to part, etc.

A part is compared to a whole:

FINGER	:	HAND	::	room	:	house
(part)		*(whole)*		*(part)*		*(whole)*

A whole is compared to a part:

DECK	:	CARD	::	novel	:	chapter
(whole)		*(part)*		*(whole)*		*(part)*

c. COMPONENTS—elements of a compound, ingredients of a recipe, etc.

An ingredient is compared to its finished result:

FLOUR	:	CAKE	::	sulphur	:	gunpowder
(ingredient)		*(finished product)*		*(ingredient)*		*(finished product)*
HYDROGEN	:	WATER	::	sodium	:	salt
(element)		*(compound)*		*(element)*		*(compound)*

d. OPERATIONALS—time sequence, operations, stages, phases, beginning to ending, before to after, etc.

One element of time is compared to another element of time:

DAWN	:	DUSK	::	sunrise	:	sunset
(time element)		*(time element)*		*(time element)*		*(time element)*

A time sequence relationship is expressed:

PROLOGUE	:	EPILOGUE	::	birth	:	death
(beginning)		*(ending)*		*(beginning)*		*(ending)*

A complete operation is compared to a stage:

FOOTBALL GAME	:	QUARTER	::	baseball game	:	inning
(operation)		*(stage)*		*(operation)*		*(stage)*

NOTE: Many analogies will overlap into more than one of the above basic types and will have to be analyzed by their purpose, use, cause-effect relationship, etc.

PRACTICE SET 1

Select the best answer to each question and write the letter of your choice in the space provded.

1. APPOINTMENT is related to CANCEL as BUILDING is related to _____
   A) construct   C) demolish
   B) conference   D) design

2. SPORT is related to SPECTATOR as TELE-VISION is related to _____
   A) vision   C) viewer
   B) tube   D) channel

3. PURITY is related to WHITE as ANGER is re-lated to _____
   A) yellow   C) mad
   B) red   D) mean

4. WALL is related to PAINTING as FLOOR is re-lated to _____
   A) sweeping   C) house
   B) dirty   D) ironing

5. PLUMBER is related to WRENCH as LION-TAMER is related to _____
   A) lion   C) cage
   B) whip   D) fear

6. AUTOMOBILE is related to IGNITION as LAMP is related to _____
   A) bulb   C) switch
   B) wheel   D) steering wheel

7. IMPORTANT is related to INSIGNIFICANT as INTENDED is related to _____
   A) purpose   C) meaningless
   B) required   D) accidental

8. CUISINE is related to KITCHEN as EXPERI-MENT is related to _____
   A) living room   C) stadium
   B) airport   D) laboratory

9. ORE is related to MINE as SAP is related to _____
   A) syrup   C) branch
   B) fluid   D) tree

10. WINDOW is related to AWNING as EYES is related to _____
    A) glasses   C) visor
    B) feet   D) hand

11. SALVAGE is related to TREASURE as RESCUE is related to _____
    A) ambulance   C) squad
    B) victim   D) hospital

12. ALLIES is related to ADVERSARIES as FRIENDS is related to _____
    A) foes   C) arbitrators
    B) helpers   D) peacemakers

13. LAGOON is related to BAY as BROOK is re-lated to _____
    A) puddle   C) ocean
    B) river   D) aqueduct

14. TASK is related to FATIGUE as FASTING is related to _____
    A) food   C) weakness
    B) strength   D) slowness

15. DRAPE is related to WINDOW as COSTUME is related to _____
    A) seamstress   C) character
    B) Halloween   D) mask

16. DAWN is related to DAY as PREFACE is related to _____
    A) epilogue   C) book
    B) index   D) chapter

17. TRIAL is related to COURTROOM as BALL-GAME is related to _____
    A) clubhouse   C) stadium
    B) league   D) uniform

18. MARRIAGE is related to BACHELOR as EXPERIENCE is related to _____
    A) fun   C) wizard
    B) novice   D) husband

19. HEART is related to HUMAN as ENGINE is related to _____
    A) carburetor   C) automobile
    B) gasoline   D) mechanic

20. BURGLAR is related to ALARM as TRESPASSER is related to _____
    A) bark   C) air raid
    B) steal   D) property

ANSWER EXPLANATIONS FOR PRACTICE SET 1

1. (C) The first word is eliminated by the second word.
2. (C) The first word is watched by the second word.
3. (B) The second word is the color symbolizing the first word.
4. (A) The second word is done to the first word.
5. (B) The second word is a tool of the first word.

6. **(C)** The second word turns on the first word.
7. **(D)** The first word is the opposite of the second word.
8. **(D)** The first word is produced in the second word.
9. **(D)** The first word is produced in the second word.
10. **(C)** The second word shades the first word.
11. **(B)** The first word saves the second word.
12. **(A)** The first word is the opposite of the second word.
13. **(B)** The first word is similar to but bigger than the second word.
14. **(C)** The first word causes the second word.
15. **(C)** The first word covers the second word.
16. **(C)** The first word begins the second word.
17. **(C)** The first word takes place in the second word.
18. **(B)** The first word ends the second word.
19. **(C)** The first word is the vital center of the second word.
20. **(A)** The first word is frightened away by the second word.

PRACTICE SET 2

Select the best answer to each question and write the letter of your choice in the space provided.

1. SOLO is related to ENSEMBLE as INDIVIDUAL is related to _____
   A) committee   C) instrument
   B) performance   D) partner

2. MELANCHOLY is related to CHEERFUL as TRAGEDY is related to _____
   A) death   C) play
   B) drama   D) comedy

3. BIGOT is related to TOLERANCE as MISER is related to _____
   A) generosity   C) hoard
   B) money   D) spendthrift

4. CLAW is related to LION as TALON is related to _____
   A) snake   C) hand
   B) hawk   D) finger

5. BUSINESS is related to BANKRUPT as TEAM is related to _____
   A) fall behind   C) teamwork
   B) forfeit   D) play

6. COFFEE is related to BEAN as TEA is related to _____
   A) bag   C) instant
   B) leaf   D) iced

7. HERD is related to CATTLE as FLOCK is related to _____
   A) lions   C) mice
   B) sheep   D) gather

8. ICE is related to GLACIER as SAND is related to _____
   A) beach   C) sandstorm
   B) heat   D) water

9. CAPTAIN is related to SHIP as PUBLISHER is related to _____
   A) newspaper   C) film
   B) mint   D) airplane

10. CATASTROPHE is related to EARTHQUAKE as BIRD is related to _____
    A) robin   C) accident
    B) flight   D) nest

11. EXTINCT is related to DINOSAUR as IMAGINARY is related to _____
    A) whale   C) unicorn
    B) fantasy   D) real

12. ASTRONOMY is related to STARS as GEOLOGY is related to _____
    A) geography   C) rocks
    B) maps   D) artifacts

13. REVOLUTION is related to TYRANNY as COURAGE is related to _____
    A) fear   C) government
    B) anger   D) heroism

14. SACRIFICE is related to MARTYR as RULE is related to _____
    A) lawyer   C) despot
    B) carpenter   D) measure

15. DAY is related to SOLAR as EVENING is related to _____
    A) night   C) dawn
    B) dark   D) lunar

16. GARAGE is related to VEHICLES as VAULT is related to _____
    A) burglar   C) valuables
    B) safe   D) combination

17. LIMP is related to INJURY as LAUGH is related to _____
    A) cry   C) joke
    B) pain   D) smile

18. WATER is related to EVAPORATE as ICE is re-
    lated to _____
    A) freeze   C) cold
    B) melt   D) solid

19. MEAT is related to PROTEIN as POTATOES is
    related to _____
    A) fat   C) calories
    B) starch   D) butter

20. DISEMBARK is related to SHIP as DISMOUNT
    is related to _____
    A) train   C) horse
    B) rider   D) mountain

ANSWER EXPLANATIONS FOR PRACTICE SET 2

1. (A) The second word is the plural of the first
   word.
2. (D) The first word is the opposite of the second word.
3. (A) The first word lacks the second word.
4. (B) The second word grasps with the first
   word.
5. (B) The second word is the failure of the first
   word.
6. (B) The first word comes originally from the
   second word.
7. (B) The first word is a collection of the second word.
8. (A) The second word is composed of the first
   word.
9. (A) The first word is in charge of the second
   word.
10. (A) The second word is a specific example of
    the first word.
11. (C) The first word is a description of the sec-
    ond word.
12. (C) The first word is the study of the second
    word.
13. (A) The first word overcomes the second
    word.
14. (C) The first word is an action of the second
    word.
15. (D) The second word is the illumination of
    the first word.
16. (C) The first word stores the second word.
17. (C) The second word causes the first word.
18. (B) The first word changes by means of the
    second word.
19. (B) The first word provides the second
    word.
20. (C) The first word is the action of getting off
    the second word.

PRACTICE SET 3

Select the best answer to each question and write
the letter of your choice in the space provided.

1. DUNCE is related to SCHOLAR as TRAITOR is
   related to _____
   A) spy   C) rogue
   B) teaser   D) hero

2. SCARCITY is related to PLENTY as FOOLISH-
   NESS is related to _____
   A) wisdom   C) interests
   B) jokes   D) jesters

3. IMAGE is related to MIRAGE as FACT is re-
   lated to _____
   A) fantasy   C) thought
   B) oasis   D) reality

4. BOOK is related to INDEX as APARTMENT
   BUILDING is related to _____
   A) doorbells   C) bedroom
   B) directory   D) driveway

5. IGLOO is related to ESKIMO as NEST is re-
   lated to _____
   A) Indian   C) family
   B) bird   D) flock

6. NUN is related to HABIT as SOLDIER is re-
   lated to _____
   A) rifle   C) uniform
   B) battalion   D) infantry

7. VIAL is related to BARREL as PAMPHLET is
   related to _____
   A) volume   C) leaflet
   B) box   D) discount

8. WAITER is related to TIP as ACTOR is related
   to _____
   A) applause   C) actress
   B) drama   D) stage

9. BLADE is related to SKATE as WHEEL is re-
   lated to _____
   A) kick   C) bicycle
   B) foot   D) spoke

10. RAIN is related to DROP as SNOW is related
    to _____
    A) flake   C) ice
    B) icicle   D) hail

11. BALDNESS is related to HAIR as SILENCE is
    related to _____
    A) quiet   C) laughter
    B) noise   D) sunshine

12. CIRCLE is related to ARC as LINE is related to _____
   A) parallel   C) curve
   B) segment   D) perpendicular

13. DOG is related to WOLF as CAT is related to _____
   A) kitty   C) bear
   B) tiger   D) feline

14. FEATHERS is related to BIRD as SCALES is related to _____
   A) weigh   C) fish
   B) notes   D) animal

15. PACKAGE is related to RIBBON as CAKE is related to _____
   A) chocolate   C) icing
   B) wedding   D) sugar

16. FACE is related to EYES as HOUSE is related to _____
   A) windows   C) roof
   B) doors   D) ears

17. PUNCH is related to DUCK as QUESTION is related to _____
   A) answer   C) evade
   B) understand   D) teach

18. TREE is related to SAPLING as COW is related to _____
   A) bull   C) calf
   B) milk   D) barn

19. SOCCER is related to BALL as HOCKEY is related to _____
   A) stick   C) goal
   B) ice   D) puck

20. DROWSY is related to NAP as HUNGRY is related to _____
   A) snack   C) siesta
   B) starve   D) drink

ANSWER EXPLANATIONS FOR PRACTICE SET 3

1. (D) The first word is the opposite of the second word.
2. (A) The first word is the opposite of the second word.
3. (A) The second word is an imaginary first word.
4. (B) The second word is a contents listing of the first word.
5. (B) The second word builds and lives out of the first word.
6. (C) The first word wears the second word.

7. (A) The second word is a much larger first word.
8. (A) The second word is given in appreciation to the first word.
9. (C) The first word is a part of the second word.
10. (A) The first word falls in the form of the second word.
11. (B) The first word lacks the second word.
12. (B) The second word is a part of the first word.
13. (B) The first word is a domesticated animal in the same family as the second word.
14. (C) The first word is the body covering of the second word.
15. (C) The second word is what goes around the first word.
16. (A) The second word is the "viewing openings" of the first word.
17. (C) The second word avoids the first word.
18. (C) The second word is an immature first word.
19. (D) The second word is the object of control when playing the first word.
20. (A) The second word satisfies the biological condition of the first word.

PRACTICE SET 4

Select the best answer to each question and write the letter of your choice in the space provided.

1. LIFEGUARD is related to RESCUE as PROFESSOR is related to _____
   A) instruct   C) school
   B) college   D) student

2. JOKE is related to LAUGHTER as THREAT is related to _____
   A) fear   C) happiness
   B) discovery   D) brawny

3. DEPOSIT is related to WITHDRAWAL as POSITIVE is related to _____
   A) neutral   C) position
   B) negative   D) bankrupt

4. TREMOR is related to EARTHQUAKE as WIND is related to _____
   A) hurricane   C) clock
   B) lightning   D) thunder

5. JAR is related to JAM as SHOES is related to _____
   A) sandals   C) feet
   B) laces   D) soles

6. RADIO is related to TRANSISTOR as SAIL-BOAT is related to _____
   A) mast
   B) rudder
   C) engine
   D) wind

7. TOES is related to FOOT as HANDS is related to _____
   A) fingers
   B) clock
   C) glove
   D) house

8. PREDICTION is related to MYSTIC as PROGNOSIS is related to _____
   A) diagnosis
   B) prescription
   C) doctor
   D) patient

9. MEAT is related to MILK as FORK is related to _____
   A) knife
   B) straw
   C) dish
   D) cow

10. REHEARSE is related to IMPROVEMENT as PRACTICE is related to _____
    A) perfection
    B) study
    C) failure
    D) audition

11. HOUSE is related to ROOF as BOX is related to _____
    A) wall
    B) face
    C) side
    D) lid

12. TEETHING is related to PAIN as TICKLING is related to _____
    A) tenderness
    B) laughter
    C) friendship
    D) soothing

13. THROTTLE is related to GASOLINE as FAUCET is related to _____
    A) hose
    B) garden
    C) water
    D) car

14. WRING is related to WASHCLOTH as SQUEEZE is related to _____
    A) mop
    B) sponge
    C) pail
    D) pillow

15. STAMP is related to POSTAGE as PREMIUM is related to _____
    A) insurance
    B) accident
    C) coupon
    D) exceptional

16. WEIGHT is related to SCALE as LENGTH is related to _____
    A) speedometer
    B) tape measure
    C) clock
    D) width

17. SCULPTOR is related to MARBLE as NOVELIST is related to _____
    A) books
    B) paper
    C) literature
    D) characters

18. MODEST is related to HUMBLE as CAUTIOUS is related to _____
    A) accident
    B) careful
    C) reliable
    D) braggart

19. SAFARI is related to GAME as POSSE is related to _____
    A) animal
    B) human
    C) fugitive
    D) western

20. LULLABY is related to BABY as TAPS is related to _____
    A) trumpet
    B) soldier
    C) bedtime
    D) sleep

ANSWER EXPLANATIONS FOR PRACTICE SET 4

1. **(A)** The second word is the job task of the first word.
2. **(A)** The second word is the result of the first word.
3. **(B)** The first word is the opposite of the second word.
4. **(A)** The second word is larger in size than the first word.
5. **(C)** The first word contains the second word.
6. **(D)** The second word powers the first word.
7. **(B)** The first word is on or a part of the second word.
8. **(C)** The first word is a statement made by the second word.
9. **(B)** The first word relates to solid food; the second word to liquid food.
10. **(A)** The second word is the goal of the first word.
11. **(D)** The second word is atop the first word.
12. **(B)** The second word is a result of the first word.
13. **(C)** The first word regulates the flow of the second word.
14. **(B)** The first word empties the liquid from the second word.
15. **(A)** The first word pays for the second word.
16. **(B)** The second word measures the first word.
17. **(B)** The second word is the raw material used by the first word.
18. **(B)** The first word is a synonym for the second word.
19. **(C)** The second word is the object of capture of the first word.
20. **(B)** The first word precedes the sleeping of the second word.

Select the best answer to each question and write the letter of your choice in the space provided.

1. NURSE is related to DOCTOR as SECRETARY is related to _____
   A) man
   B) office
   C) typewriter
   D) executive

2. ENCOURAGE is related to RIDICULE as SMILE is related to _____
   A) scowl
   B) happy
   C) rely
   D) wink

3. AMNESIA is related to MEMORIES as SILENCE is related to _____
   A) operation
   B) hearing
   C) melodies
   D) quiet

4. APPRENTICE is related to MASTER as STUDENT is related to _____
   A) scholar
   B) academic
   C) teacher
   D) studies

5. SIGNATURE is related to FORGERY as ORIGINAL is related to _____
   A) facsimile
   B) verbatim
   C) reasonable
   D) criminal

6. ACCIDENT is related to RECKLESSNESS as HUMILIATION is related to _____
   A) resoluteness
   B) tactlessness
   C) cleanliness
   D) determination

7. NAVIGATOR is related to SEXTANT as WOODSMAN is related to _____
   A) novel
   B) work
   C) axe
   D) timber

8. BOOK is related to CHAPTER as SYMPHONY is related to _____
   A) musician
   B) conductor
   C) movement
   D) instrument

9. ONION is related to TEARS as TIREDNESS is related to _____
   A) body
   B) bed
   C) yawn
   D) exercise

10. GALLOP is related to HORSE as SLITHER is related to _____
    A) snail
    B) rat
    C) spider
    D) snake

11. IRON is related to RUST as TOOTH is related to _____
    A) incisor
    B) toothpaste
    C) decay
    D) clean

12. TROPICAL is related to RAIN as ARCTIC is related to _____
    A) ice
    B) snow
    C) igloo
    D) water

13. ENGINE is related to FUEL as BODY is related to _____
    A) organs
    B) limb
    C) food
    D) breath

14. SCARCE is related to EXPENSIVE as PLENTIFUL is related to _____
    A) invaluable
    B) cheap
    C) rotten
    D) valuable

15. ENORMOUS is related to MINUTE as REWARD is related to _____
    A) reprimand
    B) value
    C) restitution
    D) hour

16. RECKLESS is related to CAREFUL as FACT is related to _____
    A) novel
    B) new
    C) fiction
    D) antique

17. GINGER is related to ROOT as CHOCOLATE is related to _____
    A) bar
    B) candy
    C) bean
    D) milk

18. BULLSEYE is related to TARGET as NOSE is related to _____
    A) eyes
    B) ears
    C) face
    D) body

19. BUTTER is related to MARGARINE as SUGAR is related to _____
    A) sweet
    B) salt
    C) saccharin
    D) oleomargarine

20. BIRD is related to WORM as CAT is related to _____
    A) dog
    B) mouse
    C) pet
    D) animal

ANSWER EXPLANATIONS FOR PRACTICE SET 5

1. (D) The first word assists the second word.
2. (A) The first word is the opposite of the second word.
3. (C) The first word is the absence of the second word.
4. (C) The first word learns from the second word.
5. (A) The second word is a copy of the first word.
6. (B) The first word results from the second word.

7. (C) The second word is a tool of the first word.
8. (C) The second word is a part of the first word.
9. (C) The first word causes the second word.
10. (D) The first word is how the second word moves.
11. (C) The second word is the corrosion of the first word.
12. (B) The second word is the precipitation occurring in the region of the first word.
13. (C) The second word powers the first word.
14. (B) The second word is the cost of the first word.
15. (A) The first word is the opposite of the second word.
16. (C) The first word is the opposite of the second word.
17. (C) The second word is the origin of the first word.
18. (C) The first word is the center of the second word.
19. (C) The second word is a substitute for the first word.
20. (B) The second word is the prey of the first word.

PRACTICE SET 6

Select the best answer to each question and write the letter of your choice in the space provided.

1. COACH is related to TEAM as CONDUCTOR is related to _____
   A) electricity   C) instruments
   B) orchestra   D) music

2. EWE is related to RAM as CHICKEN is related to _____
   A) hen   C) rooster
   B) chick   D) fowl

3. SWORD is related to KNIGHT as RIFLE is related to _____
   A) gun   C) pistol
   B) soldier   D) weapon

4. PAPER is related to INK as BLACKBOARD is related to _____
   A) writing   C) schoolroom
   B) lesson   D) chalk

5. COOL is related to FRIGID as WARM is related to _____
   A) torrid   C) crisp
   B) lukewarm   D) balmy

6. NEWS is related to HEARSAY as FACT is related to _____
   A) ideas   C) science
   B) newspaper   D) fiction

7. CROCUS is related to SPRING as THUNDER-CLOUD is related to _____
   A) sky   C) winter
   B) storm   D) dark

8. OBESE is related to SLENDER as BABBLING is related to _____
   A) brook   C) talkative
   B) quiet   D) slim

9. LEMON is related to CITRUS as CHICKEN is related to _____
   A) rooster   C) fowl
   B) hen   D) barnyard

10. INFANTS is related to NURSERY as MINNOWS is related to _____
    A) hospital   C) babies
    B) hatchery   D) fish

11. WATER is related to JUG as LETTER is related to _____
    A) alphabet   C) stamp
    B) envelope   D) literate

12. HICK is related to SOPHISTICATION as BOOR is related to _____
    A) tactfulness   C) interesting
    B) money   D) rudeness

13. THUG is related to GUN as BULL is related to _____
    A) steer   C) matador
    B) horns   D) sports

14. SCHOLAR is related to ENCYCLOPEDIA as MECHANIC is related to _____
    A) dictionary   C) manual
    B) tools   D) transistor

15. OVERALLS is related to TRACTOR as TUXEDO is related to _____
    A) farming   C) cummerbund
    B) limousine   D) sportscar

16. FAME is related to DISGRACE as HERO is related to _____
    A) criminal   C) fortune
    B) friendship   D) popularity

17. PIANO is related to TUNED as HAIR is related to _____
    A) grown   C) blonde
    B) trimmed   D) shaggy

18. PODIUM is related to SPEAKER as STAGE is related to _____
    A) coach   C) cowboy
    B) actor   D) soldier

19. ANGLER is related to TROUT as WOLF is related to _____
    A) cub   C) lair
    B) hunter   D) rabbit

20. CRINGE is related to COWARD as DECEIVE is related to _____
    A) spy   C) actor
    B) soldier   D) hero

ANSWER EXPLANATIONS FOR PRACTICE SET 6

1. **(B)** The first word prepares and leads the second word.
2. **(C)** The first word is the female of the species; the second word is the male.
3. **(B)** The first word is the weapon used by the second word.
4. **(D)** The second word is the substance used to write on the first word.
5. **(A)** The second word is a greater degree of the first word.
6. **(D)** The first word is nearer the truth; the second word lacks truth.
7. **(B)** The first word is a sign of the second word.
8. **(B)** The first word is the opposite of the second word.
9. **(C)** The first word is a specific variety of the second word.
10. **(B)** The first word is where the second word lives immediately after birth.
11. **(B)** The second word contains the first word.
12. **(A)** The first word is lacking the second word.
13. **(B)** The second word is the weapon used by the first word.
14. **(C)** The second word is the reference book of the first word.
15. **(B)** The first word is the attire worn by the person using the second word.
16. **(A)** The first word is the opposite of the second word.
17. **(B)** The second word puts the first word "in order."
18. **(B)** The first word is where the second word performs.
19. **(D)** The second word is the prey of the first word.
20. **(A)** The first word is the action of the second word.

PRACTICE SET 7

Select the best answer to each question and write the letter of your choice in the space provided.

1. SCALPEL is related to KNIFE as NURSE is related to _____
   A) doctor   C) hospital
   B) assistant   D) operation

2. BEGGAR is related to POOR as FOX is related to _____
   A) skunk   C) large
   B) slow   D) sly

3. FELONY is related to MISDEMEANOR as KILL is related to _____
   A) maim   C) murder
   B) bury   D) guilty

4. RETRACT is related to STATEMENT as VOID is related to _____
   A) escape   C) contract
   B) avoidance   D) empty

5. STOOPED is related to POSTURE as SLURRED is related to _____
   A) diction   C) music
   B) stance   D) action

6. MOVIES is related to PROJECTOR as RECORDS is related to _____
   A) speakers   C) phonograph
   B) tape recorder   D) radio

7. CHEMIST is related to LABORATORY as ARTIST is related to _____
   A) canvas   C) easel
   B) museum   D) studio

8. AGILE is related to NIMBLE as FAST is related to _____
   A) swift   C) perpetual
   B) slow   D) racy

9. DELICACY is related to GOURMET as INSECT is related to _____
   A) bee   C) frog
   B) pollen   D) hive

10. BOOK is related to CHAPTER as SONG is related to _____
    A) stanza   C) music
    B) sing   D) instrument

11. AMBIGUOUS is related to CLARITY as TEMPORARY is related to _____
    A) transient   C) clear
    B) permanence   D) fragile

12. SAW is related to CUT as YARDSTICK is related to _____
   A) foot
   B) inch
   C) measure
   D) tool

13. PROBLEM is related to SOLUTION as POISON is related to _____
   A) hemlock
   B) nitrate
   C) arsenic
   D) antidote

14. SUGGEST is related to REQUIRED as REQUEST is related to _____
   A) ask
   B) demand
   C) suspect
   D) allow

15. AUTOMOBILE is related to HIGHWAY as LOCOMOTIVE is related to _____
   A) station
   B) train
   C) track
   D) engine

16. DISTANCE is related to MILE as LIQUID is related to _____
   A) milk
   B) quart
   C) water
   D) meter

17. TAILOR is related to NEEDLE as MECHANIC is related to _____
   A) engineer
   B) screwdriver
   C) toolchest
   D) brush

18. PORCINE is related to PIG as BOVINE is related to _____
   A) boy
   B) cow
   C) sheep
   D) iodine

19. BREAD is related to BUTTER as POTATOES is related to _____
   A) gravy
   B) steak
   C) margarine
   D) lamb

20. GNASH is related to TEETH as LISTEN is related to _____
   A) hear
   B) ears
   C) resolve
   D) dissuade

ANSWERS AND EXPLANATIONS FOR PRACTICE SET 7

1. **(B)** The first word is the medical term for the second word.
2. **(D)** The second word is a characteristic of the first word.
3. **(A)** The first word is a more serious degree of the second word.
4. **(C)** The first word nullifies the second word.
5. **(A)** The first word is an impairment of the second word.
6. **(C)** The second word plays the first word.
7. **(D)** The second word is where the first word works.
8. **(A)** The first word is a synonym for the second word.
9. **(C)** The first word is eaten by the second word.
10. **(A)** The second word is a part of the first word.
11. **(B)** The first word is the opposite of the second word.
12. **(C)** The first word is the tool to do the second word.
13. **(D)** The second word overcomes the first word.
14. **(B)** The second word is an imperative ("must") of the first word.
15. **(C)** The first word travels on the second word.
16. **(B)** The second word is a measure of the first word.
17. **(B)** The second word is a tool of the first word.
18. **(B)** The first word means "pertaining to" the second word.
19. **(A)** The second is usually put on the first word.
20. **(B)** The first word is the action of the second word.

REVIEWING THE KEY STRATEGIES

Remember to:

1. Determine the relationship in the first pair.
2. Use "in the same way" to set up relationships.
3. Keep the order similar.
4. Keep parts of speech consistent.
5. Disregard subject matter; only relationship is important.
6. Look at all the choices before selecting one.
7. Eliminate wrong choices immediately.
8. Use categories to recognize relationships.

GRAMMAR

This question type tests your ability to recognize language that is unsuitable for a formal letter or written report. Knowledge of the rules and conventions of Standard Written English is necessary.

Each question consists of four different sentences. Three of them contain errors; one does not. Consider the following example:

A) Those who can remember well after a period of practice has an advantage over others.
B) Through regular practice, it is possible to develop a good memory, which can be very useful.
C) A good memory is not enjoyed by many people which do not practice at it.
D) Practice is required, being that memory is so difficult to get ahold of.

The correct answer is (B); it demonstrates grammar and usage suitable for a formal letter or report. An explanation of the errors in each of the other choices is included in the following discussion of helpful techniques and strategies.

HELPFUL TECHNIQUES AND STRATEGIES

1. Read all four sentences before considering which one is best. Don't jump to conclusions.
2. Sentences that are incorrect will often contain one of the following types of errors:
   a. INCORRECT VERBS—Pay special attention to the verbs in each sentence. One type of verb error occurs in choice (A) of the preceding example: "*Those* who can remember well after a period of practice *has* an advantage over others." In this case, the subject is "those," which is plural, and therefore the verb should also be plural, "have" instead of "has." In this case, the danger lies in presuming that "practice" is the subject of the sentence and concluding that because "practice has" is correct, the sentence is correct. When examining the verb in any sentence, be careful to identify correctly the subject (the "doer" of the action). Here is another sentence in which the subject does not agree with the verb:

   INCORRECT: A *crate* of office supplies have been stored in the closet, until some other space is found.

   CORRECT: A *crate* of office supplies has been stored in the closet, until some other space is found.

   Besides checking for subject-verb agreement, make sure that the verb tense is correct. Consider the following example:

   By the end of the year, every employee *will had been given* a 10 percent raise.

   In this case, "had" is incorrect; the correct verb is "have."

   b. MISUSE OF PRONOUNS—Pay special attention to pronouns: he, she, him, her, we, us, you, who, whom, which, that. Choice (C) of the example contains a pronoun error: "A good memory is not enjoyed by many people *which* do not practice at it." The pronoun "which" does not refer correctly to "people"; the correct pronoun here is "who." The following sentences also illustrate pronoun errors.

   INCORRECT: When *one* has given dedicated service to the company for so many years, *you* expect a gift upon retirement.

   CORRECT: When *one* has given dedicated service to the company for so many years, *one* expects a gift upon retirement.

   It would also be correct, in this case, to write "he expects" or "she expects." "He" and "she" agree with "one."

   INCORRECT: The man *whom* delivered the new copier to the office also installed it.

   CORRECT: The man *who* delivered the new copier to the office also installed it.

   The pronoun "whom" refers to those who *receive action*, and the pronoun "who" refers to those who do an action. In this case, the man is doing an action, delivering the copier, so "who" is correct.
   Another example of this:

   INCORRECT: I will give the bonus to whomever fixes the machine.
   In this sentence, *whomever* is incorrect. Al-

though it appears that "whomever" is the object of the preposition "to" and therefore should be correct, it is not the object of "to." The entire phrase, "whomever fixes the machine," is the object of "to," and within that phrase, "whomever" is doing the action: "*whomever* fixes the machine." Therefore, "whomever," as the doer, is incorrect. It should be changed to "whoever."

CORRECT: I will give the bonus to whoever fixes the machine.

c. INCORRECT USAGE—A number of expressions commonly used in conversation are incorrect in Standard Written English. Choice (D) in the original example contains two such expressions: "Practice is required, *being that* memory is so difficult to *get ahold of.*" Here is one way to rewrite this sentence correctly: "Because the improvement of memory is so difficult, practice is required." The following are some expressions that represent incorrect usage:

all the farther	hisself	ought to of
being as how	in regards	theirselves
being that	that	use to,
had to of	irregardless	suppose to
	no such a	

d. VAGUE OR UNCLEAR MEANING—The meaning of a sentence may be vague or unclear because (1) certain words in the sentence are not used clearly or (2) the structure of the sentence makes the meaning illogical or unclear. Consider the following set of four choices:

A) While proofreading the letter, a mistake was detected in the third line.
B) While proofreading a letter, one should be able to do this perfectly.
C) Through careful proofreading, a number of mistakes can appear in a letter.
D) Those who carefully proofread letters detect errors easily.

The correct choice is (D); the meaning of each of the other choices is unclear. In choice (B), the meaning of "this" is uncertain; "this" may or may not refer to proofreading. In choice (A), the structure of the sentence makes it seem as if "a mistake" is doing the proofreading! Choice (C) makes the inaccurate and illogical statement that mistakes "appear" through proofreading; it is more logical and accurate to say that mistakes are *detected* through proofreading.

e. REPETITION—A sentence is incorrect when it is unnecessarily wordy or repetitious. Consider the following examples:

The memorandum was sent to those who received it, the manager and me.
Everyone was asked to arrive for work early in the morning, at 6 A.M.

Here are less repetitious and wordy versions of the same sentences:

The memorandum was received by the manager and me.
Everyone was asked to arrive for work at 6 A.M.

A few more examples of common errors:

A) The quantity of child care centers have increased during the last decade, along with the increase in working parents.
B) For the work of parents, more child care centers have appeared during the last decade.
C) With more during the last decade, working parents appreciate child care centers.
D) During the last decade, the appearance of more working parents has coincided with the appearance of more child care centers.

Choice (D) is correct. In (A), the verb "have" should be replaced with "has," in order to agree with the subject, "quantity." In (B), "for the work of parents" is an unclear phrase. In (C), the meaning of "more" is unclear.

A) The sales force ought to of achieved much higher sales last week, but were not able to do so.
B) The sales force, who is usually very successful, did a very poor job last week.
C) Selling much less than usual, the weeks ahead might be more productive for the company sales force.

D) Putting a week of poor results behind them, the sales force hoped that the weeks ahead would be more productive.

Choice (D) is correct. In (A), "ought to of" is incorrect usage. In (B), the pronoun "who" is incorrect; "which" is the correct pronoun for referring to "the sales force." The structure of choice (C) makes it seem as if "the weeks ahead," rather than the sales force, are "selling much less than usual."

A) The lobby of the Brinker Building use to of been much less crowded than it is now.

B) If the lobby of the Brinker Building would have had been enlarged years ago, it would not be so crowded today.
C) The lobby of the Brinker Building is much more crowded now than it used to be.
D) When one enters the lobby of the Brinker Building, you immediately enter a crowd.

Choice (C) is correct. In (A), "use to of been" is incorrect usage. In (B), "would have had been" is an incorrect verb tense; "had been" is correct. In (D), the pronoun "you" is incorrect; "you" should be replaced with "one," "he," or "she," and "enter" should be changed to "enters."

PRACTICE SET 1

Decide which sentence is preferable with respect to grammar and usage suitable for a formal letter or report. Write the letter of your choice in the space provided.

1. A) The prohibition against laying down _____ on the furniture is posted in several places throughout the company lounge.
   B) During lunch and breaks, although laying one down in the company-lounge may be inviting, it is prohibited.
   C) Lying down on furniture in the company lounge is not allowed.
   D) With reference to the furnishings in the lounge, lying down or laying on it cannot be permitted.

2. A) Having the drinking of wine fre- _____ quently in Italy and France contrasts with the regular drinking of water in the United States.
   B) With water the frequent drink in the United States, wine is for Italy and France also a frequent drink.
   C) Drinking wine such as we in the United States drink water are the people of which are in Italy and France.
   D) Many people in Italy and France drink wine as frequently as we in the United States drink water.

3. A) Modern business psychologists, _____ with information on creativity and stress more than long ago, have contributed to improved morale and productivity.
   B) With valuable information on creativity and stress, modern business psychologists have contributed to improved morale and productivity.
   C) Improved morale and productivity has been of modern business psychology, with information on creativity and stress.
   D) Creativity and stress have improved morale and productivity, with information from modern business psychologists.

4. A) A longer lunch period will be pro- _____ vided, after it was reported that hastily eating lunch caused an upset stomach.
   B) Eating lunch too quickly, an upset stomach resulted in lengthening the lunch period.
   C) Returning from lunch feeling upset, a longer lunch period was instituted for everyone.
   D) Convinced that eating a hasty lunch is not healthy for anyone, we are instituting a longer lunch period.

5. A) People often read a book merely to _____ pass the time, to prove their intelligence, avoiding the real world, and many other ridiculous reasons.
   B) There are many good reasons for reading, and some ridiculous ones as well.
   C) Merely passing the time, to prove their intelligence, and to avoid the real world, many people read a book.
   D) Reading for ridiculous reasons are merely to pass the time, to prove their intelligence, and to avoid the real world, among others.

6. A) Manikins, each dressed in an expen- _____ sive outfit, makes the store window attractive to passersby.
   B) There are two manikins, dressed in expensive clothes, in the store window.
   C) As shoppers pass the store window, expensively dressed manikins pass their view.
   D) As for clothes that are attractive and expensive, manikins are on display in the store window.

7. A) Empty since it appeared, a number _____ of you have requested a suggestion box for the office.
   B) The suggestion box that a number of you requested has remained empty since it appeared.
   C) The request for a suggestion box, to which was responded with one, has not as yet resulted with a suggestion.

D) Suggestions for the suggestion box have not appeared as yet, and it is still empty even though a number of you have requested it.

8. A) Having mislain the calendar, the appointments calendar was unable to verify where they should be and when. _____

B) Scheduling was impossible because the appointments secretary had mislain the appointments calendar.

C) The calendar listing everyone's appointments could not be found, with the result being that no one knew where to be and when.

D) The appointments secretary mislaid his calendar, so no one knew whether any appointments had been scheduled.

9. A) Associates who we have not contacted for months should be informed of all recent decisions. _____

B) Inform associates whom we have not contacted for months of all recent decisions.

C) Of all associates that we have not contacted for months, inform them of recent decisions.

D) Not contacting associates for months, we are informing them of all recent decisions.

10. A) When one has all ready publicized a decision, it is difficult to revoke it. _____

B) With an already publicized decision, revoking it is difficult.

C) With the revoking of a decision already publicized, revoking it is difficult.

D) It is difficult to revoke a decision that has already been publicized.

ANSWER EXPLANATIONS FOR PRACTICE SET 1

1. **(C)** The most prominent error in each of the other choices is the incorrect use of "laying" for "lying."

2. **(D)** "Having" should be omitted in (A). (B) is both vague and repetitious (for example, "frequent drink"). "Such as we" is one incorrect phrase in (C).

3. **(B)** The sentence structure in each of the other choices is incoherent, and the meaning of several phrases is unclear.

4. **(D)** Choice (B) seems to say that an upset stomach is eating lunch, and (C) that the lunch period returns from lunch. The verb tenses in (A) are inconsistent.

5. **(B)** (A) and (C) have parallelism errors. (D) should begin, "Ridiculous reasons for reading . . ."

6. **(B)** In (A), the verb "makes" does not agree with the subject "manikins." (C) contains the illogical phrase "manikins pass." In (D), the connection between the first half of the sentence and the second half is unclear.

7. **(B)** The phrase "empty since it appeared" in (A) is misplaced. (C) contains awkward and wordy phrases, for instance, "to which was responded." (D) is wordy and repetitious.

8. **(D)** "Mislain" is incorrect in both (A) and (B). In (C), "with the result being that" is wordy and awkward.

9. **(B)** In (A), "who" is incorrect. In (C), the sentence structure is wordy and awkward, and "that" is used incorrectly. In (D), the verb tense of "not contacting" is incorrect.

10. **(D)** In (A), "all ready" is incorrect; "already" would be correct. Although (B) and (C) do use "already" correctly, both sentences are vague and wordy. The most clear, direct, and correct expression is (D).

PRACTICE SET 2

Decide which sentence is preferable with respect to grammar and usage suitable for a formal letter or report. Write the letter of your choice in the space provided.

1. A) Everyone differs greatly in the way they listen to and benefit from information. _____

B) Listening closely to important information, in order to benefit from it, vary from person to person.

C) Listening carefully is an important skill, especially when vital information is involved.

D) Skillful listening is important, while everyone does theirs differently.

2. A) Neither wealth nor power are the desires of those majoring in business, according to a recent poll. _____

B) Business majors polled recently denied that either wealth or power are their desire.

C) Business majors desire neither wealth nor power as such in a recent poll.

D) Wealth and power were not the stated goals of business majors polled recently.

3. A) Both the inventor and the manufacturer _____ received credit for the success of the product.

   B) The inventor was as responsible for the success of the product, with the manufacturer.

   C) High sales figures for the new product delighted not only their inventor, but also the manufacturer.

   D) The inventor and the manufacturer was given publicity for the popularity of their new product.

4. A) Government institutions have become _____ more powerful, but they have also lost the respect of many citizens.

   B) A rapidly decreasing respect for government institutions and that such institutions are becoming more powerful is a cause of concern.

   C) The status of government institutions, that has changed recently, can result in less respect.

   D) As for the status of government institutions, theirs is not as strong as it was formerly.

5. A) Dealing directly with the question are _____ minor errors in typing to be allowed.

   B) Some people question whether minor errors in typing should be allowed.

   C) The allowance of imperfectly typed manuscripts are not to be permitted.

   D) Although typing errors are difficult to avoid, it cannot be permitted.

6. A) Many will agree with the new retirement _____ policy, and many will disagree with it, taking the other side of the issue.

   B) Some changes in the retirement policy provokes both positive and negative responses.

   C) Those who drafted the new retirement policy welcome both positive and negative responses from all concerned.

   D) Retirement is an issue to get both pro and con viewpoints.

7. A) The City Council, consisting of twelve _____ members, were scheduled to meet for several hours.

   B) With all twelve members of the City Council scheduled to meet, several hours were scheduled.

   C) A City Council meeting may be scheduled soon, if all of the council members are available at a convenient time.

   D) Finding several hours for a meeting of the City Council members were not at all easy.

8. A) To type a letter accurately, spelling must _____ be part of what is watched.

   B) Accurate typing and correct spelling are both absolutely necessary.

   C) With accuracy, both for typing and for spelling, a letter will be acceptable.

   D) Typing, spelling, and accuracy are those which any letter must demonstrate.

9. A) Adam is a successful student who never _____ thinks of anything but grades.

   B) Adam is a successful student whom never thinks of anything but grades.

   C) Adam is a successful student for who grades are all that is important.

   D) Adam, for who grades are most important, is a successful student.

10. A) The people who neglect important tasks _____ until the last minute are usually unable to do a careful job.

    B) Those type of people which neglect important tasks usually rush to complete them.

    C) Types of people which neglect important tasks until the last minute do so in a rush.

    D) With the neglect of important tasks by those who prefer to rush, the last minute is popular.

ANSWER EXPLANATIONS FOR PRACTICE SET 2

1. **(C)** In (A), the pronoun "they" and the verbs "listen" and "benefit" should agree with the singular "everyone." One error in (B) is the incorrect use of "vary"; the verb should be "varies." In (D), "theirs" is a plural pronoun, but "everyone" is singular.

2. **(D)** In both (A) and (B), the verb "are" should be changed to "is." In (C), "as such" is awkward.

3. **(A)** In (B), either the "as" or the "with" is incorrect. In (C), "their" should be replaced with "its." In (D), the verb "was given" should be replaced with "were given," in order to agree with the plural subject.

4. **(A)** The sentence structure of (B) is awkward, and "is" is incorrect. (C) is unclear, and (D) is wordy.

5. **(B)** Choice (A) is not a complete sentence. In (C), "are" should be changed to "is" in order to agree with "allowance." In (D), "it" is an incorrect pronoun; "they" would be correct, to agree with "errors."

6. **(C)** Choice (A) is repetitious. In (B), "provokes" should be changed to "provoke," to agree with "changes." In (D), "to get" is an awkward phrase.

7. **(C)** In (A), the verb "were" does not agree with the subject, "City Council." In (B), the repetition of "scheduled" is awkward. In (D), the verb "were" should be changed to "was."

8. (B) Choice (A) seems to say that the "spelling" is doing the "typing"! In (C), both instances of "for" may be changed to "in." In (D), "those which" is an incomplete, unclear phrase.

9. (A) In the incorrect choices, "whom" and "for who" are used incorrectly.

10. (A) In (B), "those type" and "which" are incorrect. In (C), "which" is incorrect ("who" and "whom" are used to refer to people). In (D), "the last minute is popular" has no clear relation to the first part of the sentence.

PRACTICE SET 3

Decide which sentence is preferable with respect to grammar and usage suitable for a formal letter or report. Write the letter of your choice in the space provided.

1. A) The Back & Hammer Corporation has designed a new building that is round in shape and large in size. _____
   B) The new Back & Hammer building will be round and very large, according to the architect's design.
   C) With the new building's design submitted by the architect, Back & Hammer can look forward to a new size and shape.
   D) While conventional buildings are somewhat smaller and more square, the new Back & Hammer building's roundness and size is a reason it is different.

2. A) Whichever of the two companies submits the lowest bid will receive the contract. _____
   B) The contract will be awarded to whoever bids lowest.
   C) Bidding lower than the competitors, the contract will go to whomever does so.
   D) The contract bids are being reviewed by myself, who will select the lowest.

3. A) Those in the company who had worked all the hardest to handle the Christmas rush, were rewarded with large bonuses. _____
   B) Those who worked hardest to handle the Christmas rush will receive large bonuses.
   C) A well-deserved bonus was paid by the company to the hardest-working employees among them, during the Christmas rush
   D) Working hardly during the very busy Christmas season brought bonuses to a number of workers.

4. A) Whoever answers the phone must do so _____ courteously.
   B) Courtesy is important, both away from it and on the phone.
   C) Without courtesy on the telephone, any secretary is lacking with a vital skill.
   D) A courteous phone voice, for whomever answers the phone, has great importance.

5. A) Although hundreds of people complained when they changed the taste of their soft drink, sales remained steady. _____
   B) Sales did not decrease after the company "improved" the taste of its soft drinks, but hundreds of people complained.
   C) The complaints of hundreds of people in the fact of a new taste for the cola had no effect on sales.
   D) Selling cola was no more difficult after changing their taste than before it.

6. A) After establishing its home office in Los Angeles, the small company failed to compete successfully with larger firms in the area. _____
   B) Although they intended to offer competition to larger firms in the Los Angeles area, the new company was not successful.
   C) Among successful competition among successful firms in the Los Angeles area, a smaller company is unlikely to be successful.
   D) Achieving success in the competitive Los Angeles area, the new company was not able to do so.

7. A) Child safety groups are demanding legislation forbidding the use of glass containers in public places. _____
   B) Fearing for the safety of children who might be injured by them, child safety groups are forbidding the public use of glass containers.
   C) Because broken glass containers may injure a child, they are demanding legislation prohibiting their public use.
   D) Children, because they may break, should not have access to glass containers.

8. A) One new employee was accused of complaining too much, but denied that he had done so. _____
   B) One new employee was overheard complaining about his job, but he claimed that he said no such a thing.

C) Accused of complaining too much, a new employee denied himself.
D) Complaining excessively, the job was obviously unpleasant for the new employee.

9. A) Everyone on the staff, as well as Jerry and _____ I, supports the new proposal.
   B) Everyone on the staff, as well as Jerry and me, supports the new proposal.
   C) The support of the new proposal by Jerry as well as me goes along with the support of the staff.
   D) Me and Jerry and everyone on the staff support the new proposal.

10. A) Choosing every word carefully, a writer _____ can communicate even complex ideas with clarity and precision.
    B) Choosing every word carefully, even complex ideas can be written with clarity and precision.
    C) Writing complex ideas with clarity and precision, choosing every word carefully.
    D) As for clarity and precision, it is the task of choosing every word carefully.

ANSWER EXPLANATIONS FOR PRACTICE SET 3

1. **(B)** In (A), "in shape" and "in size" are repetitious. In (C) there is no clear reference to a building, so "a new size and shape" is vague. In (D), the subjects "roundness and size" require a plural verb and "reasons."
2. **(B)** In (A) "lowest" should be "lower" (C) seems to say that the contract itself is doing the bidding, and "whomever" is not the correct form. In (D), "me" should be used, instead of "myself."
3. **(B)** In (A), "all the hardest" is incorrect. In (C), the meaning of "them" is not clear. In (D), "working hardly" is incorrect.
4. **(A)** Choices (B) and (D) both contain pronoun errors: in (B), "it" is vague, and in (D), "whomever" is incorrect. In (C), "lacking with" should be replaced with "lacking in."
5. **(B)** In (A), the meaning of "they" and "their" is not clear. In (C), "in the fact of" is an incorrect phrase. In (D), the meaning of "it" is not clear, and "their" should be "its."
6. **(A)** In (B), "they" is used incorrectly to refer to "company." In (C), "Among successful competition among" is repetitious. Choice (D) seems to contradict itself.
7. **(A)** In each of the other choices, the use of pronouns "they" and "them" is unclear.
8. **(A)** In (B), "no such a thing" is incorrect. In (C), "denied himself" is not the appropriate phrase.

Choice (D), with its unclear sentence structure, seems to say that the "job" was "complaining excessively."
9. **(A)** In both (B) and (D), "me" is incorrect; "I" is the correct pronoun in both cases. (C) is an unnecessarily wordy expression.
10. **(A)** In (B), the "complex ideas" seem to be doing the "choosing." Choice (C) is not a complete sentence. In (D), "it" is a vague term.

PRACTICE SET 4

Decide which sentence is preferable with respect to grammar and usage suitable for a formal letter or report. Write the letter of your choice in the space provided.

1. A) If the report would have been completed _____ on schedule, everyone would have been able to take the weekend off.
   B) Everyone will be required to work this weekend if the report is not completed on time.
   C) With the possibility of completing the report in order to avoid working all weekend, everyone would have tried staying on schedule.
   D) A report not completed by this weekend, the weekend off will not be available.

2. A) Both men and women, whomever are interested in administrative experience, are invited to apply for a summer internship program.
   B) We are pleased to announce a summer internship program that offers substantial administrative experience.
   C) Those whom are after administrative experience should apply for the summer internship program.
   D) With administrative experience, the summer internship program invites applications from both men and women.

3. A) The special talents of every team member are rarely acknowledged by the coach.
   B) Each member of the team is theirself a unique talent, even though the coach rarely gives anyone credit.
   C) Without any credit of the coach, the unique talent of each team member goes unnoticed.
   D) Talented and unique, the team goes without the acknowledgment of them by the coach.

4. A) In the opinion of the general public, it _____
believes that major corporations are not
ethical.
   B) The general public questions the ethics
of major corporations, in their opinion.
   C) With a belief regarding major corporations that their ethics are questionable,
the general public voices its opinion.
   D) The general public believes that the
practices of most major corporations are
not ethical.

5. A) Most popular in relation to the flexible _____
interest rate is the fixed rate, even
though it is often higher.
   B) With flexible versus fixed rates, the more
popular one is the higher of the two.
   C) Flexible interest rates are less popular
than fixed rates, even though fixed rates
are usually higher.
   D) Less popularity has made flexible interest rates less appealing than the higher
fixed rates.

6. A) Because Stupple & Whipple Industries _____
has discontinued the production of microcomputers, they are giving full attention to other possible products.
   B) Having decided to investigate other possibilities, Stupple & Whipple Industries
is no longer producing microcomputers.
   C) Microcomputer production is not for
Stupple & Whipple Industries any
longer, after whose decision to explore
other possibilities.
   D) Without microcomputers in production,
other possibilities than the computer is
the interest of Stupple & Whipple
Industries.

7. A) As far as political forces were concerned, _____
industrial growth as well as business
grows stronger before 1950.
   B) During the first half of this century, business and industry were becoming domi-
nant political forces in the United States.
   C) As the growth of the United States pro-
gressed during the first half of the century, both business and industry was in
the forefront.
   D) With the early years of this century came
a dominant industry, as a political force,
along with business.

8. A) The memorandum was addressed to the _____
office manager, the division supervisor,
and me.

B) Those receiving the communication included myself, along with the division
manager, and in addition, the office
manager.
   C) A memo—routed to the office manager
via the division supervisor and me—was
received.
   D) After receiving a memo addressed also
to the office manager and me, the division supervisor did also.

9. A) The president of the Rotary Club won re- _____
election being that his past achievements
were so many.
   B) Being that his past achievements were so
many, the president of the Rotary Club
won reelection.
   C) The president of the Rotary Club won reelection because of his many past
achievements.
   D) With his many past achievements in
mind, reelection of the Rotary Club president was because of them.

10. A) In the court's judgment, the cause of the _____
accident was negligence rather than
speeding.
    B) The cause of the accident was negligence
rather than speeding in the court's
judgment.
    C) The cause of the accident was negligence
instead of speeding in the court's
judgment.
    D) Negligence rather than speeding was the
cause of the accident in the court
judgment.

ANSWER EXPLANATIONS FOR PRACTICE SET 4

1. (B) In (A), "report would have been" should be
"report had been." In both (C) and (D), the sentence structure is obviously confusing.
2. (B) "Whomever" and whom" are incorrect pronouns in (A) and (C). The sentence structure of (D)
suggests that the "summer program" has "administrative experience."
3. (A) In (B), the pronoun "theirself" is incorrect,
and in (D), the pronoun "them" is incorrect. In (C),
"of the coach" should be "from the coach."
4. (D) In (A), "it believes" is repetitious. "Their" is
incorrect in (B). In (C) "with a belief regarding . . . that" is awkward usage.
5. (C) In (A), "in relation to" is awkward. In (B), the
meaning of the sentence is unclear. In (D), "less
popularity" is an awkward phrase.

6. **(B)** In (A) and (C) there are pronoun errors: "they" is incorrect in (A), and "whose" contributes to poor sentence structure in (C). In (D), "is" should be "are" ("possibilities are").

7. **(B)** Both (A) and (C) contain incorrect verbs: "grows" in (A), and "was" in (C). The relationship between "business" and "industry" is not precisely stated in (D).

8. **(A)** Each of the other is wordy or awkward.

9. **(C)** In both (A) and (B), "being that" is an incorrect phrase; "because" is correct. Choice (D) is awkward and unclear.

10. **(A)** In (B), "speeding in the court's judgment" seems to say that the speeding took place in the court; this same confusing phrase occurs in (C). In (D), the comma is missing before the final phrase; "court" should be "court's."

PRACTICE SET 5

Decide which sentence is preferable with respect to grammar and usage suitable for a formal letter or report. Write the letter of your choice in the space provided.

1. A) A meeting was called for we project supervisors and our assistants. _____
    B) It was important to all concerned that a meeting having been called for both supervisors and assistants be scheduled.
    C) Project supervisors and their assistants were called to a meeting.
    D) Meeting regularly, on the part of both supervisors and assistants, were important to all concerned.

2. A) Not likely to repeat what he had said a moment ago, the teacher was not sure if whether the class understood him or not. _____
    B) Making an important point more than once, the class was not sure of the teacher's meaning until he had repeated it.
    C) Uncertain about whether the class had understood him, the teacher repeated what he had said a moment ago.
    D) After a few moments past, and the class still did not express any understanding, the teacher had repeated himself.

3. A) Several friends have decided to jog on a weekend basis, which can gradually be increased as their heart and lungs grow stronger. _____

    B) Several friends have decided to jog together every Saturday, and perhaps more often as their hearts and lungs grow stronger.
    C) To jog more often as their heart and lungs grow stronger, several friends have decided to jog every Saturday.
    D) With every Saturday, several friends have begun jogging as their hearts and lungs grow stronger.

4. A) Finding the most efficient method for completing a routine task can make it more pleasant. _____
    B) Routine assignments can be very unpleasant without which effort to find a method that is efficient.
    C) The founding of a method, although it does not change the requirement to do a routine task, can be more pleasant.
    D) Routine though they may be, a task can be much better if one is given an efficient method for completing it.

5. A) Friends for years, they suddenly began arguing frequently and loudly. _____
    B) Arguments can upset years of friendship, as a frequent and loud one seemed to prove in a recent case.
    C) With years behind a friendship of frequent and loud arguments, those involved are often not capable of continuing the relationship.
    D) How violent an argument must be before a friendship is affected, and those involved in it must change their relationship.

6. A) As for other appliances, those installed newly have energy efficiency ratings surpassed the older ones. _____
    B) Each of the appliances installed in the new offices is energy-efficient.
    C) New appliances, even though more expensive, compare favorably over those that required more energy in the past.
    D) Although new, the energy used by each new appliance in each new office could not be described as efficient.

7. A) All of his sentences are well constructed, and it contributes to the clarity of his writing. _____
    B) His well-constructed sentences contribute to the clarity of his writing.
    C) Clear sentences, well-constructed, are contributory to clarity of writing.

D) All of his sentences are well-constructed, that being the contribution to the clarity of his writing.

8. A) Both days being the same birthday for _____ both Jean and Joan, we baked only one cake.
   B) On the same day as Joan, whose birthday falls along with Jean's, more than one cake for both of them was not necessary.
   C) We baked a cake for Jean, whose birthday fell on the same day as Joan's.
   D) With the other's birthday on the same day as Jean, namely Joan, we had already baked a cake for only one.

9. A) Reading the newspaper carefully, I no- _____ ticed that an old English sheepdog was advertised in the column labeled "Pets for Sale."
   B) Reading the newspaper carefully, an old English Sheepdog was advertised in the column labeled "Pets for Sale."
   C) By reading the newspaper carefully, an old English sheepdog was advertised in the column labeled "Pets for Sale."
   D) In the column labeled "Pets for Sale," reading carefully, I noticed an old English sheepdog.

10. A) Everyone should be commended for _____ performing admirable well during a recent evaluation of the department.
    B) Everyone should be commended for performing admirably well during a recent evaluation of the department.
    C) With an admirably well performance, everyone in the department should be commended.
    D) An admirable good performance deserves commending everyone in the department.

ANSWER EXPLANATIONS FOR PRACTICE SET 5

1. (C) In (A), "for we" is incorrect; "for us" would be correct. In (B) the verb "having been called" is both unnecessary and incorrect. In (D), the verb "were" does not agree with the subject, "meeting"; "Meeting . . . *was* important" would be correct.
2. (C) In (A), "if whether" is incorrect; "if" alone would be sufficient. The sentence structure of (B) seems to say that the class, not the teacher, is "making a important point." In (D), both "past" and "had repeated" are incorrect.
3. (B) An error in (A) is "heart"; it should be "hearts." An obvious error in (C) is the repetition of "to jog." Choice (D) is unclear.
4. (A) In (B), "without which effort" is incorrect. One error in (C) is the incorrect use of "founding." In (D), "they" is used incorrectly to refer to "task."
5. (A) (B) is not as clear a statement as (A); the word "one" makes no sense with "frequent." In (C), "with years behind" is awkward. In (D), the sentence structure is not clear.
6. (B) In (A), "surpassed," "as for other appliances," and "installed newly" are used incorrectly. In (C), "compare favorably over" should be "compare favorably to". In (D), "new" seems to refer to "energy"; this is an illogical reference.
7. (B) "It" is an incorrect pronoun in (A); "they contribute" or just "contribute" would be correct. In (C), "contributory" is incorrect. In (D), "that being" is a vague phrase.
8. (C) The sentence structure of each of the other choices is obviously wordy, vague, and confusing.
9. (A) Both (B) and (C) seem to say that a sheepdog was reading the paper. In (D), "reading carefully" is placed in an awkward position in the sentence.
10. (B) In (A), "admirable" is incorrect. In (C), "admirably well performance" is incorrect. In (D), "admirable good" is incorrect. "Performing admirably well," in (B), is the correct expression.

PRACTICE SET 6

Decide which sentence is preferable with respect to grammar and usage suitable for a formal letter or report. Write the letter of your choice in the space provided.

1. A) A letterhead that is colorful but not hav- _____ ing adequate information is useless.
   B) Letterhead design is not nearly as important as the sufficiency of informing them who read it.
   C) If the information on the company letterhead is insufficient, they serve no purpose.
   D) Along with a colorful design, the company letterhead must include sufficient information.

2. A) Visitors are asked to park their cars away _____ from the main building during rush-hour traffic.
   B) Access to the main building during rush-hour traffic is prohibited on visitors.
   C) Parking space is available a long ways from the main building during rush-hour traffic.
   D) Finding a parking space near the main building for visitors is impossible during the rush hour.

3. A) After talking to the accountant, Mr. _____ Wright felt he should audit the report prior to the noon conference.
   B) Mr. Wright asked his accountant whether auditing the report before his conference at noon was possible.
   C) If he could audit the report before the noon conference was what Mr. Wright needed to know of his accountant.
   D) Mr. Wright wondered if his accountant would have time to audit the report prior to the noon conference.

4. A) The final draft of a report should dem- _____ onstrate not only correct English, with logical organization as well.
   B) Correct English, as well as logical organization, are important in the final draft of a report.
   C) When drafting the final version of a report, writers must pay close attention to both correct English and logical organization.
   D) As for final matters, correctness and effective organization should be the focus of any writer concerned with it.

5. A) Neither welfare benefits nor an im- _____ proved health plan was discussed by the board members.
   B) Neither welfare benefits or an improved health plan was on the agenda at the board meeting.
   C) With more important matters to consider, the board members discussed not welfare benefits or even an improved health plan.
   D) Without discussion of either welfare benefits or an improved health plan at the board meeting.

6. A) Those who require emergency medical _____ attention may do so without loss of pay.
   B) When emergency medical attention is necessary to interrupt the workday, no loss of pay results.
   C) Anyone who must leave work for emergency medical attention will not suffer any loss of pay.
   D) Loss of pay is not given to those who need emergency medical attention during the workday.

7. A) "To Whom It May Concern" is one of _____ many popular grammatically correct phrases.
   B) Among grammatically popular and correct expressions, "To Whom It May Concern" is one of many.

C) When beginning correspondence with "To Whom It May Concern," they can be sure of a popular and grammatical phrase.
D) A number of phrases are both popular and grammatically correct; "To Whom It May Concern" is one of which.

8. A) This year's expenditure for advertising _____ ought to of been much lower.
   B) The firm must devote fewer of its budget to advertising.
   C) The advertising budget should be reduced.
   D) Reduction in the budget for advertising would of been a good idea.

9. A) When only one security officer is on duty _____ in the building, there are those of which take special precautions.
   B) Those who work after hours should be very cautious, being as how only one security officer is on duty.
   C) Only one security officer patrols the building after working hours, so everyone staying late should be very cautious.
   D) All should take precautions over any emergency after hours, rather than to depend on only one security officer.

10. A) An unused office, full of obsolete equip- _____ ment and discarded files, were made ready for the newest member of the firm.
    B) To find office space for someone new, an unused area full of old files and useless equipment is available.
    C) New office space is scarce, except of an area that had been used for storage.
    D) A previously unused office will be renovated for the use of the firm's newest member.

ANSWER EXPLANATIONS FOR PRACTICE SET 6

1. **(D)** In (A), to be parallel, "not having" should read "does not have." In (B), "sufficiency of informing them" is incorrect. In (C), "they serve" should be replaced with "it serves."
2. **(A)** In (B), "prohibited on" is incorrect. In (C), "ways" is incorrect. In (D), "for visitors" is awkwardly placed.
3. **(D)** In each of the other choices, the reference of the pronoun "he" or "his" is not clear.
4. **(C)** In (A), the words following the comma are incorrectly phrased; correct phrasing would be "but also logical organization." In (B), "are"

should be replaced with "is," in order to agree with the singular subject, "correct English." In (D), "it" is a vague pronoun.

5. **(A)** Both (B) and (C) are incorrect because they do not use "neither/not . . . nor" correctly. (D) is not a complete sentence.

6. **(C)** In (A), "may do so" is an inappropriate phrase. In (B), "to interrupt the workday" is illogical. Choice (D) is also illogical, because "loss of pay" is not something that is "given."

7. **(A)** In (B), "grammatically popular" is an illogical phrase. In (C), "they" is unclear. In (D), "of which" is unnecessary.

8. **(C)** In (A), "ought to of" is incorrect. In (B), "fewer" should be replaced with "less." In (D), "would of been" is incorrect.

9. **(C)** In (A), "those of which" is an incorrect phrase. In (B), "being as how" is incorrect. In (D), one error is "precautions over," which should be replaced with "precautions for"; another is "rather than *to* depend"—"to" is incorrect.

10. **(D)** In (A), "were" should be replaced with "was," in order to agree with the subject, "office." (B) illustrates unclear sentence structure and seems to say that the "unused area" is "to find office space." In (C), "except of" should be replaced with "except for."

REVIEWING THE KEY STRATEGIES

Remember to:

1. Read all four sentences before selecting answer.

2. Look for common errors first:

    — incorrect verbs

    — misuse of pronouns

    — incorrect usage

    — unclear meaning

    — repetition

SPELLING

This question type tests your ability to recognize correct spelling. You are given three different spellings of a certain word and are required to choose the correct spelling, if it appears. If it does not appear, you are to choose answer D.

Helpful Techniques and Strategies

1. SEE the word. Very often, we do not recognize words that are misspelled because of the way they are pronounced. For instance, "accidentally" is pronounced "accident-ly" and may be misspelled for that reason.

    After looking at the three choices you are given, look away from the test page and attempt to *see* the word in your mind. Write the word mentally, letter by letter. Doing so may help you to avoid a misspelling based on pronunciation alone.

2. Before taking the test, study a list of commonly misspelled words, such as the following. The common trouble spots are underlined.

3. One way to prepare for this part of the test is to create your own sample questions, using the preceding list of commonly misspelled words. Keeping in mind some basic spelling rules and common spelling errors (some examples follow), devise possible misspellings of these words. This way you will become familiar not only with the correct spelling, but also with possible types of incorrect spellings that may appear on the test. Examples:

absolutely	absalutely	absolootly
foresee	forsee	foursea
vegetable	vegtable	vegetible

TABLE 3
SOME COMMONLY MISSPELLED WORDS

absence	bicycle	correspondence	equipped	independence	necessary	pursuing	sophomore
accept	bulletin	courageous	evidently	influential	neither	quarreling	specimen
accidentally	bureau	course	excitement	ingenious	nickel	really	speech
accommodate	cafeteria	courteous	existence	inoculate	niece	receipt	stomach
accordance	calendar	courtesy	expense	interesting	ninety	received	strength
achievement	campaign	criticism	extension	interfere	ninth	recognize	succeed
acknowledge	captain	crowd	familiar	jealous	noticeable	recommend	success
acquainted	careful	crucial	fascinating	jewelry	occasion	referee	sufficient
acquired	carriage	deceive	fatigue	judgment	occurred	referred	superintendent
across	ceiling	decided	forcibly	justice	often	refugee	surely
advice	cemetery	defendant	forehead	kindergarten	omitted	relieve	surprise
advisable	changeable	dependent	foreign	knowledge	owing	religious	suspense
advise	chaos	descent	foresee	laboratory	pamphlet	remittance	technical
affectionately	chief	desirable	forty	legible	parallel	repetition	terrible
aisle	climbed	despair	forward	lettuce	pastime	reservoir	therefore
allege	cloth	desperate	freight	library	permanent	resistance	thorough
all right	clothes	device	fugitive	lieutenant	personally	restaurant	tobacco
almost	college	disastrous	fundamental	lightning	personnel	rhyme	toward
already	colonel	discipline	further	losing	physically	rhythm	tragedy
altogether	column	disease	generally	lying	planning	ridiculous	transferred
amateur	committee	divided	government	maintenance	possesses	salary	twelfth
annual	common	doubt	grateful	magazine	possibility	sandwich	typical
anxious	comparative	duly	grievance	marriage	possible	scarcely	unusual
apparatus	competition	dying	guarantee	merchandise	preceding	schedule	useful
arctic	confident	effect	guard	miniature	prejudice	secretary	vegetable
article	congratulations	efficiency	handful	mischievous	privilege	seize	village
ascertain	conquer	eighth	harassed	misspelled	probably	sergeant	villain
assistance	conscience	eligible	height	mortgage	procedure	severely	weight
athletic	conscientious	embarrass	heroes	mournful	proceeded	shriek	weird
attacked	conscious	eminent	immediately	movable	prominent	siege	welfare
attendance	consequently	endeavor	incidentally	murmur	proved	sincerely	woman
beggar	convenience	environment	indefinitely	muscle	psychology	skiing	yield
benefited	coolly	equipment					

4. Be familiar with basic spelling rules. Study the following:
   a. ADDING ENDINGS—When a word ends with "e," drop the "e" if the ending begins with a vowel (a, e, i, o, u), but do not drop the "e" if the ending begins with a consonant (b, c, d, f, g, h, etc.). Examples:

   age—aging (drop the "e" when adding "ing")
   manage—management (keep the "e" when adding "ment")

   Change "y" to "i" when adding an ending, except when the ending is "ing." Examples:

   study—studies—studying

   Keep the final "l" when you add "ly." Example:

   personal—personally

   b. "I" BEFORE "E" EXCEPT AFTER "C." Examples:

   field   perceive
   relief   ceiling

   When the sound of "ie" is not ē (ee), the usual spelling is "ei." Examples:

   neighbor
   weigh
   height

   Exceptions to these rules: weird, leisure, friend, mischief

5. Be familiar with types of common spelling errors. We have already cautioned you to become familiar with words that are pronounced differently from the way they are spelled. Besides the confusion of pronunciation and spelling, another common error is *confusing words with the same sound but different spellings.* Study the following list:

TABLE 4
SOME COMMONLY CONFUSED WORDS

air; ere; heir	buy; by
ate; eight	cent; scent; sent
blew; blue	coarse; course
bough; bow	for; four
brake; break	forth; fourth
grate; great	right; write
groan; grown	road; rode
hear; here	sew; so; sow
him; hymn	scene; seen
hole; whole	stationary; stationery
hour; our	steal; steel
its; it's	straight; strait
knew; new	some; sum
know; no	son; sun
lead; led	sweet; suite
mail; male	their; there; they're
meat; meet	threw; through
pail; pale	to; too; two
pair; pare; pear	way; weigh
peace; piece	whose; who's
principal; principle	wood; would
read; red	

6. Keep a personal list of troublesome words. Jot down those words that give you particular spelling problems, and review them regularly.

Sample Questions

Find the correct spelling of the word and write the letter of your choice in the space provided. If no suggested spelling is correct, write choice D.

1. A) accomadate   C) accommodate   _____
   B) accomodate   D) none of these

2. A) calander   C) calendur   _____
   B) calendar   D) none of these

3. A) priviledge   C) privledge   _____
   B) privilege   D) none of these

4. A) recommend   C) recomend   _____
   B) reccommend   D) none of these

5. A) developement   C) devellopment   _____
   B) development   D) none of these

6. A) nickel   C) nickil   _____
   B) nickle   D) none of these

7. A) catagory   C) cattagory   _____
   B) category   D) none of these

Answers to Sample Questions

1. C		5. B	
2. B		6. A	
3. B		7. B	
4. A			

PRACTICE SET 1

Find the correct spelling of the word and write the letter of your choice in the space provided. If no suggested spelling is correct, write choice D.

1. A) fourty C) forety _____
   B) forty D) none of these

2. A) acheivement C) acheivment _____
   B) achievement D) none of these

3. A) accross C) acros _____
   B) across D) none of these

4. A) advertizement C) advertisement _____
   B) adverticement D) none of these

5. A) salary C) sallary _____
   B) salery D) none of these

6. A) permenent C) purmenent _____
   B) permanent D) none of these

7. A) ajourn C) adjourn _____
   B) edjourn D) none of these

8. A) artikle C) articul _____
   B) artical D) none of these

9. A) scarcley C) scarcly _____
   B) scarcely D) none of these

10. A) intresting C) interesting _____
    B) intrestting D) none of these

11. A) magasine C) magazine _____
    B) maggazine D) none of these

12. A) referance C) reference _____
    B) refrence D) none of these

13. A) posible C) posibel _____
    B) possible D) none of these

14. A) gentlemen C) gentelmen _____
    B) gentalmen D) none of these

15. A) consequently C) consecuentally _____
    B) consequentally D) none of these

16. A) captian C) captein _____
    B) captin D) none of these

17. A) carrage C) carriage _____
    B) cariage D) none of these

18. A) aquired C) ackwiered _____
    B) acuired D) none of these

19. A) lutenant C) liutenant _____
    B) lieutenent D) none of these

20. A) independance C) independince _____
    B) independence D) none of these

ANSWERS FOR PRACTICE SET 1

1. (B) forty
2. (B) achievement
3. (B) across
4. (C) advertisement
5. (A) salary
6. (B) permanent
7. (C) adjourn
8. (D) Correct spelling: article
9. (B) scarcely
10. (C) interesting
11. (C) magazine
12. (C) reference
13. (B) possible
14. (A) gentlemen
15. (A) consequently
16. (D) Correct spelling: captain
17. (C) carriage
18. (D) Correct spelling: acquired
19. (D) Correct spelling: lieutenant
20. (B) independence

PRACTICE SET 2

Find the correct spelling of the word and write the letter of your choice in the space provided. If no suggested spelling is correct, write choice D.

1. A) stomach C) stommack _____
   B) stomack D) none of these

2. A) jewlrey C) jewelry _____
   B) jewlry D) none of these

3. A) superentendent C) superentendant _____
   B) superintendant D) none of these

4. A) virticle C) vertical _____
   B) verticle D) none of these

5. A) sofomore C) sophmore _____
   B) sophomore D) none of these

6. A) sarjent C) sargant _____
   B) sargeant D) none of these

7. A) vegtable   C) vegetable   _____
   B) vegtabel   D) none of these

8. A) tobaco   C) tabacco   _____
   B) tobacco   D) none of these

9. A) moregage   C) morgage   _____
   B) mortgage   D) none of these

10. A) merchandice C) merchandise _____
    B) merchandize D) none of these

11. A) omited   C) ommitted   _____
    B) omitted   D) none of these

12. A) memmorandem C) memmorandum _____
    B) memorandum   D) none of these

13. A) minature C) minatoor   _____
    B) miniature D) none of these

14. A) greatful C) graitful   _____
    B) grateful D) none of these

15. A) fudjitive C) fugative   _____
    B) fudgitive D) none of these

16. A) preperations C) preprarations _____
    B) preparations D) none of these

17. A) equiptment   C) equipment   _____
    B) eqwuiptment D) none of these

18. A) buereau   C) bureau   _____
    B) beaureau D) none of these

19. A) accordance C) acordance   _____
    B) accordence D) none of these

20. A) assistence C) assistance _____
    B) assistince D) none of these

ANSWERS FOR PRACTICE SET 2

1. (A) stomach
2. (C) jewelry
3. (D) Correct spelling: superintendent
4. (C) vertical
5. (B) sophomore
6. (D) Correct spelling: sergeant
7. (C) vegetable
8. (B) tobacco
9. (B) mortgage
10. (C) merchandise
11. (B) omitted
12. (B) memorandum

13. (B) miniature
14. (B) grateful
15. (D) Correct spelling: fugitive
16. (B) preparations
17. (C) equipment
18. (C) bureau
19. (A) accordance
20. (C) assistance

PRACTICE SET 3

Find the correct spelling of the word and write the letter of your choice in the space provided. If no suggested spelling is correct, write choice D.

1. A) artic   C) Artic   _____
   B) arctic   D) none of these

2. A) marrage   C) marriage   _____
   B) marraige   D) none of these

3. A) chiminey   C) chimeny   _____
   B) chimney   D) none of these

4. A) perfession C) profession _____
   B) profesion D) none of these

5. A) excape   C) escape   _____
   B) exkape   D) none of these

6. A) surprize   C) surprise   _____
   B) serprise   D) none of these

7. A) congradalations C) congratulations _____
   B) congradulations D) none of these

8. A) reconize   C) recconise   _____
   B) recognize D) none of these

9. A) tomorow   C) tomorrow   _____
   B) tommorrow D) none of these

10. A) atheltics C) athletics   _____
    B) atheletics D) none of these

11. A) disasterous C) desasterous _____
    B) disastrous   D) none of these

12. A) prespire   C) perspire   _____
    B) pirspire   D) none of these

13. A) secratery C) secratary   _____
    B) secretery D) none of these

14. A) umberella C) umberela   _____
    B) umbrella   D) none of these

15. A) lightining C) litening   _____
    B) lightning   D) none of these

16. A) goverment   C) government   _____
    B) govrenment D) none of these

17. A) affectionitely C) affectionately _____
    B) affectionatly   D) none of these

18. A) requirment C) requiremint   _____
    B) requirement D) none of these

19. A) choclate   C) chocolit   _____
    B) chocolet   D) none of these

20. A) asociate   C) assoshiate   _____
    B) associate   D) none of these

ANSWERS FOR PRACTICE SET 3

1. (B) arctic
2. (C) marriage
3. (B) chimney
4. (C) profession
5. (C) escape
6. (C) surprise
7. (C) congratulations
8. (B) recognize
9. (C) tomorrow
10. (C) athletics
11. (B) disastrous
12. (C) perspire
13. (D) Correct spelling: secretary
14. (B) umbrella
15. (B) lightning
16. (C) government
17. (C) affectionately
18. (B) requirement
19. (D) Correct spelling: chocolate
20. (B) associate

PRACTICE SET 4

Find the correct spelling of the word and write the letter of your choice in the space provided. If no suggested spelling is correct, write choice D.

1. A) dependent C) dependint   _____
   B) dependunt D) none of these

2. A) equasion   C) equazion   _____
   B) equation   D) none of these

3. A) excitment C) excitement   _____
   B) exsitement D) none of these

4. A) presense   C) prescence   _____
   B) presence   D) none of these

5. A) envirement C) environment   _____
   B) enviernment D) none of these

6. A) campaine   C) campaign   _____
   B) campain   D) none of these

7. A) corespondence C) corraspondence _____
   B) corispondence D) none of these

8. A) benefit   C) benafit   _____
   B) benifit   D) none of these

9. A) consequentally C) consekwentally _____
   B) consequently   D) none of these

10. A) attendence C) attendance   _____
    B) atendance   D) none of these

11. A) promanent   C) promenint   _____
    B) promenent   D) none of these

12. A) height   C) heighth   _____
    B) hieght   D) none of these

13. A) dropt   C) dropped   _____
    B) droped   D) none of these

14. A) carefull   C) carful   _____
    B) careful   D) none of these

15. A) busness   C) business   _____
    B) bizness   D) none of these

16. A) suceed   C) succed   _____
    B) succede   D) none of these

17. A) english   C) English   _____
    B) Englesh   D) none of these

18. A) cooperation C) cooparation   _____
    B) coaparation D) none of these

19. A) vackume   C) vaccuum   _____
    B) vaccume   D) none of these

20. A) afourmentioned C) aformentioned _____
    B) aforementioned D) none of these

ANSWERS FOR PRACTICE SET 4

1. (A) dependent
2. (B) equation
3. (C) excitement

4. (B) presence
5. (C) environment
6. (C) campaign
7. (D) Correct spelling: correspondence
8. (A) benefit
9. (B) consequently
10. (C) attendance
11. (D) Correct spelling: prominent
12. (A) height
13. (C) dropped
14. (B) careful
15. (C) business
16. (D) Correct spelling: succeed
17. (C) English
18. (A) cooperation
19. (D) Correct spelling: vacuum
20. (B) aforementioned

PRACTICE SET 5

Find the correct spelling of the word and write the letter of your choice in the space provided. If no suggested spelling is correct, write choice D.

1. A) relience   C) reliance   _____
    B) relyance   D) none of these

2. A) adition   C) addittion   _____
    B) addition   D) none of these

3. A) innoculate   C) inocculate   _____
    B) inoculate   D) none of these

4. A) probubly   C) probably   _____
    B) probly   D) none of these

5. A) Febuary   C) February   _____
    B) Febrary   D) none of these

6. A) testimonial   C) testemonial   _____
    B) testamonial   D) none of these

7. A) eficient   C) efficcient   _____
    B) effishient   D) none of these

8. A) necesary   C) necessary   _____
    B) nessesary   D) none of these

9. A) temprature   C) temperature   _____
    B) tempereture   D) none of these

10. A) corperation   C) corporation   _____
     B) corparation   D) none of these

11. A) comittment   C) commitment   _____
     B) committment   D) none of these

12. A) facetously   C) fascetiously   _____
     B) facitiously   D) none of these

13. A) barter   C) bartur   _____
     B) bartar   D) none of these

14. A) recquisite   C) recwisite   _____
     B) requisite   D) none of these

15. A) inteligent   C) intelligint   _____
     B) entelegent   D) none of these

16. A) transatory   C) transitory   _____
     B) transitorry   D) none of these

17. A) langauge   C) langwage   _____
     B) language   D) none of these

18. A) liberry   C) library   _____
     B) libary   D) none of these

19. A) resplendent   C) resplendint   _____
     B) resplendant   D) none of these

20. A) propelor   C) propeller   _____
     B) propellor   D) none of these

ANSWERS FOR PRACTICE SET 5

1. (C) reliance
2. (B) addition
3. (B) inoculate
4. (C) probably
5. (C) February
6. (A) testimonial
7. (D) Correct spelling: efficient
8. (C) necessary
9. (C) temperature
10. (C) corporation
11. (C) commitment
12. (D) Correct spelling: facetiously
13. (A) barter
14. (B) requisite
15. (D) Correct spelling: intelligent
16. (C) transitory
17. (B) language
18. (C) library
19. (A) resplendent
20. (C) propeller

PRACTICE SET 6

Find the correct spelling of the word and write the letter of your choice in the space provided. If no suggested spelling is correct, write choice D.

1. A) wield   C) weilde   _____
   B) weild   D) none of these

2. A) exhilarate   C) exhilerate   _____
   B) exilarate   D) none of these

3. A) misspell   C) misspel   _____
   B) mispell   D) none of these

4. A) grammer   C) grammar   _____
   B) gramar   D) none of these

5. A) existance   C) exsistence   _____
   B) existence   D) none of these

6. A) missile   C) misile   _____
   B) missle   D) none of these

7. A) procede   C) proseed   _____
   B) proceed   D) none of these

8. A) repitition   C) repittition   _____
   B) repetition   D) none of these

9. A) wierd   C) weerd   _____
   B) weird   D) none of these

10. A) embaras   C) embarrass   _____
    B) embarass   D) none of these

11. A) perogative   C) prerogotive   _____
    B) prerogative   D) none of these

12. A) their's   C) theyr's   _____
    B) theirs   D) none of these

13. A) guage   C) gaige   _____
    B) gauge   D) none of these

14. A) aggression   C) aggresion   _____
    B) agression   D) none of these

15. A) restarant   C) restaurant   _____
    B) restrant   D) none of these

16. A) marshul   C) marshalle   _____
    B) marshal   D) none of these

17. A) ristrain   C) restrain   _____
    B) restrane   D) none of these

18. A) cemetary   C) cemetery   _____
    B) cemitery   D) none of these

19. A) irresistible   C) irrisistable   _____
    B) irresistable   D) none of these

20. A) occassion   C) occasion   _____
    B) ocassion   D) none of these

ANSWERS FOR PRACTICE SET 6

1. (A) wield
2. (A) exhilarate
3. (A) misspell
4. (C) grammar
5. (B) existence
6. (A) missile
7. (B) proceed
8. (B) repetition
9. (B) weird
10. (C) embarrass
11. (B) prerogative
12. (B) theirs
13. (B) gauge
14. (A) aggression
15. (C) restaurant
16. (C) marshalle
17. (C) restrain
18. (C) cemetery
19. (A) irresistible
20. (C) occasion

REVIEWING THE KEY STRATEGIES

Remember to:

1. "See" the word.

2. Review your list of commonly misspelled words.

3. Be familiar with basic spelling rules.

4. Be familiar with types of common errors.

5. Keep a personal list of troublesome words.

READING

This question type tests your ability to understand the essential meaning of brief paragraphs. No outside information or knowledge is required to answer each question.

Each paragraph is very brief, sometimes no more than one sentence. One question follows each paragraph, with four answer choices.

Helpful Techniques and Strategies for Reading Each Paragraph

1. Each paragraph usually contains only one main idea, often stated in the first sentence. Identify the main idea in the following sample paragraph:

   > As the legal profession becomes more specialized and complex, clerical assistance must become more specialized as well. One legal secretary might be an expert in bankruptcy law, another an expert in criminal justice.

   The first sentence, a general statement about increasing specialization in the legal profession, states the main idea. It is followed by a more specific statement, which gives additional information. You should practice recognizing this structure: *main idea + additional information*.

2. As you finish reading each paragraph, try to summarize the paragraph mentally, in a few words. For example, after reading the sample paragraph just given, you might summarize it by saying to yourself, "Legal secretaries specialize in different types of law."

3. Note whether the paragraph states a particular attitude toward the subject. Typically, the author will either *approve* or *disapprove* of the main point or remain *neutral*. In the sample passage just given, the author takes no position pro or con, but delivers the additional information in a matter-of-fact way. Consider the following sample passage:

   > In the majority of modern families, both husband and wife work full-time. However, many of these couples become more devoted to their jobs than to each other.

   Here, the main point receives criticism rather than support. The key to the author's attitude here is the contrast word "however"; when a *contrast word* follows the main point, it may indicate the author's disapproval of the main point.

4. If necessary, read the paragraph twice so that you understand it fully. These paragraphs are so brief that an *occasional* rereading will not seriously shorten your allotted time. However, never reread a paragraph until you have read it completely.

5. Don't dwell on unfamiliar words. Usually the context of a paragraph will help you to understand such words. Consider the following sample passage:

   > A regular diet of pizza and beer may have deleterious effects. These foods are loaded with fats and carbohydrates, and add more to one's waistline than to physical well-being.

   Although "deleterious" may be an unfamiliar word, the remainder of the paragraph makes it clear that the effects of pizza and beer are unhealthy, and suggests that "deleterious" has a meaning similar to "unhealthy."

Helpful Techniques and Strategies for Choosing an Answer

Consider once again a sample paragraph that we examined earlier, this time including a question:

> As the legal profession becomes more specialized and complex, clerical assistance must become more specialized as well. One legal secretary might be an expert in bankruptcy law, another an expert in criminal justice.

The paragraph best supports the statement that a legal secretary
A) may understand subjects other than law
B) may have special training in a particular branch of law
C) must be an expert in several types of law
D) is of no use to attorneys

1. When considering the answer choices, try first to eliminate incorrect answers. An incorrect answer often falls into one of three categories:

   a. IRRELEVANT, OR NOT ADDRESSED—Choice (A) is an irrelevant choice. Although particular types of law are mentioned, subjects other than law are not. Note that this statement may certainly be true for some legal secretaries, but receives no support *from the paragraph*.

   b. *CONTRADICTORY*—Choice (C) contradicts information in the passage. The paragraph discusses legal secretaries who specialize in *one* type of law, not several.

   c. *UNREASONABLE*—Choice (D) is an altogether unreasonable statement, according to the paragraph. The passage stresses the special expertise of legal secretaries thus making it unreasonable to conclude that they are useless.

2. In many cases, the correct answer choice will repeat the main point from the paragraph. In this case, the main point is that legal secretaries are becoming more specialized, and the correct answer emphasizes "special training." Notice also that the correct answer here refers as well to the second sentence, which contains additional information about particular branches of law.

   A few more samples:

A regular diet of pizza and beer may have deleterious effects. These foods are loaded with fats and carbohydrates, and add more to one's waistline than to physical well-being.

The paragraph best supports the statement that pizza and beer
A) should be consumed regularly if they are to have the proper effects
B) should definitely be eaten occasionally
C) can be harmful if they make up the main part of every meal
D) should be consumed separately rather than together

The correct answer is (C); it repeats the main point that pizza and beer, if eaten regularly, can have deleterious (harmful to health) effects. Choice (A) contradicts this point. Choice (B) contradicts the author's negative attitude toward pizza and beer. Choice (D) is irrelevant; the issue whether pizza and beer should be consumed separately or together is not addressed by the passage.

The belief that positive thinking is the key to success can lead to laziness. It encourages some people to engage in slipshod work, in the hope that an optimistic mental attitude will take the place of hard, careful, dedicated work.

The paragraph best supports the statement that laziness
A) is always the result of positive thinking
B) is practiced by successful people
C) is only permissible after one has completed a hard day's work
D) may result from a reliance on positive thinking

The correct choice is (D), which repeats the main point that "positive thinking . . . can lead to laziness." However, the paragraph does not say that laziness is *always* the result; therefore (A) is not the best answer. Choice (A) *overstates* the main point of the paragraph; the overstatement is evident in the use of the word "always." Choice (B) is unreasonable and is certainly contradicted by the paragraph. Choice (C) is irrelevant; the paragraph does not discuss *when* laziness is permissible.

PRACTICE SET 1

Select the best answer to each question and write the letter of your choice in the space provided.

1. Hundreds of new self-help books have been _____ published over the last decade. These books generally reflect a positive, optimistic approach to modern problems and challenges, informed by current research in psychology.

   The paragraph best supports the statement that the authors of self-help books

   A) are psychologists
   B) may be aware of current research in psychology
   C) are of greatest value to psychologists
   D) have only been published over the last ten years

2. The recent popularity of hot-air ballooning _____ is yet another instance of nostalgia for the past. Certainly these brightly colored floating globes of air are not modern inventions; rather, they recall the spectacle of county fairs and carnivals from the turn of the century.

   The paragraph best supports the statement that hot-air balloons

   A) could be seen at county fairs and carnivals of the past
   B) are more brightly colored today than they were at the turn of the century
   C) are most popular among those who lived at the turn of the century
   D) have been popular in every century

3. It has been said that a weed is a flower whose _____ virtue has not yet been discovered. As if to prove this point, a number of homeowners who are tired of constantly maintaining a pretty lawn and shrubbery have decided to let weeds run wild in their yards. The result, in some cases, has been quite an attractive array of lively shapes and colors.

   The paragraph best supports the statement that

   A) weeds are not flowers
   B) weeds make a pretty lawn even prettier
   C) weeds can be beautiful
   D) most homeowners prefer to let weeds run wild

4. Although every individual is thinking constantly during the course of every day, no one _____ is aware of his thoughts very often. Just walking a few steps entails a number of mental choices and activities that are performed more or less unconsciously. To become conscious of everything going on in the mind would be immobilizing.

   The paragraph best supports the statement that unconscious mental choices

   A) are performed by everyone every day
   B) are most dangerous when one is not thinking
   C) are immobilizing
   D) occur every few steps

5. Science fiction and fantasy have always appealed to the desire to escape from the boredom of conventional life and to experience the adventure and danger of a new environment. Thrilling to the excitement of "Star Wars" is a way of "getting away from it all."

   The paragraph best supports the statement that "Star Wars"

   A) is popular only with those who are bored with life
   B) provides excitement that conventional life does not
   C) is the best example of science fiction and fantasy
   D) is more thrilling than any other science fiction movie

6. Hitting a baseball is certainly one of the most _____ difficult feats in sports. Even the greatest hitters of all time have been able only to hit safely once for every three trips to the plate. In other words, even great hitters fail more often than they succeed.

   The paragraph best supports the statement that

   A) nothing succeeds like success
   B) it is unrealistic to expect to get a hit more than once in three tries
   C) great hitters must get used to being failures
   D) the difficulty of hitting a baseball causes many potential ballplayers to avoid the sport

7. The microwave oven has become a standard _____ appliance in many kitchens, mainly because it offers a fast way of cooking food, and therefore appeals to the growing number of households whose members maintain busy schedules, and have little time for the slow, conventional preparation of a meal.

   The paragraph best supports the statement that the microwave oven appeals to

A) everyone living in a busy household

B) those who need time to maintain a busy schedule in the kitchen

C) those who need more standard appliances in the kitchen

D) those who are not able to spend much time cooking

8. Clarity, correctness, and coherence are certainly elements of good writing, but interest is the most important element of all; writing that does not provoke and hold a reader's attention rarely succeeds as effective communication. _____

The paragraph best supports the statement that

A) clarity, correctness, and coherence are not important elements of good writing

B) good writers are always interesting people

C) it is possible for writing to be correct without being interesting

D) writing is the most effective means of communication

9. Because so many educators have concluded that interacting with students is more effective than dominating and commanding them, student-centered classrooms (typified by open discussion and sharing) have become more numerous than teacher-centered classrooms (typified by passive attention to lectures). _____

The paragraph best supports the statement that the number of student-centered classrooms

A) is larger than the number of teacher-centered classrooms

B) has been approved by educators

C) means that students are learning more than they ever have before

D) suggests that there are more students dominating teachers than there are teachers dominating students

10. Despite numerous medical studies that publicize health risks associated with caffeine, Americans continue to consume coffee in huge quantities. For most, the benefits of coffee apparently outweigh the dangers. _____

The paragraph best supports the statement that caffeine

A) is included in all brands of coffee

B) is a popular drink in America

C) receives unwarranted attention from the medical profession

D) is the victim of careless scientific research

ANSWER EXPLANATIONS FOR PRACTICE SET 1

1. **(B)** The paragraph states that self-help books are "generally . . . informed by current research in psychology." However, just because these books may contain research in psychology, they are not necessarily authored by psychologists, so (A) is not the best choice.

2. **(A)** The paragraph associates present-day hot-air balloons with those seen at county fairs and carnivals at the turn of the century.

3. **(C)** The passage states that a collection of weeds can be quite attractive.

4. **(A)** The paragraph states that every day "a number of mental choices" are performed "more or less unconsciously."

5. **(B)** The paragraph states that science fiction and fantasy (of which "Star Wars" is an example) provide "escape from the boredom of conventional life."

6. **(B)** Since even the greatest hitters hit safely only once in three tries, we may logically conclude that it is unrealistic to expect to do better than this.

7. **(D)** The paragraph says that the microwave oven appeals to those who have "little time" for the slow preparation of a meal.

8. **(C)** By emphasizing that interest is more important than correctness, the paragraph strongly implies that it is possible for writing to be correct without being interesting.

9. **(A)** Each of the other choices requires assumptions not supported by the paragraph. The paragraph does explicitly state that student-centered classrooms "have become more numerous" than teacher-centered classrooms.

10. **(B)** The paragraph explicitly states that "Americans . . . consume coffee in huge quantities."

PRACTICE SET 2

Select the best answer to each question and write the letter of your choice in the space provided.

1. Comedy is an art that is constantly changing. _____ What was funny a few years ago seems merely silly now, mainly because the public tastes and public issues that are the substance of comedy have themselves changed. New events result in new blunders, and provide the material for new jokes.

The paragraph best supports the statement that

A) today's jokes are different than they were years ago
B) today's jokes refer only to current events
C) comedians are finding it difficult to write new material
D) comedy writers are constantly changing

2. Being new and different does not ensure the _____ success of a product. Advertisers must see to it that buyers who will use the product hear about it; they must place their advertising in the right spot. Little is gained by advertising denture adhesive during a Saturday morning cartoon show.

The paragraph best supports the statement that

A) Saturday morning cartoon shows do not contain advertisements
B) Saturday morning cartoon shows only advertise products that are not new and different
C) most buyers are shopping rather than watching television on Saturday mornings
D) those who use denture adhesive are not likely to be the viewers of Saturday morning cartoon shows

3. Some American auto factories are beginning _____ to resemble their Japanese counterparts. In many Japanese factories, the workers enjoy the same status and privileges as their bosses. Everyone works in harmony, and there is much less of the tension and anger that results when one group dominates another.

The paragraph best supports the statement that

A) everyone works in harmony in Japan
B) workers and bosses share the same status in some American factories
C) there is one main cause of tension and anger
D) Japanese factories have been influenced by the success of the American auto industry

4. Scientists persist in their efforts to improve _____ on nature. Making advances in genetic engineering, some researchers expect to invent new forms of life soon. One bacterium under development can consume and digest toxic wastes, and thus help clean up the environment.

The paragraph best supports the statement that

A) toxic wastes pose the most serious environmental problem, as far as scientists are concerned

B) it is the responsibility of scientists to improve on nature
C) a bacterium that can consume and digest toxic wastes would be a new form of life
D) inventing new forms of life takes persistence

5. The foliage and ground cover growing along _____ the nation's superhighways serve at least two functions. They help make traveling a more pleasant visual experience, and they help absorb the noise of thousands of automobile engines.

The paragraph best supports the statement that

A) foliage and ground cover are planted along superhighways for more than one reason
B) automobile engines become less noisy on superhighways
C) there are only two reasons for planting foliage and ground cover along superhighways
D) pleasant scenery results in safer driving

6. An emphasis on orderly behavior and discipline _____ in junior high school and high school prepares young adults to join the work force upon graduation, where they must adhere to rules and regulations. But a school experience that does not encourage free expression, individuality, and creativity may produce obedient workers who are not able to think for themselves.

The paragraph best supports the statement that junior high school and high school

A) are not educating young adults properly
B) do not employ teachers who can think for themselves
C) should encourage qualities other than orderly behavior and discipline
D) punish those who are creative

7. Comic strips can often provide a commentary _____ on everyday life, along with entertainment. The characters from "Peanuts," for instance, represent types of people that everyone encounters regularly: the bumbling nice guy; the brash, insensitive loudmouth; and the student for whom school is a bore.

The paragraph best supports the statement that the characters in "Peanuts"

A) do not represent particular individuals
B) handle real life better than real people
C) represent the three most common types of people one encounters in everyday life
D) appear in other comic strips as well

8. In the 1930s, the first modern health spas _____ were built, complete with efficient exercise equipment, swimming pools, and full-service locker rooms. But health spas did not become wildly popular until the 1980s; now one cannot travel very far in any big city without seeing one.

The paragraph best supports the statement that the popularity of health spas

A) is the result of improved exercise equipment
B) could not be measured in the 1930s
C) has increased since the 1930s
D) only exists in big cities

9. Poets who wish to compose a Japanese haiku _____ must follow a formula: There are three lines in all, a first line of five syllables, a second line of seven syllables, and a third line of five syllables. The restriction to precisely seventeen syllables makes the haiku form quite difficult to master.

The paragraph best supports the statement that writing a haiku

A) is difficult for someone who is not Japanese
B) may include more than three lines
C) extends beyond thirty-five syllables in special cases
D) is not an easy task, even though the form of the poem is simple

10. The length and structure of the workweek _____ have undergone a good deal of change in recent years. Workers who once labored eight hours each day, forty hours each week, Monday through Friday, are now allowed to determine their own schedules to some extent. Those who are able to complete assigned tasks efficiently and effectively during a shortened or irregular schedule, or those who can work better during different hours from the standard ones, are allowed an adjusted schedule by some companies.

The paragraph best supports the statement that some workers

A) are unable to work efficiently and effectively
B) may work on Saturday or Sunday
C) are employed by old-fashioned companies
D) work much more than forty hours each week

ANSWER EXPLANATIONS FOR PRACTICE SET 2

1. **(A)** The paragraph repeatedly stresses that what is funny now is different from what was funny in the past.
2. **(D)** The paragraph stresses that advertising must be placed in the "right spots" and concludes by implying that a cartoon show is not the right spot to appeal to "buyers who will use the product."
3. **(B)** The passage states that some American factories are beginning to operate like those in Japan, relative to the relationship between workers and bosses.
4. **(C)** The "bacterium under development" is mentioned as an example of "new forms of life."
5. **(A)** The passage states that foliage and ground cover "serve at least two functions."
6. **(C)** The passage calls for the encouragement of "free expression, individuality, and creativity."
7. **(A)** The passage states that the comic strip's characters represent "types of people," thus strongly implying that they do not represent particular individuals.
8. **(C)** The paragraph states that health spas became "wildly popular" in the 1980s.
9. **(D)** The paragraph states explicitly that the haiku form is "quite difficult to master."
10. **(B)** The paragraph stresses that some workers no longer work during the standard, Monday through Friday, workweek; this fact strongly implies that some workers may work on Saturday or Sunday. The paragraph does not suggest, however, that the workweek has become longer than forty hours, so (D) is not the best answer.

PRACTICE SET 3

Select the best answer to each question and write the letter of your choice in the space provided.

1. The relationship between architecture and _____ geometry becomes apparent once one surveys the newest buildings under construction in metropolitan areas. Each structure is a precise combination of triangles, rectangles, and trapezoids, arranged so that angles jut out in unusual places, in an array of lively designs.

The paragraph best supports the statement that new buildings

A) are more pleasant to look at than old ones
B) utilize a number of geometric shapes
C) were constructed to reflect a love of geometry
D) are designed to teach geometry to observers

2. Fast food is becoming more nutritious. Salad _____
bars are appearing at places that only served
hamburgers once, offering diners the benefits of fresh vegetables. And the menus are
expanding in other directions as well, offering chicken sandwiches on whole wheat
buns, and low-fat yogurt desserts. With families cooking less often and eating out more
often, the diet provided by fast-food chains
has a great impact on the health of the nation;
it would seem that the budget restaurants are
taking seriously their responsibility to nour-
ish us.

The paragraph best supports the statement that the
improved nutrition of fast food is

A) affecting the health of many people
B) probably only a temporary trend
C) mainly based on the availability of more fresh
vegetables
D) a response to widespread malnutrition

3. Few people understand poetry, and few pre- _____
fer to read it. Although English professors
speak in glowing terms about the greatness
of Pope's *Rape of the Lock* and Tennyson's
Ulysses, it seems that only other professors
share their enthusiasm. To appreciate the
greatness of difficult poetry, readers must exercise great patience and concentration, and
must tolerate the unusual, compressed language of rhythm and rhyme; with so many
urgent issues demanding our attention at almost every hour of the day, choosing to figure out a poem seems an unlikely possibility.

The paragraph best supports the statement that poetry is popular

A) because so many people love the satisfaction
that comes from understanding a great poem
B) because English professors have generated en-
thusiasm in so many of their students
C) with those who love rhymes
D) with a small, specialized group

4. Those who try to increase their vocabulary _____
by memorizing words and definitions are
wasting time. Only by employing language in
real situations do we make it familiar. Therefore, the most effective way to learn a new
word is to use it, again and again.

The paragraph best supports the statement that people can increase their vocabulary by

A) memorizing more than just word lists and definitions

B) using only the words they need to use
C) creating situations that require unusual lan-
guage
D) using new words whenever possible

5. Meteorology may qualify as a science, but _____
there is a great deal of guesswork involved as
well. Even with tremendous knowledge
about wind currents and weather patterns,
and the most sophisticated equipment, fore-
casters' predictions are often wrong. The
movement of a phenomenon as prominent as
a hurricane cannot even be determined very
far in advance. We remain the servants and
victims of the weather, not its masters.

The paragraph best supports the statement that the
science of weather prediction

A) is only accurate when the weather is fair
B) is useless when it comes to hurricanes
C) is not yet sophisticated enough to achieve accu-
racy consistently
D) does not qualify as a science

6. More children die each year from automo- _____
bile accidents than from any other single
cause. This fact should be sufficient to force
each of the 50 states to enact a mandatory seat
belt law, but such laws have not yet swept the
country. If we are to preserve our most precious natural resource, however, we must
take steps that make buckling up imperative
everywhere.

The paragraph best supports the statement that children are

A) our most precious natural resource
B) ignored in most states
C) not willing to wear seat belts
D) dying more frequently than ever

7. A baseball game can be described as a series _____
of solo performances: at any given moment,
attention is focused on one player and one
play. On the other hand, soccer involves all
of the team most of the time: each player in-
teracts with others constantly, so that no single individual seems responsible for success
or failure. It is perhaps because spectators
enjoy concentrating on individual personalities that baseball remains a much more popular spectator sport than soccer.

The paragraph best supports the statement that the
popularity of baseball

A) will always be greater than the popularity of soccer
B) cannot be compared to the popularity of soccer
C) may be related to the preferences of spectators
D) will remain strong as long as individual players maintain their skills

8. Modern word processing equipment makes _____ the preparation of business correspondence easier and more efficient, perhaps. Typing errors disappear from the monitor at the touch of a button, and the final printout takes only seconds to produce. However, some typists have not yet become comfortable with staring at a text displayed on a screen; they are used to black letters on a white background, and cannot perceive textual errors as readily when faced with white letters on a dark background.

The paragraph best supports the statement that the typing errors that appear on a word processor screen

A) are more serious than those that appear on paper
B) are more difficult for some typists to recognize
C) disappear before they can be corrected
D) are more modern than errors produced on a typewriter

9. Student protesters are more polite than they _____ used to be. One need only recall the violent riots of the 1960s, led by ragged, long-haired political activists, to notice the difference that prevails today: while the demonstrators of yesteryear yelled obscenities at the police and openly flouted civic regulations, today's demonstrators cooperate almost meekly with law enforcement officials, maintaining a neat, orderly, peaceful display while they express political dissent.

The paragraph best supports the statement that

A) today's protesters are not as effective as the protesters of the 1960s
B) law enforcement officials encounter less hostility from protesters now than they did in the 1960s
C) today's protesters wear nice clothes and have short hair
D) civic regulations have changed since the 1960s, and are not so offensive to protesters anymore

10. Everyone who collects books is not an avid _____ reader. Some prefer to fill their homes with shelves of novels, travelogues, and self-help

guides for the purpose of display and decoration only. They enjoy the accessibility of knowledge and information, but rarely partake of the storehouse.

The paragraph best supports the statement that those who buy books

A) prefer only novels, travelogues, and self-help guides
B) decorate their homes with books alone
C) have added a storehouse onto their home
D) do not necessarily read them

ANSWER EXPLANATIONS FOR PRACTICE SET 3

1. **(B)** The passage states that new buildings display geometric shapes: triangles, rectangles, and trapezoids.
2. **(A)** The paragraph states that the availability of more nutritious fast food "has a great impact on the health of the nation."
3. **(D)** The paragraph states that poetry seems to be popular mainly with professors (2nd sentence); professors are a small, specialized group.
4. **(D)** All the other choices contradict the information in the passage; (D) repeats the point of the third sentence.
5. **(C)** Several times the passage makes the point that predicting the weather involves "a great deal of guesswork" and can be inaccurate.
6. **(A)** The value of children is stressed throughout the passage, and they are called "our most precious natural resource" in the final sentence.
7. **(C)** The final sentence of the paragraph proposes that what the spectators enjoy (individual personalities) may determine the greater popularity of baseball.
8. **(B)** The passage states that "some typists . . . cannot perceive textual errors as readily" on a word processor screen.
9. **(B)** The major change emphasized in the passage is the increased cooperation with law enforcement officials.
10. **(D)** The paragraph explicitly states that every collector of books "is not an avid reader."

PRACTICE SET 4

Select the best answer to each question and write the letter of your choice in the space provided.

1. The federal government is becoming more _____ vigilant when it comes to toxic waste. Probably as a result of widespread press coverage

of the Love Canal disaster a few years ago, politicians and bureaucrats are more sensitive to heightened public attention to mismanaged chemical dumps and the health hazards they pose. Heavy fines are being imposed upon those who have ignored regulations about safe waste disposal.

The paragraph best supports the statement that the Love Canal disaster

A) was the first disaster of its kind
B) led to a number of other, more serious disasters involving unsafe waste disposal
C) was the first disaster that attracted the attention of the federal government
D) involved the issue of toxic waste

2. Sociologists have noted that children today _____ are less "childish" than ever; when they are still very young, perhaps only six or seven years old, children are already mimicking adult fashions and leading relatively independent lives. Dressed in designer jeans, an elementary school child is likely to spend much of every day fending for herself, taking charge of her own life while waiting for her working parents to arrive home. Less dependent on adults for their day-to-day decisions, children "grow up" faster.

The paragraph best supports the statement that children today are

A) likely to wear only fashion jeans
B) likely to be more intelligent than children of six or seven years ago
C) not interested in the opinions of their parents
D) likely to have parents who are employed outside the home during the day

3. The new American revolution is an electronic one. Advances in sophisticated circuitry have yielded more gadgets than anyone could have imagined only a few years ago: calculators as small as a wristwatch and automobile dashboards full of digital readouts are two of the many products that have enhanced the quality of life. There is some fear, however, that we may become so dependent on solid-state circuits to do our thinking that we may forget how to do it ourselves.

The paragraph best supports the statement that although progress in electronic progress has improved the quality of life, it

A) may affect our ability to think independently

B) has merely provided gadgets
C) has made those who use electronic devices more afraid of them than ever
D) is not nearly as sophisticated as it will become in the next century

4. There are advantages and disadvantages to _____ clear, simple writing. Sentences that are easy to understand are processed more quickly and efficiently by readers; those who can express themselves in simple terms are rarely misunderstood. However, prose that is crystal clear often lacks both complexity and imagination. Whether one chooses a style that is simple and clear or complex and unusual often depends upon the tolerance of one's readers.

The paragraph best supports the statement that more tolerant readers will

A) be less willing to read simple and clear writing
B) be more willing to read complex and unusual writing
C) be confused easily
D) demand writing that is complex, unusual, and easy to misunderstand

5. Years ago, a nationwide poll concluded that _____ there are more televisions than there are bathtubs in American homes. No doubt that fact remains today, especially in light of the growing popularity of home computers. Now, in addition to owning televisions for entertainment, more and more families are purchasing TV monitors for use with a personal computer. We can guess safely that there are still many more people staring at a picture tube than singing in the shower.

The paragraph best supports the statement that

A) cleanliness is less important to Americans than it used to be
B) most homes do not require more than one bathtub
C) the general results of the nationwide poll taken years ago are still true
D) few people have televisions in the bathroom

6. Some have called Californians the nomads of _____ America. While those living in the Midwest, the South, and the East tend to reside in the same place for a number of years, Californians change addresses regularly. The constant mobility of California residents helps to keep the real estate industry in that state thriving.

The paragraph best supports the statement that real estate sales

A) are related to how frequently a population changes addresses
B) have always been better in California than in any other state
C) are more important to Californians than to the residents of other states
D) are virtually nonexistent outside California

7. Recently, cable television firms have faced _____ stiff competition from the home video industry. Given the choice of either renting movies for home viewing or subscribing to a cable service that offers recent films, consumers are choosing the rentals. Many say that local video stores offer a wider choice of movies than any cable station, and that renting movies allows viewers the freedom to watch them at any time, so they are not tied to the cable station schedule.

The paragraph best supports the statement that consumers

A) prefer to rent movies rather than buy them
B) value freedom of choice
C) would like to upgrade the quality of cable television firms
D) watch a greater number of movies than cable television firms have been able to provide

8. A recent experiment in psychology yielded _____ results that are difficult to interpret. Researchers found that whenever the light bulbs were changed in the workplace, production increased. Although the brightness in the room neither increased nor decreased, the workers worked better each time a custodial crew changed the bulbs. Perhaps just the sight of the light bulbs being changed led the workers to feel that conditions had improved, and to work better.

The paragraph best supports the statement that the results of the psychology experiment

A) will lead to a continual increase in production
B) had no effect on the work of the custodial crew
C) lead to no definite conclusions
D) will be used to improve working conditions in a number of companies

9. Some teachers prefer "creative" writers, and _____ some prefer "correct" writers. Rarely does one encounter a student who writes unconventional and exciting prose while also obey-

ing all the rules and conventions of standard written English. It may be impossible for any writer to be both radical and obedient at the same time.

The paragraph best supports the statement that a writer who is both creative and correct

A) is rarely successful in school
B) is preferred by half of the teachers he encounters
C) tends to confuse being radical with being obedient
D) knows how to deviate from the rules of standard written English

10. Many aviators are also avid sailors, perhaps _____ because the principles of flying are so similar to the principles of sailing, so that participants in both sports enjoy the thrill of riding the wind.

The paragraph best supports the statement that

A) learning to sail qualifies one to fly an airplane
B) flying is most thrilling on windy days
C) many aviators are sailors, but no sailors are aviators
D) many aviators, when not flying, enjoy sailing

ANSWER EXPLANATIONS FOR PRACTICE SET 4

1. **(D)** The paragraph discusses government attention to toxic waste, and the Love Canal disaster is cited as a specific example.
2. **(D)** The individual who represents "children today" in the paragraph waits "for her working parents to arrive home"; the strong implication here is that the parents are employed outside the home.
3. **(A)** The final sentence of the paragraph contrasts the enhanced quality of life with the possibility that electronic devices may "do our thinking" for us.
4. **(B)** The paragraph associates a writer's chosen style with the tolerance of readers and implies that complex and unusual writing requires more tolerant readers because it is not understood as "quickly and efficiently" as simple and clear writing.
5. **(C)** The paragraph states that the "fact remains today" that there are more televisions than bathtubs in American homes.
6. **(A)** The passage associates the "mobility of California residents" with a thriving real estate industry, but does not support any of the other possible choices.
7. **(B)** The paragraph states that consumers prefer the freedom to choose both their movies and their viewing time.

8. **(C)** Although the paragraph reaches a conclusion that is "perhaps" true, it emphasizes that the results of the experiment "are difficult to interpret," and states no *definite* conclusions.

9. **(D)** The creative and correct writer knows the rules and also knows how to write "unconventional" prose, that is, prose that deviates from the rules.

10. **(D)** The paragraph explicitly states that "many aviators are also avid sailors."

PRACTICE SET 5

Select the best answer to each question and write the letter of your choice in the space provided.

1. Historians accept the fact that writing history _____ requires interpreting the past, not just cataloguing it. As a mere collection of facts, the history of the Civil War means nothing; only when the facts are analyzed and explained does this event become significant.

   The paragraph best supports the statement that a list of facts about the Civil War is

   A) what most historians are interested in
   B) mistaken for history by those who are not historians
   C) not so important as the analysis and explanation of those facts
   D) usually too dull for any historian

2. The automobile engine is an unappreciated _____ marvel. Consider its durability alone, as it endures tens of thousands of miles of wear and tear over years and years, and still starts up every morning.

   The paragraph best supports the statement that those who drive automobiles

   A) abuse their automobile engines
   B) do not usually consider the amazing durability of the engine
   C) run the engine longer than they should
   D) know almost nothing about how an automobile engine works

3. Babe Ruth still holds the official record for _____ the most home runs hit in one season. Roger Maris hit 61 home runs, to top Ruth's record of 60, but Maris batted in 162 games, compared to 154 games for Ruth.

   The paragraph best supports the statement that Roger Maris

   A) played in a number of unofficial baseball games, but hit home runs in none of them
   B) did not hit a home run again after the season in which he hit 61
   C) probably had more chances to hit home runs, during the season, than Babe Ruth did
   D) was a more powerful hitter than Babe Ruth, despite the existence of Ruth's record

4. Many gamblers seem unwilling to admit that _____ chance and luck largely determine who wins and loses. Many develop elaborate schemes and systems for winning at blackjack and roulette, but only very few leave the casino wealthier than when they entered.

   The paragraph best supports the statement that a system for winning at blackjack

   A) depends to a great extent upon chance and luck for its success
   B) should only be used by gamblers who consider themselves lucky
   C) can also be useful for winning at roulette and other casino games
   D) has been tried by many gamblers who have relied on chance and luck as well

5. Secretaries must be experts in human relations as well as office procedures. Much of their time every day is spent advising and counseling others about programs and policies, and repeatedly adjusting to the variety of persons and personalities that visits the office each day.

   The paragraph best supports the statement that the ability to interact effectively with a variety of different people

   A) should not be expected of a secretary, even though it is a valuable skill
   B) is only useful during the times that the office is very busy
   C) is a very important and necessary secretarial skill
   D) should only be demanded of secretaries who have had extensive training in human relations

6. Social observers have noted that "stress," _____ which is such a popular affliction in this decade, was virtually unheard-of in the recent past. Our grandparents accorded no special status to everyday tension, and they seem to have experienced less of such tension than we do now. If "stress" did not receive so much publicity these days, perhaps many of us would not feel compelled to suffer from it.

The paragraph best supports the statement that the widespread publicity of stress

A) is something that those of past generations would not have allowed
B) may actually influence the occurrence of stress
C) never compelled our grandparents to pay any attention to everyday tension
D) has gone unnoticed by many of us

7. A neat, orderly workplace encourages calmness and efficiency, just as a messy workplace provokes tension and wastefulness. In other words, the qualities of the workplace draw out related qualities in the workers.

The paragraph best supports the statement that the appearance of a workplace

A) is usually neat and orderly
B) is completely dependent on the abilities of the workers
C) can affect the behavior of the workers
D) must be maintained on a regular basis, just as personal qualities such as wastefulness must be maintained on a regular basis.

8. For inexperienced writers, often the most difficult task is writing an introduction. Therefore, it is sometimes best to delay writing the introductory paragraph until after the body, or "middle" of the essay, is complete.

The paragraph best supports the statement that

A) experienced writers may not need to delay writing the introductory paragraph
B) experienced writers must always write the introductory paragraph before writing the body of the essay
C) without first reading the body of the essay, inexperienced writers cannot tell what they are supposed to write about
D) the introductory paragraph is always a disaster for inexperienced writers

9. As digital clocks replace traditional, radial timepieces, the connection between time and the rotation of the earth is less evident. As the hands of a radial clock move in a circle, from hour to hour, they mimic the turning of the earth on its axis, during the course of each twenty-four-hour day.

The paragraph best supports the statement that the movement of a radial clock

A) reminds everyone of the rotation of the sun around the earth
B) is less accurate, but more natural, than the movement of a digital clock
C) only pretends to duplicate the rotation of the earth
D) is significantly different from the movement of a digital clock

10. The interior design of a restaurant can invite _____ customers to either dine leisurely, or eat and run. Dark, soft upholstery and soft lighting are conducive to a long, relaxed meal; on the other hand, stiff, thinly padded chairs and brightly illuminated dining areas seem to keep people from remaining for very long.

The paragraph best supports the statement that the length of time that one spends at a restaurant meal

A) is usually spent relaxing in a dark atmosphere
B) can vary with the quality of the food as well as the interior design of the restaurant
C) may be affected by the interior design of the restaurant
D) is never pleasant when the room is brightly lit and the chairs are thinly padded

ANSWER EXPLANATIONS FOR PRACTICE SET 5

1. (C) The paragraph stresses that analysis and explanation, rather than facts alone, are important to historians.
2. (B) The passage calls the automobile engine an "unappreciated marvel" and follows with a discussion of engine durability, thus implying that drivers do not usually consider the durability of the engine.
3. (C) The paragraph states that Maris hit 61 home runs in a season that was longer than the season during which Ruth set his record; therefore, we may conclude that Maris probably had more chances than Ruth to hit home runs.
4. (A) The paragraph states explicitly that "chance and luck largely determine who wins and loses."
5. (C) The importance of "adjusting to the variety of persons and personalities" is emphasized in the paragraph.
6. (B) The final sentence suggests a relationship between the publicity of stress and the occurrence of it.

7. (C) The paragraph compares the appearance of the workplace with the "qualities in the workers," pointing out that the workers are affected by the workplace.

8. (A) The paragraph suggests that inexperienced writers may need to delay writing the introductory paragraph, and thus implies that experienced writers may not need to delay writing the introductory paragraph.

9. (D) The passage contrasts digital clocks with radial timepieces, in the first sentence.

10. (C) It is the interior design of the restaurant that invites customers "to either dine leisurely, or eat and run."

REVIEWING THE KEY STRATEGIES

Remember to:

1. Eliminate incorrect answers first. They may be:
   — irrelevant
   — contradictory
   — unreasonable

2. Look for correct answer choices that repeat or re-emphasize main points of the passage.

CHAPTER 3

Three Verbal Abilities Model Tests
with Answer Explanations

This chapter contains three complete full-length model tests with answers and explanations. The purpose of this chapter is to help you master the techniques for working quickly under time pressure. After correcting each model test, assess your strengths and weaknesses and return to the specific review section for additional review.

The model tests should be taken under strict test conditions. This means:

—no scratch paper permitted

—any scratch work must be done on test booklet

—answers must be marked on answer sheet

—use #2 pencils with erasers

—follow time limits exactly. (Use an alarm clock.) Thirty-five minutes for each test. You may not proceed to test #2 until 35 minutes are up for test #1. Then you may not return to test #1.

—no interruptions allowed

—no aids permitted (such as dictionary, calculator, etc.)

NOTE: Sample questions are usually distributed with the announcement and if so may not be given in the official examinations.

Remember to tear out your answer sheet preceding each model test.

ANSWER SHEET

SIGNATURE: _____
(Please Sign)

EXAMINATION TITLE: _____

PLACE OF EXAMINATION: _____
City _____ State _____

TODAY'S DATE: _____

SAMPLE Ⓐ ● Ⓒ Ⓓ Ⓔ

DIRECTIONS FOR MARKING ANSWER SHEET

Use only a **No. 2 (or softer) lead pencil**. Darken completely the circle corresponding to your answer. You **must** keep your mark within the circle. Stray marks may be counted as errors. Erase **completely** all marks except your answer.

SAMPLE NAME GRID

		F.I.	M.I.
	LAST NAME	C	A

1. In the boxes below, **PRINT** your name. Print only as many letters as will fit within the areas for the last name, first initial (F.I.), and middle initial (M.I.) Below each box, darken the circle containing the same letter. SEE SAMPLE NAME GRID

LAST NAME | F.I. | M.I.

2. In the boxes below, enter your 9-digit Social Security Number. Below each box, darken the circle in each column corresponding to the number you have entered.

SOCIAL SECURITY NUMBER

3. OCCUPATIONAL GROUP NUMBER

SECTION 1

Make no marks or entries in the columns to the right until you receive instructions from the administrator.

P A R T

TEST SERIES

TEST NUMBER

1 Ⓐ Ⓑ Ⓒ Ⓓ Ⓔ	11 Ⓐ Ⓑ Ⓒ Ⓓ Ⓔ	31 Ⓐ Ⓑ Ⓒ Ⓓ Ⓔ	51 Ⓐ Ⓑ Ⓒ Ⓓ Ⓔ	71 Ⓐ Ⓑ Ⓒ Ⓓ Ⓔ	91 Ⓐ Ⓑ Ⓒ Ⓓ Ⓔ	111 Ⓐ Ⓑ Ⓒ Ⓓ Ⓔ
2 Ⓐ Ⓑ Ⓒ Ⓓ Ⓔ	12 Ⓐ Ⓑ Ⓒ Ⓓ Ⓔ	32 Ⓐ Ⓑ Ⓒ Ⓓ Ⓔ	52 Ⓐ Ⓑ Ⓒ Ⓓ Ⓔ	72 Ⓐ Ⓑ Ⓒ Ⓓ Ⓔ	92 Ⓐ Ⓑ Ⓒ Ⓓ Ⓔ	112 Ⓐ Ⓑ Ⓒ Ⓓ Ⓔ
3 Ⓐ Ⓑ Ⓒ Ⓓ Ⓔ	13 Ⓐ Ⓑ Ⓒ Ⓓ Ⓔ	33 Ⓐ Ⓑ Ⓒ Ⓓ Ⓔ	53 Ⓐ Ⓑ Ⓒ Ⓓ Ⓔ	73 Ⓐ Ⓑ Ⓒ Ⓓ Ⓔ	93 Ⓐ Ⓑ Ⓒ Ⓓ Ⓔ	113 Ⓐ Ⓑ Ⓒ Ⓓ Ⓔ
4 Ⓐ Ⓑ Ⓒ Ⓓ Ⓔ	14 Ⓐ Ⓑ Ⓒ Ⓓ Ⓔ	34 Ⓐ Ⓑ Ⓒ Ⓓ Ⓔ	54 Ⓐ Ⓑ Ⓒ Ⓓ Ⓔ	74 Ⓐ Ⓑ Ⓒ Ⓓ Ⓔ	94 Ⓐ Ⓑ Ⓒ Ⓓ Ⓔ	114 Ⓐ Ⓑ Ⓒ Ⓓ Ⓔ
5 Ⓐ Ⓑ Ⓒ Ⓓ Ⓔ	15 Ⓐ Ⓑ Ⓒ Ⓓ Ⓔ	35 Ⓐ Ⓑ Ⓒ Ⓓ Ⓔ	55 Ⓐ Ⓑ Ⓒ Ⓓ Ⓔ	75 Ⓐ Ⓑ Ⓒ Ⓓ Ⓔ	95 Ⓐ Ⓑ Ⓒ Ⓓ Ⓔ	115 Ⓐ Ⓑ Ⓒ Ⓓ Ⓔ
6 Ⓐ Ⓑ Ⓒ Ⓓ Ⓔ	16 Ⓐ Ⓑ Ⓒ Ⓓ Ⓔ	36 Ⓐ Ⓑ Ⓒ Ⓓ Ⓔ	56 Ⓐ Ⓑ Ⓒ Ⓓ Ⓔ	76 Ⓐ Ⓑ Ⓒ Ⓓ Ⓔ	96 Ⓐ Ⓑ Ⓒ Ⓓ Ⓔ	116 Ⓐ Ⓑ Ⓒ Ⓓ Ⓔ
7 Ⓐ Ⓑ Ⓒ Ⓓ Ⓔ	17 Ⓐ Ⓑ Ⓒ Ⓓ Ⓔ	37 Ⓐ Ⓑ Ⓒ Ⓓ Ⓔ	57 Ⓐ Ⓑ Ⓒ Ⓓ Ⓔ	77 Ⓐ Ⓑ Ⓒ Ⓓ Ⓔ	97 Ⓐ Ⓑ Ⓒ Ⓓ Ⓔ	117 Ⓐ Ⓑ Ⓒ Ⓓ Ⓔ
8 Ⓐ Ⓑ Ⓒ Ⓓ Ⓔ	18 Ⓐ Ⓑ Ⓒ Ⓓ Ⓔ	38 Ⓐ Ⓑ Ⓒ Ⓓ Ⓔ	58 Ⓐ Ⓑ Ⓒ Ⓓ Ⓔ	78 Ⓐ Ⓑ Ⓒ Ⓓ Ⓔ	98 Ⓐ Ⓑ Ⓒ Ⓓ Ⓔ	118 Ⓐ Ⓑ Ⓒ Ⓓ Ⓔ
9 Ⓐ Ⓑ Ⓒ Ⓓ Ⓔ	19 Ⓐ Ⓑ Ⓒ Ⓓ Ⓔ	39 Ⓐ Ⓑ Ⓒ Ⓓ Ⓔ	59 Ⓐ Ⓑ Ⓒ Ⓓ Ⓔ	79 Ⓐ Ⓑ Ⓒ Ⓓ Ⓔ	99 Ⓐ Ⓑ Ⓒ Ⓓ Ⓔ	119 Ⓐ Ⓑ Ⓒ Ⓓ Ⓔ
10 Ⓐ Ⓑ Ⓒ Ⓓ Ⓔ	20 Ⓐ Ⓑ Ⓒ Ⓓ Ⓔ	40 Ⓐ Ⓑ Ⓒ Ⓓ Ⓔ	60 Ⓐ Ⓑ Ⓒ Ⓓ Ⓔ	80 Ⓐ Ⓑ Ⓒ Ⓓ Ⓔ	100 Ⓐ Ⓑ Ⓒ Ⓓ Ⓔ	120 Ⓐ Ⓑ Ⓒ Ⓓ Ⓔ
	21 Ⓐ Ⓑ Ⓒ Ⓓ Ⓔ	41 Ⓐ Ⓑ Ⓒ Ⓓ Ⓔ	61 Ⓐ Ⓑ Ⓒ Ⓓ Ⓔ	81 Ⓐ Ⓑ Ⓒ Ⓓ Ⓔ	101 Ⓐ Ⓑ Ⓒ Ⓓ Ⓔ	121 Ⓐ Ⓑ Ⓒ Ⓓ Ⓔ
	22 Ⓐ Ⓑ Ⓒ Ⓓ Ⓔ	42 Ⓐ Ⓑ Ⓒ Ⓓ Ⓔ	62 Ⓐ Ⓑ Ⓒ Ⓓ Ⓔ	82 Ⓐ Ⓑ Ⓒ Ⓓ Ⓔ	102 Ⓐ Ⓑ Ⓒ Ⓓ Ⓔ	122 Ⓐ Ⓑ Ⓒ Ⓓ Ⓔ
	23 Ⓐ Ⓑ Ⓒ Ⓓ Ⓔ	43 Ⓐ Ⓑ Ⓒ Ⓓ Ⓔ	63 Ⓐ Ⓑ Ⓒ Ⓓ Ⓔ	83 Ⓐ Ⓑ Ⓒ Ⓓ Ⓔ	103 Ⓐ Ⓑ Ⓒ Ⓓ Ⓔ	123 Ⓐ Ⓑ Ⓒ Ⓓ Ⓔ
	24 Ⓐ Ⓑ Ⓒ Ⓓ Ⓔ	44 Ⓐ Ⓑ Ⓒ Ⓓ Ⓔ	64 Ⓐ Ⓑ Ⓒ Ⓓ Ⓔ	84 Ⓐ Ⓑ Ⓒ Ⓓ Ⓔ	104 Ⓐ Ⓑ Ⓒ Ⓓ Ⓔ	124 Ⓐ Ⓑ Ⓒ Ⓓ Ⓔ
	25 Ⓐ Ⓑ Ⓒ Ⓓ Ⓔ	45 Ⓐ Ⓑ Ⓒ Ⓓ Ⓔ	65 Ⓐ Ⓑ Ⓒ Ⓓ Ⓔ	85 Ⓐ Ⓑ Ⓒ Ⓓ Ⓔ	105 Ⓐ Ⓑ Ⓒ Ⓓ Ⓔ	125 Ⓐ Ⓑ Ⓒ Ⓓ Ⓔ
	26 Ⓐ Ⓑ Ⓒ Ⓓ Ⓔ	46 Ⓐ Ⓑ Ⓒ Ⓓ Ⓔ	66 Ⓐ Ⓑ Ⓒ Ⓓ Ⓔ	86 Ⓐ Ⓑ Ⓒ Ⓓ Ⓔ	106 Ⓐ Ⓑ Ⓒ Ⓓ Ⓔ	126 Ⓐ Ⓑ Ⓒ Ⓓ Ⓔ
	27 Ⓐ Ⓑ Ⓒ Ⓓ Ⓔ	47 Ⓐ Ⓑ Ⓒ Ⓓ Ⓔ	67 Ⓐ Ⓑ Ⓒ Ⓓ Ⓔ	87 Ⓐ Ⓑ Ⓒ Ⓓ Ⓔ	107 Ⓐ Ⓑ Ⓒ Ⓓ Ⓔ	127 Ⓐ Ⓑ Ⓒ Ⓓ Ⓔ
	28 Ⓐ Ⓑ Ⓒ Ⓓ Ⓔ	48 Ⓐ Ⓑ Ⓒ Ⓓ Ⓔ	68 Ⓐ Ⓑ Ⓒ Ⓓ Ⓔ	88 Ⓐ Ⓑ Ⓒ Ⓓ Ⓔ	108 Ⓐ Ⓑ Ⓒ Ⓓ Ⓔ	128 Ⓐ Ⓑ Ⓒ Ⓓ Ⓔ
	29 Ⓐ Ⓑ Ⓒ Ⓓ Ⓔ	49 Ⓐ Ⓑ Ⓒ Ⓓ Ⓔ	69 Ⓐ Ⓑ Ⓒ Ⓓ Ⓔ	89 Ⓐ Ⓑ Ⓒ Ⓓ Ⓔ	109 Ⓐ Ⓑ Ⓒ Ⓓ Ⓔ	129 Ⓐ Ⓑ Ⓒ Ⓓ Ⓔ
	30 Ⓐ Ⓑ Ⓒ Ⓓ Ⓔ	50 Ⓐ Ⓑ Ⓒ Ⓓ Ⓔ	70 Ⓐ Ⓑ Ⓒ Ⓓ Ⓔ	90 Ⓐ Ⓑ Ⓒ Ⓓ Ⓔ	110 Ⓐ Ⓑ Ⓒ Ⓓ Ⓔ	130 Ⓐ Ⓑ Ⓒ Ⓓ Ⓔ

MODEL TEST 1

Time allotted—35 minutes

Directions

Each question has four suggested answers. Decide which one is the best answer. Find the question number on the Answer Sheet. Show your answer to the question by darkening completely the space corresponding to the letter that is the same as the letter of your answer. Keep your mark within the space. If you have to erase a mark, be sure to erase it completely. Mark only one answer for each question. Do NOT mark space E for any question.

Word Meaning

1. *Integrity* means most nearly
   A) wealth   C) honesty
   B) temper   D) understanding

2. *Frugal* means most nearly
   A) free   C) pretentious
   B) thrifty   D) profane

3. *Depravity* means most nearly
   A) corruption   C) greed
   B) slavery   D) boldness

4. *Awry* means most nearly
   A) distant   C) not straight
   B) bitter   D) ironic

5. *Unkempt* means most nearly
   A) neat   C) swollen
   B) untidy   D) closed

Analogies

6. ALUMNUS is related to ALUMNA as ROOSTER is related to
   A) hen   C) barnyard
   B) crow   D) chick

7. PRUNE is related to PLUM as RAISIN is related to
   A) kumquat   C) peach
   B) grape   D) cereal

8. RUNG is related to LADDER as STEP is related to
   A) march   C) stairway
   B) halt   D) prong

9. INTERSECTION is related to RED LIGHT as PROMONTORY is related to
   A) lighthouse   C) archipelago
   B) peninsula   D) island

Grammar

Decide which sentence is preferable with respect to grammar and usage suitable for a formal letter or report.

10. A) Each of the senior staff members regards his work serious enough to excel in every task, according to a recent evaluation.
    B) According to a recent evaluation, each senior staff member regards his work so seriously that he excels in every task.
    C) With a serious regard, according to a recent evaluation, each senior staff member excels in every task.
    D) The excelling in every task by each of the senior staff members is the result of taking work seriously according to a recent evaluation.

11. A) Although the floral arrangement smelled sweetly, several people complained about its gaudiness.
    B) Smelling sweetly, the floral arrangement still received complaints from those objecting to its gaudiness.
    C) The sweet-smelling floral arrangement had complaints of gaudiness.
    D) Although gaudy, the floral arrangement smelled sweet.

Spelling

Find the correct spelling of the word and darken the proper answer space. If no suggested spelling is correct, darken space D.

12. A) recieved   C) received
    B) receeved   D) none of these

13. A) posibility   C) possibility
    B) possibillity D) none of these

14. A) musile   C) muscle
    B) musscle   D) none of these

15. A) kindergarten C) kindergardin
    B) kindergarden D) none of these

Reading

16. Any voice heard over the phone is associated with a face and personality, which are sometimes not at all appropriate to the actual person who is speaking. In other words, the telephone can be both an invaluable tool for communication and a source of mistaken impressions.

    The paragraph best supports the statement that the way a person sounds over the phone
    A) will lead a listener to accurately imagine a face and personality
    B) will always fool a listener who is curious about what face and personality match the voice
    C) is often distorted by the mistaken impressions of the telephone
    D) may not always match the face and personality of the person

17. Teachers in several regions are being asked to take competency tests in order to demonstrate their educational preparation and literacy skills. Recently, some officials emphasized the need for a national test for teachers, and some teachers' groups responded angrily.

    The paragraph best supports the statement that
    A) some teachers' groups do not believe that teachers can pass a competency test
    B) the competency tests already in use have received no angry responses
    C) the institution of a national competency test for teachers is a controversial issue
    D) the results of competency tests accurately reflect the educational preparation and literacy skills of teachers

18. *Unique* means most nearly
    A) singular   C) twisted
    B) sexless   D) clownish

19. *Proficient* means most nearly
    A) quick   C) skilled
    B) dubious   D) reliable

20. *Judicious* means most nearly
    A) trial   C) debatable
    B) wise   D) sweet

21. *Meticulous* means most nearly
    A) careful   C) asinine
    B) imitative   D) healthful

22. *Prognosis* means most nearly
    A) sickness   C) forecast
    B) difficulty   D) forked

23. SUNDIAL is related to CLOCK as ABACUS is related to
    A) stopwatch   C) calculator
    B) barometer   D) thermometer

24. TADPOLE is related to FROG as CATERPILLAR is related to
    A) worm   C) butterfly
    B) fur   D) forest

25. MAYOR is related to CITY as GOVERNOR is related to
    A) country   C) village
    B) nation   D) state

26. MARS is related to RED as SATURN is related to
    A) Jupiter   C) planet
    B) rings   D) moons

27. A) The most demanding professor on campus always requires term papers, insists on field studies, and reads all lab reports personally.
    B) The most demanding professor on campus always requires term papers, insists on field studies, and reading all lab reports personally.
    C) Personally reading all lab reports, insisting on field studies, and to require term papers make this professor the most demanding.
    D) With demanding term papers, insisting on field studies, and the reading of all lab reports, this professor is requiring.

28. A) The agency overseas sent several representatives, who present new ideas for marketing there after they arrived.
    B) The overseas representatives presented new ideas for marketing when they arrived here.
    C) The overseas representatives' arrival presented new ideas for marketing.
    D) Having had arrived here, the overseas representatives present new ideas.

29. A) hankerchef   C) hankerchefe
    B) handkerchief   D) none of these

30. A) proceedural   C) procederal
    B) procedural   D) none of these

31. A) pschology   C) psycholagy
     B) pschylogy   D) none of these

32. A) proffesor   C) professor
     B) profesor   D) none of these

33. Those who find themselves without the time to sit down and read a good book are listening to books instead. A number of literary classics have been recorded on audio cassettes and have become popular with busy professionals as well as with homemakers.

The paragraph best supports the statement that the time required to read books
     A) may be used by some people for tasks other than reading
     B) is better spent listening to books on audio cassettes
     C) is less available today than it was earlier in this century
     D) is probably spent on audio and video entertainment

34. The dozens of different languages spoken today may have a common root. A number of linguists and historians believe that the Indo-European language, spoken thousands of years ago, was the basis for many of the languages of more modern times. The precise nature of the Indo-European language is, however, very difficult to determine.

The paragraph best supports the statement that
     A) Indo-European is no longer spoken anywhere in the world
     B) there were dozens of different ancient languages that were all called Indo-European
     C) linguists and historians are no longer interested in the precise nature of Indo-European
     D) Indo-European is not the only language that was spoken

35. *Introverted* means most nearly
     A) unarguable   C) strong
     B) withdrawn   D) upset

36. *Heterogeneous* means most nearly
     A) perverted   C) varied
     B) healthy   D) recondite

37. *Feasible* means most nearly
     A) practical   C) stealable
     B) expensive   D) ridiculous

38. To *emulate* means most nearly to
     A) imitate   C) require
     B) disown   D) disparage

39. *Hirsute* means most nearly
     A) historic   C) mounted
     B) hairy   D) armored

40. PROFESSOR is related to CAMPUS as LIFEGUARD is related to
     A) rescue   C) beach
     B) save   D) summer

41. TELESCOPE is related to CLOSE as MICROSCOPE is related to
     A) small   C) far
     B) large   D) near

42. CHILD is related to BIB as ADULT is related to
     A) wipe   C) napkin
     B) neck   D) food

43. PEN is related to QUILL as PAPER is related to
     A) pencil   C) ink
     B) parchment   D) book

44. A) Waste can be eliminated, or at least reduced, if less pencils, pens, and paper clips are left lying around.
     B) Waste can be eliminated, or at least reduced, if fewer pencils, pens, and paper clips are left lying around.
     C) The fewer the pencils, pens, and paper clips, the more of waste is eliminated.
     D) With pencils, pens, and paper clips less wasted, the more it can be eliminated or reduced.

45. A) When only six months old, the committee will review the success of the new management plan.
     B) After the new management plan has been implemented for six months, the committee will have had it under review.
     C) With six months behind them, the new management plan's success came under the review of the committee.
     D) In six months the committee will review the effects of the new management plan.

46. A) heros   C) heroes
     B) heeroes   D) none of these

47. A) imediately   C) immediately
    B) immedietly   D) none of these

48. A) influential   C) influensial
    B) influencial   D) none of these

49. A) eradicate   C) irradicate
    B) iradicate   D) none of these

50. Although reference books such as a dictionary, thesaurus, and grammar handbook are part of any writer's library, they are not usually consulted with regularity. Too much time looking into reference works leaves little time for the writing itself.

The paragraph best supports the statement that a writer's reference books
A) are best left untouched by any writer who wishes to be productive
B) may be books other than a dictionary, thesaurus, and grammar handbook
C) always require a great deal of time to consult
D) are indispensable for writers, but do not often improve the quality of any writer's work

51. When one is pressed to complete a writing task within a brief time limit, it is often useful to rely on a standard formula for organizing the writing. One very useful formula for writing the first paragraph of an essay is abbreviated TRI, topic-restriction-illustration. Using this formula, one first writes a very general sentence (topic), and then follows with a more focused statement (restriction) and a mention of the examples that will be discussed (illustration).

The paragraph best supports the statement that
A) writing within a brief time limit is very difficult for anyone who does not use a standard formula
B) the time available for writing may determine whether using a formula is necessary
C) those who rely on TRI for writing paragraphs will complete writing tasks more quickly than those who do not
D) there are no standard formulas for writing the paragraphs that follow the first one

52. *Pastoral* means most nearly
A) ancient   C) melodic
B) rural   D) starving

53. *Homage* means most nearly
A) honor   C) settle
B) estate   D) vision

54. *Aghast* means most nearly
A) fueled   C) horrified
B) exhaust   D) left over

55. *Innate* means most nearly
A) human   C) simplistic
B) overwrought   D) in-born

56. *Fetid* means most nearly
A) stinking   C) fallen
B) productive   D) satiated

57. APARTMENT is related to RENT as HOME is related to
A) paint   C) live
B) purchase   D) build

58. JOCKEY is related to SMALL as RACEHORSE is related to
A) big   C) fast
B) brown   D) old

59. PREFACE is related to BOOK as PREFIX is related to
A) novel   C) suffix
B) word   D) repair

60. RADIO is related to TELEVISION as AURAL is related to
A) oral   C) film
B) visual   D) station

61. A) Arriving at the office early, the sun was rising as the manager began work.
B) The sun rising and arriving at the office early, the manager began work.
C) The manager arrived at the office before sunrise and began work.
D) Managing a sunrise arrival at the office to begin work, the manager had been working.

62. A) Juries usually make correct decisions and perform their duties both correctly and effectively.
B) Juries usually make correct decisions.
C) Making correct decisions keep juries both correct and effective.
D) Juries usually make correct decisions and perform their duties both correct and effective.

63. A) garanteed   C) gauranteed
    B) guaranteed   D) none of these

64. A) fundimental   C) fundementel
    B) fundamental   D) none of these

65. A) murmer   C) mermer
    B) mermur   D) none of these

66. A) mornful   C) mournfull
    B) mournful   D) none of these

67. A skillful typist is much more than a transcriber of words. Given a rough draft filled with scribbles and awkward phrases, the typist must not only type the copy, but also decipher and make clear ideas that the original writer left vague.

The paragraph best supports the statement that
A) typists do not always receive rough drafts that are neat and clear
B) typists prefer to revise and correct the writer's rough draft
C) all typists have worked for writers who were imaginative but not able to produce a clear rough draft
D) most typists expect that a rough draft will be difficult to read

68. At most major universities, the availability of parking spaces is a substantial problem. There are always far fewer spaces than there are students, faculty, and staff who drive to school, and unless one arrives very early in the morning, the likelihood of securing a space is slim indeed.

The paragraph best supports the statement that many people who attend major universities
A) arrive early in the morning
B) do not park on campus
C) are not bothered by parking problems
D) prefer to walk to school

69. To *embellish* means most nearly to
A) signal   C) ornament
B) stomach   D) mortify

70. *Paraphernalia* means most nearly
A) spirits   C) fear
B) equipment   D) illegal

71. To *hinder* means most nearly to
A) restrain   C) sharpen
B) imply   D) pray

72. To *cull* means most nearly to
A) cut   C) select
B) desert   D) decay

73. *Chaste* means most nearly
A) pursuit   C) satisfaction
B) pure   D) punishment

74. PERSON is related to SURNAME as BOOK is related to
A) author   C) chapter
B) subject   D) title

75. ROOM is related to LAMP as SKY is related to
A) cloud   C) sun
B) night   D) day

76. CLOTHING is related to CLOSET as AMMUNITION is related to
A) armory   C) garage
B) general   D) storeroom

77. INDUSTRY is related to POLLUTION as TRAFFIC is related to
A) cars   C) highway
B) accidents   D) speed

78. A) Referring to known and proven facts is important in any effective argument.
B) To know and proving facts for an effective argument is important.
C) One should include persuasive facts in any argument.
D) One should put persuasive facts in their argument whenever possible.

79. A) Thirty-six hours, give or take a few minutes, are the length of time required for the special project.
B) Required for the special project are thirty-six hours, give or take a few minutes.
C) The special project will require approximately thirty-six hours.
D) With a requirement of thirty-six hours, more or less, the special project requires a precise length of time.

80. A) preperations   C) prepurations
    B) prepirations   D) none of these

81. A) predjudice   C) prejudice
    B) pregjudice   D) none of these

82. A) meaness   C) meenness
    B) meanness   D) none of these

83. A) matteriel   C) material
    B) meterial   D) none of these

84. When individual personalities conflict, the best solution is honesty and compromise. Only by airing the problem and discussing mutually agreeable terms for solving it, can a group put conflict behind them and get on with useful work.

The paragraph best supports the statement that when a conflict arises between individuals,
    A) honesty on the part of either individual is unusual
    B) solving the problem is much more difficult than continuing to work together
    C) one of the individuals is not willing to be honest and compromise
    D) an individual who refuses to compromise is an obstacle to solving the problem

85. With advances in medical technology, and increased public interest in exercise and nutrition, the average life expectancy in America continues to increase, and consequently, the average age of the population continues to rise. America is getting older.

The paragraph best supports the statement that exercise and nutrition
    A) have offset the decay of American culture
    B) are less advanced than medical technology, but more interesting to the public
    C) have contributed to longer lives, and affected the average age of the population
    D) are most valuable before one passes the average age of the population

ANSWER KEY FOR MODEL TEST 1

Word Meaning

1. C	18. A	35. B	52. B	69. C
2. B	19. C	36. C	53. A	70. B
3. A	20. B	37. A	54. C	71. A
4. C	21. A	38. A	55. D	72. C
5. B	22. C	39. B	56. A	73. B

Analogies

6. A	23. C	40. C	57. B	74. D
7. B	24. C	41. B	58. C	75. C
8. C	25. D	42. C	59. B	76. A
9. A	26. B	43. B	60. B	77. B

Grammar

10. B	27. A	44. B	61. C	78. C
11. D	28. B	45. D	62. B	79. C

Spelling

12. C	29. B	46. C	63. B	80. D
13. C	30. B	47. C	64. B	81. C
14. C	31. D	48. A	65. D	82. B
15. A	32. C	49. A	66. B	83. C

Reading

16. D	33. A	50. B	67. A	84. D
17. C	34. A	51. B	68. B	85. C

ANALYSIS CHART FOR MODEL TEST 1

Now that you've corrected your exam, use the following chart to carefully analyze your results and spot your strengths and weaknesses. This analysis should help you focus your study and review efforts.

Section	Total Number of Questions	Number Correct	Number Incorrect	Number Unanswered*
Word Meaning	25			
Analogies	20			
Grammar	10			
Spelling	20			
Reading Comprehension	10			
TOTAL	85			

*Since there is no penalty for incorrect answers on the Verbal Abilities Test, you should have left no question unanswered. Even if you didn't have time to answer a question, at least you should have filled in the answer space with a guess.

ANSWER EXPLANATIONS FOR MODEL TEST 1

1. **(C)** honesty
2. **(B)** thrifty
3. **(A)** corruption
4. **(C)** not straight
5. **(B)** untidy
6. **(A)** The first word is the male version; the second word is the female version.
7. **(B)** The first word is the second word dried up.
8. **(C)** The first word is one of the parts of the second word.

9. **(A)** The second word is the signal located at the first word.

10. **(B)** In (A), "serious" should be "seriously." In (C), "with a serious regard" is unclear. Choice (D) is wordy.

11. **(D)** In both (A) and (B), "sweetly" should be "sweet." In (C), "had complaints of gaudiness" is an unclear phrase.

12. **(C)** received

13. **(C)** possibility

14. **(C)** muscle

15. **(A)** kindergarten

16. **(D)** The paragraph implies that listeners will not always *accurately* imagine the face and personality associated with a voice on the telephone, so (A) is not the best choice. (D) sums up the overall point of the paragraph.

17. **(C)** The paragraph states that "some officials" and "some teachers' groups" disagree about the need for a national competency test; such disagreement makes the issue controversial, rather than agreeable to all.

18. **(A)** singular

19. **(C)** skilled

20. **(B)** wise

21. **(A)** careful

22. **(C)** forecast

23. **(C)** The first word is an ancient version of the second word.

24. **(C)** The first word changes into the second word.

25. **(D)** The first word is the elected leader of the second word.

26. **(B)** The second word is a characteristic of the first word.

27. **(A)** Choices (B), (C), and (D) all exhibit faulty parallelism; for instance, in (C), "to require" should be "requiring."

28. **(B)** In both (A) and (D), the verbs are incorrect: "present" in both (A) and (D) should be "presented"; also, "having had" in (D) should be "having." In (C), the "arrival" rather than the "representatives" presented the new ideas.

29. **(B)** handkerchief

30. **(B)** procedural

31. **(D)** Correct spelling: psychology

32. **(C)** professor

33. **(A)** The paragraph stresses the popularity of books on cassettes and suggests that some people are listening to books rather than reading them, thus spending the time during which they might be reading in other ways.

34. **(A)** While (D) may be true, in general, it is not supported by information in the passage. Because the passage states that Indo-European is an ancient language that remains more or less unknown today, we may conclude that it is no longer spoken; otherwise, its nature would not be "difficult to determine."

35. **(B)** withdrawn

36. **(C)** varied

37. **(A)** practical

38. **(A)** imitate

39. **(B)** hairy

40. **(C)** The second word is where the first word works.

41. **(B)** The second word is the resulting action of the first word.

42. **(C)** The second word is used while the first word eats.

43. **(B)** The second word is an ancient version of the first word.

44. **(B)** In (A), "less" is used incorrectly; when describing items that are *countable,* "fewer" is correct. (C) is an illogical sentence, and "more of waste" is a vague expression. In (D), "less wasted" and "it" are unclear.

45. **(D)** In (A), the sentence seems to say that the committee is "only six months old." (B) contains a verb error: "will have had" is incorrect. (C) is awkward and not clear; "them" should be "it."

46. **(C)** heroes

47. **(C)** immediately

48. **(A)** influential

49. **(A)** eradicate

50. **(B)** Each of the other choices is an extreme conclusion that extends beyond the information in the paragraph. In the paragraph, the particular books mentioned are offered as examples of reference books in general and are not referred to as the *only* reference books useful or available to a writer.

51. **(B)** The paragraph mentions "time limit" as a factor related to using a formula for writing. Each of the other choices may be true in general, but none is supported by the paragraph.

52. **(B)** rural

53. **(A)** honor

54. **(C)** horrified

55. **(D)** in-born

56. **(A)** stinking

57. **(B)** The second word is the common way of obtaining the first word.

58. **(C)** The second word is a characteristic of the first word.

59. **(B)** The first word is the first part of the second word.

60. **(B)** The first word refers to hearing; the second word refers to sight.

61. **(C)** Choices (A) and (B) seem to say that the sun was arriving at the office early. Choice (D) is vague and wordy.

62. **(B)** Choices (A), (C) and (D) are unnecessarily repetitious. In (C), "keep" should be "keeps." In (D), "correct and effective" should be "correctly and effectively."

63. **(B)** guaranteed

64. **(B)** fundamental

65. **(D)** Correct spelling: murmur

66. **(B)** mournful

67. **(A)** The paragraph describes a rough draft that is neither neat nor clear as something that a typist may receive.

68. **(B)** The availability of "far fewer spaces" than drivers allows us to conclude that many people do not park on campus.

69. **(C)** ornament

70. **(B)** equipment

71. **(A)** restrain

72. **(C)** select

73. **(B)** pure

74. **(D)** The second word is the identifying name for the first word.

75. **(C)** The second word illuminates the first word.

76. **(A)** The first word is stored in the second word.

77. **(B)** The second word is a harmful result of the first word.

78. **(C)** In (A), "known and proven facts" is an unnecessarily wordy phrase. In (B), "proving" should be "to prove," and the verb should be plural ("are"). In (D), "their" is incorrect; "one's," "his," or "her" is correct in this case.

79. **(C)** In (A) and (B), the verb "are" should be singular, to agree with the single-unit subject. The sentence structure in (B) is also awkward. Choice (D) is repetitious and also illogical, because "thirty-six hours, more or less" is not a *precise* length of time."

80. **(D)** Correct spelling is preparations

81. **(C)** prejudice

82. **(B)** meanness

83. **(C)** material

84. **(D)** The paragraph connects compromise with the "best solution" and allows us to conclude that a solution is blocked by one who is unwilling to compromise.

85. **(C)** The passage explicitly states that exercise and nutrition have caused Americans to live longer.

ANSWER SHEET

SIGNATURE: _____
(Please Sign)

EXAMINATION TITLE: _____

PLACE OF EXAMINATION: _____
City _____ State _____

TODAY'S DATE: _____

SAMPLE ⒶⒷⒸⒹⒺ

SAMPLE Ⓐ●ⒸⒹⒺ

DIRECTIONS FOR MARKING ANSWER SHEET

Use only a **No. 2 (or softer) lead pencil**. Darken completely the circle corresponding to your answer. You **must** keep your mark within the circle. Stray marks may be counted as errors. Erase **completely** all marks except your answer.

SAMPLE NAME GRID

1. In the boxes below, **PRINT** your name. Print only as many letters as will fit within the areas for the last name, first initial (F.I.), and middle initial (M.I.). Below each box, darken the circle containing the same letter. SEE SAMPLE NAME GRID

2. In the boxes below, enter your 9-digit Social Security Number. Below each box, darken the circle in each column corresponding to the number you have entered.

SOCIAL SECURITY NUMBER

3. OCCUPATIONAL GROUP NUMBER

LAST NAME   F.I.   M.I.

SECTION 1

Make no marks or entries in the columns to the right until you receive instructions from the administrator.

TEST NUMBER | TEST SERIES | PART

1 ⒶⒷⒸⒹⒺ	11 ⒶⒷⒸⒹⒺ	31 ⒶⒷⒸⒹⒺ	51 ⒶⒷⒸⒹⒺ	71 ⒶⒷⒸⒹⒺ	91 ⒶⒷⒸⒹⒺ	111 ⒶⒷⒸⒹⒺ
2 ⒶⒷⒸⒹⒺ	12 ⒶⒷⒸⒹⒺ	32 ⒶⒷⒸⒹⒺ	52 ⒶⒷⒸⒹⒺ	72 ⒶⒷⒸⒹⒺ	92 ⒶⒷⒸⒹⒺ	112 ⒶⒷⒸⒹⒺ
3 ⒶⒷⒸⒹⒺ	13 ⒶⒷⒸⒹⒺ	33 ⒶⒷⒸⒹⒺ	53 ⒶⒷⒸⒹⒺ	73 ⒶⒷⒸⒹⒺ	93 ⒶⒷⒸⒹⒺ	113 ⒶⒷⒸⒹⒺ
4 ⒶⒷⒸⒹⒺ	14 ⒶⒷⒸⒹⒺ	34 ⒶⒷⒸⒹⒺ	54 ⒶⒷⒸⒹⒺ	74 ⒶⒷⒸⒹⒺ	94 ⒶⒷⒸⒹⒺ	114 ⒶⒷⒸⒹⒺ
5 ⒶⒷⒸⒹⒺ	15 ⒶⒷⒸⒹⒺ	35 ⒶⒷⒸⒹⒺ	55 ⒶⒷⒸⒹⒺ	75 ⒶⒷⒸⒹⒺ	95 ⒶⒷⒸⒹⒺ	115 ⒶⒷⒸⒹⒺ
6 ⒶⒷⒸⒹⒺ	16 ⒶⒷⒸⒹⒺ	36 ⒶⒷⒸⒹⒺ	56 ⒶⒷⒸⒹⒺ	76 ⒶⒷⒸⒹⒺ	96 ⒶⒷⒸⒹⒺ	116 ⒶⒷⒸⒹⒺ
7 ⒶⒷⒸⒹⒺ	17 ⒶⒷⒸⒹⒺ	37 ⒶⒷⒸⒹⒺ	57 ⒶⒷⒸⒹⒺ	77 ⒶⒷⒸⒹⒺ	97 ⒶⒷⒸⒹⒺ	117 ⒶⒷⒸⒹⒺ
8 ⒶⒷⒸⒹⒺ	18 ⒶⒷⒸⒹⒺ	38 ⒶⒷⒸⒹⒺ	58 ⒶⒷⒸⒹⒺ	78 ⒶⒷⒸⒹⒺ	98 ⒶⒷⒸⒹⒺ	118 ⒶⒷⒸⒹⒺ
9 ⒶⒷⒸⒹⒺ	19 ⒶⒷⒸⒹⒺ	39 ⒶⒷⒸⒹⒺ	59 ⒶⒷⒸⒹⒺ	79 ⒶⒷⒸⒹⒺ	99 ⒶⒷⒸⒹⒺ	119 ⒶⒷⒸⒹⒺ
10 ⒶⒷⒸⒹⒺ	20 ⒶⒷⒸⒹⒺ	40 ⒶⒷⒸⒹⒺ	60 ⒶⒷⒸⒹⒺ	80 ⒶⒷⒸⒹⒺ	100 ⒶⒷⒸⒹⒺ	120 ⒶⒷⒸⒹⒺ
	21 ⒶⒷⒸⒹⒺ	41 ⒶⒷⒸⒹⒺ	61 ⒶⒷⒸⒹⒺ	81 ⒶⒷⒸⒹⒺ	101 ⒶⒷⒸⒹⒺ	121 ⒶⒷⒸⒹⒺ
	22 ⒶⒷⒸⒹⒺ	42 ⒶⒷⒸⒹⒺ	62 ⒶⒷⒸⒹⒺ	82 ⒶⒷⒸⒹⒺ	102 ⒶⒷⒸⒹⒺ	122 ⒶⒷⒸⒹⒺ
	23 ⒶⒷⒸⒹⒺ	43 ⒶⒷⒸⒹⒺ	63 ⒶⒷⒸⒹⒺ	83 ⒶⒷⒸⒹⒺ	103 ⒶⒷⒸⒹⒺ	123 ⒶⒷⒸⒹⒺ
	24 ⒶⒷⒸⒹⒺ	44 ⒶⒷⒸⒹⒺ	64 ⒶⒷⒸⒹⒺ	84 ⒶⒷⒸⒹⒺ	104 ⒶⒷⒸⒹⒺ	124 ⒶⒷⒸⒹⒺ
	25 ⒶⒷⒸⒹⒺ	45 ⒶⒷⒸⒹⒺ	65 ⒶⒷⒸⒹⒺ	85 ⒶⒷⒸⒹⒺ	105 ⒶⒷⒸⒹⒺ	125 ⒶⒷⒸⒹⒺ
	26 ⒶⒷⒸⒹⒺ	46 ⒶⒷⒸⒹⒺ	66 ⒶⒷⒸⒹⒺ	86 ⒶⒷⒸⒹⒺ	106 ⒶⒷⒸⒹⒺ	126 ⒶⒷⒸⒹⒺ
	27 ⒶⒷⒸⒹⒺ	47 ⒶⒷⒸⒹⒺ	67 ⒶⒷⒸⒹⒺ	87 ⒶⒷⒸⒹⒺ	107 ⒶⒷⒸⒹⒺ	127 ⒶⒷⒸⒹⒺ
	28 ⒶⒷⒸⒹⒺ	48 ⒶⒷⒸⒹⒺ	68 ⒶⒷⒸⒹⒺ	88 ⒶⒷⒸⒹⒺ	108 ⒶⒷⒸⒹⒺ	128 ⒶⒷⒸⒹⒺ
	29 ⒶⒷⒸⒹⒺ	49 ⒶⒷⒸⒹⒺ	69 ⒶⒷⒸⒹⒺ	89 ⒶⒷⒸⒹⒺ	109 ⒶⒷⒸⒹⒺ	129 ⒶⒷⒸⒹⒺ
	30 ⒶⒷⒸⒹⒺ	50 ⒶⒷⒸⒹⒺ	70 ⒶⒷⒸⒹⒺ	90 ⒶⒷⒸⒹⒺ	110 ⒶⒷⒸⒹⒺ	130 ⒶⒷⒸⒹⒺ

MODEL TEST 2

Time allotted—35 minutes

Directions

Each question has four suggested answers. Decide which one is the best answer. Find the question number on the Answer Sheet. Show your answer to the question by darkening completely the space corresponding to the letter that is the same as the letter of your answer. Keep your mark within the space. If you have to erase a mark, be sure to erase it completely. Mark only one answer for each question. Do NOT mark space E for any question.

Word Meaning

1. *Criterion* means most nearly
   - A) armor
   - B) standard
   - C) soldier
   - D) fuel

2. *Slothful* means most nearly
   - A) three-toed
   - B) intermittent
   - C) lazy
   - D) ghostly

3. *Queasy* means most nearly
   - A) nauseous
   - B) enthusiastic
   - C) quiet
   - D) reliable

4. To *interject* means most nearly to
   - A) upset
   - B) hint
   - C) interrupt
   - D) fear

5. To *renounce* means most nearly to
   - A) give up
   - B) remember
   - C) enjoy
   - D) rectify

Analogies

6. TEETH is related to CHEW as NOSE is related to
   - A) sweet
   - B) smell
   - C) center
   - D) nostril

7. BAT is related to BASEBALL as DRUMSTICK is related to
   - A) instrument
   - B) triangle
   - C) band leader
   - D) drum

8. WOOD is related to GLASS as PAPER is related to
   - A) cellophane
   - B) page
   - C) ripped
   - D) book

9. STENOGRAPHER is related to WORDS as ACCOUNTANT is related to
   - A) typist
   - B) letters
   - C) numbers
   - D) terms

Grammar

10. A) Whomever reviews last month's financial statements must conclude that the company is in trouble.
    B) With a review of financial statements, one must conclude that it is all the better to see that the company is in trouble.
    C) A review of last month's financial statements suggests that the company is in trouble.
    D) The review of last month's financial statements should be referred to whomever will review it thoroughly.

11. A) The hazy ideas and concepts presented in the presentation were vague and indefinite.
    B) The presenter presented hazy ideas and concepts in a vague and indefinite way.
    C) Hazy ideas and concepts were presented only vaguely, and without definitions.
    D) The ideas presented were vague.

Spelling

12. A) rediculous
    B) ridiculious
    C) ridiculus
    D) none of these

13. A) pronunciation
    B) pronounciation
    C) pronunction
    D) none of these

14. A) desireable
    B) disireable
    C) desirable
    D) none of these

15. A) judgment
    B) judgemint
    C) jugdment
    D) none of these

Reading

16. Most college graduates do not pursue a career relevant to their college major. Part of the reason for this is a fast-changing job market, which creates new jobs and job categories, and eliminates old jobs and job categories, at such a rapid pace that college training in a particular area may become obsolete very quickly.

The paragraph best supports the statement that a student entering college today

A) will encounter a much-changed job market when she graduates

B) will be unable to find a job when she graduates

C) will need to create a new job for herself, taking account of the old jobs that have been eliminated

D) should not pursue a major that is not relevant to the future job market

17. The past is the mirror of the present. By studying history we encounter the same general problems that cultures and societies face today, and we learn possible solutions to those problems. We may also learn that some problems can never be absolutely solved.

The paragraph best supports the statement that history

A) always provides the necessary solutions to modern social problems

B) makes the solution of modern problems even more difficult

C) is a source of solutions that may be used to address problems in modern times

D) does not necessarily repeat itself

18. *Orifice* means most nearly

A) building   C) opening

B) protrusion   D) allowance

19. *Morose* means most nearly

A) gloomy   C) dissolved

B) sprawling   D) large

20. To *impede* means most nearly to

A) instruct   C) obstruct

B) construct   D) assume

21. *Fickle* means most nearly

A) pretty   C) changeable

B) sour   D) redolent

22. To *enthrall* means most nearly to

A) tease   C) captivate

B) test   D) require

23. COTTON is related to SOFT as WOOL is related to

A) sheep   C) expensive

B) warm   D) light

24. SMOKE is related to CHIMNEY as LIQUID is related to

A) funnel   C) glass

B) ocean   D) water

25. ATHLETE is related to ROOKIE as MOVIE is related to

A) screening   C) award

B) premiere   D) cancelation

26. PENDULUM is related to SWING as GYROSCOPE is related to

A) stop   C) spin

B) measure   D) boat

27. A) Because she demanded immediate improvement, the manager warned her that dismissal was a possibility.

B) Demanding immediate improvement, the manager threatened her with dismissal.

C) The manager threatened her with immediate improvement in mind.

D) Because she demanded immediate improvement, she warned her that dismissal was a possibility.

28. A) Regulations must be enforced all the farther if they are to be effective.

B) The farther enforcement of regulations will guarantee their effectiveness.

C) Going farther with the enforcement of regulations guarantees farther effectiveness.

D) Stronger enforcement will make the regulations more effective.

29. A) separate   C) seprate

B) seperate   D) none of these

30. A) publically   C) publickally

B) publicly   D) none of these

31. A) accomadate   C) accommodate

B) accomodate   D) none of these

32. A) calander   C) calender

B) calendar   D) none of these

33. Perhaps it is true, as the old saying goes, that knowledge is power. But sometimes knowledge brings pain rather than power: the more we learn and the more we read, the more we realize that the world is filled with violence and corruption. This knowledge may leave us feeling more powerless than powerful.

The paragraph best supports the statement that knowledge

A) may be possible only after violence and corruption are eliminated forever
B) is mainly the result of reading about violence and corruption
C) may not lead to power
D) really exists only in old sayings, and is rarely available from any other source

34. Office procedures are not inflexible. Although each employee has been assigned specific tasks to be performed at specific times, all must be sensitive to the needs and problems of others and help out whenever necessary. In order to be ready to help, everyone is advised to become familiar with the jobs and responsibilities of others, to become as skilled as possible in as many different tasks as possible.

The paragraph best supports the statement that

A) assisting coworkers is important and desirable
B) most employees are not willing to help one another
C) some employees are more skilled than others
D) learning many different tasks is difficult

35. *Dubious* means most nearly
   A) doubtful   C) long
   B) retired   D) dumb

36. *Ungainly* means most nearly
   A) bankrupt   C) not permanent
   B) swollen   D) awkward

37. To *lampoon* means most nearly to
   A) spear   C) ridicule
   B) harvest   D) light

38. To *fritter* means most nearly to
   A) waste   C) allow
   B) cook   D) seal

39. To *coerce* means most nearly to
   A) rely   C) force
   B) think over   D) agree

40. CHOREOGRAPHER is related to BALLET as INVENTOR is related to
   A) laboratory   C) electricity
   B) machine   D) imagination

41. BASEMENT is related to ATTIC as VALLEY is related to
   A) plateau   C) mountaintop
   B) crevasse   D) pasture

42. BOOK is related to LIBRARY as WHEAT is related to
   A) granary   C) food
   B) bread   D) milk

43. BUST is related to SCULPTOR as PLAY is related to
   A) playground   C) dramatist
   B) worker   D) entertainer

44. A) Merlo's Gift Shop and Nat's Novelty Store sells gifts created by local artists.
    B) Gifts created to local artists are sold in both Merlo's Gift Shop and Nat's Novelty Store.
    C) Merlo's and Nat's, selling gifts created by local artists.
    D) Merlo's Gift Shop and Nat's Novelty Store sell gifts created by local artists.

45. A) The office manager hired the most experienced of the two candidates who applied for a clerical position.
    B) Deciding experientially on who was better prepared clerically, the office manager decided to choose between two candidates.
    C) Primarily interested in the candidate with more experience, the office manager hired her for the new clerical position.
    D) With a clerical position in mind requiring experience, the decision was for the office manager.

46. A) curtale   C) certail
    B) curtail   D) none of these

47. A) bribery   C) bribary
    B) bribury   D) none of these

48. A) tommorow   C) tommorrow
    B) tomorrow   D) none of these

49. A) maneuver   C) manuver
    B) manuever   D) none of these

50. With expert clerical assistance, a business executive is free to concentrate on important issues and decisions, and can rely on the staff to give expert attention to correspondence, bookkeeping, and appointments. Without expert

clerical assistance, an executive must compromise her talents and her time. Clearly, it is the clerical staff that allows any executive to be an executive; a talented staff guarantees that business will thrive.

The paragraph best supports the statement that expert attention to correspondence, bookkeeping, and appointments

A) utilizes the talents and time of some business executives
B) leaves the staff free to concentrate on other issues
C) are tasks that all executives should master
D) are best accomplished by a talented staff

51. In most cases, prefer active verbs to passive verbs. A sentence such as "The salaries were raised by the board of directors," should be revised to read, "The board of directors raised the salaries." In this case, and in so many others, the active construction results in a more economical statement, one that is understood more quickly and clearly. Of course, passive constructions cannot and should not be discarded altogether.

The paragraph best supports the statement that passive constructions

A) will be thought incorrect by most readers
B) are useful at times
C) can be understood more clearly than active constructions
D) must always be revised

52. *Frigid* means most nearly
A) white   C) cold
B) smart   D) thick

53. *Bloated* means most nearly
A) shipwrecked   C) swollen
B) hollow   D) embalmed

54. To *relish* means most nearly to
A) anger   C) protest
B) enjoy   D) upset

55. *Ailing* means most nearly
A) affected   C) ill
B) disordered   D) worn

56. *Cognizant* means most nearly
A) aware   C) hardy
B) wheeling   D) terminal

57. FLOWER is related to GARDEN as TREE is related to
A) stump   C) weeds
B) orchard   D) branches

58. SHEEP is related to WOOL as GOOSE is related to
A) gander   C) down
B) flock   D) beak

59. BLEEDING is related to TOURNIQUET as TRAFFIC is related to
A) green light   C) automobile
B) red light   D) detour

60. FOOD is related to FASTING as EXERCISE is related to
A) conditioning   C) resting
B) warming up   D) stretching

61. A) In order to cut expenses, the supervisor must decide whether to reduce the workload, lay off several employees, or forbid private use of the duplicating machine.
B) Reducing the workload, laying off several employees, or to forbid private use of the duplicating machine were several options open to the supervisor cutting employees.
C) Reduced workload, or employees, or no private duplication crossed the mind of the supervisor cutting expenses.
D) The supervisor thought about several ways to cut expenses: workload, employee reduction, or in the area of duplication.

62. A) Having been promoted suddenly, the board of directors extended their congratulations to the new vice-president.
B) The board of directors congratulated the new vice-president on his sudden promotion.
C) To the new vice-president, with promotion so sudden, the board of directors congratulated him.
D) The board of directors will have had congratulated the new vice-president after his sudden promotion.

63. A) histeria   C) hystaria
B) hysteria   D) none of these

64. A) misconseption   C) misconception
B) misconcepsion   D) none of these

65. A) disburce
    B) disberse
    C) disburse
    D) none of these

66. A) revinue
    B) revenue
    C) revenew
    D) none of these

67. County clerks, who issue marriage licenses and retain records of confidential marriages, have reported numerous abuses of the confidential marriage law. In San Diego, for instance, the Immigration and Naturalization Service has found that illegal aliens take advantage of the law's privacy to wed citizens they may never have met, in order to gain legal residency status.

    The paragraph best supports the statement that the confidential marriage law
    A) can be abused by illegal aliens who want to become legal residents
    B) is often abused by the county clerks who issue marriage licenses
    C) is used by illegal aliens to marry citizens outside the United States
    D) privately issues licenses and records of marriage

68. By investing $10 million in the shuttle salvage operation, underwriters for the Palapa and Westar now have a chance to recover some of the $100 million they paid to the Indonesian government and to Western Union after the satellite launch fizzled last February.

    The paragraph best supports the statement that the salvage operation
    A) was a failure last February
    B) will earn $100 million from the Indonesian government
    C) may help reduce the losses incurred by the underwriters
    D) will recover $100 million paid by Western Union

69. *Compunction* means most nearly
    A) remorse
    B) timely
    C) grammar
    D) gall

70. *Mundane* means most nearly
    A) commonplace
    B) awkward
    C) religious
    D) formidable

71. *Verbatim* means most nearly
    A) babbling
    B) argument
    C) word-for-word
    D) enticing

72. *Unequivocal* means most nearly
    A) clear
    B) advantageous
    C) mute
    D) mistaken

73. *Clemency* means most nearly
    A) redundancy
    B) illumination
    C) leniency
    D) tendency

74. HAIR is related to HEAD as NAIL is related to
    A) hammer
    B) finger
    C) arm
    D) cut

75. FENCE is related to YARD as BRACELET is related to
    A) wrist
    B) ring
    C) neck
    D) belt

76. SOLDIER is related to BARRACKS as ESKIMO is related to
    A) Iceland
    B) arctic
    C) snow
    D) igloo

77. SOCKET is related to PLUG as HOLE is related to
    A) peg
    B) pencil
    C) shovel
    D) axe

78. A) Promising a bright future, and to celebrate a wonderful past, the Hardy Company awarded each of its employees a bonus.
    B) To promise a bright future and a wonderful past, the Hardy Company awarded each of its employees a bonus.
    C) The future bright and the past wonderful, the bonus awarded to each of the Hardy Company employees.
    D) The Hardy Company awarded each of its employees a bonus, promising them a bright future and thanking them for a wonderful past.

79. A) The lunch he ordered tasted better than the coworkers.
    B) The lunch he ordered tasted better than the others' lunches.
    C) The lunch he ordered tasted better than the coworkers lunching.
    D) Lunching with the coworkers, the one he ordered tasted best.

80. A) modren
    B) modurn
    C) modern
    D) none of these

81. A) aparatis
    B) aparatus
    C) apparatus
    D) none of these

82. A) sumation   C) summation
    B) summashun   D) none of these

83. A) forein   C) foriegn
    B) foreign   D) none of these

84. With the growing popularity of radio talk shows, it becomes possible to spend most of the day listening to interesting conversations on a variety of significant topics, even while working at a solitary job. Listening to music all day may not be nearly as rewarding or informative.

The paragraph best supports the statement that listening to music

A) has become a popular alternative to listening to talk shows

B) is never as interesting as participating in a conversation

C) may be less preferable than listening to radio talk shows

D) makes it impossible to listen to radio talk shows

85. Those who have difficulty reading are usually those who have not read much. The habit of reading is probably instilled during childhood; those children with parents who like to read also tend to acquire a fondness for books. Adults who have never learned to like reading are likely to avoid it.

The paragraph best supports the statement that those who have avoided reading during childhood

A) will probably not find reading easier as they get older

B) will transmit a hateful attitude toward books and reading to their children

C) were probably kept from reading by their parents

D) did so only because interesting reading material was not made available by their parents

ANSWER KEY FOR MODEL TEST 2

Word Meaning

1. B	18. C	35. A	52. C	69. A
2. C	19. A	36. D	53. C	70. A
3. A	20. G	37. C	54. B	71. C
4. C	21. C	38. A	55. C	72. A
5. A	22. C	39. C	56. A	73. C

Analogies

6. B	23. B	40. B	57. B	74. B
7. D	24. A	41. C	58. C	75. A
8. A	25. B	42. A	59. B	76. D
9. C	26. C	43. C	60. C	77. A

Grammar

10. C	27. B	44. D	61. A	78. D
11. D	28. D	45. C	62. B	79. B

Spelling

12. D	29. A	46. B	63. B	80. C
13. A	30. B	47. A	64. C	81. C
14. C	31. C	48. B	65. C	82. C
15. A	32. B	49. A	66. B	83. B

Reading

16. A	33. C	50. D	67. A	84. C
17. C	34. A	51. B	68. C	85. A

ANALYSIS CHART FOR MODEL TEST 2

Now that you've corrected your exam, use the following chart to carefully analyze your results and spot your strengths and weaknesses. This analysis should help you focus your study and review efforts.

Section	Total Number of Questions	Number Correct	Number Incorrect	Number Unanswered*
Word Meaning	25			
Analogies	20			
Grammar	10			
Spelling	20			
Reading Comprehension	10			
TOTAL	85			

*Since there is no penalty for incorrect answers on the Verbal Abilities Test, you should have left no question unanswered. Even if you didn't have time to answer a question, at least you should have filled in the answer space with a guess.

ANSWER EXPLANATIONS FOR MODEL TEST 2

1. (B) standard
2. (C) lazy
3. (A) nauseous
4. (C) interrupt
5. (A) give up

6. **(B)** The second word is the action of the first word.
7. **(D)** The first word hits the second word.
8. **(A)** The second word has clear, "see-through" qualities, differentiating it from the first word.
9. **(C)** The first word works professionally with the second word.
10. **(C)** In (A), "whomever" is incorrect; "whoever" would be correct. In (B), "all the better" is an incorrect expression. In (D), "whomever" should be "whoever."
11. **(D)** Each of the other choices is repetitious; for instance, "vague" repeats unnecessarily the meaning of "hazy."
12. **(D)** Correct spelling: ridiculous
13. **(A)** pronunciation
14. **(C)** desirable
15. **(A)** judgment
16. **(A)** The passage stresses the "fast-changing job market."
17. **(C)** The passage stresses the similarity between the "general problems" of the past and those of the present, but does not suggest that the study of history will answer all questions or solve all problems.
18. **(C)** opening
19. **(A)** gloomy
20. **(C)** obstruct
21. **(C)** changeable
22. **(C)** captivate
23. **(B)** The second word is a quality of the first word.
24. **(A)** The first word travels through the second word.
25. **(B)** The second word is the initial introduction of the first word.
26. **(C)** The second word is the movement of the first word.
27. **(B)** In both (A) and (D), the reference of "her" and of "she" is vague. In (C), the meaning of "in mind" is not clear.
28. **(D)** "All the farther" and "farther" are incorrect in each of the other choices; "further" would be a better choice in all three cases.
29. **(A)** separate
30. **(B)** publicly
31. **(C)** accommodate
32. **(B)** calendar
33. **(C)** The passage states that having knowledge may leave the holder of such knowledge feeling "more powerless than powerful."
34. **(A)** None of the other choices is supported by information in the paragraph. (A) repeats the overall point of the paragraph.

35. **(A)** doubtful
36. **(D)** awkward
37. **(C)** ridicule
38. **(A)** waste
39. **(C)** force
40. **(B)** The first word creates the second word.
41. **(C)** The first word is at the bottom; the second word is at the top.
42. **(A)** The first word is stored in the second word.
43. **(C)** The second word creates the first word.
44. **(D)** In (A), the subject of the sentence is plural, so the verb should be plural, "sell" instead of "sells." In (B), "to" should be "by." (C) is not a complete sentence.
45. **(C)** In (A), the correct phrase for comparing two people is "more experienced" rather than "most experienced." In (B), "experientially" improperly refers to the office manager. (D) is vague and illogical, saying that the decision had a mind and that the clerical position was given to the office manager!
46. **(B)** curtail
47. **(A)** bribery
48. **(B)** tomorrow
49. **(A)** maneuver
50. **(D)** This choice restates the overall point of the paragraph.
51. **(B)** The final sentence states that "passive constructions . . . should not be discarded altogether" and thus implies that passive constructions are useful at times.
52. **(C)** cold
53. **(C)** swollen
54. **(B)** enjoy
55. **(C)** ill
56. **(A)** aware
57. **(B)** The first word grows in the second word.
58. **(C)** The second word covers the first word.
59. **(B)** The second word stops the flow of the first word.
60. **(C)** The second word is the opposite of the first word.
61. **(A)** In (B), "to forbid" should be "forbidding" (so that it is parallel with "reducing" and "laying"). Both (C) and (D) are incomplete and unclear.
62. **(B)** In both (A) and (C), the sentence structure is awkward and unclear. Also in (A), the board of directors seems to have been promoted. In (D), "will have had congratulated" is an incorrect verb; "congratulated" alone would be sufficient here.
63. **(B)** hysteria
64. **(C)** misconception

65. **(C)** disburse
66. **(B)** revenue
67. **(A)** The passage states that illegal aliens take advantage of the law "in order to gain legal residency status."
68. **(C)** The paragraph states that the underwriters "now have a chance to recover" some of the money they lost because of the failed launch.
69. **(A)** remorse
70. **(A)** commonplace
71. **(C)** word-for-word
72. **(A)** clear
73. **(C)** leniency
74. **(B)** The first word grows out of the second word.
75. **(A)** The second word encircles the first word.
76. **(D)** The second word is the structure in which the first word lives.
77. **(A)** The second word fits into the first word.

78. **(D)** In (A), "to celebrate" should be "celebrating," parallel to "promising." Choice (B) is illogical: one cannot *promise* a "wonderful past." (C) is not a complete sentence.
79. **(B)** Choices (A) and (C) compare the taste of lunch with the taste of coworkers. In (D), "one" appears to refer to "coworkers."
80. **(C)** modern
81. **(C)** apparatus
82. **(C)** summation
83. **(B)** foreign
84. **(C)** The paragraph states that listening to music "may not be nearly as rewarding or informative" as listening to radio talk shows.
85. **(A)** The paragraph reveals that children who have not read much will probably become adults who avoid reading and have difficulty reading. Each of the other choices makes assumptions about parents that are not expressed or implied in the paragraph.

ANSWER SHEET

SIGNATURE: _____
(Please Sign)

EXAMINATION TITLE: _____

PLACE OF EXAMINATION: _____
City   State

TODAY'S DATE: _____

SAMPLE Ⓐ ● Ⓒ Ⓓ Ⓔ

DIRECTIONS FOR MARKING ANSWER SHEET

Use only a **No. 2 (or softer) lead pencil.** Darken completely the circle corresponding to your answer. You **must** keep your mark within the circle. Stray marks may be counted as errors. Erase **completely** all marks except your answer.

SAMPLE NAME GRID

M.I.
F.I.
LAST NAME

MCCABE

1. In the boxes below, **PRINT** your name. Print only as many letters as will fit within the areas for the last name, first initial (F.I.), and middle initial (M.I.). Below each box, darken the circle containing the same letter. SEE SAMPLE NAME GRID

2. In the boxes below, enter your 9-digit Social Security Number. Below each box, darken the circle in each column corresponding to the number you have entered.

3. OCCUPATIONAL GROUP NUMBER

SOCIAL SECURITY NUMBER

LAST NAME
F.I.
M.I.

SECTION 1

Make no marks or entries in the columns to the right until you receive instructions from the administrator.

PART
Ⓐ Ⓑ Ⓒ Ⓓ Ⓔ Ⓕ Ⓖ Ⓗ Ⓘ Ⓙ

TEST SERIES
⓪①②③④⑤⑥⑦⑧⑨
⓪①②③④⑤⑥⑦⑧⑨
⓪①②③④⑤⑥⑦⑧⑨

TEST NUMBER
⓪①②③④⑤⑥⑦⑧⑨
⓪①②③④⑤⑥⑦⑧⑨
⓪①②③④⑤⑥⑦⑧⑨

1 Ⓐ Ⓑ Ⓒ Ⓓ Ⓔ
2 Ⓐ Ⓑ Ⓒ Ⓓ Ⓔ
3 Ⓐ Ⓑ Ⓒ Ⓓ Ⓔ
4 Ⓐ Ⓑ Ⓒ Ⓓ Ⓔ
5 Ⓐ Ⓑ Ⓒ Ⓓ Ⓔ
6 Ⓐ Ⓑ Ⓒ Ⓓ Ⓔ
7 Ⓐ Ⓑ Ⓒ Ⓓ Ⓔ
8 Ⓐ Ⓑ Ⓒ Ⓓ Ⓔ
9 Ⓐ Ⓑ Ⓒ Ⓓ Ⓔ
10 Ⓐ Ⓑ Ⓒ Ⓓ Ⓔ

11 Ⓐ Ⓑ Ⓒ Ⓓ Ⓔ
12 Ⓐ Ⓑ Ⓒ Ⓓ Ⓔ
13 Ⓐ Ⓑ Ⓒ Ⓓ Ⓔ
14 Ⓐ Ⓑ Ⓒ Ⓓ Ⓔ
15 Ⓐ Ⓑ Ⓒ Ⓓ Ⓔ
16 Ⓐ Ⓑ Ⓒ Ⓓ Ⓔ
17 Ⓐ Ⓑ Ⓒ Ⓓ Ⓔ
18 Ⓐ Ⓑ Ⓒ Ⓓ Ⓔ
19 Ⓐ Ⓑ Ⓒ Ⓓ Ⓔ
20 Ⓐ Ⓑ Ⓒ Ⓓ Ⓔ

21 Ⓐ Ⓑ Ⓒ Ⓓ Ⓔ
22 Ⓐ Ⓑ Ⓒ Ⓓ Ⓔ
23 Ⓐ Ⓑ Ⓒ Ⓓ Ⓔ
24 Ⓐ Ⓑ Ⓒ Ⓓ Ⓔ
25 Ⓐ Ⓑ Ⓒ Ⓓ Ⓔ
26 Ⓐ Ⓑ Ⓒ Ⓓ Ⓔ
27 Ⓐ Ⓑ Ⓒ Ⓓ Ⓔ
28 Ⓐ Ⓑ Ⓒ Ⓓ Ⓔ
29 Ⓐ Ⓑ Ⓒ Ⓓ Ⓔ
30 Ⓐ Ⓑ Ⓒ Ⓓ Ⓔ

31 Ⓐ Ⓑ Ⓒ Ⓓ Ⓔ
32 Ⓐ Ⓑ Ⓒ Ⓓ Ⓔ
33 Ⓐ Ⓑ Ⓒ Ⓓ Ⓔ
34 Ⓐ Ⓑ Ⓒ Ⓓ Ⓔ
35 Ⓐ Ⓑ Ⓒ Ⓓ Ⓔ
36 Ⓐ Ⓑ Ⓒ Ⓓ Ⓔ
37 Ⓐ Ⓑ Ⓒ Ⓓ Ⓔ
38 Ⓐ Ⓑ Ⓒ Ⓓ Ⓔ
39 Ⓐ Ⓑ Ⓒ Ⓓ Ⓔ
40 Ⓐ Ⓑ Ⓒ Ⓓ Ⓔ

41 Ⓐ Ⓑ Ⓒ Ⓓ Ⓔ
42 Ⓐ Ⓑ Ⓒ Ⓓ Ⓔ
43 Ⓐ Ⓑ Ⓒ Ⓓ Ⓔ
44 Ⓐ Ⓑ Ⓒ Ⓓ Ⓔ
45 Ⓐ Ⓑ Ⓒ Ⓓ Ⓔ
46 Ⓐ Ⓑ Ⓒ Ⓓ Ⓔ
47 Ⓐ Ⓑ Ⓒ Ⓓ Ⓔ
48 Ⓐ Ⓑ Ⓒ Ⓓ Ⓔ
49 Ⓐ Ⓑ Ⓒ Ⓓ Ⓔ
50 Ⓐ Ⓑ Ⓒ Ⓓ Ⓔ

51 Ⓐ Ⓑ Ⓒ Ⓓ Ⓔ
52 Ⓐ Ⓑ Ⓒ Ⓓ Ⓔ
53 Ⓐ Ⓑ Ⓒ Ⓓ Ⓔ
54 Ⓐ Ⓑ Ⓒ Ⓓ Ⓔ
55 Ⓐ Ⓑ Ⓒ Ⓓ Ⓔ
56 Ⓐ Ⓑ Ⓒ Ⓓ Ⓔ
57 Ⓐ Ⓑ Ⓒ Ⓓ Ⓔ
58 Ⓐ Ⓑ Ⓒ Ⓓ Ⓔ
59 Ⓐ Ⓑ Ⓒ Ⓓ Ⓔ
60 Ⓐ Ⓑ Ⓒ Ⓓ Ⓔ

61 Ⓐ Ⓑ Ⓒ Ⓓ Ⓔ
62 Ⓐ Ⓑ Ⓒ Ⓓ Ⓔ
63 Ⓐ Ⓑ Ⓒ Ⓓ Ⓔ
64 Ⓐ Ⓑ Ⓒ Ⓓ Ⓔ
65 Ⓐ Ⓑ Ⓒ Ⓓ Ⓔ
66 Ⓐ Ⓑ Ⓒ Ⓓ Ⓔ
67 Ⓐ Ⓑ Ⓒ Ⓓ Ⓔ
68 Ⓐ Ⓑ Ⓒ Ⓓ Ⓔ
69 Ⓐ Ⓑ Ⓒ Ⓓ Ⓔ
70 Ⓐ Ⓑ Ⓒ Ⓓ Ⓔ

71 Ⓐ Ⓑ Ⓒ Ⓓ Ⓔ
72 Ⓐ Ⓑ Ⓒ Ⓓ Ⓔ
73 Ⓐ Ⓑ Ⓒ Ⓓ Ⓔ
74 Ⓐ Ⓑ Ⓒ Ⓓ Ⓔ
75 Ⓐ Ⓑ Ⓒ Ⓓ Ⓔ
76 Ⓐ Ⓑ Ⓒ Ⓓ Ⓔ
77 Ⓐ Ⓑ Ⓒ Ⓓ Ⓔ
78 Ⓐ Ⓑ Ⓒ Ⓓ Ⓔ
79 Ⓐ Ⓑ Ⓒ Ⓓ Ⓔ
80 Ⓐ Ⓑ Ⓒ Ⓓ Ⓔ

81 Ⓐ Ⓑ Ⓒ Ⓓ Ⓔ
82 Ⓐ Ⓑ Ⓒ Ⓓ Ⓔ
83 Ⓐ Ⓑ Ⓒ Ⓓ Ⓔ
84 Ⓐ Ⓑ Ⓒ Ⓓ Ⓔ
85 Ⓐ Ⓑ Ⓒ Ⓓ Ⓔ
86 Ⓐ Ⓑ Ⓒ Ⓓ Ⓔ
87 Ⓐ Ⓑ Ⓒ Ⓓ Ⓔ
88 Ⓐ Ⓑ Ⓒ Ⓓ Ⓔ
89 Ⓐ Ⓑ Ⓒ Ⓓ Ⓔ
90 Ⓐ Ⓑ Ⓒ Ⓓ Ⓔ

91 Ⓐ Ⓑ Ⓒ Ⓓ Ⓔ
92 Ⓐ Ⓑ Ⓒ Ⓓ Ⓔ
93 Ⓐ Ⓑ Ⓒ Ⓓ Ⓔ
94 Ⓐ Ⓑ Ⓒ Ⓓ Ⓔ
95 Ⓐ Ⓑ Ⓒ Ⓓ Ⓔ
96 Ⓐ Ⓑ Ⓒ Ⓓ Ⓔ
97 Ⓐ Ⓑ Ⓒ Ⓓ Ⓔ
98 Ⓐ Ⓑ Ⓒ Ⓓ Ⓔ
99 Ⓐ Ⓑ Ⓒ Ⓓ Ⓔ
100 Ⓐ Ⓑ Ⓒ Ⓓ Ⓔ

101 Ⓐ Ⓑ Ⓒ Ⓓ Ⓔ
102 Ⓐ Ⓑ Ⓒ Ⓓ Ⓔ
103 Ⓐ Ⓑ Ⓒ Ⓓ Ⓔ
104 Ⓐ Ⓑ Ⓒ Ⓓ Ⓔ
105 Ⓐ Ⓑ Ⓒ Ⓓ Ⓔ
106 Ⓐ Ⓑ Ⓒ Ⓓ Ⓔ
107 Ⓐ Ⓑ Ⓒ Ⓓ Ⓔ
108 Ⓐ Ⓑ Ⓒ Ⓓ Ⓔ
109 Ⓐ Ⓑ Ⓒ Ⓓ Ⓔ
110 Ⓐ Ⓑ Ⓒ Ⓓ Ⓔ

111 Ⓐ Ⓑ Ⓒ Ⓓ Ⓔ
112 Ⓐ Ⓑ Ⓒ Ⓓ Ⓔ
113 Ⓐ Ⓑ Ⓒ Ⓓ Ⓔ
114 Ⓐ Ⓑ Ⓒ Ⓓ Ⓔ
115 Ⓐ Ⓑ Ⓒ Ⓓ Ⓔ
116 Ⓐ Ⓑ Ⓒ Ⓓ Ⓔ
117 Ⓐ Ⓑ Ⓒ Ⓓ Ⓔ
118 Ⓐ Ⓑ Ⓒ Ⓓ Ⓔ
119 Ⓐ Ⓑ Ⓒ Ⓓ Ⓔ
120 Ⓐ Ⓑ Ⓒ Ⓓ Ⓔ

121 Ⓐ Ⓑ Ⓒ Ⓓ Ⓔ
122 Ⓐ Ⓑ Ⓒ Ⓓ Ⓔ
123 Ⓐ Ⓑ Ⓒ Ⓓ Ⓔ
124 Ⓐ Ⓑ Ⓒ Ⓓ Ⓔ
125 Ⓐ Ⓑ Ⓒ Ⓓ Ⓔ
126 Ⓐ Ⓑ Ⓒ Ⓓ Ⓔ
127 Ⓐ Ⓑ Ⓒ Ⓓ Ⓔ
128 Ⓐ Ⓑ Ⓒ Ⓓ Ⓔ
129 Ⓐ Ⓑ Ⓒ Ⓓ Ⓔ
130 Ⓐ Ⓑ Ⓒ Ⓓ Ⓔ

Time allotted—35 minutes

Directions

Each question has four suggested answers. Decide which one is the best answer. Find the quesiton number on the Answer Sheet. Show your answer to the question by darkening completely the space corresponding to the letter that is the same as the letter of your answer. Keep your mark within the space. If you have to erase a mark, be sure to erase it completely. Mark only one answer for each question. Do NOT mark space E for any question.

Word Meaning

1. *Harried* means most nearly
   A) rapid   C) rushed
   B) disturbed   D) distant

2. To *scald* means most nearly to
   A) climb   C) raise
   B) censure   D) burn

3. To *decipher* means most nearly to
   A) translate   C) funnel
   B) number   D) determine

4. *Rationale* means most nearly
   A) motive   C) reality
   B) emotion   D) amount

5. *Antidote* means most nearly
   A) joke   C) cure
   B) hospital   D) story

Analogies

6. BANK is related to MONEY as ARMORY is related to
   A) iron   C) ammunition
   B) coins   D) soldiers

7. ADOLESCENCE is related to YOUNGSTER as MATURITY is related to
   A) adult   C) teenager
   B) child   D) corpse

8. CRIME is related to WITNESS as EVENT is related to
   A) police   C) spectator
   B) judge   D) stadium

9. BOTTLE is related to CORK as POT is related to
   A) pan   C) stove
   B) handle   D) lid

Grammar

Decide which sentence is preferable with respect to grammar and usage suitable for a formal letter or report.

10. A) All of them decided it would not be as good for the girls to stay home rather than go to the party.
    B) The girls all decided it would be best to stay at home rather to go to the party.
    C) All the girls decided it would be better to stay home than to go to the party.
    D) To stay home instead of going to the party was decided to be the best according to all the girls.

11. A) When a person reads the instructions, they should remember to follow directions as complete as possible.
    B) When reading the instructions, a person should follow directions as completely as possible.
    C) Following directions as completely as possible, a person reading the instructions.
    D) Remember when reading instructions and following directions as completely as possible.

Spelling

Find the correct spelling of the word and darken the proper answer space. If no suggested spelling is correct, darken space D.

12. A) juvenil   C) juvinil
    B) juvanile   D) none of these

13. A) drapht   C) draph
    B) draft   D) none of these

14. A) defence   C) defensce
    B) defense   D) none of these

15. A) territorrial   C) territorial
    B) teritorial   D) none of these

Reading

16. Noting that drug abuse has increased markedly since the 1960s, we must ask why. Put simply, people use drugs because the complexity and difficulty of modern life is simply overwhelming, and the temptation to escape from it all with cocaine is often impossible to resist.

    The paragraph best supports the statement that cocaine

    A) was not used previous to the 1960s
    B) is part of the complexity and difficulty of modern life
    C) is a temptation that can be resisted when life is more simple and easy
    D) is one of the drugs whose abuse has increased since the 1960s

17. The ability to recognize grammar and usage errors in the writing of others is not the same as the ability to see such errors in one's own writing. Often a writer is not aware of his own errors until they are pointed out by a good editor.

    The paragraph best supports the statement that errors in grammar and usage

    A) are difficult to recognize on one's own writing
    B) are only apparent to professional editors who are not writers
    C) are not usually a problem for an editor reading her own writing
    D) must be pointed out before they are recognized

18. *Hindrance* means most nearly
    A) secret   C) aid
    B) obstacle   D) medication

19. To *pacify* means most nearly to
    A) cross   C) placate
    B) attempt   D) conceal

20. *Maxim* means most nearly
    A) amount   C) giant
    B) proverb   D) poison

21. *Cavity* means most nearly
    A) quill   C) sting
    B) decay   D) hole

22. *Torrid* means most nearly
    A) slow   C) fearful
    B) hot   D) determined

23. PRESCRIPTION is related to PHARMACIST as BLUEPRINT is related to
    A) builder   C) landlord
    B) architect   D) tenant

24. GUILT is related to INNOCENCE as VICE is related to
    A) crime   C) sin
    B) punishment   D) virtue

25. ZOO is related to ANIMAL as GALLERY is related to
    A) patrons   C) art
    B) guards   D) building

26. CLOCK is related to HOUR as CALENDAR is related to
    A) minute   C) month
    B) hour   D) June

27. A) Be sure to double check your ticket location to make certain you are in the proper seat.
    B) To make sure you are in the proper seat, double checking your ticket location is to be done.
    C) Making certain you are in the proper seat, your ticket is to be double checked.
    D) To double check your ticket location and to be certain you are in the proper seat.

28. A) Whatever he does or doesn't do, it's for sure that he really truly enjoys his work.
    B) Depending on what he does or doesn't do, he sure likes his work.
    C) Not mattering what he does or doesn't do, he enjoys his work.
    D) Whatever he does or doesn't do, he at least enjoys his work.

29. A) tolerence   C) tolerance
    B) tollerance   D) none of these

30. A) tommorrow   C) tomorrow
    B) tommorow   D) none of these

31. A) lightening   C) litening
    B) lightning   D) none of these

32. A) likeable   C) likible
    B) likable   D) none of these

33. Since 1890, the federal government and the states have passed a number of laws against corrupt political practices. But today many feel that political corruption is a regular occurrence, and deeply mistrust their public leaders.

The paragraph best supports the statement that many citizens

A) are not in favor of laws against corrupt political practices
B) changed their attitude toward political corruption after 1890
C) think that their political leaders are probably corrupt
D) are even more corrupt than their political leaders

34. People who easily adapt themselves to different social situations, who mingle easily with many different personalities, might be compared to the chameleon, that lizard who changes color to match the environment.

The paragraph best supports the statement that

A) it is possible to compare people with animals
B) adaptable people tend to resemble reptiles
C) the chameleon is a very social animal
D) the ability to change color is not limited to the chameleon

35. *Garish* means most nearly
A) gaudy   C) worthless
B) decorative   D) abundant

36. *Regal* means most nearly
A) normal   C) young
B) immense   D) kingly

37. *Occult* means most nearly
A) youthful   C) swift
B) mysterious   D) fraudulent

38. *Parody* means most nearly
A) spoof   C) flock
B) equality   D) trap

39. To *beckon* means most nearly
A) desire   C) delight
B) reverse   D) summon

40. SAILBOAT is related to WIND as BICYCLE is related to
A) feet   C) road
B) wheels   D) chain

41. BLUNDER is related to MISCUE as PRECISION is related to
A) .error   C) slang
B) accuracy   D) illusion

42. HORSE is related to STABLE as TENANT is related to
A) city   C) apartment
B) landlord   D) lease

43. RECIPE is related to INGREDIENTS as CAST is related to
A) play   C) arm
B) stage   D) characters

44. A) Typical of their species, the parrot will thrive where they can find enough fruits and nuts.
B) Like their species, parrots will thrive wherever it can find enough fruits and nuts.
C) Finding enough fruits and nuts will enable parrots to thrive like their species.
D) Typical of their species, parrots will thrive wherever they can find enough fruits and nuts.

45. A) Bernhouse obviously treasured the memory of his father's happiness as much as he did the memory of his own childhood.
B) The memory of his father's happiness was obviously treasured by Bernhouse as much as he did his father's treasured happiness.
C) Obviously treasuring his father's happiness as much as the memory of Bernhouse's own childhood.
D) Bernhouse treasured obviously the memory of his father's happiness as much as his own childhood memory.

46. A) allright   C) allrite
B) alright   D) none of these

47. A) hazardous   C) hazzardice
B) hazzardous   D) none of these

48. A) congradulatons   C) congratalations
B) congradalations D) none of these

49. A) mannakin   C) mannequin
B) mannaquin   D) none of these

50. Some scientists have proposed that, over two hundred million years ago, one giant land mass—rather than various continents and islands—covered one-third of the earth.

The paragraph best supports the statement that the different continents that exist now

A) were all larger in the past
B) may not have always existed as such
C) have been challenged by scientists
D) now occupy two-thirds of the earth

51. Antifreeze lowers the melting point of any liquid to which it is added, so that the liquid will not freeze in cold weather. It is commonly used to maintain the cooling system in automobile radiators. Of course, the weather may become so cold that even antifreeze is not effective, but such a severe climatic condition rarely occurs in well-traveled places.

The paragraph best supports the statement that antifreeze is

A) usually effective only in automobile radiators
B) usually effective wherever automobile travel is common
C) usually effective even in the coldest climates on earth
D) not nearly as effective as it could be

52. *Frivolous* means most nearly
A) lighthearted   C) close
B) likable   D) equivalent

53. *Macabre* means most nearly
A) parrot   C) biblical
B) grotesque   D) paper

54. To *exert* means most nearly to
A) consume   C) forgive
B) acquit   D) exercise

55. To *infiltrate* means most nearly to
A) limit   C) disbelieve
B) intrude   D) deduce

56. *Callous* means most nearly
A) rough   C) sore
B) insensitive   D) conventional

57. HELIUM is related to BALLOON as WATER is related to
A) shore   C) aquarium
B) rain   D) fish

58. STONE is related to CHERRY as ATOM is related to
A) nucleus   C) molecule
B) electron   D) bomb

59. LAMB is related to SHEEP as CUB is related to
A) calf   C) bear
B) colt   D) den

60. DRY is related to PARCHED as WET is related to
A) soaked   C) dank
B) damp   D) rain

61. A) Music and films with a strong Latin theme has helped to unite the community.
B) Music, as well as films with a strong Latin theme, have been mostly helpful for the uniting of the community.
C) Music and films with a strong Latin theme have helped to unite the community.
D) Uniting the community, music and films with a strong Latin theme have been helpful.

62. A) Sitting in what he called his home away from home, Arnold thought concerning about his future.
B) Sitting in what he called his home away from home, concerning his future Arnold thought.
C) Having sat in what he is calling his home away from home, Arnold thinks about his future.
D) Sitting in what he called his home away from home, Arnold thought about the future.

63. A) musichan   C) musisian
B) musician   D) none of these

64. A) practicle   C) practical
B) practicul   D) none of these

65. A) servent   C) servant
B) servint   D) none of these

66. A) sincerly   C) sincerely
B) sinserely   D) none of these

67. In the twelfth century, people used the abacus (a simple device made of beads strung on wire) to perform complex calculations. Today we use electronic calculators, and the abacus has become obsolete. One thousand years from now, who knows?

The paragraph best supports the statement that

A) the abacus is useless for performing calculations today
B) in the distant future, the electronic calculator of today may seem obsolete
C) devices used for calculating undergo a vast improvement every 1,000 years
D) modern calculations are more complex than ancient calculations

68. It has been estimated that only one out of 500 drunken drivers on the highway is flagged down by the police. The odds against being arrested make it tempting for drinkers to give themselves the benefit of the doubt when they are considering whether they should get behind the wheel.

The paragraph best supports the statement that drinkers are

A) usually not driving when they are detained by the police
B) likely to drive even though they are drunk
C) quite frequently stopped by the police while on the highway
D) never stopped by the police while driving on the highway

69. To *elucidate* means most nearly to
A) explain   C) tighten
B) lose   D) forget

70. *Tawny* means most nearly
A) quiet   C) brown
B) soft   D) rowdy

71. *Despot* means most nearly
A) tyrant   C) inkwell
B) oasis   D) morsel

72. To *tarry* means most nearly to
A) hurry   C) blacken
B) linger   D) soil

73. *Lank* means most nearly
A) piece   C) amount
B) slender   D) common

74. CATERPILLAR is related to BUTTERFLY as TADPOLE is related to
A) lilypad   C) egg
B) pond   D) frog

75. PATRON is related to SUPPORT as ADMIRER is related to
A) compliment   C) contribution
B) money   D) desire

76. HOUSE is related to BASEMENT as CASTLE is related to
A) moat   C) dungeon
B) tower   D) parapet

77. MOTH is related to FLAME as IRON is related to
A) solder   C) filing
B) magnet   D) brass

78. A) Many at the time believed that the alliance with the allies is a trick to confuse their enemy.
B) Many at the time believes that the alliance with the allies was a trick to confuse their enemies.
C) Many at the time believed that their alliance with the allies confused the enemy as a trick.
D) Many at the time believed that their alliance with the allies was a trick to confuse their enemies.

79. A) Going a long way towards improvement of efficiency, they are no doubt useless, computers without humans.
B) Though they have gone a long way towards improvement of efficiency, computers are no doubt useless, having no humans.
C) Though they've made major improvements in efficiency, computers are useless without humans.
D) Being without humans, in spite of their improvements in efficiency, computers have gone a long way.

80. A) deceive   C) decieve
B) deceeve   D) none of these

81. A) vilence   C) violense
B) violence   D) none of these

82. A) misry   C) missery
    B) misary   D) none of these

83. A) heighth   C) hieght
    B) height   D) none of these

84. One of the most important works of the Middle Ages was *The Principles of Letter Writing*, authored by an anonymous Italian educator. It became the basis for formal communication, and many of the principles it advocates have become part of clerical education today.

The paragraph best supports the statement that clerical workers today

A) should be more familiar with relevant books from the Middle Ages
B) study some principles of communication that were available in the Middle Ages
C) are not familiar with *The Principles of Letter Writing*
D) study some principles that contradict those proposed in the Middle Ages

85. Although the acceptable format for writing reports varies from profession to profession, certain rules are invariable. For example, all writers must avoid faulty parallelism and misplaced modifiers; such grammatical errors are incorrect in any context.

The paragraph best supports the statement that different professions

A) tend to disapprove of grammatical errors in written reports
B) are only concerned with errors involving parallelism and modifiers
C) consult grammatical rules before the preparation of any written report
D) follow the same basic format for written reports, although there are variations

ANSWER KEY FOR MODEL TEST 3

Word Meaning

1. B	18. B	35. A	52. A	69. A
2. D	19. C	36. D	53. B	70. C
3. A	20. B	37. B	54. D	71. A
4. A	21. D	38. A	55. B	72. B
5. C	22. B	39. D	56. B	73. B

Analogies

6. C	23. A	40. A	57. C	74. D
7. A	24. D	41. B	58. A	75. A
8. C	25. C	42. C	59. C	76. C
9. D	26. C	43. D	60. A	77. B

Grammar

10. C	27. A	44. D	61. C	78. D
11. B	28. D	45. A	62. D	79. C

Spelling

12. D	29. C	46. D	63. B	80. A
13. B	30. C	47. A	64. C	81. B
14. B	31. B	48. D	65. C	82. D
15. C	32. B	49. C	66. C	83. B

Reading

16. D	33. C	50. B	67. B	84. B
17. A	34. A	51. B	68. B	85. A

ANALYSIS CHART FOR MODEL TEST 3

Now that you've corrected your exam, use the following chart to carefully analyze your results and spot your strengths and weaknesses. This analysis should help you focus your study and review efforts.

Section	Total Number of Questions	Number Correct	Number Incorrect	Number Unanswered*
Word Meaning	25			
Analogies	20			
Grammar	10			
Spelling	20			
Reading Comprehension	10			
TOTAL	85			

*Since there is no penalty for incorrect answers on the Verbal Abilities Test, you should have left no question unanswered. Even if you didn't have time to answer a question, at least you should have filled in the answer space with a guess.

ANSWER EXPLANATIONS FOR MODEL TEST 3

1. **(B)** disturbed
2. **(D)** burn
3. **(A)** translate
4. **(A)** motive
5. **(C)** cure

6. **(C)** The second word is stored in the first word.
7. **(A)** The first word is a condition of the second word.
8. **(C)** The second word observes the first word.
9. **(D)** The first word is closed up by the second word.
10. **(C)** In (A), "not be as good...rather than" is incorrect. In (B), "best" is incorrect when comparing two options. It should be "better." In (D), "according to" is awkward, and the sentence is better stated in the active, rather than passive.
11. **(B)** In (A), "they" incorrectly refers to "a person." (C) and (D) are sentence fragments.
12. **(D)** Correct spelling: juvenile
13. **(B)** draft
14. **(B)** defense
15. **(C)** territorial
16. **(D)** Cocaine is mentioned as a specific example of the general increase in drug abuse.
17. **(A)** The paragraph's second sentence strongly supports this choice.
18. **(B)** obstacle
19. **(C)** placate
20. **(B)** proverb
21. **(D)** hole
22. **(B)** hot
23. **(A)** The first word is given to the second word.
24. **(D)** The first word is the opposite of the second word.
25. **(C)** The first word displays the second word.
26. **(C)** The first word measures the second word.
27. **(A)** In (B), the sentence would be vastly improved if the phrases were in reverse order. In (C), "Making certain" should be "To make certain." (D) is a sentence fragment.
28. **(D)** In (A), "for sure" and "really truly" are unacceptable idioms, as is "Not mattering" in (C). In (B), "sure" should be "certainly."
29. **(C)** tolerance
30. **(C)** tomorrow
31. **(B)** lightning
32. **(B)** likable
33. **(C)** The passage states that "many...deeply mistrust their public leaders."
34. **(A)** The paragraph is itself a comparison between people and animals, thus supporting the statement that people and animals can be compared.
35. **(A)** gaudy
36. **(D)** kingly
37. **(B)** mysterious
38. **(A)** spoof
39. **(D)** summon
40. **(A)** The second word powers the first word.

41. **(B)** The first word is a synonym for the second word.
42. **(C)** The first word lives in the second word.
43. **(D)** The first word is composed of the second word.
44. **(D)** In (A), "the parrot" (singular) does not agree with "their" and "they." Similarly in (B), "parrots" does not agree with "it." In (C), "to thrive like their species" is vague.
45. **(A)** In (B), "as much as he did" is vague. (C) is a sentence fragment. In (D), "treasured obviously" is incorrect sentence structure.
46. **(D)** Correct spelling: all right
47. **(A)** hazardous
48. **(D)** Correct spelling: congratulations
49. **(C)** mannequin
50. **(B)** The paragraph discusses the possibility that the various continents of today were once contained in "one giant land mass."
51. **(B)** The final sentence implies that antifreeze is effective in "well-traveled places," that is, places where automobile travel is common.
52. **(A)** lighthearted
53. **(B)** grotesque
54. **(D)** exercise
55. **(B)** intrude
56. **(B)** insensitive
57. **(C)** The second word is filled with the first word.
58. **(A)** The second word is the center of the first word.
59. **(C)** The first word is a young second word.
60. **(A)** The second word is the extreme of the first word.
61. **(C)** In (A), "Music and films" (plural) require a plural verb, "have helped" instead of "has helped." In (B), the opposite is required: "Music...*has* helped," a singular subject takes a singular verb. Notice in (B) that "films" are not part of the subject. In (D), "have been helpful" is vague.
62. **(D)** In (A), "concerning about" is incorrect usage. (B) uses awkward structure. In (C), verb tenses are inconsistent.
63. **(B)** musician
64. **(C)** practical
65. **(C)** servant
66. **(C)** sincerely
67. **(B)** The paragraph concludes by questioning what sort of calculation device will exist in 1,000 years, strongly implying that the electronic calculator, like the abacus, will become obsolete.

68. **(B)** The paragraph states that drunken drivers are tempted to "give themselves the benefit of the doubt" when deciding whether to drive; in other words, drunken drivers are tempted to drive in spite of their condition.

69. **(A)** explain

70. **(C)** brown

71. **(A)** tyrant

72. **(B)** linger

73. **(B)** slender

74. **(D)** The first word transforms into the second word.

75. **(A)** The first word gives the second word.

76. **(C)** The second word is in the bottom of the first word.

77. **(B)** The first word is attracted to the second word.

78. **(D)** In (A), "is" should be "was." In (B), "believes" should be "believed." In (C), "confused the enemy as a trick" is awkward structure.

79. **(C)** In (A), "they" is vague, and the structure is awkward. In (B), "having no humans" is a vague phrase, as is "being without humans" in (D).

80. **(A)** deceive

81. **(B)** violence

82. **(D)** correct spelling: misery

83. **(B)** height

84. **(B)** The paragraph states that principles from the Middle Ages "have become part of clerical education today."

85. **(A)** The paragraph stresses the incorrectness of grammatical errors in all professions, saying that certain rules are "invariable."

PART TWO

The Clerical Abilities Test

CHAPTER 4

General Strategies
A Diagnostic Test
with Answer Explanations
Analysis of Strengths and Weaknesses

THE CLERICAL ABILITIES TEST

The Clerical Abilities Test is a test of speed and accuracy on four clerical tasks. There are 120 questions with a *time limit of 15 minutes*. The categories are as follows:

Name and number checking	30 questions
Alphabetical order	30 questions
Arithmetic	30 questions
Letters and numbers	30 questions

The question types are "scrambled" throughout the test; that is, there are 5 questions of each type, repeated until they total 120 questions. Each question has equal value toward your final score. Your score on the Clerical Abilities Test, unlike that on the Verbal Abilities Test, is penalized for incorrect answers. (See the section on "Guessing" that follows.)

PROCEDURE

You will have 10 minutes to study the directions and sample questions on the front of your test booklet and to mark the answers to these sample questions in the space provided. (However, since time is at a premium on this test, it is important that you become familiar with the test question types *long before you take the actual exam*.) You will be told when to begin the actual test, for which you will have only 15 minutes.

GENERAL STRATEGIES

Since there is a limited amount of time (15 minutes) for 120 questions, some essential considerations come into play. We recommend that you reread the general strategies explained in the Verbal Abilities Test section of this book (pages 3–

5). There is one very *important* difference in the strategies for the Clerical Abilities Test, however, in regard to guessing.

Guessing

The score for this test, unlike the Verbal Abilities Test, is determined by the number of right answers *minus one-fourth* the number of wrong answers. Blank answers are given neither plus nor minus credit. Therefore every filled-in but incorrect answer lowers your test score very slightly. For example, if on this test you answer

90 questions correctly,
20 questions incorrectly, and leave
10 questions unanswered,

you will get 90 credits for your correct answers, minus 5 points for your incorrect answers ($\frac{1}{4} \times$ 20), for a total of 85 points. Notice that your final score is 5 points lower because of the 20 wrong answers.

Because of this adjustment, it is not wise to guess blindly on the Clerical Abilities Test, as a wrong choice can decrease your total score. (A "blind" guess is answering a question where you have no insight into the problem and no way of eliminating any choices.)

But if you are able to eliminate even one of the answer choices as incorrect, then you will have increased the odds of guessing correctly and, in the long run, you should get more points in your favor than taken away.

Of course, if you can eliminate *two* choices as incorrect, your chances of guessing correctly are even greater.

So, to summarize, don't guess blindly on this test, but do guess when you can eliminate one or more answer choices as incorrect.

Remember, if you skip a question, be careful to place your next answer mark in the proper space on your answer sheet, *not* in the space you just skipped!

Speed

The Clerical Abilities Test is primarily a test of *speed* in carrying out relatively simple clerical tasks. While accuracy on these tasks is important and will be taken into account in the scoring, experience has shown that many persons are so concerned about accuracy that they do the test more slowly than they should. Speed as well as accuracy is important to achieve a good score. Therefore, do not spend undue time on any particular question.

HOW TO DETERMINE THE TOTAL TEST SCORE

The score on the Verbal Abilities Test is the number of right answers. The score on the Clerical Abilities Test is the number of right answers minus ¼ the number of wrong answers ($R - \frac{1}{4}W$).

The scores on both tests will be added to determine total score. The passing point on the total test will vary according to the grade and kind of position to be filled. In general, a score of approximately 60 percent of the 85 questions on the Verbal Abilities Test is considered good performance. Therefore, a score of 50 or better on the Verbal Abilities Test and a score of 100 on the Verbal and Clerical Abilities Tests combined are considered good scores. These scores will probably qualify a prospective applicant, providing all other test and experience requirements for a particular position are met. Similarly, a score of less than 50 percent of the questions on the Verbal Abilities Test is considered poor. Less than 40 on the Verbal Abilities Test and less than 80 on the Verbal and Clerical Abilities Tests combined indicate relatively poor performance.

A review of how you answered the test questions in the Model Tests will provide useful information to see whether more work is needed in spelling, grammar, etc., whether greater speed or accuracy is needed in the Clerical Abilities Test, and whether the nature of the tasks in the two tests has been clearly understood.

A Diagnostic Test with Answer Explanations

The purpose of this diagnostic test is to familiarize you with the Clerical Abilities Test. It is designed to introduce you to the testing areas and assist you in evaluating your strengths and weaknesses. This will help you focus your review. Chapter 5 will give you a more complete range of problem types and specific strategies for each section. After correcting the diagnostic exam and assessing your strengths and weaknesses, you should start your area reviews and practice in the next chapter.

The diagnostic test should be taken under strict test conditions.

NOTE: Sample questions are usually distributed with the announcement and if so may not be given in the official examination.

First take 10 minutes to review the sample questions given here before starting this exam. Now tear out your answer sheet from this book, turn to the next page, and begin the exam.

ANSWER SHEET

SIGNATURE: _____
(Please Sign)

EXAMINATION TITLE: _____

PLACE OF EXAMINATION: _____
City _____ State _____

TODAY'S DATE: _____

SAMPLE Ⓐ ● Ⓒ Ⓓ Ⓔ

DIRECTIONS FOR MARKING ANSWER SHEET

Use only a **No. 2 (or softer) lead pencil.** Darken completely the circle corresponding to your answer. **You must keep your mark within the circle.** Stray marks may be counted as errors. Erase **completely** all marks except your answer.

SAMPLE NAME GRID

M.I. | A
F.I. | C

LAST NAME
M C C A B E

1. In the boxes below, **PRINT** your name. Print only as many letters as will fit within the areas for the last name, first initial (F.I.), and middle initial (M.I.) Below each box, darken the circle containing the same letter. SEE SAMPLE NAME GRID

2. In the boxes below, enter your 9-digit Social Security Number. Below each box, darken the circle in each column corresponding to the number you have entered.

SOCIAL SECURITY NUMBER

3. OCCUPATIONAL GROUP NUMBER

M.I.

F.I.

LAST NAME

SECTION 1

PART

TEST SERIES

TEST NUMBER

Make no marks or entries in the columns to the right until you receive instructions from the administrator.

1 Ⓐ Ⓑ Ⓒ Ⓓ Ⓔ	21 Ⓐ Ⓑ Ⓒ Ⓓ Ⓔ	41 Ⓐ Ⓑ Ⓒ Ⓓ Ⓔ	61 Ⓐ Ⓑ Ⓒ Ⓓ Ⓔ	81 Ⓐ Ⓑ Ⓒ Ⓓ Ⓔ	101 Ⓐ Ⓑ Ⓒ Ⓓ Ⓔ	121 Ⓐ Ⓑ Ⓒ Ⓓ Ⓔ
2 Ⓐ Ⓑ Ⓒ Ⓓ Ⓔ	22 Ⓐ Ⓑ Ⓒ Ⓓ Ⓔ	42 Ⓐ Ⓑ Ⓒ Ⓓ Ⓔ	62 Ⓐ Ⓑ Ⓒ Ⓓ Ⓔ	82 Ⓐ Ⓑ Ⓒ Ⓓ Ⓔ	102 Ⓐ Ⓑ Ⓒ Ⓓ Ⓔ	122 Ⓐ Ⓑ Ⓒ Ⓓ Ⓔ
3 Ⓐ Ⓑ Ⓒ Ⓓ Ⓔ	23 Ⓐ Ⓑ Ⓒ Ⓓ Ⓔ	43 Ⓐ Ⓑ Ⓒ Ⓓ Ⓔ	63 Ⓐ Ⓑ Ⓒ Ⓓ Ⓔ	83 Ⓐ Ⓑ Ⓒ Ⓓ Ⓔ	103 Ⓐ Ⓑ Ⓒ Ⓓ Ⓔ	123 Ⓐ Ⓑ Ⓒ Ⓓ Ⓔ
4 Ⓐ Ⓑ Ⓒ Ⓓ Ⓔ	24 Ⓐ Ⓑ Ⓒ Ⓓ Ⓔ	44 Ⓐ Ⓑ Ⓒ Ⓓ Ⓔ	64 Ⓐ Ⓑ Ⓒ Ⓓ Ⓔ	84 Ⓐ Ⓑ Ⓒ Ⓓ Ⓔ	104 Ⓐ Ⓑ Ⓒ Ⓓ Ⓔ	124 Ⓐ Ⓑ Ⓒ Ⓓ Ⓔ
5 Ⓐ Ⓑ Ⓒ Ⓓ Ⓔ	25 Ⓐ Ⓑ Ⓒ Ⓓ Ⓔ	45 Ⓐ Ⓑ Ⓒ Ⓓ Ⓔ	65 Ⓐ Ⓑ Ⓒ Ⓓ Ⓔ	85 Ⓐ Ⓑ Ⓒ Ⓓ Ⓔ	105 Ⓐ Ⓑ Ⓒ Ⓓ Ⓔ	125 Ⓐ Ⓑ Ⓒ Ⓓ Ⓔ
6 Ⓐ Ⓑ Ⓒ Ⓓ Ⓔ	26 Ⓐ Ⓑ Ⓒ Ⓓ Ⓔ	46 Ⓐ Ⓑ Ⓒ Ⓓ Ⓔ	66 Ⓐ Ⓑ Ⓒ Ⓓ Ⓔ	86 Ⓐ Ⓑ Ⓒ Ⓓ Ⓔ	106 Ⓐ Ⓑ Ⓒ Ⓓ Ⓔ	126 Ⓐ Ⓑ Ⓒ Ⓓ Ⓔ
7 Ⓐ Ⓑ Ⓒ Ⓓ Ⓔ	27 Ⓐ Ⓑ Ⓒ Ⓓ Ⓔ	47 Ⓐ Ⓑ Ⓒ Ⓓ Ⓔ	67 Ⓐ Ⓑ Ⓒ Ⓓ Ⓔ	87 Ⓐ Ⓑ Ⓒ Ⓓ Ⓔ	107 Ⓐ Ⓑ Ⓒ Ⓓ Ⓔ	127 Ⓐ Ⓑ Ⓒ Ⓓ Ⓔ
8 Ⓐ Ⓑ Ⓒ Ⓓ Ⓔ	28 Ⓐ Ⓑ Ⓒ Ⓓ Ⓔ	48 Ⓐ Ⓑ Ⓒ Ⓓ Ⓔ	68 Ⓐ Ⓑ Ⓒ Ⓓ Ⓔ	88 Ⓐ Ⓑ Ⓒ Ⓓ Ⓔ	108 Ⓐ Ⓑ Ⓒ Ⓓ Ⓔ	128 Ⓐ Ⓑ Ⓒ Ⓓ Ⓔ
9 Ⓐ Ⓑ Ⓒ Ⓓ Ⓔ	29 Ⓐ Ⓑ Ⓒ Ⓓ Ⓔ	49 Ⓐ Ⓑ Ⓒ Ⓓ Ⓔ	69 Ⓐ Ⓑ Ⓒ Ⓓ Ⓔ	89 Ⓐ Ⓑ Ⓒ Ⓓ Ⓔ	109 Ⓐ Ⓑ Ⓒ Ⓓ Ⓔ	129 Ⓐ Ⓑ Ⓒ Ⓓ Ⓔ
10 Ⓐ Ⓑ Ⓒ Ⓓ Ⓔ	30 Ⓐ Ⓑ Ⓒ Ⓓ Ⓔ	50 Ⓐ Ⓑ Ⓒ Ⓓ Ⓔ	70 Ⓐ Ⓑ Ⓒ Ⓓ Ⓔ	90 Ⓐ Ⓑ Ⓒ Ⓓ Ⓔ	110 Ⓐ Ⓑ Ⓒ Ⓓ Ⓔ	130 Ⓐ Ⓑ Ⓒ Ⓓ Ⓔ
11 Ⓐ Ⓑ Ⓒ Ⓓ Ⓔ	31 Ⓐ Ⓑ Ⓒ Ⓓ Ⓔ	51 Ⓐ Ⓑ Ⓒ Ⓓ Ⓔ	71 Ⓐ Ⓑ Ⓒ Ⓓ Ⓔ	91 Ⓐ Ⓑ Ⓒ Ⓓ Ⓔ	111 Ⓐ Ⓑ Ⓒ Ⓓ Ⓔ	
12 Ⓐ Ⓑ Ⓒ Ⓓ Ⓔ	32 Ⓐ Ⓑ Ⓒ Ⓓ Ⓔ	52 Ⓐ Ⓑ Ⓒ Ⓓ Ⓔ	72 Ⓐ Ⓑ Ⓒ Ⓓ Ⓔ	92 Ⓐ Ⓑ Ⓒ Ⓓ Ⓔ	112 Ⓐ Ⓑ Ⓒ Ⓓ Ⓔ	
13 Ⓐ Ⓑ Ⓒ Ⓓ Ⓔ	33 Ⓐ Ⓑ Ⓒ Ⓓ Ⓔ	53 Ⓐ Ⓑ Ⓒ Ⓓ Ⓔ	73 Ⓐ Ⓑ Ⓒ Ⓓ Ⓔ	93 Ⓐ Ⓑ Ⓒ Ⓓ Ⓔ	113 Ⓐ Ⓑ Ⓒ Ⓓ Ⓔ	
14 Ⓐ Ⓑ Ⓒ Ⓓ Ⓔ	34 Ⓐ Ⓑ Ⓒ Ⓓ Ⓔ	54 Ⓐ Ⓑ Ⓒ Ⓓ Ⓔ	74 Ⓐ Ⓑ Ⓒ Ⓓ Ⓔ	94 Ⓐ Ⓑ Ⓒ Ⓓ Ⓔ	114 Ⓐ Ⓑ Ⓒ Ⓓ Ⓔ	
15 Ⓐ Ⓑ Ⓒ Ⓓ Ⓔ	35 Ⓐ Ⓑ Ⓒ Ⓓ Ⓔ	55 Ⓐ Ⓑ Ⓒ Ⓓ Ⓔ	75 Ⓐ Ⓑ Ⓒ Ⓓ Ⓔ	95 Ⓐ Ⓑ Ⓒ Ⓓ Ⓔ	115 Ⓐ Ⓑ Ⓒ Ⓓ Ⓔ	
16 Ⓐ Ⓑ Ⓒ Ⓓ Ⓔ	36 Ⓐ Ⓑ Ⓒ Ⓓ Ⓔ	56 Ⓐ Ⓑ Ⓒ Ⓓ Ⓔ	76 Ⓐ Ⓑ Ⓒ Ⓓ Ⓔ	96 Ⓐ Ⓑ Ⓒ Ⓓ Ⓔ	116 Ⓐ Ⓑ Ⓒ Ⓓ Ⓔ	
17 Ⓐ Ⓑ Ⓒ Ⓓ Ⓔ	37 Ⓐ Ⓑ Ⓒ Ⓓ Ⓔ	57 Ⓐ Ⓑ Ⓒ Ⓓ Ⓔ	77 Ⓐ Ⓑ Ⓒ Ⓓ Ⓔ	97 Ⓐ Ⓑ Ⓒ Ⓓ Ⓔ	117 Ⓐ Ⓑ Ⓒ Ⓓ Ⓔ	
18 Ⓐ Ⓑ Ⓒ Ⓓ Ⓔ	38 Ⓐ Ⓑ Ⓒ Ⓓ Ⓔ	58 Ⓐ Ⓑ Ⓒ Ⓓ Ⓔ	78 Ⓐ Ⓑ Ⓒ Ⓓ Ⓔ	98 Ⓐ Ⓑ Ⓒ Ⓓ Ⓔ	118 Ⓐ Ⓑ Ⓒ Ⓓ Ⓔ	
19 Ⓐ Ⓑ Ⓒ Ⓓ Ⓔ	39 Ⓐ Ⓑ Ⓒ Ⓓ Ⓔ	59 Ⓐ Ⓑ Ⓒ Ⓓ Ⓔ	79 Ⓐ Ⓑ Ⓒ Ⓓ Ⓔ	99 Ⓐ Ⓑ Ⓒ Ⓓ Ⓔ	119 Ⓐ Ⓑ Ⓒ Ⓓ Ⓔ	
20 Ⓐ Ⓑ Ⓒ Ⓓ Ⓔ	40 Ⓐ Ⓑ Ⓒ Ⓓ Ⓔ	60 Ⓐ Ⓑ Ⓒ Ⓓ Ⓔ	80 Ⓐ Ⓑ Ⓒ Ⓓ Ⓔ	100 Ⓐ Ⓑ Ⓒ Ⓓ Ⓔ	120 Ⓐ Ⓑ Ⓒ Ⓓ Ⓔ	

CLERICAL ABILITIES DIAGNOSTIC TEST

Time allotted—15 minutes

Directions

This test contains four kinds of questions. There are some of each kind on each page in the booklet. The time limit for the test will be announced by the examiner.

Study the sample questions carefully. Each question has five suggested answers. Decide which one is the best answer. Find the question number on the Sample Answer Sheet. Show your answer to the question by darkening completely the space corresponding to the letter that is the same as the letter of your answer. Keep your mark within the space. If you have to erase a mark, be sure to erase it completely. Mark only one answer for each question.

Sample Questions

In each line across the page there are three names or numbers that are much alike. Compare the three names or numbers and decide which ones are exactly alike. On the Sample Answer Sheet at the right, mark the answer—

A if ALL THREE names or numbers are exactly ALIKE
B if only the FIRST and SECOND names or numbers are exactly ALIKE
C if only the FIRST and THIRD names or numbers are exactly ALIKE
D if only the SECOND and THIRD names or numbers are exactly ALIKE
E if ALL THREE names or numbers are DIFFERENT

I.	Davis Hazen	David Hozen	David Hazen
II.	Lois Appel	Lois Appel	Lois Apfel
III.	June Allan	Jane Allan	Jane Allan
IV.	10235	10235	10235
V.	32614	32164	32614

SAMPLE ANSWER SHEET

1 Ⓐ Ⓑ Ⓒ Ⓓ Ⓔ
2 Ⓐ Ⓑ Ⓒ Ⓓ Ⓔ
3 Ⓐ Ⓑ Ⓒ Ⓓ Ⓔ
4 Ⓐ Ⓑ Ⓒ Ⓓ Ⓔ
5 Ⓐ Ⓑ Ⓒ Ⓓ Ⓔ
6 Ⓐ Ⓑ Ⓒ Ⓓ Ⓔ
7 Ⓐ Ⓑ Ⓒ Ⓓ Ⓔ

It will be to your advantage to learn what A, B, C, D, and E stand for. If you finish the sample questions before you are told to turn to the test, study them.

In the next group of sample questions, there is a name in a box at the left, and four other names in alphabetical order at the right. Find the correct space for the boxed name so that it will be in alphabetical order with the others, and mark the letter of that space as your answer.

VI. | Jones, Jane |
  A) →
    Goodyear, G. L.
  B) →
    Haddon, Harry
  C) →
    Jackson, Mary
  D) →
    Jenkins, William
  E) →

VII. | Kessler, Neilson |
  A) →
    Kessel, Carl
  B) →
    Kessinger, D. J.
  C) →
    Kessler, Karl
  D) →
    Kessner, Lewis
  E) →

CORRECT ANSWERS TO SAMPLE QUESTIONS

1 Ⓐ Ⓑ Ⓒ Ⓓ ●
2 Ⓐ ● Ⓒ Ⓓ Ⓔ
3 Ⓐ Ⓑ Ⓒ ● Ⓔ
4 ● Ⓑ Ⓒ Ⓓ Ⓔ
5 Ⓐ Ⓑ ● Ⓓ Ⓔ
6 Ⓐ Ⓑ Ⓒ Ⓓ ●
7 Ⓐ Ⓑ Ⓒ ● Ⓔ

In the following questions, do whatever the question says, and find your answer among the list of suggested answers for that question. Mark the Sample Answer Sheet A, B, C or D, for the answer you obtained; or if your answer is not among these, mark E for that question.

	Answers		*Answers*
VIII. Add:	A) 44 B) 45	X. Multiply:	A) 100 B) 115
22	C) 54 D) 55	25	C) 125 D) 135
+ 33	E) none of these	× 5	E) none of these

IX. Subtract:	A) 20 B) 21	XI. Divide:	A) 20 B) 22
24	C) 27 D) 29	6)‾126	C) 24 D) 26
− 3	E) none of these		E) none of these

There is one set of suggested answers for the next group of sample questions. Do not try to memorize these answers, because there will be a different set on each page in the test.

To find the answer to a question, find which suggested answer contains numbers and letters all of which appear in the question. If no suggested answer fits, mark E for that question.

XII. 8 N K 9 G T 4 6
XIII. T 9 7 Z 6 L 3 K
XIV. Z 7 G K 3 9 8 N
XV. 3 K 9 4 6 G Z L
XVI. Z N 7 3 8 K T 9

Suggested Answers
$\begin{cases} A = 7, \ 9, \ G, \ K \\ B = 8, \ 9, \ T, \ Z \\ C = 6, \ 7, \ K, \ Z \\ D = 6, \ 8, \ G, \ T \\ E = \text{none of these} \end{cases}$

After you have marked your answers to all the questions on the Sample Answer Sheets on this page and on the preceding page, check them with the answers in the boxes marked Correct Answers to Sample Questions.

Answer Explanations for Sample Questions

I. (E) Davis Hazen	David Hozen	David Hazen	VIII. (D) 55
II. (B) Lois Appel	Lois Appel	Lois Apfel	IX. (B) 21
III. (D) June Allan	Jane Allan	Jane Allan	X. (C) 125
IV. (A) 10235	10235	10235	XI. (E) 21
V. (C) 32614	32164	32614	XII. (D) 8 N K 9 G T 4 6
VI. (E) Jenkins, William			XIII. (C) T 9 7 Z 6 L 3 K
Jones, Jane			XIV. (A) Z 7 G K 3 9 8 N
VII. (D) Kessler, Karl			XV. (E) 3 K 9 4 6 G Z L
Kessler, Neilson			XVI. (B) Z N 7 3 8 K T 9
Kessner, Lewis			

THE TEST

In questions 1 through 5, compare the three names or numbers, and mark the answer—

A if ALL THREE names or numbers are exactly ALIKE
B if only the FIRST and SECOND names or numbers are exactly ALIKE
C if only the FIRST and THIRD names or numbers are exactly ALIKE
D if only the SECOND and THIRD names or numbers are exactly ALIKE
E if ALL THREE names or numbers are DIFFERENT

1. 5261383	5261383	5261338
2. 8125690	8126690	8125609
3. W. E. Johnston	W. E. Johnson	W. E. Johnson
4. Vergil L. Muller	Vergil L. Muller	Vergil L. Muller
5. Atherton R. Warde	Asheton R. Warde	Atherton P. Warde

In questions 6 through 10, find the correct place for the name in the box.

6. Hackett, Gerald

A) →
Habert, James
B) →
Hachett, J. J.
C) →
Hachetts, K. Larson
D) →
Hachettson, Leroy
E) →

7. Margenroth, Alvin

A) →
Margeroth, Albert
B) →
Margestein, Dan
C) →
Margestein, David
D) →
Margue, Edgar
E) →

8. Bobbitt, Olivier E.

A) →
Bobbitt, D. Olivier
B) →
Bobbitt, Olive B.
C) →
Bobbitt, Olivia H.
D) →
Bobbitt, R. Olivia
E) →

9. Mosely, Werner

A) →
Mosely, Albert J.
B) →
Mosley, Alvin
C) →
Mosley, S. M.
D) →
Mozley, Vinson N.
E) →

10. Youmuns, Frank L.

A) →
Youmons, Frank G.
B) →
Youmons, Frank H.
C) →
Youmons, Frank K.
D) →
Youmons, Frank M.
E) →

GO ON TO THE NEXT COLUMN.

Answers

11. Add:
   43
   + 32

   A) 55 B) 65
   C) 66 D) 75
   E) none of these

12. Subtract:
   83
   − 4

   A) 73 B) 79
   C) 80 D) 89
   E) none of these

13. Multiply:
   41
   × 7

   A) 281 B) 287
   C) 291 D) 297
   E) none of these

14. Divide:
   $6\overline{)306}$

   A) 44 B) 51
   C) 52 D) 60
   E) none of these

15. Add:
   37
   + 15

   A) 42 B) 52
   C) 53 D) 62
   E) none of these

For each question below, find which one of the suggested answers appears in that question.

16. 6 2 5 K 4 P T G

17. L 4 7 2 T 6 V K

18. 3 5 4 L 9 V T G

19. G 4 K 7 L 3 5 Z

20. 4 K 2 9 N 5 T G

Suggested Answers
A = 4, 5, K, T
B = 4, 7, G, K
C = 2, 5, G, L
D = 2, 7, L, T
E = none of these

GO ON TO THE NEXT PAGE.

In questions 21 through 25, compare the three names or numbers, and mark the answer—

A if ALL THREE names or numbers are exactly ALIKE
B if only the FIRST and SECOND names or numbers are exactly ALIKE
C if only the FIRST and THIRD names or numbers are exactly ALIKE
D if only the SECOND and THIRD names or numbers are exactly ALIKE
E if ALL THREE names or numbers are DIFFERENT

21.	2395890	2395890	2395890
22.	1926341	1926347	1926314
23.	E. Owens McVey	E. Owen McVey	E. Owen McVay
24.	Emily Neal Rouse	Emily Neal Rowse	Emily Neal Rowse
25.	H. Merritt Audubon	H. Merriott Audubon	H. Merritt Audubon

In questions 26 through 30, find the correct place for the name in the box.

26. Watters, N. O.
- A) →
  Waters, Charles L.
- B) →
  Waterson, Nina P.
- C) →
  Watson, Nora J.
- D) →
  Wattwood, Paul A.
- E) →

27. Johnston, Edward
- A) →
  Johnston, Edgar R.
- B) →
  Johnston, Edmond
- C) →
  Johnston, Edmund
- D) →
  Johnstone, Edmund A.
- E) →

28. Rensch, Adeline
- A) →
  Ramsay, Amos
- B) →
  Remschel, Augusta
- C) →
  Renshaw, Austin
- D) →
  Rentzel, Becky
- E) →

29. Schnyder, Maurice
- A) →
  Schneider, Martin
- B) →
  Schneider, Mertens
- C) →
  Schnyder, Newman
- D) →
  Schreibner, Norman
- E) →

30. Freedenburg, C. Erma
- A) →
  Freedenberg, Emerson
- B) →
  Freedenberg, Erma
- C) →
  Freedenberg, Erma E.
- D) →
  Freedinberg, Erma F.
- E) →

31. Subtract:
68
− 47

Answers
A) 10   B) 11
C) 20   D) 22
E) none of these

32. Multiply:
50
× 8

A) 400   B) 408
C) 450   D) 458
E) none of these

33. Divide:
9)180

A) 20   B) 29
C) 30   D) 39
E) none of these

34. Add:
78
+ 63

A) 131   B) 140
C) 141   D) 151
E) none of these

35. Subtract:
89
− 70

A) 9   B) 18
C) 19   D) 29
E) none of these

For each question below, find which one of the suggested answers appears in that question.

36. 9 G Z 3 L 4 6 N

37. L 5 N K 4 3 9 V

38. 8 2 V P 9 L Z 5

39. V P 9 Z 5 L 8 7

40. 5 T 8 N 2 9 V L

Suggested Answers
A = 4, 9, L, V
B = 4, 5, N, Z
C = 5, 8, L, Z
D = 8, 9, N, V
E = none of these

GO ON TO THE NEXT COLUMN.

GO ON TO THE NEXT PAGE.

In questions 41 through 45, compare the three names or numbers, and mark the answer—
A if ALL THREE names or numbers are exactly ALIKE
B if only the FIRST and SECOND names or numbers are exactly ALIKE
C if only the FIRST and THIRD names or numbers are exactly ALIKE
D if only the SECOND and THIRD names or numbers are exactly ALIKE
E if ALL THREE names or numbers are DIFFERENT

41. 6219354	6219354	6219354
42. 2312793	2312793	2312793
43. 1065407	1065407	1065047
44. Francis Ransdell	Frances Ramsdell	Francis Ramsdell
45. Cornelius Detwiler	Cornelius Detwiler	Cornelius Detwiler

In questions 46 through 50, find the correct place for the name in the box.

46. DeMattia, Jessica
A) →
  DeLong, Jesse
B) →
  DeMatteo, Jessie
C) →
  Derby, Jessie S.
D) →
  DeShazo, L. M.
E) →

47. Theriault, Louis
A) →
  Therien, Annette
B) →
  Therien, Elaine
C) →
  Thibeault, Gerald
D) →
  Thiebeault, Pierre
E) →

48. Gaston, M. Hubert
A) →
  Gaston, Dorothy M.
B) →
  Gaston, Henry N.
C) →
  Gaston, Isabel
D) →
  Gaston, M. Melvin
E) →

49. SanMiguel, Carlos
A) →
  SanLuis, Juana
B) →
  Santilli, Laura
C) →
  Stinnett, Nellie
D) →
  Stoddard, Victor
E) →

50. DeLaTour, Hall F.
A) →
  Delargy, Harold
B) →
  DeLathouder, Hilda
C) →
  Lathrop, Hillary
D) →
  LaTour, Hullbert E.
E) →

GO ON TO THE NEXT COLUMN. ⟶

Answers

51. Multiply:
  62
  × 5
A) 300 B) 310
C) 315 D) 360
E) none of these

52. Divide:
  3)153
A) 41 B) 43
C) 51 D) 53
E) none of these

53. Add:
  47
  + 21
A) 58 B) 59
C) 67 D) 68
E) none of these

54. Subtract:
  87
  − 42
A) 34 B) 35
C) 44 D) 45
E) none of these

55. Multiply:
  37
  × 3
A) 91   B) 101
C) 104 D) 114
E) none of these

For each question below, find which one of the suggested answers appears in that question.

56. N 5 4 7 T K 3 Z

57. 8 5 3 V L 2 Z N

58. 7 2 5 N 9 K L V

59. 9 8 L 2 5 Z K V

60. Z 6 5 V 9 3 9 N

Suggested Answers
A = 3, 8, K, N
B = 5, 8, N, V
C = 3, 9, V, Z
D = 5, 9, K, Z
E = none of these

GO ON TO THE NEXT PAGE.

In questions 61 through 65, compare the three names or numbers, and mark the answer—

A if ALL THREE names or numbers are exactly ALIKE
B if only the FIRST and SECOND names or numbers are exactly ALIKE
C if only the FIRST and THIRD names or numbers are exactly ALIKE
D if only the SECOND and THIRD names or numbers are exactly ALIKE
E if ALL THREE names or numbers are DIFFERENT

61.	6452054	6452654	6452054
62.	8501268	8501268	8501286
63.	Ella Burk Newham	Ella Burk Newnham	Elena Burk Newnham
64.	Jno. K. Ravencroft	Jno. H. Ravencroft	Jno. H. Ravencoft
65.	Martin Wills Pullen	Martin Wills Pulen	Martin Wills Pullen

In questions 66 through 70, find the correct place for the name in the box.

66. O'Bannon, M.J.

A) →
   O'Beirne, B. B.
B) →
   Oberlin, E. L.
C) →
   Oberneir, L. P.
D) →
   O'Brian, S. F.
E) →

67. Entsminger, Jacob

A) →
   Ensminger, J.
B) →
   Entsminger, J. A.
C) →
   Entsminger, Jack
D) →
   Entsminger, James
E) →

68. Iacone, Pete R.

A) →
   Iacone, Pedro
B) →
   Iacone, Pedro M.
C) →
   Iacone, Peter F.
D) →
   Iascone, Peter W.
E) →

69. Sheppard, Gladys

A) →
   Shepard, Dwight
B) →
   Shepard, F. H.
C) →
   Shephard, Louise
D) →
   Shepperd, Stella
E) →

70. Thackton, Melvin T.

A) →
   Thackston, Milton G.
B) →
   Thackston, Milton W.
C) →
   Thackston, Theodore
D) →
   Thackston, Thomas G.
E) →

Answers

71. Divide:

$$7 \overline{)357}$$

A) 51 B) 52
C) 53 D) 54
E) none of these

72. Add:

58
+ 27

A) 75 B) 84
C) 85 D) 95
E) none of these

73. Subtract:

86
− 57

A) 18 B) 29
C) 38 D) 39
E) none of these

74. Multiply:

68
× 4

A) 242 B) 264
C) 272 D) 274
E) none of these

75. Divide:

$$9 \overline{)639}$$

A) 71 B) 73
C) 81 D) 83
E) none of these

For each question below, find which one of the suggested answers appears in that question.

76. 6 Z T N 8 7 4 V

77. V 7 8 6 N 5 P L

78. N 7 P V 8 4 2 L

79. 7 8 G 4 3 V L T

80. 4 8 G 2 T N 6 L

Suggested
Answers

A = 2, 7, L, N
B = 2, 8, T, V
C = 6, 8, L, T
D = 6, 7, N, V
E = none of these

GO ON TO THE NEXT COLUMN.

GO ON TO THE NEXT PAGE.

In questions 81 through 85, compare the three names or numbers, and mark the answer—

A if ALL THREE names or numbers are exactly ALIKE
B if only the FIRST and SECOND names or numbers are exactly ALIKE
C if only the FIRST and THIRD names or numbers are exactly ALIKE
D if only the SECOND and THIRD names or numbers are exactly ALIKE
E if ALL THREE names or numbers are DIFFERENT

81.	3457988	3457986	3457986
82.	4695682	4695862	4695682
83.	Stricklund Kanedy	Stricklund Kanedy	Stricklund Kanedy
84.	Joy Harlor Witner	Joy Harloe Witner	Joy Harloe Witner
85.	R. M. O. Uberroth	R. M. O. Uberroth	R. N. O. Uberroth

In questions 86 through 90, find the correct place for the name in the box.

86. **Dunlavey, M. Hilary**
A) →
Dunleavy, Hilary G.
B) →
Dunleavy, Hilary K.
C) →
Dunleavy, Hilary S.
D) →
Dunleavy, Hilery W.
E) →

87. **Yarbrough, Maria**
A) →
Yabroudy, Margy
B) →
Yarboro, Marie
C) →
Yarborough, Marina
D) →
Yarborough, Mary
E) →

88. **Prouty, Martha**
A) →
Proutey, Margaret
B) →
Proutey, Maude
C) →
Prouty, Myra
D) →
Prouty, Naomi
E) →

89. **Pawlowicz, Ruth M.**
A) →
Pawalek, Edward
B) →
Pawelek, Flora G.
C) →
Pawlowski, Joan M.
D) →
Pawtowski, Wanda
E) →

90. **Vanstory, George**
A) →
Vanover, Eva
B) →
VanSwinderen, Floyd
C) →
VanSyckle, Harry
D) →
Vanture, Laurence
E) →

GO ON TO THE NEXT COLUMN.

Answers

91. Add:
28
+ 35

A) 53   B) 62
C) 64   D) 73
E) none of these

92. Subtract:
78
− 69

A) 7   B) 8
C) 18   D) 19
E) none of these

93. Multiply:
86
× 6

A) 492   B) 506
C) 516   D) 526
E) none of these

94. Divide:
8) 648

A) 71   B) 76
C) 81   D) 89
E) none of these

95. Add:
97
+ 34

A) 131   B) 132
C) 140   D) 141
E) none of these

For each question below, find which one of the suggested answers appears in that question.

96. V 5 7 Z N 9 4 T

97. 4 6 P T 2 N K 9

98. 6 4 N 2 P 8 Z K

99. 7 P 5 2 4 N K T

100. K T 8 5 4 N 2 P

Suggested Answers
A = 2, 5, N, Z
B = 4, 5, N, P
C = 2, 9, P, T
D = 4, 9, T, Z
E = none of these

GO ON TO THE NEXT PAGE.

In questions 101 through 105, compare the three names or numbers, and mark the answer—
A if ALL THREE names or numbers are exactly ALIKE
B if only the FIRST and SECOND names or numbers are exactly ALIKE
C if only the FIRST and THIRD names or numbers are exactly ALIKE
D if only the SECOND and THIRD names or numbers are exactly ALIKE
E if ALL THREE names or numbers are DIFFERENT

101. 1592514	1592574	1592574
102. 2010202	2010202	2010220
103. 6177396	6177936	6177396
104. Drusilla S. Ridgeley	Drusilla S. Ridgeley	Drusilla S. Ridgeley
105. Andrei I. Toumantzev	Andrei I. Tourmantzev	Aṅdrei I. Toumantzov

In questions 106 through 110, find the correct place for the name in the box.

106. | Fitzsimmons, Hugh |

A) →
Fitts, Harold
B) →
Fitzgerald, June
C) →
FitzGibbon, Junius
D) →
FitzSimons, Martin
E) →

107. | D'Amato, Vincent |

A) →
Daly, Steven
B) →
D'Amboise, S. Vincent
C) →
Daniel, Vail
D) →
DeAlba, Valentina
E) →

108. | Schaeffer, Roger D. |

A) →
Schaffert, Evelyn M.
B) →
Schaffner, Margaret M.
C) →
Schafhirt, Milton G.
D) →
Shafer, Richard E.
E) →

109. | White-Lewis, Cecil |

A) →
Whitelaw, Cordelia
B) →
White-Leigh, Nancy
C) →
Whitely, Rodney
D) →
Whitlock, Warren
E) →

110. | VanDerHeggen, Don |

A) →
VanDemark, Doris
B) →
Vandenberg, H. E.
C) →
VanDercook, Marie
D) →
vanderLinden, Robert
E) →

GO ON TO THE NEXT COLUMN.

Answers

111. Add:
$$75$$
$$+ 49$$
A) 124 B) 125
C) 134 D) 225
E) none of these

112. Subtract:
$$69$$
$$- 45$$
A) 14 B) 23
C) 24 D) 26
E) none of these

113. Multiply:
$$36$$
$$\times 8$$
A) 246 B) 262
C) 288 D) 368
E) none of these

114. Divide:
$$8\overline{)328}$$
A) 31 B) 41
C) 42 D) 48
E) none of these

115. Multiply:
$$58$$
$$\times 9$$
A) 472 B) 513
C) 521 D) 522
E) none of these

For each question below, find which one of the suggested answers appears in that question.

116. Z 3 N P G 5 4 2

117. 6 N 2 8 G 4 P T

118. 6 N 4 T V G 8 2

119. T 3 P 4 N 8 G 2

120. 6 7 K G N 2 L 5

Suggested
Answers
A = 2, 3, G, N
B = 2, 6, N, T
C = 3, 4, G, K
D = 4, 6, K, T
E = none of these

IF YOU FINISH BEFORE THE TIME IS UP, YOU MAY GO BACK AND CHECK YOUR ANSWERS.

ANSWER KEY FOR DIAGNOSTIC TEST

Alike or Different

1. B	21. A	41. A	61. C	81. D	101. D
2. E	22. E	42. A	62. B	82. C	102. B
3. D	23. E	43. B	63. E	83. A	103. C
4. A	24. D	44. E	64. E	84. D	104. A
5. E	25. C	45. A	65. C	85. B	105. E

Alphabetizing

6. E	26. D	46. C	66. A	86. A	106. D
7. A	27. D	47. A	67. D	87. E	107. B
8. D	28. C	48. D	68. C	88. C	108. A
9. B	29. C	49. B	69. D	89. C	109. C
10. E	30. D	50. C	70. E	90. B	110. D

Arithmetic

11. D	31. E	51. B	71. A	91. E	111. A
12. B	32. A	52. C	72. C	92. E	112. C
13. B	33. A	53. D	73. B	93. C	113. C
14. B	34. C	54. D	74. C	94. C	114. B
15. B	35. C	55. E	75. A	95. A	115. D

Letters and Numbers

16. A	36. E	56. E	76. D	96. D	116. A
17. D	37. A	57. B	77. D	97. C	117. B
18. E	38. C	58. E	78. A	98. E	118. B
19. B	39. C	59. D	79. E	99. B	119. A
20. A	40. D	60. C	80. C	100. B	120. E

ANALYSIS CHART FOR DIAGNOSTIC TEST

Now that you've corrected your exam, use the following chart to carefully analyze your results and spot your strengths and weaknesses. This analysis should help you focus your study and review efforts.

Section	Total Number of Questions	Number Correct	Number Incorrect	Number Unanswered*
Alike or Different	30			
Alphabetizing	30			
Arithmetic	30			
Letters and Numbers	30			
TOTAL	120			

*Since there is a small penalty for incorrect answers on the Clerical Abilities Test, you should not guess blindly. Try to eliminate one or more of the choices before you take your educated guess.

ANSWER EXPLANATIONS FOR DIAGNOSTIC TEST

1. (B) 5261383 | 5261383 | 5261338
2. (E) 8125690 | 8126690 | 8125609
3. (D) W. E. Johnston | W. E. Johnson | W. E. Johnson
4. (A) Vergil L. Muller | Vergil L. Muller | Vergil L. Muller
5. (E) Atherton R. Warde | Asheton R. Warde | Atherton P. Warde
6. (E) Hachettson, Leroy
   Hackett, Gerald
7. (A) *Margenroth, Alvin*
   Margeroth, Albert
8. (D) Bobbitt, Olivia H.
   Bobbit, Olivier E.
   Bobbitt, R. Olivia
9. (B) Mosely, Albert J.
   Mosely Werner
   Mosley, Alvin
10. (E) Youmons, Frank M.
    Youmuns, Frank L.
11. (D) 75
12. (B) 79
13. (B) 287
14. (B) 51
15. (B) 52
16. (A) 6 2 5 K 4 P T G
17. (D) L 4 7 2 T 6 V K
18. (E) 3 5 4 L 9 V T G
19. (B) G 4 K 7 L 3 5 Z
20. (A) 4 K 2 9 N 5 T G
21. (A) 2395890 | 2395890
22. (E) 1926341 | 1926347 | 1926314
23. (E) E. Owens McVey | E. Owen McVey | E. Owen McVay
24. (D) Emily Neal Rouse | Emily Neal Rouse | Emily Neal Rowse
25. (C) H. Merritt Audubon | H. Merriott Audubon | H. Merritt Audubon
26. (D) Watson, Nora J.
    Watters, N. O.
    Wattwood, Paul A.
27. (D) Johnston, Edmund
    Johnston, Edward
    Johnstone, Edmund A.
28. (C) Remschel, Augusta
    Rensch, Adeline
    Renshaw, Austin

29. (C) Schneider, Mertens
    Schnyder, Maurice
    Schnyder, Newman
30. (D) Freedenberg, Erma E.
    Freedenburg, C. Erma
    Freedinberg, Erma F.
31. (E) 21
32. (A) 400
33. (A) 20
34. (C) 141
35. (C) 19
36. (E) 9 G Z 3 L 4 6 N
37. (A) L 5 N K 4 3 9 V
38. (C) 8 2 V P 9 L Z 5
39. (C) V P 9 Z 5 L 8 7
40. (D) 5 T 8 N 2 9 V L
41. (A) 6219354 | 6219354 | 6219354
42. (A) 2312793 | 2312793 | 2312793
43. (B) 1065407 | 1065047 | 1065407
44. (E) Francis Ransdell | Francis Ramsdell | Frances Ramsdell
45. (A) Cornelius Detwiler | Cornelius Detwiler | Cornelius Detwiler
46. (C) DeMatteo, Jessie
    DeMattia, Jessica
    Derby, Jessie S.
47. (A) *Theriault, Louis*
    Therien, Annette
48. (D) Gaston, Isabel
    Gaston, M. Hubert
    Gaston, M. Melvin
49. (B) SanLuis, Juana
    San Miguel, Carlos
    Santilli, Laura
50. (C) DeLathouder, Hilda
    DeLaTour, Hall F.
    Lathrop, Hillary
51. (B) 310
52. (C) 51
53. (D) 68
54. (D) 45
55. (E) 111
56. (E) N 5 4 7 T K 3 Z
57. (B) 8 5 3 V L 2 Z N
58. (E) 7 2 5 N 9 K L V
59. (D) 9 8 L 2 5 Z K V

60. (C) Z65V93PN
61. (C) 6452054 6452654 6452054
62. (B) 8501268 8501268 8501286
63. (E) Ella Burk Newham Ella Burk Newham Ella Burk Newham
64. (E) Jno. K. Ravencroft Jno. H. Ravencroft Jno. H. Ravencroft
65. (C) Martin Wills Pullen Martin Wills Pulen Martin Wills Pullen
66. (A) O'Bannon, M. J.
    O'Beirne, B. B.
67. (D) Entsminger, Jack
    Entsminger, Jacob
    Entsminger, James
68. (C) Iacone, Pedro M.
    Iacone, Pete R.
    Iacone, Peter F.
69. (D) Shephard, Louise
    Sheppard, Gladys
    Shepperd, Stella
70. (E) Thackston, Thomas G.
    Thackton, Melvin T.
71. (A) 51
72. (C) 85
73. (B) 29
74. (C) 272
75. (A) 71
76. (D) 6ZTN874V
77. (D) V786N5PL
78. (A) N7PV842L
79. (E) 78G43VLT
80. (C) 48G2TN6L
81. (D) 3457988 3457986
82. (C) 4695682 4695862
83. (A) Stricklund, Kanedy Stricklund, Kanedy
84. (D) Joy Harlor Witner Joy Harloe Witner
85. (B) R. M. O. Uberroth R. M. O. Uberroth
86. (A) Dunlavey, M. Hilary
    Dunleavy, Hilary G.
87. (E) Yarborough, Mary
    Yarbrough, Maria
88. (C) Proutey, Maude
    Prouty, Martha
    Prouty, Myra
89. (C) Pawelek, Flora G.
    Pawlowicz, Ruth M.
    Pawlowski, Joan M.

90. (B) Vanover, Eva
    Vanstory, George
    VanSwinderen, Floyd
91. (E) 63
92. (E) 9
93. (C) 516
94. (C) 81
95. (A) 131
96. (D) V57ZN94T
97. (C) 46PT2NK9
98. (E) 64N2P8ZK
99. (B) 7P524NKT
100. (B) KT854N2P
101. (D) 1592514 1592574 1592574
102. (B) 2010202 2010202 2010220
103. (C) 6177396 6177936 6177396
104. (A) Drusilla S. Ridgeley Drusilla S. Ridgeley Drusilla S. Ridgeley
105. (E) Andrei I. Toumantzev Andrei I. Tourmantzev Andrei I. Toumantzov
106. (D) FitzGibbon, Junius
    Fitzsimmons, Hugh
    FitzSimons, Martin
107. (B) Daly, Steven
    D'Amato, Vincent
    D'Amboise, S. Vincent
108. (A) Schaeffer, Roger D.
    Schaffert, Evelyn M.
109. (C) White-Leigh, Nancy
    White-Lewis, Cecil
    Whitely, Podney
110. (D) VanDercook, Marie
    VanDerHeggen, Don
    vanderLinden, Robert
111. (A) 124
112. (C) 24
113. (C) 288
114. (B) 41
115. (D) 522
116. (A) Z3NPG542
117. (B) 6N28G4PT
118. (B) 6N4TVG82
119. (A) T3P4N8G2
120. (E) 67KGN2L5

CHAPTER 5

Understanding the Sections
Key Strategies
Practice, Practice, Practice

ALIKE OR DIFFERENT

This question type tests your observation skills. You are given three names or three sets of numbers and are asked to determine if

ALL THREE are alike (answer A)
only the FIRST and SECOND are alike (answer B)
only the FIRST and THIRD are alike (answer C)
only the SECOND and THIRD are alike (answer D)
NONE of them are alike (answer E)

For example:

Harmon A. Killebrew   Harmon A. Killebrew   Harmonn A. Killebrew

Notice that the third name has a double "n", making it different from the first two names. Therefore since only the FIRST and SECOND are alike, the answer is B.

Or another example:

3546798   3547698   3546798

Notice here that the first and third are alike, but the second set of numbers is different—the 6 and 7 are reversed. Therefore the answer is C.

HELPFUL TECHNIQUES AND STRATEGIES

1. Before you take your actual test, be sure to understand and *memorize* what each answer choice indicates. You should not have to keep looking back and forth from the problems to the directions for every question.

2. Practice the many questions in this book, finding a particular technique that works best for you. Here are some suggestions:

   For the Numbers

   a. Since there are seven numbers in each set, you may read the set as if it's a telephone number. If you are used to working with phone numbers, saying to yourself ("subvocalizing") a telephone "exchange" (the first three numbers) followed by four digits may be a helpful method.
   For example:

   2698621   2698612   2698612

   Thus, you might subvocalize "269-8621" for the first set. Then, since the beginning of the next set, "269-," sounds the same, you continue with the last four digits—"8612." These sound different from the four digits in the first set. Therefore, you know sets 1 and 2 are different, because of the last four digits. Now try the third set: "269-" (the "exchange" sounds the same) "8612." Which last four digits does the third set duplicate? Quickly checking, you find the last four digits of set 2 are also "8612." The answer is (D).

   b. This telephone technique has variations. You may wish to compare the first three digits (the "exchange") in each set separately; then compare the last four digits in each set—a divide and conquer strategy.

   c. Or you may wish to try "Odd Man Out"—checking the first two sets to determine if they're similar. If they are, you then go to the third to see whether you have an (A) answer (all ALIKE) or a (B) answer (only the first two ALIKE). If the first two are different, then proceed to the third to see if the third matches the first set (answer C), or the second set (answer D), or neither set (answer E).

   d. Whichever technique you develop, watch out for "reversals."
   For example:

   4695862   4695682   4695862

Notice that sets 1 and 3 are alike, but that 8 and 6 are reversed in set 2. Such reversals are often easily missed.

For the Names

a. Saying the names *carefully* in your mind may be helpful, but sometimes names spelled differently can sound alike.

b. You may wish to "divide and conquer": first comparing first names, then initials, then last names.

c. Watch out for the following:
Double letters. Often a letter will be single in one name but doubled in another.

Bob Uberroth   Bob Uberroth   Bob Uberoth

The third name has a single "r."
Silent letters

Emiley Smyth   Emiley Smyth   Emily Smith

Notice how all three first names will sound the same despite the last name not having the second "e."
Reversals. Especially look out for reversals of vowels, easy to miss. For example:

Annette Tharien   Annette Tharien   Annette Tharein

Notice the "i" and "e" reversed in the third name.

Different common spellings. Be aware of names (like Francis/Frances) that have more than one correct spelling. For example:

Francis Ramsdell   Frances Ramsdell   Frances Ramsdell

Only the second and the third names are alike, because "Francis" is spelled with an "i" in the first name.

Reverse letters. Some letters are the mirror image of other letters, and these can sometimes be confusing, especially if you are working at top speed. For example, "p" is the mirror image of "q." The letter "b" is the reverse of the letter "d." Some people have special difficulties with these kinds of letters. Try these:

Larry P. Dobkin   Larry P. Dobkin   Larry P. Dodkin

Notice the "d" in the last name; the others contain a "b."

Look-alike letters. And, finally, keep on your toes when you see certain letters that can be easily misread as other letters. For instance, an "m" may often be misread as an "n," and vice versa. An "s" may be misread as a "z," and a "q" as a "g." As you practice, you'll begin to spot these, and you should try to remember them. For example:

Ernest Ramsdell   Ernest Ransdell   Ernest Ramsdell

Notice that "Ramsdell" is spelled with an "n," rather than an "m," in the second case. Or:

Alfredo C. Lopes   Alfredo C. Lopez   Alfredo C. Lopez

Notice the "s" in the first name; the others end in "z."

PRACTICE SET 1

Compare the three names or numbers, and mark the answer—
    A if ALL THREE names or numbers are exactly ALIKE
    B if only the FIRST and SECOND names or numbers are exactly ALIKE
    C if only the FIRST and THIRD names or numbers are exactly ALIKE
    D if only the SECOND and THIRD names or numbers are exactly ALIKE
    E if ALL THREE names or numbers are DIFFERENT

1. 9854688	9854688	9854668	_____
2. 1003873	1003873	1003873	_____
3. 4837261	4837621	4837621	_____
4. Oswald Dunleavey	Oswald Dunleavey	Oswals Dunleavy	_____
5. Joseph Willierdite	Joseph Willierdite	Joseph Willierdite	_____
6. 6978459	6974859	6974589	_____
7. 3823145	3832145	3823145	_____
8. Stacey Baum Pleskoff	Stacy Baum Plesckoff	Stacey Baum Pleskof	_____
9. C. J. Farleighbacker	C. J. Farleighbacker	C. J. Farleighbacher	_____
10. Arnold M. Goulian	Arnold M. Goulain	Arnold M. Goulian	_____
11. 8093472	8093472	8093472	_____
12. 4768523	4765823	4765833	_____
13. 9487297	9482797	9482797	_____
14. Dona Leszyzski	Dona Leszyczski	Donna Leszyzski	_____
15. Joy Mondragon	Joy Mondragon	Joy Mondr'agan	_____
16. 7465938	7465398	7465938	_____
17. 1489235	1489325	1489325	_____
18. William E. Jerzsinski	William E. Jerszinski	William E. Jerzsinski	_____
19. Ernest VanSwickerton	Ernest VanSwikirten	Ernest VanSwickerten	_____
20. Fredda Wilmarettez	Fredda Wilmarettez	Freda Wilmarettez	_____
21. 5839287	5832987	5832987	_____
22. 9372636	9732368	9732368	_____
23. Lazaro F. Cosgrove	Lasaro F. Cosgrove	Lazaro F. Casgrove	_____
24. Lucila Fontanez	Lucila Fonanes	Lunita Fontanez	_____

25. Armand Cisalissi	Armand Cisilissi	Armand Cisalissi	_____
26. 4873983	4873983	4783983	_____
27. 9578246	9578246	9578246	_____
28. 5797358	5797358	5797538	_____
29. Robin I. Gastongauy	Robin I. Gastonguay	Robin I. Gastanquay	_____
30. Alfred Geisthardt	Alfred Geisthartd	Alfred Geisthardt	_____

ANSWER EXPLANATIONS FOR PRACTICE SET 1

1. (B) 9854688	9854688	9854668	
2. (A) 1003873	1003873	1003873	
3. (D) 4837261	4837621	4837621	
4. (B) Oswald Dunleavey	Oswald Dunleavey	Oswals Dunleavy	
5. (A) Joseph Willierdite	Joseph Willierdite	Joseph Willierdite	
6. (E) 6978459	6974859	6974589	
7. (C) 3823145	3832145	3823145	
8. (E) Stacey Baum Pleskoff	Stacy Baum Plesckoff	Stacey Baum Pleskof	
9. (B) C. J. Farleighbacker	C. J. Farleighbacker	C. J. Farleighbacher	
10. (C) Arnold M. Goulian	Arnold M. Goulain	Arnold M. Goulian	
11. (A) 8093472	8093472	8093472	
12. (E) 4768523	4765823	4765833	
13. (D) 9487297	9482797	9482797	
14. (E) Dona Leszyzski	Dona Leszyczski	Donna Leszyzski	
15. (B) Joy Mondragon	Joy Mondragon	Joy Mondragan	
16. (C) 7465938	7465398	7465938	
17. (D) 1489235	1489325	1489325	
18. (C) William E. Jerzsinski	William E. Jerszinski	William E. Jerzsinski	
19. (E) Ernest VanSwickerton	Ernest VanSwikirten	Ernest VanSwickerten	
20. (B) Fredda Wilmarettez	Fredda Wilmarettez	Freda Wilmarettez	
21. (D) 5839287	5832987	5832987	
22. (D) 9372638	9732368	9732368	
23. (E) Lazaro F. Cosgrove	Lasaro F. Cosgrove	Lazaro F. Casgrove	
24. (E) Lucila Fontanez	Lucila Fonanes	Lunita Fontanez	
25. (C) Armand Cisalissi	Armand Cisilissi	Armand Cisalissi	
26. (B) 4873983	4873983	4783983	
27. (A) 9578246	9578246	9578246	
28. (B) 5797358	5797358	5797538	
29. (E) Robin I. Gastongauy	Robin I. Gastonguay	Robin I. Gastanguay	
30. (C) Alfred Geisthardt	Alfred Geisthartd	Alfred Geisthardt	

PRACTICE SET 2

Compare the three names or numbers, and mark the answer—
    A if ALL THREE names or numbers are exactly ALIKE
    B if only the FIRST and SECOND names or numbers are exactly ALIKE
    C if only the FIRST and THIRD names or numbers are exactly ALIKE
    D if only the SECOND and THIRD names or numbers are exactly ALIKE
    E if ALL THREE names or numbers are DIFFERENT

| 1. 9358745 | 9358745 | 9357845 | _____ |
| 2. 8574690 | 8547690 | 8547690 | _____ |

3. Raymond H. Didsbury	Raymond H. Diddsbury	Raymond H. Didsburry	_____
4. Stephen M. Tranz	Stephen M. Tranz	Stephen M. Tramz	_____
5. Kevin C. Kretchmer	Kevin C. Kretchmer	Kevin C. Kretchmer	_____
6. 7534689	7354689	7534689	_____
7. 4736258	4736258	4736258	_____
8. 9273415	9274315	9274315	_____
9. Douglas S. Borghi	Douglass S. Borghi	Douglass S. Borghi	_____
10. Vartan Bergquist	Vartan Berquist	Vartan Berquist	_____
11. 7493876	4793876	4739876	_____
12. 9073484	9073484	9074384	_____
13. Shehani D. Housel	Shahani D. Housel	Shehani D. Housel	_____
14. Mansoor Hornblithe	Mansoor Hornblithe	Mansoor Hornblithe	_____
15. George Komashko	George Komashko	George Kamashko	_____
16. 7287394	7287934	7827934	_____
17. 4736297	4736297	4736297	_____
18. 5398247	5389247	5389247	_____
19. Steven P. Fuschia	Stephen P. Fuschia	Stephen P. Fuschia	_____
20. Farrah Berstmilier	Farrah Berstmilier	Farrah Berstmileir	_____
21. 3827394	3827394	3827934	_____
22. 4839271	4289271	4839271	_____
23. Powers S. Boothe	Powers S. Booth	Power S. Boothe	_____
24. Evyln Schaeffert	Evyln Shaeffert	Evyln Schaeffert	_____
25. Armantine Rogioso	Armatine Rogioso	Armatine Rogioso	_____
26. 9864837	9864387	9864837	_____
27. 8725137	8725137	8725137	_____
28. 6468931	6469831	6468931	_____
29. Rogers Hornsbrath	Rogers Hornsbrath	Rogers Hornsbrathe	_____
30. Mikael Maggliocco	Mikeal Maggliocco	Mikeal Magglioco	_____

ANSWER EXPLANATIONS FOR PRACTICE SET 2

1. (B) 9358745	9358745	9357845
2. (D) 8574690	8547690	8547690
3. (E) Raymond H. Didsbury	Raymond H. Diddsbury	Raymond H. Didsburry
4. (B) Stephen M. Tranz	Stephen M. Tranz	Stephen M. Tramz
5. (A) Kevin C. Kretchmer	Kevin C. Kretchmer	Kevin C. Kretchmer
6. (C) 7534689	7354689	7534689
7. (A) 4736258	4736258	4736258
8. (D) 9273415	9274315	9274315
9. (D) Douglas S. Borghi	Douglass S. Borghi	Douglass S. Borghi
10. (D) Vartan Bergquist	Vartan Berquist	Vartan Berquist
11. (E) 7493876	4793876	4739876
12. (B) 9073484	9073484	9074384
13. (C) Shehani D. Housel	Shahani D. Housel	Shehani D. Housel
14. (A) Mansoor Hornblithe	Mansoor Hornblithe	Mansoor Hornblithe
15. (B) George Komashko	George Komashko	George Kamashko
16. (E) 7287394	7287934	7827934
17. (A) 4736297	4736297	4736297
18. (D) 5398247	5389247	5389247
19. (D) Steven P. Fuschia	Stephen P. Fuschia	Stephen P. Fuschia
20. (B) Farrah Berstmilier	Farrah Berstmilier	Farrah Berstmileir
21. (B) 3827394	3827394	3827934
22. (C) 4839271	4289271	4839271
23. (E) Powers S. Boothe	Powers S. Booth	Power S. Boothe
24. (C) Evyln Schaeffert	Evyln Shaeffert	Evyln Schaeffert
25. (D) Armantine Rogioso	Armatine Rogioso	Armatine Rogioso
26. (C) 9864837	9864387	9864837
27. (A) 8725137	8725137	8725137
28. (C) 6468931	6469831	6468931
29. (B) Rogers Hornsbrath	Rogers Hornsbrath	Rogers Hornsbrathe
30. (E) Mikael Maggliocco	Mikeal Maggliocco	Mikael Magglioco

PRACTICE SET 3

Compare the three names or numbers, and mark the answer—
  A if ALL THREE names or numbers are exactly ALIKE
  B if only the FIRST and SECOND names or numbers are exactly ALIKE
  C if only the FIRST and THIRD names or numbers are exactly ALIKE
  D if only the SECOND and THIRD names or numbers are exactly ALIKE
  E if ALL THREE names or numbers are DIFFERENT

1. 5839478	5839478	5839478	_____
2. 9382739	9382789	9382789	_____
3. Alxis Kordumdrong	Alxis Kordumdrong	Alxis Kordomdrung	_____
4. Blossom Koneczka	Blossom Koneszka	Blossom Konezska	_____
5. Bethina Ploesser	Bethina Pleosser	Bettina Ploesser	_____
6. 3746893	3746983	3746983	_____
7. 4278345	4278345	4278345	_____
8. 2875291	2785291	2785291	_____

9. Krokor Pechakjian	Krokor Pechakjian	Krokor Pecharjian	_____
10. Lynette Preistley	Lynnette Preistley	Lynnette Priestley	_____
11. 3826387	3862837	3826837	_____
12. 4739826	4739836	4739826	_____
13. 3982635	3983625	3982635	_____
14. Rafael Morrison	Rafael Morrison	Rafael Morrisson	_____
15. Randise Rappoport	Randice Rappoport	Randice Rapopport	_____
16. 3675214	3675214	3675214	_____
17. 8672391	8673291	8672391	_____
18. Quenten C. Fischbeim	Quentin C. Fischbeim	Quentin C. Fischbiem	_____
19. Jenifer Robesgiase	Jenifer Robesgiase	Jennifer Robesgiase	_____
20. Florel Petersen	Florel Peterson	Florel Peterson	_____
21. 4872364	4873264	4873264	_____
22. 7483092	7480392	7480932	_____
23. 7348234	7348234	7348234	_____
24. G. Raymund Pafalcko	G. Ramund Pafalcko	G. Raymund Pafalcko	_____
25. M. L. K. Carrutthers	M. L. K. Carruthers	M. L. K. Carruthers	_____
26. 3678362	3687362	3687362	_____
27. 9376982	9736982	9736982	_____
28. 3892761	3892761	3892761	_____
29. Rogeiio Gonzalez	Rogeiio Gonzales	Rogeiio Gonzales	_____
30. Ferdinan Bulliekeir	Ferdinan Bulleikeir	Ferdinan Bulliekier	_____

ANSWER EXPLANATIONS FOR PRACTICE SET 3

1. (A) 5839478 5839478 5839478
2. (D) 9382739 9382789 9382789
3. (B) Alxis Kordumdrong Alxis Kordumdrong Alxis Kordomdrung
4. (E) Blossom Koneczka Blossom Koneszka Blossom Konezska
5. (E) Bethina Ploesser Bethina Pleosser Bettina Ploesser
6. (D) 3746893 3746983 3746983
7. (A) 4278345 4278345 4278345
8. (D) 2875291 2785291 2785291
9. (B) Krokor Pechakjian Krokor Pechakjian Krokor Pecharjian

10. (E) Lynette Preistley	Lynnette Preistley	Lynnette Priestley
11. (E) 3826387	3862837	3826837
12. (C) 4739826	4739836	4739826
13. (C) 3982635	3983625	3982635
14. (B) Rafael Morrison	Rafael Morrison	Rafael Morrisson
15. (E) Randise Rappoport	Randice Rappoport	Randice Rapopport
16. (A) 3675214	3675214	3675214
17. (C) 8672391	8673291	8672391
18. (E) Quenten C. Fischbeim	Quentin C. Fischbeim	Quentin C. Fischbiem
19. (B) Jenifer Robesgiase	Jenifer Robesgiase	Jennifer Robesgiase
20. (D) Florel Petersen	Florel Peterson	Florel Peterson
21. (D) 4872364	4873264	4873264
22. (E) 7483092	7480392	7480932
23. (A) 7348234	7348234	7348234
24. (C) G. Raymund Pafalcko	G. Ramund Pafalcko	G. Raymund Pafalcko
25. (D) M. L. K. Carrutthers	M. L. K. Carruthers	M. L. K. Carruthers
26. (D) 3678362	3687362	3687362
27. (D) 9376982	9736982	9736982
28. (A) 3892761	3892761	3892761
29. (D) Rogeiio Gonzalez	Rogeiio Gonzales	Rogeiio Gonzales
30. (E) Ferdinan Bulliekeir	Ferdinan Bulleikeir	Ferdinan Bulliekier

PRACTICE SET 4

Compare the three names or numbers, and mark the answer—
   A if ALL THREE names or numbers are exactly ALIKE
   B if only the FIRST and SECOND names or numbers are exactly ALIKE
   C if only the FIRST and THIRD names or numbers are exactly ALIKE
   D if only the SECOND and THIRD names or numbers are exactly ALIKE
   E if ALL THREE names or numbers are DIFFERENT

1. 5732837	5372837	5372837	_____
2. 4802736	4802736	4802376	_____
3. Michel St. Johns	Michel St. John	Mishel St. Johns	_____
4. Terrence Vanespreaux	Terrence Vanesprauex	Terrence Vanespreaux	_____
5. U. Yoshima Chaingo	U. Yoshina Chaingo	U. Yoshina Chiango	_____
6. 4869482	4869482	4869482	_____
7. 8394276	8392476	8392746	_____
8. 4829487	4829487	4892487	_____
9. Dana Cammer Lynd	Dana Cammer Lynde	Dana Cammer Lynde	_____
10. Epimena Sainzt	Epimena Saintz	Epimena Sainzt	_____
11. Louis Sagakuchi	Louis Sagsgughi	Louis Sagakuchi	_____
12. Festron Armandoff	Festron Armadoff	Festron Armadoff	_____
13. Hermine Pakhanians	Hermine Pakanians	Hermine Pakhanian	_____

14.	3846398	3846389	3846398	_____
15.	7493183	7493183	7493183	_____
16.	4839273	4832973	4839273	_____
17.	4698264	4698264	4698624	_____
18.	Nicholas Palladino	Nickolas Palladino	Nicholas Palladino	_____
19.	Jaime Prestridge	Jaime Pestridge	Jaime Pestredge	_____
20.	Alonzo Forsythe	Alonzo Forsythe	Alonzo Forthythe	_____
21.	4832472	4832472	4832472	_____
22.	3659624	2695624	2695624	_____
23.	3825983	8325938	9325983	_____
24.	Marietta Rogolizzo	Marieta Rogolizzo	Marieta Rogolizzo	_____
25.	Jacob Rietdokog	Jacob Rietdokog	Jakob Rietdokog	_____
26.	5784963	5784693	5784963	_____
27.	3124785	3124785	3124875	_____
28.	Edwardo Pimpernott	Edwardo Pimpernott	Eduardo Pimpernott	_____
29.	Frencesca Moisely	Francesca Moisely	Francesca Moisely	_____
30.	Olivier R. Dudlees	Oliver R. Dudlees	Oliver R. Dudless	_____

ANSWER EXPLANATIONS FOR PRACTICE SET 4

1. (D)	5732837	5372837	5372837
2. (B)	4802736	4802736	4802376
3. (E)	Michel St. Johns	Michel St. John	Mishel St. Johns
4. (C)	Terrence Vanespreaux	Terrence Vanesprauex	Terrence Vanespreaux
5. (E)	U. Yoshima Chaingo	U. Yoshina Chaingo	U. Yoshina Chiango
6. (A)	4869482	4869482	4869482
7. (E)	8394276	8392476	8392746
8. (B)	4829487	4829487	4892487
9. (D)	Dana Cammer Lynd	Dana Cammer Lynde	Dana Cammer Lynde
10. (C)	Epimena Sainzt	Epimena Saintz	Epimena Sainzt
11. (C)	Louis Sagakuchi	Louis Sagsgughi	Louis Sagakuchi
12. (D)	Festron Armandoff	Festron Armadoff	Festron Armadoff
13. (E)	Hermine Pakhanians	Hermine Pakanians	Hermine Pakhanian
14. (C)	3846398	3846389	3846398
15. (A)	7493183	7493183	7493183
16. (C)	4839273	4832973	4839273
17. (B)	4698264	4698264	4698624
18. (C)	Nicholas Palladino	Nickolas Palladino	Nicholas Palladino
19. (E)	Jaime Prestridge	Jaime Pestridge	Jaime Pestredge
20. (B)	Alonzo Forsythe	Alonzo Forsythe	Alonzo Forthythe

21. (A) 4832472	4832472	4832472
22. (D) 3659624	2695624	2695624
23. (E) 3825983	8325938	9325983
24. (D) Marietta Rogolizzo	Marieta Rogolizzo	Marieta Rogolizzo
25. (B) Jacob Rietdokog	Jacob Rietdokog	Jakob Rietdokog
26. (C) 5784963	5784693	5784963
27. (B) 3124785	3124785	3124875
28. (B) Edwardo Pimpernott	Edwardo Pimpernott	Eduardo Pimpernott
29. (D) Frencesca Moisely	Francesca Moisely	Francesca Moisely
30. (E) Olivier R. Dudlees	Oliver R. Dudlees	Oliver R. Dudless

PRACTICE SET 5

Compare the three names or numbers, and mark the answer—
  A if ALL THREE names or numbers are exactly ALIKE
  B if only the FIRST and SECOND names or numbers are exactly ALIKE
  C if only the FIRST and THIRD names or numbers are exactly ALIKE
  D if only the SECOND and THIRD names or numbers are exactly ALIKE
  E if ALL THREE names or numbers are DIFFERENT

1. 9374653	9374653	9374653	_____
2. 4763981	4769381	4769831	_____
3. 5847291	5847291	5842791	_____
4. Atherton Jacquesman	Atherton Jaquesman	Atherton Jacqueman	_____
5. Willis Undertopper	Willis Undertopper	Willes Undertopper	_____
6. 6493759	6439759	6439759	_____
7. 3928404	3298404	3928404	_____
8. Langer F. Feltmann	Langer F. Feltman	Langar F. Feltman	_____
9. Oskar Fischman	Oskar Fischman	Oskar Ficshman	_____
10. Norris Feuchtwangar	Norris Feuchtwanger	Norris Fuechtwanger	_____
11. 4736948	4376948	4376948	_____
12. 4257389	4257389	4257389	_____
13. 8294735	2894735	8294735	_____
14. Arthur Fidelibus	Arthur Fidelibus	Arther Fidelibus	_____
15. Gerald M. Dudkins	Gerald M. Dudkins	Gerard M. Dudkins	_____
16. 4879326	4873926	4879326	_____
17. 6948732	6948732	6948732	_____
18. Haruko Kamakura	Hurako Kamakura	Hurako Kamakura	_____

19. Simmons Werthingten	Simmons Werthington	Simmins Werthington	_____
20. DeRonda Nocerino	DeRonda Nocerino	DaRonda Nocerino	_____
21. Marc Nochiela	Marc Nocheila	Marc Nochiela	_____
22. Cleveland Noburski	Cleveland Nobruski	Cleveland Nobruski	_____
23. 2839747	2839747	2839747	_____
24. 9372875	9732875	9732875	_____
25. 3729854	3729584	3798254	_____
26. 4839734	4839734	4837934	_____
27. 3526791	3526971	3526891	_____
28. 3749825	3749825	2949825	_____
29. Mallery J. Pearre	Mallory J. Peare	Mallory J. Pearre	_____
30. Stacey Rudashmann	Stacy Rudashmann	Stacey Rudashmann	_____

ANSWER EXPLANATIONS FOR PRACTICE SET 5

1. (A) 9374653	9374653	9374653
2. (E) 4763981	4769381	4769831
3. (B) 5847291	5847291	5842791
4. (E) Atherton Jacquesman	Atherton Jaquesman	Atherton Jacqueman
5. (B) Willis Undertopper	Willis Undertopper	Willes Undertopper
6. (D) 6493759	6439759	6439759
7. (C) 3928404	3298404	3928404
8. (E) Langer F. Feltmann	Langer F. Feltman	Langar F. Feltman
9. (B) Oskar Fischman	Oskar Fischman	Oskar Ficshman
10. (E) Norris Feuchtwangar	Norris Feuchtwanger	Norris Fuechtwanger
11. (D) 4736948	4376948	4376948
12. (A) 4257389	4257389	4257389
13. (C) 8294735	2894735	8294735
14. (B) Arthur Fidelibus	Arthur Fidelibus	Arther Fidelibus
15. (B) Gerald M. Dudkins	Gerald M. Dudkins	Gerard M. Dudkins
16. (C) 4879326	4873926	4879326
17. (A) 6948732	6948732	6948732
18. (D) Haruko Kamakura	Hurako Kamakura	Hurako Kamakura
19. (E) Simmons Werthingten	Simmons Werthington	Simmins Werthington
20. (B) DeRonda Nocerino	DeRonda Nocerino	DaRonda Nocerino
21. (C) Marc Nochiela	Marc Nocheila	Marc Nochiela
22. (D) Cleveland Noburski	Cleveland Nobruski	Cleveland Nobruski
23. (A) 2839747	2839747	2839747
24. (D) 9372875	9732875	9732875
25. (E) 3729854	3729584	3798254
26. (B) 4839734	4839734	4837934
27. (E) 3526791	3526971	3526891
28. (B) 3749825	3749825	2949825
29. (E) Mallery J. Pearre	Mallory J. Peare	Mallory J. Pearre
30. (C) Stacey Rudashmann	Stacy Rudashmann	Stacey Rudashmann

PRACTICE SET 6

Compare the three names or numbers, and mark the answer—
A if ALL THREE names or numbers are exactly ALIKE
B if only the FIRST and SECOND names or numbers are exactly ALIKE
C if only the FIRST and THIRD names or numbers are exactly ALIKE
D if only the SECOND and THIRD names or numbers are exactly ALIKE
E if ALL THREE names or numbers are DIFFERENT

1. Abebaye Tearleney	Abebaya Tearleney	Abebaya Tearleney	_____
2. Mimi P. Teisan	Mimi P. Tiesman	Mimi P. Tiesman	_____
3. Forest Peuterman	Forrest Peuterman	Forrest Peuterman	_____
4. 6483947	6483947	6438947	_____
5. 3926598	3925698	3925968	_____
6. 4378947	4378947	4378947	_____
7. 4628479	4624879	4628479	_____
8. Claude Versailes	Claude Versailles	Claude Versailles	_____
9. Phillip Waddillove	Phillip Waddillove	Philip Waddillove	_____
10. Pinkerten Chesneiy	Pinkerton Chesneiy	Pinkerton Chesniey	_____
11. 4893263	4893262	4893623	_____
12. 4832764	4832764	4832746	_____
13. 6382749	6832749	6832749	_____
14. Hugh L. Wyannicki	Huge L. Wyannicki	Hugh L. Wyannicki	_____
15. Otto C. Wichert	Otto C. Wichert	Otto C. Wichirt	_____
16. Maurice E. Tyson	Maurice E. Tyson	Maurice E. Tyson	_____
17. Tzivskos Tittlemen	Tzivzkos Tittlemen	Tzvizkos Tittlemen	_____
18. Peter E. Villasenor	Peter E. Villiasenor	Peter E. Villiasenor	_____
19. 7362456	7364256	7342456	_____
20. 3829756	3829576	3829756	_____
21. 4839876	4839876	4839876	_____
22. 7328631	7328361	7328631	_____
23. 3907356	3907356	3907365	_____
24. Illay Vischmid	Illay Vischmed	Illay Vischmed	_____

25. Benjamin Weinenger	Benjamen Weinenger	Benjamin Weininger	_____
26. 4983675	4983675	4983675	_____
27. 8109354	8109534	8109354	_____
28. Marion Wyanicki	Marian Wyanicki	Marian Wyanicki	_____
29. Whitney Williston	Whitney Willisten	Whitney Wiliston	_____
30. Garry Wohmgemuth	Garry Wohmgemuth	Garry Wohmgemuth	_____

ANSWER EXPLANATIONS FOR PRACTICE SET 6

1. (D) Abebaye Tearleney	Abebaya Tearleney	Abebaya Tearleney
2. (D) Mimi P. Teisan	Mimi P. Tiesman	Mimi P. Tiesman
3. (D) Forest Peuterman	Forrest Peuterman	Forrest Peuterman
4. (B) 6483947	6483947	6438947
5. (E) 3926598	3925698	3925968
6. (A) 4378947	4378947	4378947
7. (C) 4628479	4624879	4628479
8. (D) Claude Versailes	Claude Versailles	Claude Versailles
9. (B) Phillip Waddillove	Phillip Waddillove	Philip Waddillove
10. (E) Pinkerten Chesneiy	Pinkerton Chesneiy	Pinkerton Chesniey
11. (E) 4893263	4893262	4893623
12. (B) 4832764	4832764	4832746
13. (D) 6382749	6832749	6832749
14. (C) Hugh L. Wyannicki	Huge L. Wyannicki	Hugh L. Wyannicki
15. (B) Otto C. Wichert	Otto C. Wichert	Otto C. Wichirt
16. (A) Maurice E. Tyson	Maurice E. Tyson	Maurice E. Tyson
17. (E) Tzivskos Tittlemen	Tzivzkos Tittlemen	Tzvizkos Tittlemen
18. (D) Peter E. Villasenor	Peter E. Villiasenor	Peter E. Villiasenor
19. (E) 7362456	7364256	7342456
20. (C) 3829756	3829576	3829756
21. (A) 4839876	4839876	4839876
22. (C) 7328631	7328361	7328631
23. (B) 3907356	3907356	3907365
24. (D) Illay Vischmid	Illay Vischmed	Illay Vischmed
25. (E) Benjamin Weinenger	Benjamen Weinenger	Benjamin Weininger
26. (A) 4983675	4983675	4983675
27. (C) 8109354	8109534	8109354
28. (D) Marion Wyanicki	Marian Wyanicki	Marian Wyanicki
29. (E) Whitney Williston	Whitney Willisten	Whitney Wiliston
30. (A) Garry Wohmgemuth	Garry Wohmgemuth	Garry Wohmgemuth

REVIEWING THE KEY STRATEGIES

Remember to:

1. Understand and memorize the directions before your test.

2. Find the technique that works best for you, and practice it.

3. Watch out for those "troublesome" numbers and letters.

ALPHABETIZING

The rules for placing names in proper alphabetical order are simple and straightforward. They require you to follow several steps:

Different Last Names

1. First, alphabetize by the first letter of the last name:

   Brown, James
   Harris, Arthur
   Thomas, Peter

2. If two or more last names begin with the same letter, then look to the second letter in the last name:

   Brown, James
   Sanders, Fred
   Smith, Gloria

   Notice that both "S" names come after *Brown* and that *Sanders* comes before *Smith* because of their second letters ("a" and "m").

3. If the first *and* second letters of the last name are alike, then look to the third letter:

   Peterson, Roberta
   Pezzari, Thomas
   Ulmer, Janice

4. If the first three letters of the last name are similar, look to the fourth letter, and so on:

   Bronson, Eloise
   Brown, Ferdinand
   Browvort, Michael

   Notice in the last example that *Bron* comes before *Brow,* but *Brown* comes before *Browv*.

5. If the letters are identical in two names, but one name is longer, the shorter name, which "runs out of letters," goes first. For example,

   Prout, Marie
   Proute, Harry

   Notice that *Prout* comes before *Proute*.

6. Don't let lowercase letters, apostrophes, or hyphens in last names confuse you. Continue to follow rules 1 to 5. For example:

   Daly, Ernest
   D'Ambrose, Evelyn

   Above, *Dal* comes before *DAm*. Or:

   VanDercook, Stephen
   vanLitton, Morris
   Vans-Harrold, Martha

   Notice the order: VanD, vanL, Vans.

Identical Last Names

What happens if the last names are exactly the same? Then look at the first name or first initial and follow these rules:

7. Alphabetize, using the first letter of the first name:

   Smith, Albert
   Smith, George
   Smith, Harold

8. If the first name begins with the same letter, look to the second letter:

   Jones, Richard
   Jones, Roberta
   Jones, Ruben

9. If a first name is merely an initial, that initial will precede any first name beginning with that same letter. For example:

   White, N.
   White, Norbert

10. Even if there is a middle name after the first initial, or two initials, a first initial will always precede a full first name:

    Chan, G. Ling
    Chan, George

    Another example:

    Forrest, R. Peter
    Forrest, Rae

11. Of course, if the first initial comes after the first letter of the full first name, it must follow the usual alphabetical rules. For example:

    Johnson, Albert
    Johnson, C. David
    Johnson, Charles
    Johnson, F. K.
    Johnson, Louise

12. And, of course, given only first initials, follow the usual rules:

    Abbott, C.
    Abbott, C. A.
    Abbott, E.
    Abbott, F.
    Abbott, H.

    Note that Abbott, C. A. comes after Abbott, C.

13. Finally, if the first names are exactly the same, or the first initials are the same, then look to the middle initial or the middle name, and follow the standard rules. For example:

    Brown, John
    Brown, John A.
    Brown, John Albert
    Brown, John H.
    Brown, John Herbert
    Brown, John Thomas
    Brown, John Z.

    Notice that here the alphabetizing begins with the middle name or initial: *Brown, John* is first because there is no middle name or initial; then *A.*, then *Albert*, then *H.*, then *Herbert,* then *Thomas*, then *Z.*

PRACTICE SET 1

Find the correct place for the name in the box, and mark the letter of that space as your answer.

1. Waverley, S. Q.
- A) →
  - Watkins, Roger
- B) →
  - Watson, Gabriele
- C) → ____
  - Watsonian, Franklin
- D) →
  - Wetson, McDougle
- E) →

2. Burmingham, Emma A.
- A) →
  - Birmingham, Hal
- B) →
  - Birminghoff, Brinker
- C) → ____
  - Birminghuller, Daisy
- D) →
  - Burningham, Morris
- E) →

3. Burmun, Lardeese
- A) →
  - Berman, Robert
- B) →
  - Birmen, Francesca A.
- C) → ____
  - Burman, Kevin
- D) →
  - Burmen, Andre
- E) →

4. McCafferty, Gabriele
- A) →
  - Caffey, Michael
- B) →
  - Caffy, Benjamin
- C) → ____
  - Caffry, Alberta
- D) →
  - Caffry, Bertha
- E) →

5. Eliot, Joy
- A) →
  - Eliot, Robert
- B) →
  - Elliot, Jane P.
- C) → ____
  - Elliuse, Alan Curtis
- D) →
  - Elmer, Bruce
- E) →

6. Beaum, Carol Ann
- A) →
  - Baum, Stacey
- B) →
  - Baumm, Randy P.
- C) → ____
  - Buame, Heather
- D) →
  - Buamme, Rockwell C.
- E) →

7. Campanella, Gay
- A) →
  - Cambell, Colin M.
- B) →
  - Campbell, Cynthia
- C) → ____
  - Campbello, Cris
- D) →
  - Campersand, Dollie
- E) →

8. Bergerman, Ralph
- A) →
  - Bergquist, Peter
- B) →
  - Bergstrom, Paul
- C) → ____
  - Berguman, Alice
- D) →
  - Berqman, Fortuna D.
- E) →

9. Caliari, Thomasina P.
- A) →
  - Callahan, Bernetta
- B) →
  - Callope, Richard
- C) → ____
  - Calnan, Joseph
- D) →
  - Caloca, A. D.
- E) →

10. McKinsey, Cynthia
- A) →
  - McGuire, Martin
- B) →
  - McKinney, Jeff
- C) → ____
  - McKissick, Matthew
- D) →
  - McNamara, Karen
- E) →

11. Wayn, Melba
- A) →
  - Wain, Nelbert
- B) →
  - Waine, Chick
- C) → ____
  - Wayne, Harriet G.
- D) →
  - Waynie, Davis P.
- E) →

12. Shmitz, Thomas C
- A) →
  - Schmits, Deloris
- B) →
  - Schmitz, Francisco
- C) → ____
  - Schmitz, Hermionie
- D) →
  - Shmitz, Krikor
- E) →

13. McMahan, Patrick
- A) →
  MacMahan, Ferdie
- B) →
  MacMahon, Edward
- C) → _____
  McMahon, Arlene
- D) →
  McMann, Howard P.
- E) →

14. Whrine, Herman
- A) →
  Wride, Tellie
- B) →
  Wright, Catherine
- C) → _____
  Write, Foster
- D) →
  Wrivort, Norman
- E) →

15. Carlson, Karen
- A) →
  Carman, Ronald
- B) →
  Carr, Michael
- C) → _____
  Carstein, Freda
- D) →
  Carucci, Neil
- E) →

16. Fitznorris, Tawny
- A) →
  Fitzgammon, Harriet
- B) →
  Fitzgerald, John
- C) → _____
  Fitzsimmins, Dennis
- D) →
  Fitzsimmons, Francis
- E) →

17. Potimkin, Karen
- A) →
  Porter, Harmon
- B) →
  Posner, James L.
- C) → _____
  Potter, Neville K.
- D) →
  Potvin, Mary Allyn
- E) →

18. Sharman, Jean
- A) →
  Shall, Julia
- B) →
  Shalle, Nestor R.
- C) → _____
  Shaul, Ginger
- D) →
  Shawl, Forrest
- E) →

19. McKee, Forrest
- A) →
  McGee, Marvin
- B) →
  McGorrity, Sandra
- C) → _____
  McHarrigan, Michael
- D) →
  McHellman, Vernon
- E) →

20. Aubrey, Carlos
- A) →
  Arnold, Sidnor
- B) →
  Astrid, Minor G.
- C) → _____
  Barleycorn, Antonio
- D) →
  Davids, Florence
- E) →

21. National Merchant Co.
- A) →
  National Lumber
- B) →
  National Merchandising
- C) → _____
  National Merchants, Inc.
- D) →
  National Millinery Co.
- E) →

22. Anderson, J. Todd
- A) →
  Anderson, Michael
- B) →
  Anderson, Michael J.
- C) → _____
  Anderson, Noreen
- D) →
  Anderson, Stuart
- E) →

23. Vernon, Portia
- A) →
  Devney, Sara
- B) →
  De Vries, John
- C) → _____
  Devroe, Paul
- D) →
  De Weerdt, Marilyn
- E) →

24. Hulse, Thomas
- A) →
  Hult, Gerard
- B) →
  Hultart, Humphrey
- C) → _____
  Hulze, Luther
- D) →
  Lumahr, Lucy
- E) →

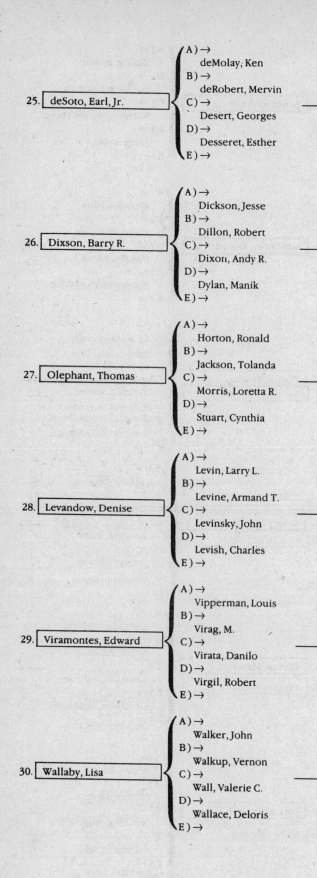

25. deSoto, Earl, Jr.
- A) →
- deMolay, Ken
- B) →
- deRobert, Mervin
- C) → _____
- Desert, Georges
- D) →
- Desseret, Esther
- E) →

26. Dixson, Barry R.
- A) →
- Dickson, Jesse
- B) →
- Dillon, Robert
- C) → _____
- Dixon, Andy R.
- D) →
- Dylan, Manik
- E) →

27. Olephant, Thomas
- A) →
- Horton, Ronald
- B) →
- Jackson, Tolanda
- C) → _____
- Morris, Loretta R.
- D) →
- Stuart, Cynthia
- E) →

28. Levandow, Denise
- A) →
- Levin, Larry L.
- B) →
- Levine, Armand T.
- C) → _____
- Levinsky, John
- D) →
- Levish, Charles
- E) →

29. Viramontes, Edward
- A) →
- Vipperman, Louis
- B) →
- Virag, M.
- C) → _____
- Virata, Danilo
- D) →
- Virgil, Robert
- E) →

30. Wallaby, Lisa
- A) →
- Walker, John
- B) →
- Walkup, Vernon
- C) → _____
- Wall, Valerie C.
- D) →
- Wallace, Deloris
- E) →

ANSWER EXPLANATIONS FOR PRACTICE SET 1

1. **(D)** Watsonian, Franklin
   Waverley, S. Q.
   Wetson, McDougle
2. **(D)** Birminghuller, Daisy
   Burmingham, Emma A.
   Burningham, Morris
3. **(E)** Burmen, Andre
   Burmun, Lardeese
4. **(E)** Caffry, Bertha
   McCafferty, Gabriele
5. **(A)** *Eliot, Joy*
   Eliot, Robert
6. **(C)** Baumm, Randy P.
   Beaum, Carol Ann
   Buame, Heather
7. **(B)** Cambell, Colin M.
   Campanella, Gay
   Campbell, Cynthia
8. **(A)** *Bergerman, Ralph*
   Bergquist, Peter
9. **(A)** *Caliari, Thomasina P.*
   Callahan, Bernetta
10. **(C)** McKinney, Jeff
    McKinsey, Cynthia
    McKissick, Matthew
11. **(C)** Waine, Chick
    Wayn, Melba
    Wayne, Harriet G.
12. **(E)** Shmitz, Krikor
    Shmitz, Thomas C.
13. **(C)** MacMahon, Edward
    McMahan, Patrick
    McMahon, Arlene
14. **(A)** *Whrine, Herman*
    Wride, Tellie
15. **(A)** *Carlson, Karen*
    Carman, Ronald
16. **(C)** Fitzgerald, John
    Fitznorris, Tawny
    Fitzsimmins, Dennis
17. **(C)** Posner, James L.
    Potimkin, Karen
    Potter, Neville K.
18. **(C)** Shalle, Nestor R.
    Sharman, Jean
    Shaul, Ginger
19. **(E)** McHellman, Vernon
    McKee, Forrest
20. **(C)** Astrid, Minor G.
    Aubrey, Carlos
    Barleycorn, Antonio
21. **(C)** National Merchandising
    National Merchant Co.
    National Merchants, Inc.

22. **(A)** *Anderson, J. Todd*
    Anderson, Michael
23. **(E)** De Weerdt, Marilyn
    Vernon, Portia
24. **(A)** *Hulse, Thomas*
    Hult, Gerard
25. **(D)** Desert, Georges
    deSoto, Earl, Jr.
    Desseret, Esther
26. **(D)** Dixon, Andy R.
    Dixson, Barry R.
    Dylan, Manik
27. **(D)** Morris, Loretta R.
    Olephant, Thomas
    Stuart, Cynthia
28. **(A)** *Levandow, Denise*
    Levin, Larry L.
29. **(C)** Virag, M.
    Viramontes, Edward
    Virata, Danilo
30. **(D)** Wall, Valerie C.
    Wallaby, Lisa
    Wallace, Deloris

PRACTICE SET 2

Find the correct place for the name in the box, and
mark the letter of that space as your answer.

1. Saxe, Antoinette
   - A) →
     - Sax, Steven
   - B) →
     - Saxon, Daniel G.
   - C) → _____
     - Saxouris, Jerome
   - D) →
     - Saxton, John
   - E) →

2. Stache, Edwin
   - A) →
     - Staahl, James
   - B) →
     - Staats, Meg
   - C) → _____
     - Stabile, Priscilla
   - D) →
     - Stabler, Jennifer
   - E) →

3. Preste, Armand H.
   - A) →
     - Presson-Allen, Jay
   - B) →
     - Preston, Allen
   - C) → _____
     - Prestuge, Victor
   - D) →
     - Pretorn, Felix
   - E) →

4. Sardoma, Anthony
   - A) →
     - Sardegna, Marie
   - B) →
     - Sardone, Gary
   - C) → _____
     - Sarenas, Maria Teresa
   - D) →
     - Sargent, D.
   - E) →

5. Mantikian, Antoine
   - A) →
     - Mantilla, Felix
   - B) →
     - Mantis, Cynthia S.
   - C) → _____
     - Mantle, John P.
   - D) →
     - Mantoura, Josephine
   - E) →

6. Patjian, Ernesto
   - A) →
     - Patinelli, Frank
   - B) →
     - Patino, Thomas
   - C) → _____
     - Patlan, Carmen
   - D) →
     - Patmar, Alexander H.
   - E) →

7. Georgian, Hal
   - A) →
     - George, Marion
   - B) →
     - Georges, Martin
   - C) → _____
     - Georgia, Ralph
   - D) →
     - Georgy, Afram
   - E) →

8. Girson, Maury
   - A) →
     - Girmala, Stephen
   - B) →
     - Gitlin, Maslow
   - C) →
     - Givargiss, Ashour
   - D) →
     - Gorshore, Bronson
   - E) →

9. Meaza, Carol H.
   - A) →
     - Mean, Russel
   - B) →
     - Meauz, Steve
   - C) → _____
     - Meazzili, Billy
   - D) →
     - Meddars, Nelie
   - E) →

10. McMinnsy, Fernon W.

A) →
McMinn, Babo
B) →
McMinnamin, Alistair D.
C) → _____
McMio, Alfred
D) →
McNeeley, Paula
E) →

11. McWilliams, Sonny

A) →
McWilliam, William
B) →
McWilliam, Wilma
C) → _____
McWilliams, Ernestine
D) →
McWilliams, Ernesto
E) →

12. McHenry, William

A) →
MacElliot, Tari
B) →
MacElliot, Una
C) → _____
MacPherson, Arnold
D) →
MacVernon, Mabel P.
E) →

13. Koralan, Isabel T.

A) →
Kornblau, David H.
B) →
Kornblum, Donald
C) → _____
Kornbluth, Sanford
D) →
Kornspan, Harvey
E) →

14. Meadow, Carla

A) →
Mead, Mary
B) →
Mead, Neville
C) → _____
Meade, Mardy
D) →
Meadville, Nancy
E) →

15. Brown, Charlene

A) →
Brown, Charles
B) →
Brown, Charley A.
C) → _____
Brown, Chas.
D) →
Brown, Cherrie
E) →

16. Bulina, Catherine

A) →
Buel, William D.
B) →
Buell, Warren
C) → _____
Buelna, Angie
D) →
Buelporos, Wesley
E) →

17. Ingars, Hyatt

A) →
Ingals, Ferdinand
B) →
Ingals, Roger
C) → _____
Ingarr, Anita
D) →
Ingarsoll, Julie A.
E) →

18. Kapov, Christopher

A) →
Kaplan, Seymour
B) →
Kaplanjian, Jacob
C) → _____
Kaplus, Asmik
D) →
Kapp, G. J.
E) →

19. Alenty, Felipe

A) →
Alejo, Maura
B) →
Aleksandian, Grigor
C) → _____
Aleman, Augusto
D) →
Alert, Anna G.
E) →

20. Hwang, Kung Jong

A) →
Hwang, Kathleen
B) →
Hwang, Kyu Chol
C) → _____
Hwang, Kyung Moon
D) →
Hwang, Soon Bong
E) →

21. Burger, Errol M.

A) →
Burcus, Gregory
B) →
Burk, Omelda
C) → _____
Burker, Cathleen
D) →
Burkette, Laura
E) →

22. Aquibas, Roger
- A) →
- Aguilar, Anna
- B) →
- Aguilar, Babo Rafael
- C) → _____
- Aguilar, Catherine
- D) →
- Aguilar, Niholas
- E) →

23. Rogers, Allen
- A) →
- Porter, Wellington
- B) →
- Quiroz, Danielle
- C) → _____
- Stevenson, Roger
- D) →
- Ulmer, Anthony
- E) →

24. Brammer, Thos.
- A) →
- Bramer, Elliot
- B) →
- Bramer, Tillie
- C) → _____
- Brammer, Timothy
- D) →
- Braumer, Dana
- E) →

25. VanderAllen, L. I.
- A) →
- Van Allen, Peter
- B) →
- VanHoven, Bud
- C) → _____
- Vannoker, Dollie F.
- D) →
- VanVenniker, Norris
- E) →

26. Brian, Bradford
- A) →
- Brainerd, M.
- B) →
- Branford, Gerry
- C) → _____
- Brassard, Jack
- D) →
- Breindon, Carol Ann
- E) →

27. Gibson, Allyn
- A) →
- Gebson, Martin A.
- B) →
- Gibsen, Roy A.
- C) → _____
- Gibsin, Boyd C.
- D) →
- Gibson, Sharyn
- E) →

28. Calhoun, John R.
- A) →
- Calder, Carla
- B) →
- Calderon, Bertie G.
- C) → _____
- Caldwell, Kenneth
- D) →
- Callwell, Ernestine
- E) →

29. Hansen, Burt
- A) →
- Hanson, A. B.
- B) →
- Hanson, Betsy
- C) → _____
- Hanson, David
- D) →
- Hanson, Georgette Y.
- E) →

30. Gruver, H. F.
- A) →
- Grunberg, Lee
- B) →
- Grundy, Allen
- C) → _____
- Grusen, Mac
- D) →
- Grutza, Carol W.
- E) →

ANSWER EXPLANATIONS FOR PRACTICE SET 2

1. (B) Sax, Steven
   Saxe, Antoinette
   Saxon, Daniel G

2. (E) Stabler, Jennifer
   Stache, Edwin

3. (B) Presson-Allen, Jay
   Preste, Armand H.
   Preston, Allen

4. (B) Sardegna, Marie
   Sardoma, Anthony
   Sardone, Gary

5. (A) *Mantikian, Antoine*
   Mantilla, Felix

6. (C) Patino, Thomas
   Patjian, Ernesto
   Patlan, Carmen

7. (D) Georgia, Ralph
   Georgian, Hal
   Georgy, Afram

8. (B) Girmala, Stephen
   Girson, Maury
   Gitlin, Maslow

9. (C) Meauz, Steve
   Meaza, Carol H.
   Meazzili, Billy

10. **(C)** McMinnamin, Alistair D.
McMinnsy, Fernon W.
McMio, Alfred

11. **(E)** McWilliams, Ernesto
McWilliams, Sonny

12. **(E)** MacVernon, Mabel R.
McHenry, William

13. **(A)** *Koralan, Isabel T.*
Kornblau, David H.

14. **(D)** Meade, Mardy
Meadow, Carla
Meadville, Nancy

15. **(A)** *Brown, Charlene*
Brown, Charles

16. **(E)** Buelporos, Wesley
Bulina, Catherine

17. **(D)** Ingarr, Anita
Ingars, Hyatt
Ingarsoll, Julie A.

18. **(D)** Kaplus, Asmik
Kapov, Christopher
Kapp, G. J.

19. **(D)** Aleman, Augusto
Alenty, Relipe
Alert, Anna G.

20. **(B)** Hwang, Kathleen
Hwang, Kung, Jong
Hwang, Kyu Chol

21. **(B)** Burcus, Gregory
Burger, Errol M.
Burk, Omelda

22. **(E)** Aguilar, Niholas
Aquibas, Roger

23. **(C)** Quiroz, Danielle
Rogers, Allen
Stevenson, Roger

24. **(C)** Bramer, Tillie
Brammer, Thos.
Brammer, Timothy

25. **(B)** Van Allen, Peter
VanderAllen, L. I.
VanHoven, Bud

26. **(E)** Breindon, Carol Ann
Brian, Bradford

27. **(D)** Gibsin, Boyd C.
Gibson, Allyn
Gibson, Sharyn

28. **(D)** Caldwell, Kenneth
Calhoun, John R.
Callwell, Ernestine

29. **(A)** *Hansen, Burt*
Hanson, A. B.

30. **(E)** Grutza, Carol W.
Gruver, H. F.

PRACTICE SET 3

Find the correct place for the name in the box, and mark the letter of that space as your answer.

1. Gardmon, Phillipe

A) →
Gardiner, Chauncy
B.) →
Gardiner, Jeffrey
C) → _____
Gardner, Helen
D) →
Gartener, Thelma Randy
E) →

2. Huntigan, Charles A.

A) →
Huntley, Derek
B.) →
Huntson, Pierre
C) → _____
Hunzigan, Kantor
D) →
Hyatt, Maurine
E) →

3. Fristel, William

A) →
Friby, Elliot
B) →
Frisbie, Celia
C) → _____
Frisch, Josef
D) →
Frisella, Carmen
E) →

4. Franklyn, Terrence

A) →
Franklin, Paul
B) →
Franklin, Robert
C) → _____
Franklin, Robin
D) →
Franklin, Stuart
E) →

5. Choung, Jackie

A) →
Chotirawa, Vinnie
B) →
Chovan, Emily
C) → _____
Choy, M.
D) →
Christena, Carla
E) →

6. Garret, Felton

A) →
Gareth, Paul
B) →
Garth, Thomas Alvin
C) → _____
Garvin, Donna Gower
D) →
Gullickson, Neil
E) →

7. | McGrath, Edwin |
   A) →
   MacGee, Milton
   B) →
   MacGuire, Mabel
   C) →
   McInerney, V. L.
   D) →
   McKinney, Neil
   E) →
   _____

8. | Christofer, Anita |
   A) →
   Choe, Wes
   B) →
   Choin, Al
   C) →
   Chorbjean, Anthony
   D) →
   Chrysler, Daniel
   E) →
   _____

9. | D'Arbanville, C. K. |
   A) →
   D'Arcy, Frances
   B) →
   Darville, Barry
   C) →
   Darwin, Thos.
   D) →
   Dary, Bernard J.
   E) →
   _____

10. | Potsdam, Freda |
    A) →
    Pottsdam, Lenia
    B) →
    Pottsy, Wallace E.
    C) →
    Poty, McGarrett
    D) →
    Pozlewski, John
    E) →
    _____

11. | Lui, David |
    A) →
    Lugo, Jaimie
    B) →
    Lui, Davis
    C) →
    Luis, Taylor
    D) →
    Lujan, Benny
    E) →
    _____

12. | McGrew, Arthur |
    A) →
    McMeekan, Jerry
    B) →
    McMillan, Paul
    C) →
    McMullan, P.
    D) →
    Mecca, Steve
    E) →
    _____

13. | Kretchmar, Arnold |
    A) →
    Krechmer, Jennifer
    B) →
    Kretchmer, Jane
    C) →
    Kretchmier, Allen
    D) →
    Kretchner, Kay
    E) →
    _____

14. | VanLaer, Robt. |
    A) →
    Vanity, Vance
    B) →
    Van Kan, Hubert
    C) →
    Van Kirk, Steven
    D) →
    Van Leeuwen, Skip
    E) →
    _____

15. | Sonpez, Kenneth |
    A) →
    Sonnet, Sherry
    B) →
    Sonnken, Jeri
    C) →
    Sonntag, Debbie
    D) →
    Soodhalter, Herman
    E) →
    _____

16. | Unified Taxi Company |
    A) →
    Unart Music Corp.
    B) →
    United Industries
    C) →
    United Recording
    D) →
    Universal Medical
    E) →
    _____

17. | Sibley, Gerard |
    A) →
    Sibella, Gloria
    B) →
    Siberny, Alvin
    C) →
    Sibfert, Harold G.
    D) →
    Sibonian, Meritt
    E) →
    _____

18. | Schrom, Jerry |
    A) →
    Shore, Steven
    B) →
    Shores, Leonard
    C) →
    Short, Michael
    D) →
    Shoup, Kathy
    E) →

19. Wader, Eugene A.
- A) →
- Waechter, Benjamin
- B) →
- Wagar, L. A.
- C) →
- Wagg, Walter
- D) →
- Wagner, Richard
- E) →

20. Vorlioz, Richard
- A) →
- Voorhis, George
- B) →
- Vornholt, John
- C) →
- Vorperian, Rose
- D) →
- Vosatka, Steve
- E) →

21. Darin, Louise
- A) →
- Darran, Robert
- B) →
- Darren, Jean Louise
- C) →
- Darrin, Sarah
- D) →
- Darryn, Josiane
- E) →

22. Cassity, Michael
- A) →
- Casady, Henry
- B) →
- Casidy, Nestor
- C) →
- Cassady, Roland
- D) →
- Cassidy, Darryl R.
- E) →

23. Carson, Adam
- A) →
- Carsen, Roger
- B) →
- Carsen, Teresa R.
- C) →
- Carsin, Foster
- D) →
- Carsini, Elaine
- E) →

24. Dolph, Ralph
- A) →
- Dogherty, Frederick
- B) →
- Dougherty, Cinthia
- C) →
- Doughrty, Benta
- D) →
- Douph, Patricia
- E) →

25. Collins, Denise
- A) →
- Collins, Collie
- B) →
- Collins, Dolley
- C) →
- Collins, Dorothy
- D) →
- Collins, Dova
- E) →

26. Homer, Nelson
- A) →
- Hooker, Dennis
- B) →
- Hooper, Margie
- C) →
- Hooper, Peter D.
- D) →
- Hoover, Phyllis
- E) →

27. Matthau, Warren
- A) →
- Mathews, Ginger
- B) →
- Matthews, Aaron
- C) →
- Matthews, Neville
- D) →
- McMathow, Lynne
- E) →

28. Dipman, Maria
- A) →
- Desmond, Ronald C.
- B) →
- Diamond, Leslie Ann
- C) →
- Dimond, Laura
- D) →
- Dizmond, Jennie
- E) →

29. Cummings, James
- A) →
- Cummings, Eric
- B) →
- Cummings, James T.
- C) →
- Cummings, Phyllis
- D) →
- Cummings, Stuart
- E) →

30. Abrahms, Corinna
- A) →
- Abrahams, Tara
- B) →
- Abrams, Marcus J.
- C) →
- Abramson, Arthur
- D) →
- Abrasnov, Clarence
- E) →

ANSWER EXPLANATIONS FOR PRACTICE SET 3

1. (C) Gardiner, Jeffrey
   Gardmon, Phillipe
   Gardner, Helen
2. (A) *Huntigan, Charles A.*
   Huntley, Derek
3. (E) Frisella, Carmen
   Fristel, William
4. (E) Franklin, Stuart
   Franklyn, Terrence
5. (B) Chotirawa, Vinnie
   Choung, Jackie
   Chovan, Emily
6. (B) Gareth, Paul
   Garret, Felton
   Garth, Thomas Alvin
7. (C) MacGuire, Mabel
   McGrath, Edwin
   McInerney, V. L.
8. (D) Chorbjean, Anthony
   Christofer, Anita
   Chrysler, Daniel
9. (A) *D'Arbanville, C. K.*
   D'Arcy, Frances
10. (A) *Potsdam, Freda*
    Pottsdam, Lenia
11. (B) Lugo, Jaimie
    Lui, David
    Lui, Davis
12. (A) *McGrew, Arthur*
    McMeekan, Jerry
13. (B) Krechmer, Jennifer
    Kretchmar, Arnold
    Kretchmer, Jane
14. (D) Van Kirk, Steven
    VanLaer, Robt.
    Van Leeuwen, Skip
15. (D) Sonntag, Debbie
    Sonpez, Kenneth
    Soodhalter, Herman
16. (B) Unart Music Corp.
    Unified Taxi Company
    United Industries
17. (D) Sibfert, Harold G.
    Sibley, Gerard
    Sibonian, Meritt
18. (A) *Schrom, Jerry*
    Shore, Steven
19. (A) *Wader, Eugene A.*
    Waechter, Benjamin
20. (B) Voorhis, George
    Vorlioz, Richard
    Vornholt, John
21. (A) *Darin, Louise*
    Darran, Robert
22. (E) Cassidy, Darryl R.
    Cassity, Michael
23. (E) Carsini, Elaine
    Carson, Adam
24. (B) Dogherty, Frederick
    Dolph, Ralph
    Dougherty, Cinthia
25. (B) Collins, Collie
    Collins, Denise
    Collins, Dolley
26. (A) *Homer, Nelson*
    Hooker, Dennis
27. (B) Mathews, Ginger
    Matthau, Warren
    Matthews, Aaron
28. (D) Dimond, Laura
    Dipman, Maria
    Dizmond, Jennie
29. (B) Cummings, Eric.
    Cummings, James
    Cummings, James T.
30. (B) Abrahams, Tara
    Abrahms, Corinna
    Abrams, Marcus J.

PRACTICE SET 4

Find the correct place for the name in the box, and mark the letter of that space as your answer.

1. Swansong, Calvin
   - A) →
     Swainson, Nellie
   - B) →
     Swanson, Caroline
   - C) → _____
     Swansonn, Kermit
   - D) →
     Swenson, Hubert
   - E) →

2. Birkler, Donald
   - A) →
     Binker, Rosa
   - B) →
     Binkier, Todd C.
   - C) → _____
     Binkler, Martha E.
   - D) →
     Bunkler, F. Alice
   - E) →

3. Faulkner, Daphne
   - A) →
     Falkner, Norman
   - B) →
     Falknor, Marvin F.
   - C) → _____
     Falkson, Albert J.
   - D) →
     Faulkner, Erica
   - E) →

4. Bellings, Marta
   - A) →
   - Bilings, V.
   - B) →
   - Bilings, William J.
   - C) → ____
   - Billings, Stella
   - D) →
   - Billings, Thomas I.
   - E) →

5. Franklin, Veñita P.
   - A) →
   - Franklin, Terrie
   - B) →
   - Franklin, U. V.
   - C) → ____
   - Franklin, Vincent
   - D) →
   - Franklin, Wallace
   - E) →

6. Abelhouszen, Alan J.
   - A) →
   - Abe, Lionel
   - B) →
   - Abel, Gregory U.
   - C) → ____
   - Abele, Joseph
   - D) →
   - Abelman, Leonore
   - E) →

7. Morroski, Andrew
   - A) →
   - Morro, Levon
   - B) →
   - Morroe, Edna F.
   - C) → ____
   - Morros, Abraham
   - D) →
   - Morrow, Millie
   - E) →

8. Sanford, Steven P.
   - A) →
   - Sanders, Fred J.
   - B) →
   - Sands, Gussie
   - C) → ____
   - Saunders, Renata
   - D) →
   - Sulnick, Samuel
   - E) →

9. Fertatta, Brad
   - A) →
   - Feratta, Francis
   - B) →
   - Feratta, Velma
   - C) → ____
   - Fertitta, Judith
   - D) →
   - Fertizza, Alma
   - E) →

10. Chakin, Roger
    - A) →
    - Chaiken, Jason
    - B) →
    - Chaikin, Roberta
    - C) → ____
    - Chaikin, Stuart
    - D) →
    - Chaikin, Ulma
    - E) →

11. Parker, James
    - A) →
    - Parker, J. Michael
    - B) →
    - Parker, J. Theodore
    - C) → ____
    - Parker, Jay Esther
    - D) →
    - Parker, Joseph Arlo
    - E) →

12. Borst, Stephen M.
    - A) →
    - Borghi, Douglas Stephen
    - B) →
    - B'Orgus, Bjorn
    - C) → ____
    - Burgess, Granville
    - D) →
    - Burgin, Edgar
    - E) →

13. Beechwood, Norris
    - A) →
    - Beachwood, Calvin
    - B) →
    - Beachwude, Edye
    - C) → ____
    - Beechwood, Kevin R.
    - D) →
    - Beechwood, Ruth M.
    - E) →

14. Pattisen, Verna
    - A) →
    - Patterson, George
    - B) →
    - Patteson, Peter
    - C) → ____
    - Pattison, Meriam
    - D) →
    - Pattisun, Selma Y.
    - E) →

15. Davis, Donnell A.
    - A) →
    - Davis, Donald
    - B) →
    - Davis, Donnell
    - C) → ____
    - Davis, Doreen
    - D) →
    - Davis, Doreit
    - E) →

16. Hooper, Homer
- A) →
- Hoort, Nicholas
- B) →
- Hoover, Jack
- C) → _____
- Hoover-Sanborn, Ernest
- D) →
- Hopkins, Mark
- E) →

17. Einstinium, Tony
- A) →
- Einstein, Charles
- B) →
- Einstien, David
- C) → _____
- Einstore, Catherine
- D) →
- Einstrum, Tina
- E) →

18. Dalton, Brenda
- A) →
- Dal Vera, John B.
- B) →
- Daly, Charles
- C) → _____
- Dalziel, Scott
- D) →
- Damar, Leonilla
- E) →

19. Davids, Jerriel
- A) →
- David, Gail
- B) →
- Davidson, Marion
- C) → _____
- Davidson, Merritt
- D) →
- Davidsten, Fran
- E) →

20. Dauvelis, Don
- A) →
- D'Attili, Ettore
- B) →
- Daues, Michael
- C) → _____
- Davalos, Susan
- D) →
- D'Avanzo, Marcus
- E) →

21. Miller, Francis A.
- A) →
- Miller, Evelyn J.
- B) →
- Miller, Evelyn P.
- C) → _____
- Miller, Frances P.
- D) →
- Miller, Frances R.
- E) →

22. O'Reilly, Bertha
- A) →
- O'Reilley, Terrence
- B) →
- O'Reilley, Vincent
- C) → _____
- O'Reilley, Wilson
- D) →
- O'Reilley, Woodrow D.
- E) →

23. Kwok, Yi
- A) →
- Kwok, Wilde F.
- B) →
- Kwok, William H.
- C) → _____
- Kwok, Ying Sum
- D) →
- Kwon, Elgin
- E) →

24. Lambson, Jessica O.
- A) →
- Lambert, Helen
- B) →
- Lambirt, Nessie
- C) → _____
- Lamburt, Petros
- D) →
- Lampurt, Jay Harriet
- E) →

25. MacClelland, Sharon
- A) →
- Macchia, Ronald
- B) →
- MacDonald, Peter C.
- C) → _____
- Macdonald, Yolanda
- D) →
- Macdonough, Brian
- E) →

26. Arsini, Mozelle T.
- A) →
- Arbitron-Mays, Wilson
- B) →
- Arion, Beverly
- C) → _____
- Arpus, Lorelle
- D) →
- Astor, Maria
- E) →

27. Hazelmen, Porter
- A) →
- Hazarian, Costan
- B) →
- Hazarian, Meriam
- C) → _____
- Hazell, David
- D) →
- Hazeltime, Daniel
- E) →

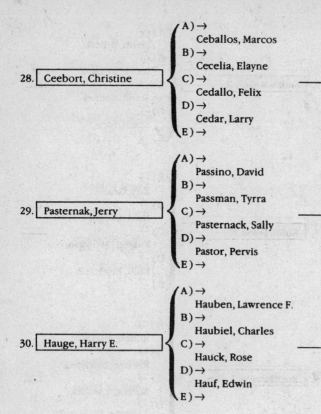

28. | Ceebort, Christine |
- A) →
  Ceballos, Marcos
- B) →
  Cecelia, Elayne
- C) → _____
  Cedallo, Felix
- D) →
  Cedar, Larry
- E) →

29. | Pasternak, Jerry |
- A) →
  Passino, David
- B) →
  Passman, Tyrra
- C) → _____
  Pasternack, Sally
- D) →
  Pastor, Pervis
- E) →

30. | Hauge, Harry E. |
- A) →
  Hauben, Lawrence F.
- B) →
  Haubiel, Charles
- C) → _____
  Hauck, Rose
- D) →
  Hauf, Edwin
- E) →

ANSWER EXPLANATIONS FOR PRACTICE SET 4

1. (C) Swanson, Caroline
   Swansong, Calvin
   Swansonn, Kermit
2. (D) Binkler, Martha E.
   Birkler, Donald
   Bunkler, F. Alice
3. (D) Falkson, Albert J.
   Faulkner, Daphne
   Faulkner, Erica
4. (A) *Bellings, Marta*
   Bilings, V.
5. (C) Franklin, U. V.
   Franklin, Venita, P.
   Franklin, Vincent
6. (D) Abele, Joseph
   Abelhouszen, Alan J.
   Abelman, Leonore
7. (D) Morros, Abraham
   Morroski, Andrew
   Morrow, Millie
8. (C) Sands, Gussie
   Sanford, Steven P.
   Saunders, Renata
9. (C) Feratta, Velma
   Fertatta, Brad
   Fertitta, Judith

10. (E) Chaikin, Ulma
    Chakin, Roger
11. (C) Parker, J. Theodore
    Parker, James
    Parker, Jay Esther
12. (C) B'Orgus, Bjorn
    Borst, Stephen M.
    Burgess, Granville
13. (D) Beechwood, Kevin R.
    Beechwood, Norris
    Beechwood, Ruth M.
14. (C) Patteson, Peter
    Pattisen, Verna
    Pattison, Meriam
15. (C) Davis, Donnell
    Davis, Donnell A.
    Davis, Doreen
16. (A) *Hooper, Homer*
    Hoort, Nicholas
17. (C) Einstien, David
    Einstinium, Tony
    Einstore, Catherine
18. (A) *Dalton, Brenda*
    Dal Vera, John B.
19. (B) David, Gail
    Davis, Jerriel
    Davidson, Marion
20. (C) Daues, Michael
    Dauvelis, Don
    Davalos, Susan
21. (E) Miller, Frances R.
    Miller, Francis A.
22. (E) O'Reilley, Woodrow D.
    O'Reilly, Bertha
23. (C) Kwok, William H.
    Kwok, Yi
    Kwok, Ying Sum
24. (C) Lambirt, Nessie
    Lambson, Jessica O.
    Lamburt, Petros
25. (B) Macchia, Ronald
    MacClelland, Sharon
    MacDonald, Peter C.
26. (D) Arpus, Lorelle
    Arsini, Mozelle T.
    Astor, Maria
27. (D) Hazell, David
    Hazelmen, Porter
    Hazeltime, Daniel
28. (E) Cedar, Larry
    Ceebort, Christine
29. (D) Pasternack, Sally
    Pasternak, Jerry
    Pastor, Pervis
30. (E) Hauf, Edwin
    Hauge, Harry E.

PRACTICE SET 5

Find the correct place for the name in the box, and
mark the letter of that space as your answer.

1. SanMarco, Antonio
   - A) →
     - SanLuis, Phillip
   - B) →
     - Sanlummis, Douglas
   - C) → ____
     - Sanlutent, Wilfred
   - D) →
     - SanMiguel, Maria
   - E) →

2. Arunges, Artin
   - A) →
     - Arto, Raoul
   - B) →
     - Artz, M. G.
   - C) → ____
     - Arutyun, Adam
   - D) →
     - Arvin, Stefanie
   - E) →

3. Felard, Stephanie
   - A) →
     - Falana, Ariel
   - B) →
     - Falardeau, George
   - C) → ____
     - Falcasantos, Lea
   - D) →
     - Falck, Raymond
   - E) →

4. Aryzinault, Paul
   - A) →
     - Arye, Israel
   - B) →
     - Aryee, Enoch
   - C) → ____
     - Arzola, Luz
   - D) →
     - Arzouman, Merry
   - E) →

5. Merlino, Flavio
   - A) →
     - Merino, Joseph
   - B) →
     - Merinoff, Anton
   - C) → ____
     - Merkley, Allen L.
   - D) →
     - Merluzzo, Paul Michael
   - E) →

6. Soleman, Brooke G.
   - A) →
     - Solmon, Sylvia
   - B) →
     - Solomon, Rose
   - C) → ____
     - Solomon, William
   - D) →
     - Soltman, Neil
   - E) →

7. Smith, Robert Z.
   - A) →
     - Smith, R. Ruth
   - B) →
     - Smith, Richard
   - C) → ____
     - Smith, Rodney
   - D) →
     - Smith, Sara
   - E) →

8. Kuhn, Frank P.
   - A) →
     - Kuh, Grace
   - B) →
     - Kuhl, Gregory
   - C) → ____
     - Kuhner, Maryann
   - D) →
     - Kulh, Eugene R.
   - E) →

9. Ruebhausen, F. Paul
   - A) →
     - Ruben, Abram
   - B) →
     - Rueben, Eva Reed
   - C) → ____
     - Ruebin, Caroline
   - D) →
     - Ruelas, Robert
   - E) →

10. Farnham, Dennis
    - A) →
      - Faris, Vernon
    - B) →
      - Farishan, Warren
    - C) → ____
      - Farley, Janet
    - D) →
      - Farmer, Susan H.
    - E) →

11. Flynt, Clinton D.
    - A) →
      - Floyd, Dorothy
    - B) →
      - Fluos, Michelle
    - C) → ____
      - Flyn, Christine
    - D) →
      - Flynn, Nina
    - E) →

12. Ruffin, Margaret G.
    - A) →
      - Rudeen, Wilma
    - B) →
      - Rudnik, M. A.
    - C) → ____
      - Rugley, Francis
    - D) →
      - Rugman, Norman
    - E) →

13. Devile, Albert

A) →
deStefano, Ann
B) →
deStepho, Pietro
C) →
deVanderveer, August
D) →
Deverend, Oscar
E) →

14. Fouhner, Esta C.

A) →
Fouchard, Joseph
B) →
Fouche, P.
C) →
Fought, Kenneth
D) →
Foulkes, Thomas
E) →

15. Carnieski, Morris

A) →
Carne, Tina
B) →
Carney, Arthur
C) →
Carnicelli, Ruben
D) →
Carnow, Martin A.
E) →

16. Floretta, Philip

A) →
Flores, Lilia
B) →
Flores, Louis
C) →
Florez, Didi S.
D) →
Florish, Kenneth
E) →

17. Irie, Kris

A) →
Irby, Ben C.
B) →
Ireland, N. A.
C) →
Irena, Perris
D) →
Iris, Carol
E) →

18. Jackson, J. P.

A) →
Jacksen, Peter
B) →
Jackson, James
C) →
Jackson, John
D) →
Jackson, William
E) →

19. Berland, Helen Ann

A) →
Berk, Lillian O.
B) →
Berker, S. R.
C) →
Berkey, Maurice
D) →
Berkquist, Peter
E) →

20. Berry, Charles

A) →
Berry, Bill
B) →
Berry, Brian
C) →
Berry, C. Douglas
D) →
Berry, Jonathan
E) →

21. McAllister, Virginia

A) →
MacMenamin, Peter
B) →
MacMullory, Nigel
C) →
McNoughton, Foster
D) →
McOleny, Santa
E) →

22. Kramer, Edward

A) →
Kramer, A.
B) →
Kramer, Allen
C) →
Kramer, E. J.
D) →
Kramer, Rubin
E) →

23. Jurimasat, Patricia

A) →
Juodeika, G. Rowena
B) →
Jura, John
C) →
Jurow, Stasia
D) →
Justice, Edgar J.
E) →

24. Harding, Gary

A) →
Hardin, Timothy
B) →
Harding, Gary D.
C) →
Harding, Gary T.
D) →
Harding, George
E) →

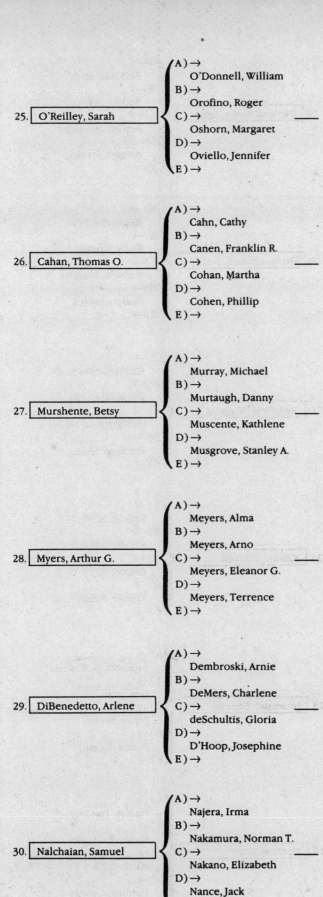

25. O'Reilley, Sarah
- A) →
- O'Donnell, William
- B) →
- Orofino, Roger
- C) → _____
- Oshorn, Margaret
- D) →
- Oviello, Jennifer
- E) →

26. Cahan, Thomas O.
- A) →
- Cahn, Cathy
- B) →
- Canen, Franklin R.
- C) → _____
- Cohan, Martha
- D) →
- Cohen, Phillip
- E) →

27. Murshente, Betsy
- A) →
- Murray, Michael
- B) →
- Murtaugh, Danny
- C) → _____
- Muscente, Kathlene
- D) →
- Musgrove, Stanley A.
- E) →

28. Myers, Arthur G.
- A) →
- Meyers, Alma
- B) →
- Meyers, Arno
- C) → _____
- Meyers, Eleanor G.
- D) →
- Meyers, Terrence
- E) →

29. DiBenedetto, Arlene
- A) →
- Dembroski, Arnie
- B) →
- DeMers, Charlene
- C) → _____
- deSchultis, Gloria
- D) →
- D'Hoop, Josephine
- E) →

30. Nalchaian, Samuel
- A) →
- Najera, Irma
- B) →
- Nakamura, Norman T.
- C) → _____
- Nakano, Elizabeth
- D) →
- Nance, Jack
- E) →

ANSWER EXPLANATIONS FOR PRACTICE SET 5

1. **(D)** Sanlutent, Wilfred
   SanMarco, Antonio
   SanMiguel, Maria
2. **(C)** Artz, M. G.
   Arunges, Artin
   Arutyun, Adam
3. **(E)** Falck, Raymond
   Felard, Stephanie
4. **(C)** Aryee, Enoch
   Aryzinault, Paul
   Arzola, Luz
5. **(D)** Merkley, Allen L.
   Merlino, Flavio
   Merluzzo, Paul Michael
6. **(A)** *Soleman, Brooke G.*
   Solmon, Sylvia
7. **(C)** Smith, Richard
   Smith, Robert Z.
   Smith, Rodney
8. **(C)** Kuhl, Gregory
   Kuhn, Frank P.
   Kuhner, Maryann
9. **(C)** Rueben, Eva Reed
   Ruebhausen, F. Paul
   Ruebin, Caroline
10. **(E)** Farmer, Susan H.
    Farnham, Dennis
11. **(E)** Flynn, Nina
    Flynt, Clinton D.
12. **(C)** Rudnik, M. A.
    Ruffin, Margaret G.
    Rugley, Francis
13. **(E)** Deverend, Oscar
    Devile, Albert
14. **(D)** Fought, Kenneth
    Fouhner, Esta C.
    Foulkes, Thomas
15. **(D)** Carnicelli, Ruben
    Carnieski, Morris
    Carnow, Martin A.
16. **(C)** Flores, Louis
    Floretta, Philip
    Florez, Didi S.
17. **(D)** Irena, Perris
    Irie, Kris
    Iris, Carol
18. **(B)** Jacksen, Peter
    Jackson, J. P.
    Jackson, James
19. **(E)** Berkquist, Peter
    Berland, Helen Ann
20. **(D)** Berry, C. Douglas
    Berry, Charles
    Berry, Jonathan
21. **(C)** MacMullory, Nigel
    McAllister, Virginia
    McNoughton, Foster

22. (D) Kramer, E. J.
    Kramer, Edward
    Kramer, Rubin
23. (C) Jura, John
    Jurimasat, Patricia
    Jurow, Stasia
24. (B) Hardin, Timothy
    Harding, Gary
    Harding, Gary D.
25. (B) O'Donnell, William
    O'Reilley, Sarah
    Orofino, Roger
26. (A) *Cahan, Thomas O.*
    Cahn, Cathy
27. (B) Murray, Michael
    Murshente, Betsy
    Murtaugh, Danny
28. (E) Meyers, Terrence
    Myers, Arthur G.
29. (E) D'Hoop, Josephine
    DiBenedetto, Arlene
30. (D) Nakano, Elizabeth
    Nalchaian, Samuel
    Nance, Jack

PRACTICE SET 6

Find the correct place for the name in the box, and mark the letter of that space as your answer.

1. Mercadante, Alicia
   - A) →
     - Mensor, Arthur C.
   - B) →
     - Meono, Michael
   - C) →
     - Mercado, Mary
   - D) →
     - Mercer, Elmer
   - E) →

2. Hawkins, Mary
   - A) →
     - Hawkins, M. C.
   - B) →
     - Hawkins, Nick
   - C) →
     - Hawkins, Odie
   - D) →
     - Hawkins, Phillipa
   - E) →

3. Bujol, Leslie
   - A) →
     - Buitrago, Belma
   - B) →
     - Buiza, Carmen
   - C) →
     - Buizzie, Ralph
   - D) →
     - Sukowski, Richard
   - E) →

4. Gomez, Anna
   - A) →
     - Gomes, Peter
   - B) →
     - Gomes, Ricardo
   - C) →
     - Gomes, Rosalina
   - D) →
     - Gomes, Steven
   - E) →

5. Rubenstein, Blanche
   - A) →
     - Rubey, Michelle
   - B) →
     - Rubins, Brady
   - C) →
     - Rubrick, Michael
   - D) →
     - Ruffert, Maggy
   - E) →

6. Sobel, Allyn D.
   - A) →
     - Snow, Wade
   - B) →
     - Snyder, Libbie
   - C) →
     - Sonsini, P.
   - D) →
     - Soria, Erica
   - E) →

7. SanBenito, Adele
   - A) →
     - Sabo, George
   - B) →
     - Sabocur, Dwight
   - C) →
     - Sabosian, Dorothy
   - D) →
     - Saobine, Judith
   - E) →

8. McEnninger, Vivian
   - A) →
     - McElleny, Thomas
   - B) →
     - McElroy, Anna
   - C) →
     - McEnney, Hazel
   - D) →
     - McEntosh, Belle
   - E) →

9. MacLoughlin, Tom
   - A) →
     - McLin, Susan
   - B) →
     - McLing, James
   - C) →
     - McLoughlin, Peter
   - D) →
     - McMahan, Daisy
   - E) →

10. Mechira, MaryLou
- A) →
- McWilliams, Robt.
- B) →
- Mead, Clark
- C) → ____
- Meador, Wilma
- D) →
- Means, T. R.
- E) →

11. Jacksen, H. Olive
- A) →
- Jacksen, Jennie
- B) →
- Jacksen, Rob
- C) → ____
- Jackson, Eric
- D) →
- Jakcson, Frances
- E) →

12. Kimstein, Dae
- A) →
- Kimsey, T.
- B) →
- Kimura, Kane
- C) → ____
- Kinard, Ernie
- D) →
- Kindred, Daryl
- E) →

13. vanEgan, Gino
- A) →
- Vanegas, Jose
- B) →
- Vaneman, Peter
- C) → ____
- Vanen, Caroline
- D) →
- vanGas, Ruta
- E) →

14. Hansen, Martin
- A) →
- Hansen, Mark
- B) →
- Hansen, Martha
- C) → ____
- Hansen, Mel
- D) →
- Hansen, O. Richard
- E) →

15. Townsley, Yoko
- A) →
- Townsend, Douglas
- B) →
- Townsends, Bart
- C) → ____
- Townshend, Faith
- D) →
- Townshend, Teresa
- E) →

16. Vann, David
- A) →
- VanLuchem, Stanley
- B) →
- Van Mar, Derry
- C) → ____
- van Northwick, Evelyn
- D) →
- Vanowen, Victor
- E) →

17. Cutler, Phillis
- A) →
- Cutler, Morris
- B) →
- Cutler, P. Ernest
- C) → ____
- Cutler, Verna
- D) →
- Cutler, Yolanda
- E) →

18. Menzer, Gary
- A) →
- Mentzer, Toni
- B) →
- Mentzies, Pauolo
- C) → ____
- Menzies, Aaron
- D) →
- Menzies, Caren
- E) →

19. Axelrod, Petros
- A) →
- Awad, Henry
- B) →
- Awaya, Robert
- C) → ____
- Awburn, Dorothy
- D) →
- Awramento, N. G.
- E) →

20. Worster, Judith
- A) →
- Wolfe, Thomas
- B) →
- Wolfeson, Harmon
- C) → ____
- Wolfestein, Terry
- D) →
- Wortman, Ed
- E) →

21. Koro, Lena
- A) →
- Korkey, Herbert
- B) →
- Korkie, Andrew W.
- C) → ____
- Korman, Don
- D) →
- Kornay, Leslie
- E) →

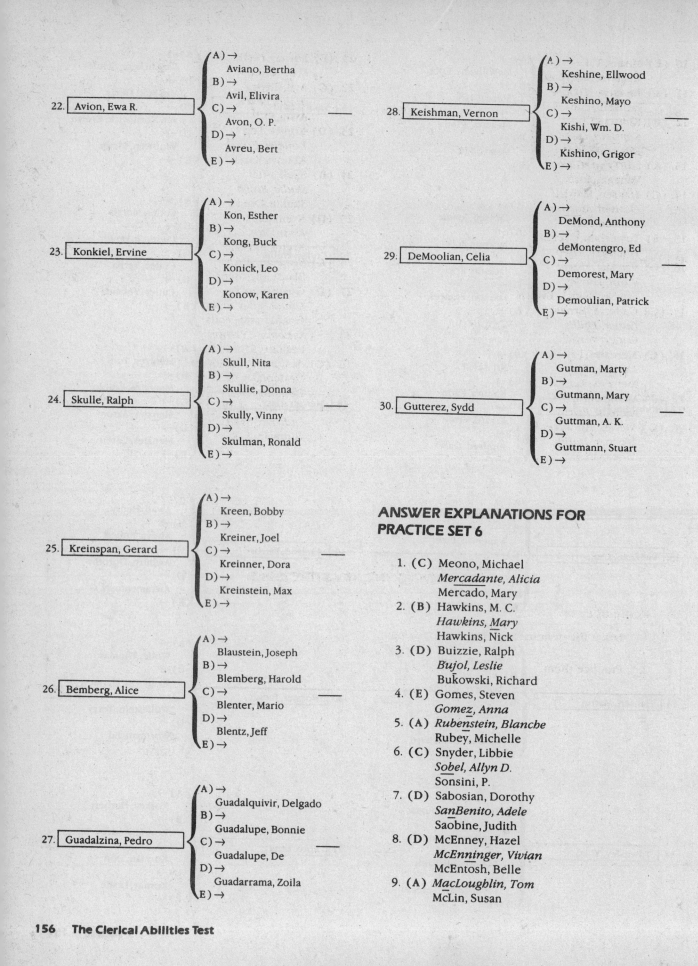

22. Avion, Ewa R.
- A) →
- Aviano, Bertha
- B) →
- Avil, Elivira
- C) →
- Avon, O. P.
- D) →
- Avreu, Bert
- E) →
_____

23. Konkiel, Ervine
- A) →
- Kon, Esther
- B) →
- Kong, Buck
- C) →
- Konick, Leo
- D) →
- Konow, Karen
- E) →
_____

24. Skulle, Ralph
- A) →
- Skull, Nita
- B) →
- Skullie, Donna
- C) →
- Skully, Vinny
- D) →
- Skulman, Ronald
- E) →
_____

25. Kreinspan, Gerard
- A) →
- Kreen, Bobby
- B) →
- Kreiner, Joel
- C) →
- Kreinner, Dora
- D) →
- Kreinstein, Max
- E) →
_____

26. Bemberg, Alice
- A) →
- Blaustein, Joseph
- B) →
- Blemberg, Harold
- C) →
- Blenter, Mario
- D) →
- Blentz, Jeff
- E) →
_____

27. Guadalzina, Pedro
- A) →
- Guadalquivir, Delgado
- B) →
- Guadalupe, Bonnie
- C) →
- Guadalupe, De
- D) →
- Guadarrama, Zoila
- E) →
_____

28. Keishman, Vernon
- A) →
- Keshine, Ellwood
- B) →
- Keshino, Mayo
- C) →
- Kishi, Wm. D.
- D) →
- Kishino, Grigor
- E) →
_____

29. DeMoolian, Celia
- A) →
- DeMond, Anthony
- B) →
- deMontengro, Ed
- C) →
- Demorest, Mary
- D) →
- Demoulian, Patrick
- E) →
_____

30. Gutterez, Sydd
- A) →
- Gutman, Marty
- B) →
- Gutmann, Mary
- C) →
- Guttman, A. K.
- D) →
- Guttmann, Stuart
- E) →
_____

ANSWER EXPLANATIONS FOR PRACTICE SET 6

1. (C) Meono, Michael
   Mercadante, Alicia
   Mercado, Mary
2. (B) Hawkins, M. C.
   Hawkins, Mary
   Hawkins, Nick
3. (D) Buizzie, Ralph
   Bujol, Leslie
   Bukowski, Richard
4. (E) Gomes, Steven
   Gomez, Anna
5. (A) *Rubenstein, Blanche*
   Rubey, Michelle
6. (C) Snyder, Libbie
   Sobel, Allyn D.
   Sonsini, P.
7. (D) Sabosian, Dorothy
   SanBenito, Adele
   Saobine, Judith
8. (D) McEnney, Hazel
   McEnninger, Vivian
   McEntosh, Belle
9. (A) *MacLoughlin, Tom*
   McLin, Susan

10. **(E)** Means, T. R.
Mechira, MaryLou

11. **(A)** *Jacksen, H. Olive*
Jacksen, Jennie

12. **(B)** Kimsey, T.
Kimstein, Dae
Kimura, Kane

13. **(A)** *vanEgan, Gino*
Vanegas, Jose

14. **(C)** Hansen, Martha
Hansen, Martin
Hansen, Mel

15. **(E)** Townshend, Teresa
Townsley, Yoko

16. **(C)** Van Mar, Derry
Vann, David
van Northwick, Evelyn

17. **(C)** Cutler, P. Ernest
Cutler, Phillis
Cutler, Verna

18. **(C)** Mentzies, Pauolo
Menzer, Gary
Menzies, Aaron

19. **(E)** Awramento, N. G.
Axelrod, Petros

20. **(D)** Wolfestein, Terry
Worster, Judith
Wortman, Ed

21. **(E)** Kornay, Leslie
Koro, Lena

22. **(C)** Avil, Elivira
Avion, Ewa R.
Avon, O. P.

23. **(D)** Konick, Leo
Konkiel, Ervine
Konow, Karen

24. **(B)** Skull, Nita
Skulle, Ralph
Skullie, Donna

25. **(D)** Kreinner, Dora
Kreinspan, Gerard
Kreinstein, Max

26. **(A)** *Bemberg, Alice*
Blaustein, Joseph

27. **(D)** Guadalupe, De
Guadalzina, Pedro
Guadarrama, Zoila

28. **(A)** *Keishman, Vernon*
Keshine, Ellwood

29. **(C)** deMontengro, Ed
DeMoolian, Celia
Demorest, Mary

30. **(C)** Gutmann, Mary
Gutterez, Sydd
Guttman, A. K.

REVIEWING THE KEY STRATEGIES

Remember to:

1. Learn the definite rules for alphabetizing.

2. Practice them.

ARITHMETIC COMPUTATIONAL SKILLS

These question types measure your ability to do simple computations, without the use of an adding machine or calculator. There are four types of questions: addition, subtraction, multiplication, and division.

ADDITION

Add: 19
    + 23

To answer this question type you must be familiar with basic addition facts (for example, 9 + 3 = 12). You should also know how to "carry." In the example just given, for the ones column 9 + 3 equals 12. The 2 is written in the total ones column, but the 1 (from the 12) is carried to the tens column, which now equals 1 + 1 + 2 = 4. The answer is 42.

$$
\begin{array}{r}
^1 19 \\
+ 23 \\
\hline
42
\end{array}
$$

SUBTRACTION

Subtract: 92
        − 37

To answer this question type, you must be familiar with basic subtraction facts (for example, 12 − 7 = 5). You should also know how to "borrow." Notice in the example just given, in the one's column, you cannot compute 2 − 7. Therefore, you must borrow a 1 (which means 10) from the 9 (ninety), and add it to the 2, which now becomes 12:

$$
\begin{array}{r}
8 \\
9^1 2 \\
− 3 7
\end{array}
$$

When you borrow 1 (ten) from the 9 (tens), the 9 (ninety) now becomes 8 (eighty), and the 2 becomes 12. Now you can subtract in the ones column, 12 − 7 = 5, and in the tens column, 8 − 3 = 5. The answer is 55.

$$
\begin{array}{r}
8 \\
9^1 2 \\
− 3 7 \\
\hline
5 5
\end{array}
$$

A TIP: You may check your subtraction, by adding up from the total. In this example:

$$
\begin{array}{r}
9 2 \\
− 3 7 \\
\hline
5 5
\end{array}
$$

Does 55 + 37 = 92? It should, if 55 is the correct answer. If it does not, then you have made a calculation error.

MULTIPLICATION

Multiply: 46
        × 3

To answer this question type, you must be familiar with basic multiplication skills (times tables). You should also know how to "carry." In the example just given, the 3 is first multiplied with the 6:

$$
\begin{array}{r}
^1 46 \\
× 3 \\
\hline
8
\end{array}
$$

3 × 6 = 18. Notice that the 8 is placed in the ones column, but the 1 (ten) is carried to the tens column. Now the 4 is multiplied by the 3: 3 × 4 = 12. And the "1" (ten) carried over is added on to the 12: 12 + 1 = 13.

$$
\begin{array}{r}
^1 46 \\
× 3 \\
\hline
138
\end{array}
$$

DIVISION

Divide: 6) 258

To answer this question type, you must be familiar with basic division skills (for example, 15 divided by 3 = 5). You should also know how to do simple "long division." In the example just given, 6 does not go into 2, but it will go into 25 a total of 4 times. Write the 4 above the 5 in 25:

$$
\begin{array}{r}
4 \\
6) \overline{258}
\end{array}
$$

Now multiply 4 × 6, and write the answer, 24, below the 25:

$$
\begin{array}{r}
4 \\
6) \overline{258} \\
24
\end{array}
$$

Now subtract:

$$
\begin{array}{r}
4 \\
6\,\overline{)\,258} \\
\underline{24} \\
1
\end{array}
$$

Now "bring down" the next digit, 8:

$$
\begin{array}{r}
4 \\
6\,\overline{)\,258} \\
\underline{24} \\
18
\end{array}
$$

Does 6 go into 18? Yes, 3 times. Therefore, write 3 on the line above the 8:

$$
\begin{array}{r}
43 \\
6\,\overline{)\,258} \\
\underline{24} \\
18
\end{array}
$$

Now multiply, as before: $3 \times 6 = 18$. Write that below the 18 and subtract:

$$
\begin{array}{r}
43 \\
6\,\overline{)\,258} \\
\underline{24} \\
18 \\
\underline{18} \\
0
\end{array}
$$

Since the difference is 0, there is no remainder. (The questions on your test will not have any remainder answer.) The final answer is 43.

A TIP: One quick way to check your answer is to multiply it by the divisor: in this case, 43×6. The result should be 258.

HELPFUL TECHNIQUES AND STRATEGIES

1. Review the basic addition and subtraction facts, as well as the multiplication (times tables) and division facts, long before taking your exam. If you are weak in any area, try to strengthen your skills in that area so that it will not slow you down when you are taking the test.

2. Practice the many arithmetic question types in this book to increase your speed, skill, and confidence.

3. Although the words "add," "subtract," "divide," or "multiply" are printed above each arithmetic question on the actual test, it is wise also to look at the "sign" in the question. For example:
   Subtract:

   $$
   \begin{array}{r}
   85 \\
   -\ 32
   \end{array}
   $$

The minus sign reinforces this as a subtraction problem. Under time and test pressure it can be easy to make a careless mistake and *add* when you should be *subtracting*. Looking at the sign will help reinforce the operation required.

4. All the problems have answer (E), "none of these." If the answer you arrive at is not listed in choices (A), (B), (C), or (D), then you are to choose answer (E).

5. As with the other question types on the test, if any particular question gives you trouble, then skip it; if you can eliminate one choice take a guess, or come back to it later if time permits.

PRACTICE SET 1

Make the following computations, and indicate which of the answer choices is the correct one.

Answers

1. Add:
82
+ 41

A) 121 B) 123
C) 133 D) 141
E) none of these

_____

2. Subtract:
90
− 31

A) 59 B) 61
C) 63 D) 69
E) none of these

_____

3. Multiply:
57
× 2

A) 104 B) 114
C) 124 D) 134
E) none of these

_____

4. Divide:
7) 602

A) 68 B) 76
C) 86 D) 88
E) none of these

_____

5. Add:
24
+ 16

A) 30 B) 40
C) 50 D) 60
E) none of these

_____

6. Subtract:
86
− 21

A) 57 B) 65
C) 67 D) 78
E) none of these

_____

7. Multiply:
85
× 5

A) 405 B) 415
C) 425 D) 435
E) none of these

_____

8. Divide:
2) 682

A) 324 B) 340
C) 341 D) 342
E) none of these

_____

9. Add:
123
+ 348

A) 461 B) 463
C) 471 D) 473
E) none of these

_____

10. Subtract:
88
− 31

A) 57 B) 59
C) 67 D) 119
E) none of these

_____

11. Multiply:
72
× 3

A) 213 B) 246
C) 261 D) 266
E) none of these

_____

12. Divide:
6) 630

A) 102 B) 105
C) 150 D) 160
E) none of these

_____

Answers

13. Add:
91
+ 45

A) 126 B) 136
C) 146 D) 156
E) none of these

_____

14. Subtract:
72
− 14

A) 52 B) 58
C) 62 D) 68
E) none of these

_____

15. Multiply:
52
× 8

A) 406 B) 412
C) 416 D) 418
E) none of these

_____

16. Divide:
9) 981

A) 19 B) 101
C) 109 D) 190
E) none of these

_____

17. Add:
82
+ 14

A) 76 B) 84
C) 86 D) 92
E) none of these

_____

18. Subtract:
89
− 14

A) 73 B) 75
C) 85 D) 93
E) none of these

_____

19. Multiply:
23
× 7

A) 141 B) 151
C) 171 D) 181
E) none of these

_____

20. Divide:
6) 204

A) 34 B) 36
C) 44 D) 48
E) none of these

_____

21. Add:
36
+ 57

A) 81 B) 83
C) 91 D) 93
E) none of these

_____

22. Subtract:
162
− 87

A) 65 B) 75
C) 77 D) 85
E) none of these

_____

23. Multiply:
28
× 5

A) 140 B) 144
C) 160 D) 164
E) none of these

_____

24. Divide:
5) 350

A) 70 B) 71
C) 75 D) 80
E) none of these

_____

25. Add:
36
+ 52

A) 84 B) 86
C) 88 D) 98
E) none of these

_____

26. Subtract:
    82
  − 17

Answers
A) 63   B) 65
C) 73   D) 75
E) none of these
_____

27. Multiply:
    72
  × 4

A) 282   B) 284
C) 288   D) 298
E) none of these
_____

28. Divide:

  4)860

A) 205   B) 215
C) 225   D) 235
E) none of these
_____

29. Add:
    29
  + 35

A) 64   B) 66
C) 68   D) 74
E) none of these
_____

30. Subtract:
    134
  − 21

A) 113   B) 118
C) 123   D) 128
E) none of these
_____

ANSWERS FOR PRACTICE SET 1

1. (B) 123
2. (A) 59
3. (B) 114
4. (C) 86
5. (B) 40
6. (B) 65
7. (C) 425
8. (C) 341
9. (C) 471
10. (A) 57
11. (E) Correct answer: 216.
12. (B) 105
13. (B) 136
14. (B) 58
15. (C) 416
16. (C) 109
17. (E) Correct answer: 96.
18. (B) 75
19. (E) Correct answer: 161.
20. (A) 34
21. (D) 93
22. (B) 75
23. (A) 140
24. (A) 70
25. (C) 88
26. (B) 65
27. (C) 288
28. (B) 215
29. (A) 64
30. (A) 113

PRACTICE SET 2

Make the following computations, and indicate which of the answer choices is the correct one.

Answers

1. Multiply:
    30
  × 4

A) 12   B) 102
C) 120   D) 140
E) none of these
_____

2. Divide:

  9)810

A) 19   B) 91
C) 99   D) 100
E) none of these
_____

3. Add:
    32
  + 84

A) 106   B) 108
C) 110   D) 118
E) none of these
_____

4. Subtract:
    93
  − 15

A) 77   B) 78
C) 88   D) 93
E) none of these
_____

5. Multiply:
    82
  × 5

A) 401   B) 410
C) 411   D) 420
E) none of these
_____

6. Divide:

  7)497

A) 17   B) 70
C) 71   D) 77
E) none of these
_____

7. Add:
    15
  + 82

A) 83   B) 87
C) 93   D) 98
E) none of these
_____

8. Subtract:
    89
  − 34

A) 54   B) 55
C) 65   D) 66
E) none of these
_____

9. Multiply:
    54
  × 4

A) 216   B) 226
C) 236   D) 264
E) none of these
_____

10. Divide:

  3)219

A) 71   B) 72
C) 73   D) 75
E) none of these
_____

11. Add:
    74
  + 18

A) 82   B) 84
C) 92   D) 94
E) none of these
_____

12. Subtract:
    71
  − 13

A) 58   B) 62
C) 63   D) 68
E) none of these
_____

13. Multiply:
    38
    × 5
    A) 150 B) 154
    C) 180 D) 190
    E) none of these
    _____

26. Divide:
    8) 648
    A) 80 B) 81
    C) 88 D) 91
    E) none of these
    _____

14. Divide:
    9) 720
    A) 8   B) 18
    C) 80 D) 81
    E) none of these
    _____

27. Add:
    26
    + 39
    A) 64 B) 65
    C) 67 D) 75
    E) none of these
    _____

15. Add:
    39
    + 52
    A) 81 B) 87
    C) 91 D) 97
    E) none of these
    _____

28. Subtract:
    93
    − 51
    A) 38 B) 42
    C) 48 D) 52
    E) none of these
    _____

16. Subtract:
    92
    − 36
    A) 46 B) 48
    C) 56 D) 58
    E) none of these
    _____

29. Multiply:
    84
    × 3
    A) 222 B) 322
    C) 332 D) 342
    E) none of these
    _____

17. Multiply:
    23
    × 6
    A) 128 B) 135
    C) 136 D) 148
    E) none of these
    _____

30. Divide:
    5) 325
    A) 55 B) 61
    C) 65 D) 68
    E) none of these
    _____

18. Divide:
    7) 357
    A) 50 B) 51
    C) 53 D) 57
    E) none of these
    _____

ANSWERS FOR PRACTICE SET 2

19. Add:
    38
    + 45
    A) 73 B) 78
    C) 80 D) 83
    E) none of these
    _____

20. Subtract:
    95
    − 32
    A) 60 B) 62
    C) 67 D) 73
    E) none of these
    _____

21. Multiply:
    15
    × 7
    A) 85   B) 95
    C) 105 D) 115
    E) none of these
    _____

22. Divide:
    6) 366
    A) 60 B) 61
    C) 66 D) 71
    E) none of these
    _____

23. Add:
    19
    + 57
    A) 76 B) 79
    C) 84 D) 86
    E) none of these
    _____

24. Subtract:
    93
    − 48
    A) 35 B) 45
    C) 55 D) 58
    E) none of these
    _____

25. Multiply:
    19
    × 7
    A) 103 B) 113
    C) 133 D) 153
    E) none of these
    _____

1. (C) 120
2. (E) Correct answer: 90.
3. (E) Correct answer: 116.
4. (B) 78
5. (B) 410
6. (C) 71
7. (E) Correct answer: 97.
8. (B) 55
9. (A) 216
10. (C) 73
11. (C) 92
12. (A) 58
13. (D) 190
14. (C) 80
15. (C) 91
16. (C) 56
17. (E) Correct answer: 138.
18. (B) 51
19. (D) 83
20. (E) Correct answer: 63.
21. (C) 105
22. (B) 61
23. (A) 76
24. (B) 45
25. (C) 133
26. (B) 81
27. (B) 65
28. (B) 42
29. (E) Correct answer: 252
30. (C) 65

PRACTICE SET 3

Make the following computations, and indicate which of the answer choices is the correct one.

Answers

1. Add:
   25
   + 36

   A) 51 B) 61
   C) 63 D) 71
   E) none of these _____

2. Subtract:
   71
   − 35

   A) 34 B) 36
   C) 46 D) 56
   E) none of these _____

3. Multiply:
   17
   × 4

   A) 28 B) 48
   C) 58 D) 68
   E) none of these _____

4. Divide:
   7) 287

   A) 41 B) 47
   C) 51 D) 57
   E) none of these _____

5. Add:
   44
   + 71

   A) 105 B) 113
   C) 115 D) 125
   E) none of these _____

6. Multiply:
   23
   × 9

   A) 181 B) 191
   C) 201 D) 207
   E) none of these _____

7. Subtract:
   53
   − 21

   A) 21 B) 23
   C) 32 D) 33
   E) none of these _____

8. Divide:
   8) 168

   A) 12 B) 20
   C) 21 D) 22
   E) none of these _____

9. Add:
   19
   + 56

   A) 65 B) 77
   C) 78 D) 85
   E) none of these _____

10. Multiply:
    22
    × 3

    A) 60 B) 62
    C) 66 D) 69
    E) none of these _____

11. Subtract:
    92
    − 13

    A) 71 B) 75
    C) 79 D) 81
    E) none of these _____

12. Divide:
    8) 248

    A) 13 B) 23
    C) 30 D) 31
    E) none of these _____

Answers

13. Add:
    49
    + 34

    A) 73 B) 81
    C) 85 D) 93
    E) none of these _____

14. Multiply:
    13
    × 6

    A) 48 B) 68
    C) 78 D) 88
    E) none of these _____

15. Subtract:
    89
    − 64

    A) 23 B) 27
    C) 35 D) 37
    E) none of these _____

16. Divide:
    7) 357

    A) 41 B) 50
    C) 55 D) 61
    E) none of these _____

17. Add:
    53
    + 25

    A) 77 B) 78
    C) 87 D) 88
    E) none of these _____

18. Subtract:
    84
    − 17

    A) 67 B) 69
    C) 75 D) 77
    E) none of these _____

19. Multiply:
    23
    × 3

    A) 66 B) 68
    C) 69 D) 96
    E) none of these _____

20. Divide:
    4) 256

    A) 61 B) 62
    C) 64 D) 66
    E) none of these _____

21. Add:
    17
    + 81

    A) 76 B) 88
    C) 97 D) 98
    E) none of these _____

22. Subtract:
    84
    − 13

    A) 61 B) 69
    C) 71 D) 73
    E) none of these _____

23. Multiply:
    24
    × 7

    A) 148 B) 158
    C) 168 D) 188
    E) none of these _____

24. Divide:
    8) 648

    A) 81 B) 82
    C) 83 D) 84
    E) none of these _____

25. Add:
    28
    + 54

    A) 72 B) 74
    C) 82 D) 84
    E) none of these _____

26. Subtract:
93
− 31

Answers
A) 60   B) 61
C) 62   D) 63
E) none of these
_____

27. Multiply:
93
× 4

A) 362   B) 366
C) 372   D) 376
E) none of these
_____

28. Divide:
7)805

A) 113   B) 120
C) 125   D) 127
E) none of these
_____

29. Add:
83
+ 59

A) 132   B) 138
C) 142   D) 144
E) none of these
_____

30. Subtract:
169
− 23

A) 144   B) 146
C) 156   D) 158
E) none of these
_____

ANSWERS FOR PRACTICE SET 3

1. **(B)** 61
2. **(B)** 36
3. **(D)** 68
4. **(A)** 41
5. **(C)** 115
6. **(D)** 207
7. **(C)** 32
8. **(C)** 21
9. **(E)** Correct answer: 75.
10. **(C)** 66
11. **(C)** 79
12. **(D)** 31
13. **(E)** Correct answer: 83.
14. **(C)** 78
15. **(E)** Correct answer: 25.
16. **(E)** Correct answer: 51.
17. **(B)** 78
18. **(A)** 67
19. **(C)** 69
20. **(C)** 64
21. **(D)** 98
22. **(C)** 71
23. **(C)** 168
24. **(A)** 81
25. **(C)** 82
26. **(C)** 62
27. **(C)** 372
28. **(E)** Correct answer: 115.
29. **(C)** 142
30. **(B)** 146

PRACTICE SET 4

Make the following computations, and indicate which of the answer choices is the correct one.

Answers

1. Multiply:
82
× 7

A) 546   B) 564
C) 568   D) 574
E) none of these
_____

2. Divide:
5)850

A) 107   B) 130
C) 170   D) 190
E) none of these
_____

3. Add:
23
+ 81

A) 104   B) 106
C) 108   D) 114
E) none of these
_____

4. Subtract:
812
− 408

A) 402   B) 404
C) 408   D) 410
E) none of these
_____

5. Multiply:
92
× 3

A) 216   B) 236
C) 256   D) 276
E) none of these
_____

6. Divide:
8)648

A) 18   B) 80
C) 88   D) 89
E) none of these
_____

7. Add:
81
+ 18

A) 98   B) 99
C) 100   D) 109
E) none of these
_____

8. Subtract:
98
− 31

A) 37   B) 39
C) 67   D) 69
E) none of these
_____

9. Multiply:
72
× 4

A) 238   B) 288
C) 328   D) 368
E) none of these
_____

10. Divide:
7)497

A) 17   B) 70
C) 71   D) 701
E) none of these
_____

11. Add:
35
+ 81

A) 106   B) 111
C) 116   D) 119
E) none of these
_____

12. Subtract:
52
− 19

A) 31   B) 33
C) 41   D) 43
E) none of these
_____

13. Multiply:
106
× 5

A) 53   B) 503
C) 530 D) 630
E) none of these
_____

14. Divide:
6)612

A) 21   B) 102
C) 111 D) 112
E) none of these

15. Add:
123
+ 304

A) 227 B) 337
C) 427 D) 437
E) none of these
_____

16. Subtract:
82
− 31

A) 31   B) 41
C) 51   D) 61
E) none of these

17. Multiply:
72
× 8

A) 562 B) 566
C) 568 D) 574
E) none of these
_____

18. Divide:
4)256

A) 44   B) 46
C) 64   D) 66
E) none of these

19. Add:
19
+ 82

A) 81   B) 83
C) 91   D) 101
E) none of these
_____

20. Subtract:
101
− 48

A) 43   B) 45
C) 55   D) 58
E) none of these
_____

21. Multiply:
21
× 8

A) 160 B) 168
C) 169 D) 186
E) none of these
_____

22. Divide:
6)906

A) 115 B) 150
C) 151 D) 155
E) none of these
_____

23. Add:
56
+ 81

A) 135 B) 137
C) 139 D) 147
E) none of these
_____

24. Subtract:
92
− 31

A) 61   B) 63
C) 67   D) 71
E) none of these
_____

25. Multiply:
23
× 5

A) 105 B) 115
C) 135 D) 155
E) none of these
_____

26. Divide:
7)784

A) 112 B) 114
C) 118 D) 121
E) none of these
_____

27. Add:
62
+ 35

A) 93   B) 97
C) 107 D) 111
E) none of these
_____

28. Subtract:
148
− 74

A) 64   B) 68
C) 72   D) 74
E) none of these
_____

29. Multiply:
74
× 3

A) 144 B) 212
C) 222 D) 224
E) none of these
_____

30. Divide:
3)936

A) 302 B) 311
C) 313 D) 318
E) none of these
_____

ANSWERS FOR PRACTICE SET 4

1. (D) 574
2. (C) 170
3. (A) 104
4. (B) 404
5. (D) 276
6. (E) Correct answer: 81.
7. (B) 99
8. (C) 67
9. (B) 288
10. (C) 71
11. (C) 116
12. (B) 33
13. (C) 530
14. (B) 102
15. (C) 427
16. (C) 51
17. (E) Correct answer: 576.
18. (C) 64
19. (D) 101
20. (E) Correct answer: 53.
21. (B) 168
22. (C) 151
23. (B) 137
24. (A) 61
25. (B) 115
26. (A) 112
27. (B) 97
28. (D) 74
29. (C) 222
30. (E) Correct answer: 312.

PRACTICE SET 5

Make the following computations, and indicate which of the answer choices is the correct one.

1. Add:
   82
   + 21

   Answers
   A) 102 B) 113
   C) 137 D) 143
   E) none of these
   _____

2. Subtract:
   96
   − 41

   A) 45 B) 47
   C) 55 D) 57
   E) none of these
   _____

3. Multiply:
   81
   × 3

   A) 241 B) 243
   C) 253 D) 283
   E) none of these
   _____

4. Divide:
   8)840

   A) 15 B) 51
   C) 105 D) 150
   E) none of these
   _____

5. Add:
   87
   + 83

   A) 160 B) 170
   C) 180 D) 190
   E) none of these
   _____

6. Subtract:
   182
   − 31

   A) 111 B) 141
   C) 143 D) 151
   E) none of these
   _____

7. Multiply:
   71
   × 5

   A) 350 B) 355
   C) 365 D) 375
   E) none of these
   _____

8. Divide:
   7)910

   A) 13 B) 103
   C) 130 D) 133
   E) none of these
   _____

9. Add:
   283
   + 46

   A) 229 B) 289
   C) 329 D) 349
   E) none of these
   _____

10. Subtract:
    261
    − 130

    A) 130 B) 131
    C) 138 D) 141
    E) none of these
    _____

11. Multiply:
    23
    × 8

    A) 164 B) 174
    C) 184 D) 194
    E) none of these
    _____

12. Divide:
    4)484

    A) 112 B) 120
    C) 121 D) 122
    E) none of these
    _____

13. Add:
    92
    + 18

    Answers
    A) 100 B) 106
    C) 108 D) 110
    E) none of these
    _____

14. Subtract:
    82
    − 15

    A) 57 B) 59
    C) 67 D) 77
    E) none of these
    _____

15. Multiply:
    18
    × 3

    A) 34 B) 44
    C) 54 D) 64
    E) none of these
    _____

16. Divide:
    8)168

    A) 12 B) 22
    C) 24 D) 31
    E) none of these
    _____

17. Add:
    42
    + 57

    A) 92 B) 95
    C) 99 D) 109
    E) none of these
    _____

18. Subtract:
    130
    − 42

    A) 68 B) 78
    C) 88 D) 98
    E) none of these
    _____

19. Multiply:
    19
    × 7

    A) 123 B) 132
    C) 143 D) 153
    E) none of these
    _____

20. Divide:
    6)366

    A) 61 B) 66
    C) 71 D) 76
    E) none of these
    _____

21. Add:
    32
    + 81

    A) 131 B) 133
    C) 137 D) 141
    E) none of these
    _____

22. Subtract:
    122
    − 38

    A) 76 B) 84
    C) 86 D) 94
    E) none of these
    _____

23. Multiply:
    23
    × 4

    A) 82 B) 88
    C) 92 D) 104
    E) none of these
    _____

24. Divide:
    3)243

    A) 18 B) 38
    C) 80 D) 81
    E) none of these
    _____

25. Add:
    56
    + 32

    A) 84 B) 86
    C) 94 D) 98
    E) none of these
    _____

26. Subtract:
84
− 31

Answers
A) 47   B) 53
C) 55   D) 57
E) none of these
_____

27. Multiply:
96
× 4

A) 342   B) 344
C) 364   D) 384
E) none of these
_____

28. Divide:
$7\overline{)392}$

A) 52   B) 53
C) 54   D) 55
E) none of these
_____

29. Add:
472
+ 319

A) 781   B) 783
C) 791   D) 797
E) none of these
_____

30. Subtract:
94
− 25

A) 69   B) 71
C) 77   D) 79
E) none of these
_____

ANSWERS FOR PRACTICE SET 5

1. **(E)** Correct answer: 103.
2. **(C)** 55
3. **(B)** 243
4. **(C)** 105
5. **(B)** 170
6. **(D)** 151
7. **(B)** 355
8. **(C)** 130
9. **(C)** 329
10. **(B)** 131
11. **(C)** 184
12. **(C)** 121
13. **(D)** 110
14. **(C)** 67
15. **(C)** 54
16. **(E)** Correct answer: 21.
17. **(C)** 99
18. **(C)** 88
19. **(E)** Correct answer: 133.
20. **(A)** 61
21. **(E)** Correct answer: 113.
22. **(B)** 84
23. **(C)** 92
24. **(D)** 81
25. **(E)** Correct answer: 88.
26. **(B)** 53
27. **(D)** 384
28. **(E)** Correct answer: 56.
29. **(C)** 791
30. **(A)** 69

PRACTICE SET 6

Make the following computations, and indicate which of the answer choices is the correct one.

Answers

1. Multiply:
32
× 5

A) 150   B) 155
C) 160   D) 170
E) none of these
_____

2. Divide:
$8\overline{)248}$

A) 13   B) 30
C) 31   D) 41
E) none of these
_____

3. Add:
52
+ 49

A) 91   B) 97
C) 101   D) 103
E) none of these
_____

4. Subtract:
44
− 13

A) 19   B) 21
C) 31   D) 39
E) none of these
_____

5. Multiply:
28
× 6

A) 148   B) 168
C) 188   D) 208
E) none of these
_____

6. Divide:
$6\overline{)384}$

A) 34   B) 44
C) 64   D) 74
E) none of these
_____

7. Add:
123
+ 38

A) 141   B) 151
C) 161   D) 171
E) none of these
_____

8. Subtract:
47
− 19

A) 18   B) 26
C) 28   D) 36
E) none of these
_____

9. Multiply:
31
× 3

A) 39   B) 36
C) 91   D) 93
E) none of these
_____

10. Divide:
$2\overline{)572}$

A) 266   B) 271
C) 281   D) 286
E) none of these
_____

11. Add:
84
+ 32

A) 114   B) 118
C) 126   D) 132
E) none of these
_____

12. Subtract:
92
− 35

A) 57   B) 59
C) 63   D) 67
E) none of these
_____

13. Multiply:
81
× 4

A) 314   B) 324
C) 342   D) 432
E) none of these   _____

14. Divide:
3) 372
A) 122   B) 126
C) 128   D) 132
E) none of these   _____

15. Add:
95
+ 28
A) 121   B) 123
C) 131   D) 133
E) none of these   _____

16. Subtract:
142
− 71
A) 61   B) 71
C) 73   D) 79
E) none of these   _____

17. Multiply:
56
× 7
A) 352   B) 372
C) 392   D) 402
E) none of these   _____

18. Divide:
4) 108
A) 23   B) 27
C) 29   D) 32
E) none of these   _____

19. Add:
28
+ 91
A) 111   B) 119
C) 121   D) 127
E) none of these   _____

20. Subtract:
88
− 32
A) 54   B) 55
C) 56   D) 57
E) none of these   _____

21. Multiply:
17
× 7
A) 109   B) 119
C) 129   D) 131
E) none of these   _____

22. Divide:
9) 918
A) 92   B) 98
C) 102   D) 120
E) none of these   _____

23. Add:
57
+ 93
A) 141   B) 144
C) 153   D) 157
E) none of these   _____

24. Subtract:
108
− 21
A) 77   B) 78
C) 87   D) 97
E) none of these   _____

25. Multiply:
28
× 8
A) 164   B) 194
C) 204   D) 224
E) none of these   _____

26. Divide:
8) 624

A) 73   B) 78
C) 79   D) 83
E) none of these   _____

27. Add:
78
+ 45
A) 127   B) 132
C) 133   D) 143
E) none of these   _____

28. Subtract:
92
− 44
A) 46   B) 48
C) 52   D) 56
E) none of these   _____

29. Multiply:
18
× 4
A) 42   B) 52
C) 62   D) 72
E) none of these   _____

30. Divide:
7) 539
A) 73   B) 77
C) 79   D) 83
E) none of these   _____

ANSWERS FOR PRACTICE SET 6

1. (C) 160
2. (C) 31
3. (C) 101
4. (C) 31
5. (B) 168
6. (C) 64
7. (C) 161
8. (C) 28
9. (D) 93
10. (D) 286
11. (E) Correct answer: 116.
12. (A) 57
13. (B) 324
14. (E) Correct answer: 124.
15. (B) 123
16. (B) 71
17. (C) 392
18. (B) 27
19. (B) 119
20. (C) 56
21. (B) 119
22. (C) 102
23. (E) Correct answer: 150.
24. (C) 87
25. (D) 224
26. (B) 78
27. (E) Correct answer: 123.
28. (B) 48
29. (D) 72
30. (B) 77

PRACTICE SET 7

Make the following computations, and indicate which of the answer choices is the correct one.

Answers

1. Add:
   29
   + 47

   A) 66   B) 67
   C) 76   D) 78
   E) none of these   _____

2. Subtract:
   108
   − 32

   A) 66   B) 76
   C) 78   D) 88
   E) none of these   _____

3. Multiply:
   19
   × 8

   A) 132   B) 138
   C) 152   D) 158
   E) none of these   _____

4. Divide:
   8) 472

   A) 57   B) 58
   C) 59   D) 61
   E) none of these   _____

5. Add:
   147
   + 204

   A) 321   B) 331
   C) 341   D) 441
   E) none of these   _____

6. Subtract:
   75
   − 38

   A) 33   B) 37
   C) 39   D) 43
   E) none of these   _____

7. Multiply:
   210
   × 4

   A) 480   B) 640
   C) 840   D) 1040
   E) none of these   _____

8. Divide:
   9) 369

   A) 38   B) 39
   C) 41   D) 49
   E) none of these   _____

9. Add:
   27
   + 98

   A) 123   B) 125
   C) 127   D) 129
   E) none of these   _____

10. Subtract:
    92
    − 18

    A) 76   B) 78
    C) 84   D) 86
    E) none of these   _____

11. Multiply:
    35
    × 9

    A) 275   B) 295
    C) 305   D) 315
    E) none of these   _____

12. Divide:
    4) 3240

    A) 801   B) 810
    C) 811   D) 880
    E) none of these   _____

13. Add:
    483
    + 235

    A) 618   B) 638
    C) 718   D) 738
    E) none of these   _____

14. Subtract:
    92
    − 31

    A) 59   B) 61
    C) 69   D) 71
    E) none of these   _____

15. Multiply:
    19
    × 6

    A) 94   B) 96
    C) 104   D) 114
    E) none of these   _____

16. Divide:
    4) 488

    A) 64   B) 82
    C) 108   D) 112
    E) none of these   _____

17. Add:
    203
    + 318

    A) 511   B) 515
    C) 521   D) 535
    E) none of these   _____

18. Subtract:
    106
    − 48

    A) 54   B) 56
    C) 58   D) 62
    E) none of these   _____

19. Multiply:
    27
    × 7

    A) 169   B) 183
    C) 191   D) 199
    E) none of these   _____

20. Divide:
    3) 903

    A) 31   B) 301
    C) 311   D) 313
    E) none of these   _____

21. Add:
    39
    + 64

    A) 93   B) 95
    C) 103   D) 105
    E) none of these   _____

22. Subtract:
    98
    − 32

    A) 64   B) 66
    C) 68   D) 74
    E) none of these   _____

23. Multiply:
    32
    × 4

    A) 124   B) 128
    C) 132   D) 136
    E) none of these   _____

24. Divide:
    8) 656

    A) 80   B) 81
    C) 82   D) 83
    E) none of these   _____

25. Add:
    94
    + 32

    A) 124   B) 126
    C) 136   D) 144
    E) none of these   _____

26. Subtract:
    29
  − 14

Answers
A) 5   B) 13
C) 18 D) 19
E) none of these
_____

27. Multiply:
    13
  × 8

A) 84   B) 94
C) 104 D) 114
E) none of these
_____

28. Divide:
  7$\overline{)385}$

A) 51   B) 53
C) 55   D) 61
E) none of these
_____

29. Add:
    85
  + 66

A) 141 B) 143
C) 151 D) 153
E) none of these
_____

30. Subtract:
    92
  − 37

A) 53   B) 55
C) 65   D) 67
E) none of these
_____

ANSWERS FOR PRACTICE SET 7

1. (C) 76
2. (B) 76
3. (C) 152
4. (C) 59
5. (E) Correct answer: 351
6. (B) 37
7. (C) 840
8. (C) 41
9. (B) 125
10. (E) Correct answer: 74.
11. (D) 315
12. (B) 810
13. (C) 718
14. (B) 61
15. (D) 114
16. (E) Correct answer: 122.
17. (C) 521
18. (C) 58
19. (E) Correct answer: 189
20. (B) 301
21. (C) 103
22. (B) 66
23. (B) 128
24. (C) 82
25. (B) 126
26. (E) Correct answer: 15.
27. (C) 104
28. (C) 55
29. (C) 151
30. (B) 55

PRACTICE SET 8

Make the following computations, and indicate which of the answer choices is the correct one.

Answers

1. Multiply:
    23
  × 6

A) 122 B) 128
C) 138 D) 198
E) none of these
_____

2. Divide:
  4$\overline{)168}$

A) 41   B) 42
C) 43   D) 48
E) none of these
_____

3. Add:
    46
  + 31

A) 74   B) 75
C) 87   D) 89
E) none of these
_____

4. Subtract:
    98
  − 41

A) 55   B) 57
C) 67   D) 73
E) none of these
_____

5. Multiply:
    72
  × 8

A) 562 B) 566
C) 568 D) 576
E) none of these
_____

6. Divide:
  7$\overline{)637}$

A) 90   B) 91
C) 92   D) 97
E) none of these
_____

7. Add:
    23
  + 84

A) 107 B) 109
C) 117 D) 119
E) none of these
_____

8. Subtract:
    96
  − 31

A) 64   B) 65
C) 75   D) 86
E) none of these
_____

9. Multiply:
    19
  × 6

A) 54   B) 64
C) 104 D) 114
E) none of these
_____

10. Divide:
  6$\overline{)660}$

A) 11   B) 101
C) 112 D) 118
E) none of these
_____

11. Add:
    28
  + 57

A) 55   B) 65
C) 75   D) 85
E) none of these
_____

12. Subtract:
    92
  − 86

A) 2   B) 4
C) 6   D) 16
E) none of these
_____

13. Multiply:
    26
    × 4

Answers
A) 84   B) 88
C) 94   D) 114
E) none of these   ——

14. Divide:
   3)288

A) 92   B) 94
C) 96   D) 98
E) none of these   ——

15. Add:
   93
  + 41

A) 123   B) 134
C) 143   D) 144
E) none of these   ——

16. Subtract:
   75
  − 18

A) 53   B) 57
C) 63   D) 67
E) none of these   ——

17. Multiply:
   58
  × 3

A) 154   B) 164
C) 174   D) 182
E) none of these   ——

18. Divide:
   8)824

A) 13   B) 18
C) 103   D) 108
E) none of these   ——

19. Add:
   28
  + 38

A) 64   B) 66
C) 68   D) 76
E) none of these   ——

20. Subtract:
   81
  − 17

A) 64   B) 68
C) 74   D) 78
E) none of these   ——

21. Multiply:
   19
  × 8

A) 72   B) 92
C) 132   D) 152
E) none of these   ——

22. Divide:
   7)784

A) 111   B) 121
C) 122   D) 128
E) none of these   ——

23. Add:
   93
  + 81

A) 172   B) 174
C) 176   D) 178
E) none of these   ——

24. Subtract:
   82
  − 14

A) 62   B) 66
C) 68   D) 72
E) none of these   ——

25. Multiply:
   23
  × 4

A) 82   B) 102
C) 112   D) 122
E) none of these   ——

26. Divide:
   3)138

Answers
A) 42   B) 46
C) 64   D) 68
E) none of these   ——

27. Add:
   83
  + 95

A) 172   B) 175
C) 178   D) 183
E) none of these   ——

28. Subtract:
   134
  − 62

A) 70   B) 72
C) 78   D) 82
E) none of these   ——

29. Multiply:
   28
  × 5

A) 140   B) 150
C) 170   D) 190
E) none of these   ——

30. Divide:
   9)108

A) 12   B) 21
C) 28   D) 81
E) none of these   ——

ANSWERS FOR PRACTICE SET 8

1. (C) 138
2. (B) 42
3. (E) Correct answer: 77.
4. (B) 57
5. (D) 576
6. (B) 91
7. (A) 107
8. (B) 65
9. (D) 114
10. (E) Correct answer: 110.
11. (D) 85
12. (C) 6
13. (E) Correct answer: 104.
14. (C) 96
15. (B) 134
16. (B) 57
17. (C) 174
18. (C) 103
19. (B) 66
20. (A) 64
21. (D) 152
22. (E) Correct answer: 112.
23. (B) 174
24. (C) 68
25. (E) Correct answer: 92.
26. (B) 46
27. (C) 178
28. (B) 72
29. (A) 140
30. (A) 12

REVIEWING THE KEY STRATEGIES

Remember to:

1. Review the basic addition, subtraction, multiplication, and division facts.

2. Practice arithmetic questions to increase speed.

3. Look at the "sign" in each problem.

4. Note all problems also contain a choice (E), "none of the these."

5. Leave the difficult questions for last.

NUMBER AND LETTER SCRAMBLE

This question type tests your observation skills. You are given five sets of eight letters and numbers (four of each), followed by five suggested answers, (A), (B), (C), (D), and (E). Answer (E) is always "none of these." For example:

1. V 5 7 Z N 9 4 T

2. 4 6 P T 2 N K 9

3. 6 4 N 2 P 8 Z K

4. 7 P 5 2 4 N K T

5. K T 8 5 4 N 2 P

Suggested Answers
$$\begin{cases} A = 2, & 5, & N, & Z \\ B = 4, & 5, & N, & P \\ C = 2, & 9, & P, & T \\ D = 4, & 9, & T, & Z \\ E = \text{none of these} \end{cases}$$

For each numbered question, you must find which of the suggested answers contains letters and numbers *all,* of which appear in that question. For example, the answer to question 1 is (D), because all of the numbers and letters in answer (D) (4, 9, T, Z) appear in question 1.

SUGGESTED STRATEGY

Since the first problem is solved, let's go on to question 2. Place your finger so that it points to the numbers in question 2, and now look at the two numbers in (A): 2 and 5. Are they contained in question 2? The 2 is, but 5 is not, so go on to answer (B). The two numbers there are 4 and 5. The 4 is in question 2, but the 5 is not, so go on to answer (C). The two numbers there are 2 and 9, *both* of which are contained in question 2. So keep going in answer (C) to the letters: P and T. Are they contained in question 2? They are, so you can stop—the answer to question 2 is (C).

If either P or T were *not* contained in the question, you would then have gone on to answer (D). If the numbers and letters in (D) were not contained in question 2, you would then choose answer (E).

Now try practicing this technique to increase your skill and speed.

Reminders:

1. Only one suggested answer will be correct for each question.
2. A suggested answer, (A), (B), (C), (D), or (E), may be used more than once for different questions in each five-question set. For example, the answers to 1, 2, 3, 4 and 5 are (D), (C), (E), (B), and (B). Notice that the (B) answer appears twice in this set of five questions.

PRACTICE SET 1

For each of the following questions, find which one of the suggested answers appears in that question.

1. F 2 Q S W 4 3 9 _____

2. 5 Q 9 7 W 3 S Z _____

3. 5 Q 3 Z X W 7 9 _____

4. Z 2 S 3 Q 7 W 9 _____

5. 5 7 H W Q 9 J 4 _____

Suggested Answers
$\begin{cases} A = 9, \ 2, \ W, \ Q \\ B = 9, \ 5, \ Q, \ Z \\ C = 2, \ 3, \ W, \ H \\ D = 3, \ 5, \ H, \ Z \\ E = \text{none of these} \end{cases}$

6. Q 4 3 6 Z H 2 F _____

7. 7 4 2 X J 9 F Q _____

8. 6 9 4 Q 8 H J X _____

9. 8 7 J 9 4 F H X _____

10. F 5 4 X 8 2 S Q _____

Suggested Answers
$\begin{cases} A = 2, \ 7, \ H, \ Q \\ B = 4, \ 7, \ Q, \ X \\ C = 2, \ 8, \ X, \ F \\ D = 4, \ 8, \ H, \ F \\ E = \text{none of these} \end{cases}$

11. 5 9 4 H 3 S Z W _____

12. J 3 6 9 Z 5 X H _____

13. 2 4 3 J 8 X Z W _____

14. W 3 H 6 J 2 4 F _____

15. 3 H 9 8 Q 4 Z W _____

Suggested Answers
$\begin{cases} A = 3, \ 4, \ H, \ Z \\ B = 3, \ 6, \ W, \ H \\ C = 9, \ 4, \ W, \ J \\ D = 9, \ 6, \ J, \ Z \\ E = \text{none of these} \end{cases}$

16. 8 W F 2 J 3 5 Q _____

17. J 4 Q H 3 2 8 X _____

18. 7 9 X S 8 J F 4 _____

19. X S 8 F 4 J 7 6 _____

20. 4 Z 7 Q 9 8 X J _____

Suggested Answers
$\begin{cases} A = 3, \ 8, \ J, \ X \\ B = 3, \ 4, \ Q, \ F \\ C = 4, \ 7, \ J, \ F \\ D = 7, \ 8, \ Q, \ X \\ E = \text{none of these} \end{cases}$

21. 5 F Z Q 7 6 3 X _____

22. X 6 7 5 Q 4 S J _____

23. Q 6 S X 7 3 9 J _____

24. 6 7 W 3 2 X J Z _____

25. 3 7 W 9 Z Q 5 J _____

Suggested Answers
$\begin{cases} A = 9, \ 6, \ J, \ Q \\ B = 9, \ 7, \ Z, \ X \\ C = 5, \ 7, \ J, \ Z \\ D = 5, \ 6, \ Q, \ X \\ E = \text{none of these} \end{cases}$

26. X 4 6 F Q 8 3 Z _____

27. 3 5 S Z 9 Q H 8 _____

28. 5 3 Q 9 S 7 F H _____

29. 6 S 4 9 3 Q H Z _____

30. H Z 7 4 3 Q 9 S _____

Suggested Answers
$\begin{cases} A = 9, \ 4, \ Q, \ F \\ B = 3, \ 4, \ Q, \ S \\ C = 9, \ 8, \ S, \ Z \\ D = 3, \ 8, \ Z, \ F \\ E = \text{none of these} \end{cases}$

8. 5 7 6 M 3 I Z H   _____

9. H 6 X 9 M 5 7 Y   _____

10. 6 X 4 3 R 7 Z H   _____

Suggested Answers
$\begin{cases} A = 6, & 7, & X, & Z \\ B = 6, & 9, & H, & X \\ C = 4, & 7, & H, & M \\ D = 4, & 9, & M, & Z \\ E = \text{none of these} \end{cases}$

9.
10. (C) F
11. (A) 5 9 4 H 3 S Z W
12. (D) J 3 6 9 Z 5 X H
13. (E) 2 4 3 J 8 X Z W
14. (B) W 3 H 6 J 2 4 F
15. (A) 3 H 9 8 Q 4 Z W
16. (E) 8 W F 2 J 3 5 Q
17. (A) J 4 Q H 3 2 8 X
18. (C) 7 9 X S 8 J F 4
19. (C) X S 8 F 4 J 7 6
20. (D) 4 Z 7 Q 9 8 X J
21. (D) 5 F Z Q 7 6 3 X
22. (D) X 6 7 5 Q 4 S J
23. (A) Q 6 S X 7 3 9 J
24. (E) 6 7 W 3 2 X J Z
25. (C) 3 7 W 9 Z Q 5 J
26. (D) X 4 6 F Q 8 3 Z
27. (C) 3 5 S Z 9 Q H 8
28. (E) 5 3 Q 9 S 7 F H
29. (B) 6 S 4 9 3 Q H Z
30. (B) H Z 7 4 3 Q 9 S

11. 3 H Y 5 M 6 8 R   _____

12. M 7 R X 6 5 3 I   _____

13. 2 4 I U 3 M Y 7   _____

14. I U 3 Y 7 M 2 9   _____

15. 7 Z 2 R 4 3 I M   _____

Suggested Answers
$\begin{cases} A = 6, & 3, & M, & I \\ B = 6, & 7, & R, & Y \\ C = 7, & 2, & M, & Y \\ D = 2, & 3, & R, & I \\ E = \text{none of these} \end{cases}$

PRACTICE SET 2

For each of the following questions, find which one of the suggested answers appears in that question.

1. Y 5 R U H 7 6 4   _____

16. 8 Y Z R 2 9 6 I   _____

17. I 9 2 8 R 7 U M   _____

18. R 9 U I 2 6 4 M   _____

2. 8 R 4 2 H 6 U Z   _____

19. 9 2 H 6 5 I M Z   _____

3. 8 R 6 Z I H 2 4   _____

20. 6 2 H 4 Z R 8 M   _____

4. Z 5 U 6 R 2 H 4   _____

5. 8 9 X H R 4 M 7   _____

Suggested Answers
$\begin{cases} A = 4, & 5, & H, & R \\ B = 4, & 8, & R, & Z \\ C = 5, & 6, & H, & X \\ D = 6, & 8, & X, & Z \\ E = \text{none of these} \end{cases}$

Suggested Answers
$\begin{cases} A = 4, & 9, & M, & R \\ B = 4, & 2, & Z, & I \\ C = 8, & 2, & M, & Z \\ D = 8, & 9, & R, & I \\ E = \text{none of these} \end{cases}$

21. I 7 9 Y R 3 6 Z   _____

22. 6 8 U Z 4 R X 3   _____

6. 8 4 7 X 6 U Z H   _____

23. 8 6 R 4 U 2 Y X   _____

7. M 6 9 4 Z 8 I X   _____

24. 9 U 7 4 R X Z   _____

25. X Z 2 7 6 R 4 U   _____

Suggested Answers
$\begin{cases} A = 4, 7, R, Y \\ B = 6, 7, R, U \\ C = 4, 3, U, Z \\ D = 6, 3, Z, Y \\ E = \text{none of these} \end{cases}$

26. R 7 6 9 Z X 5 Y   ——

27. 2 7 5 I M 4 Y R   ——

28. 9 4 7 R 3 X M I   ——

29. 3 2 M 4 7 Y X I   ——

30. Y 8 7 I 3 5 U R   ——

Suggested Answers
$\begin{cases} A = 5, 2, X, R \\ B = 7, 2, R, I \\ C = 5, 3, I, Y \\ D = 7, 3, X, Y \\ E = \text{none of these} \end{cases}$

ANSWER EXPLANATIONS FOR PRACTICE SET 2

1. (A) Y 5 R U H 7 6 4
2. (B) 8 R 4 2 H 6 U Z
3. (B) 8 R 6 Z I H 2 4
4. (A) Z 5 U 6 R 2 H 4
5. (E) 8 9 X H R 4 M 7
6. (A) 8 4 7 X 6 U Z H
7. (D) M 6 9 4 Z 8 I X
8. (E) 5 7 6 M 3 I Z H
9. (B) H 6 X 9 M 5 7 Y
10. (A) 6 X 4 3 R 7 Z H
11. (E) 3 H Y 5 M 6 8 R
12. (A) M 7 R X 6 5 3 I
13. (C) 2 4 I U 3 M Y 7
14. (C) I U 3 Y 7 M 2 9
15. (D) 7 Z 2 R 4 3 I M
16. (D) 8 Y Z R 2 9 6 I
17. (D) I 9 2 8 R 7 U M
18. (A) R 9 U I 2 6 4 M
19. (E) 9 2 H 6 5 I M Z
20. (C) 6 2 H 4 Z R 8 M
21. (D) I 7 9 Y R 3 6 Z
22. (C) 6 8 U Z 4 R X 3
23. (E) 8 6 R 4 U 2 Y X
24. (E) 9 U 7 4 R X Z
25. (B) X Z 2 7 6 R 4 U
26. (E) R 7 6 9 Z X 5 Y
27. (B) 2 7 5 I M 4 Y R
28. (E) 9 4 7 R 3 X M I
29. (D) 3 2 M 4 7 Y X I
30. (C) Y 8 7 I 3 5 U R

PRACTICE SET 3

For each of the following questions, find which one of the suggested answers appears in that question.

1. Q 9 8 3 X Z 7 M   ——

2. 4 9 7 U W 6 M Q   ——

3. 3 6 9 Q 5 Z W U   ——

4. 5 4 W 6 9 M Z U   ——

5. M 2 9 U 5 7 R Q   ——

Suggested Answers
$\begin{cases} A = 7, 4, Z, Q \\ B = 9, 4, Q, U \\ C = 7, 5, U, M \\ D = 9, 5, Z, M \\ E = \text{none of these} \end{cases}$

6. U 9 3 M Q 5 8 X   ——

7. 8 2 R X 6 Q Z 5   ——

8. 2 8 Q 6 R 4 M Z   ——

9. 3 R 9 6 8 Q Z X   ——

10. Z X 4 9 8 Q 6 R   ——

Suggested Answers
$\begin{cases} A = 6, 9, Q, M \\ B = 8, 9, Q, R \\ C = 6, 5, R, X \\ D = 8, 5, X, M \\ E = \text{none of these} \end{cases}$

11. 2 M X Q 4 3 8 U   ——

12. U 3 4 2 Q 9 R W   ——

13. Q 3 R U 4 8 6 W   ——

14. 3 4 F 8 7 U W X   ——

15. 8 4 F 6 X Q 2 W   ——

Suggested Answers
$\begin{cases} A = 6, 3, W, Q \\ B = 6, 4, X, U \\ C = 2, 4, W, X \\ D = 2, 3, Q, U \\ E = \text{none of these} \end{cases}$

16. 5 F M 7 W 8 2 Q   ——

17. W 9 Q Z 8 7 5 U   ——

18. 4 6 U R 5 W M 9   ——

19. U R 5 M 9 W 4 3   ——

20. 9 X 4 Q 6 5 U W   ——

Suggested Answers
$\begin{cases} A = 8, & 5, & W, & U \\ B = 8, & 9, & Q, & M \\ C = 9, & 4, & W, & M \\ D = 4, & 5, & Q, & U \\ E = \text{none of these} \end{cases}$

21. 2 6 9 Z 8 R X F   ——

22. W 8 3 6 X 2 U Z   ——

23. 7 9 8 W 5 U X F   ——

24. F 8 Z 3 W 7 9 M   ——

25. 8 Z 6 5 Q 9 X F   ——

Suggested Answers
$\begin{cases} A = 8, & 9, & Z, & X \\ B = 8, & 3, & F, & Z \\ C = 6, & 9, & F, & W \\ D = 6, & 3, & W, & X \\ E = \text{none of these} \end{cases}$

26. M 7 Q R F 9 8 6   ——

27. 2 Q 6 4 F 8 R X   ——

28. 2 Q 8 X U F 4 6   ——

29. X 7 R 8 Q 4 F 6   ——

30. 2 3 Z F Q 6 W 9   ——

Suggested Answers
$\begin{cases} A = 6, & 7, & F, & Q \\ B = 6, & 2, & Q, & X \\ C = 7, & 8, & F, & Z \\ D = 8, & 2, & Z, & X \\ E = \text{none of these} \end{cases}$

ANSWER EXPLANATIONS FOR PRACTICE SET 3

1. (E) Q 9 8 3 X Z 7 M
2. (B) 4 9 7 U W 6 M Q
3. (E) 3 6 9 Q 5 Z W U
4. (D) 5 4 W 6 9 M Z U
5. (C) M 2 9 U 5 7 R Q
6. (D) U 9 3 M Q 5 8 X
7. (C) 8 2 R X 6 Q Z 5
8. (E) 2 8 Q 6 R 4 M Z
9. (B) 3 R 9 6 8 Q Z X
10. (B) Z X 4 9 8 Q 6 R
11. (D) 2 M X Q 4 3 8 U
12. (D) U 3 4 2 Q 9 R W
13. (A) Q 3 R U 4 8 6 W
14. (E) 3 4 F 8 7 U W X
15. (C) 8 4 F 6 X Q 2 W
16. (E) 5 F M 7 W 8 2 Q
17. (A) W 9 Q Z 8 7 5 U
18. (C) 4 6 U R 5 W M 9
19. (C) U R 5 M 9 W 4 3
20. (D) 9 X 4 Q 6 5 U W
21. (A) 2 6 9 Z 8 R X F
22. (D) W 8 3 6 X 2 U Z
23. (E) 7 9 8 W 5 U X F
24. (B) F 8 Z 3 W 7 9 M
25. (A) 8 Z 6 5 Q 9 X F
26. (A) M 7 Q R F 9 8 6
27. (B) 2 Q 6 4 F 8 R X
28. (B) 2 Q 8 X U F 4 6
29. (A) X 7 R 8 Q 4 F 6
30. (E) 2 3 Z F Q 6 W 9

PRACTICE SET 4

For each of the following questions, find which one of the suggested answers appears in that question.

1. 4 5 J Q M 8 H 3   ——

2. Y 9 R 2 M 6 Q 8   ——

3. 4 M 2 Y W Q 6 8   ——

4. 4 M 8 6 Q 2 R Y   ——

5. S 9 M R Q 3 2 8   ——

Suggested Answers
$\begin{cases} A = 8, & 9, & Q, & M \\ B = 8, & 4, & M, & Y \\ C = 9, & 2, & Q, & J \\ D = 2, & 4, & J, & Y \\ E = \text{none of these} \end{cases}$

6. 2 J 8 7 M 3 Y Q   ——

7. Q 2 J 5 H 9 3 S   ——

8. 9 3 2 H 7 W Y Q   ——

9. H 2 5 8 Y 4 W J   ——

10. 4 8 3 J 2 R Y Q   ——

Suggested Answers
{
A = 2, 3, J, Y
B = 2, 5, Q, J
C = 8, 3, Q, H
D = 8, 5, H, Y
E = none of these
}

11. 3 Y 6 M 8 7 W H   ——

12. W R 7 S 3 H 6 5   ——

13. 6 8 W R 7 H S 3   ——

14. H 3 M J 2 9 7 W   ——

15. 7 Q S 9 H 2 4 M   ——

Suggested Answers
{
A = 2, 7, H, W
B = 2, 3, M, S
C = 3, 6, H, S
D = 6, 7, M, W
E = none of these
}

16. 2 6 Q 8 Y M 4 H   ——

17. 5 6 Q 2 9 W H Y   ——

18. M 5 R W 6 2 8 H   ——

19. W 5 6 4 M 3 R H   ——

20. 4 S Y M 6 5 2 W   ——

Suggested Answers
{
A = 8, 5, H, M
B = 8, 6, Y, W
C = 4, 6, H, Y
D = 4, 5, M, W
E = none of these
}

21. J Y 6 3 2 M 8 R   ——

22. 5 R 3 8 2 M J Y   ——

23. 4 2 M 8 R 6 S J   ——

24. 2 4 R Y 8 M J 7   ——

25. W 3 5 S M 7 2 Y   ——

Suggested Answers
{
A = 8, 3, M, S
B = 2, 3, M, R
C = 8, 7, R, Y
D = 2, 7, Y, S
E = none of these
}

26. S 4 3 W 7 9 R M   ——

27. 7 6 H 8 3 S J W   ——

28. 5 8 3 M 7 J H W   ——

29. 6 3 9 W H 8 S M   ——

30. M 3 2 5 Y J 9 S   ——

Suggested Answers
{
A = 9, 6, J, M
B = 3, 6, M, W
C = 9, 7, W, S
D = 3, 7, J, S
E = none of these
}

ANSWER EXPLANATIONS FOR PRACTICE SET 4

1. (E) 4 5 J Q M 8 H 3
2. (A) Y 9 R 2 M 6 Q 8
3. (B) 4 M 2 Y W Q 6 8
4. (B) 4 M 8 6 Q 2 R Y
5. (A) S 9 M R Q 3 2 8
6. (A) 2 J 8 7 M 3 Y Q
7. (B) Q 2 J 5 H 9 3 S
8. (E) 9 3 2 H 7 W Y Q
9. (D) H 2 5 8 Y 4 W J
10. (A) 4 8 3 J 2 R Y Q
11. (D) 3 Y 6 M 8 7 W H
12. (C) W R 7 S 3 H 6 5
13. (C) 6 8 W R 7 H S 3
14. (A) H 3 M J 2 9 7 W
15. (E) 7 Q S 9 H 2 4 M
16. (C) 2 6 Q 8 Y M 4 H
17. (E) 5 6 Q 2 9 W H Y
18. (A) M 5 R W 6 2 8 H
19. (D) W 5 6 4 M 3 R H
20. (D) 4 S Y M 6 5 2 W
21. (B) J Y 6 3 2 M 8 R
22. (B) 5 R 3 8 2 M J Y
23. (E) 4 2 M 8 R 6 S J
24. (C) 2 4 R Y 8 M J 7
25. (D) W 3 5 S M 7 2 Y
26. (C) S 4 3 W 7 9 R M
27. (D) 7 6 H 8 3 S J W
28. (E) 5 8 3 M 7 J H W
29. (B) 6 3 9 W H 8 S M
30. (E) M 3 2 5 Y J 9 S

PRACTICE SET 5

For each of the following questions, find which one of the suggested answers appears in that question.

1. T 3 2 G 6 8 L K   ————

2. 6 5 P 7 2 T N G   ————

3. 4 7 2 K 6 N P G   ————

4. 5 2 8 G P 7 T K   ————

5. K 2 9 4 Z N 8 T   ————

Suggested Answers
$\begin{cases} A = 8, & 5, & N, & K \\ B = 2, & 5, & K, & G \\ C = 8, & 6, & G, & T \\ D = 2, & 6, & N, & T \\ E = \text{none of these} \end{cases}$

6. N Z 5 2 9 K 7 L   ————

7. 4 L 2 7 9 K N Z   ————

8. 3 9 K 7 L 5 T N   ————

9. 9 3 L Z 7 K N 6   ————

10. G 2 4 T K 6 9 Z   ————

Suggested Answers
$\begin{cases} A = 7, & 6, & Z, & T \\ B = 9, & 2, & K, & L \\ C = 7, & 6, & L, & Z \\ D = 9, & 6, & Z, & T \\ E = \text{none of these} \end{cases}$

11. 9 5 V 7 Z K 3 P   ————

12. 4 5 V 9 8 G P Z   ————

13. K 4 L G 5 9 7 P   ————

14. G 4 5 3 K 2 L P   ————

15. 3 T Z K 5 4 9 G   ————

Suggested Answers
$\begin{cases} A = 7, & 4, & P, & K \\ B = 7, & 5, & Z, & G \\ C = 3, & 5, & P, & Z \\ D = 3, & 4, & K, & G \\ E = \text{none of these} \end{cases}$

16. 2 Z 5 K 7 6 G P   ————

17. G L 6 T 2 P 5 4   ————

18. 5 7 G L 6 P T 2   ————

19. P 2 K N 9 8 6 G   ————

20. 6 V T 8 P 9 3 K   ————

Suggested Answers
$\begin{cases} A = 9, & 6, & P, & G \\ B = 9, & 2, & K, & T \\ C = 2, & 5, & P, & T \\ D = 5, & 6, & K, & G \\ E = \text{none of these} \end{cases}$

21. 9 N 7 6 K 2 Z V   ————

22. V 9 N 4 P 8 2 T   ————

23. 8 2 9 P 6 G Z V   ————

24. P 9 3 7 Z 3 G N   ————

25. 3 7 2 N 9 L Z V   ————

Suggested Answers
$\begin{cases} A = 9, & 2, & N, & Z \\ B = 9, & 3, & V, & N \\ C = 7, & 2, & V, & P \\ D = 7, & 3, & P, & Z \\ E = \text{none of these} \end{cases}$

26. 3 4 N V K 7 P 2   ————

27. Z 8 L 9 K 5 V 7   ————

28. 3 K 9 Z G V 5 7   ————

29. 3 K 7 5 V 9 L Z   ————

30. T 8 K L V 2 9 7   ————

Suggested Answers
$\begin{cases} A = 7, & 8, & V, & K \\ B = 7, & 3, & K, & Z \\ C = 8, & 9, & V, & N \\ D = 9, & 3, & N, & Z \\ E = \text{none of these} \end{cases}$

1. (C) T 3 2 G 6 8 L K
2. (D) 6 5 P 7 2 T N G
3. (E) 4 7 2 K 6 N P G
4. (B) 5 2 8 G P 7 T K
5. (E) K 2 9 4 Z N 8 T
6. (B) N Z 5 2 9 K 7 L
7. (B) 4 L 2 7 9 K N Z
8. (E) 3 9 K 7 L 5 T N
9. (C) 9 3 L Z 7 K N 6
10. (D) G 2 4 T K 6 9 Z
11. (C) 9 5 V 7 Z K 3 P
12. (E) 4 5 V 9 8 G P Z
13. (A) K 4 L G 5 9 7 P
14. (D) G 4 5 3 K 2 L P
15. (D) 3 T Z K 5 4 9 G

16. (D) 2 Z 5 K 7 6 G P
17. (C) G L 6 T 2 P 5 4
18. (C) 5 7 G L 6 P T 2
19. (A) P 2 K N 9 8 6 G
20. (E) 6 V T 8 P 9 3 K
21. (A) 9 N 7 6 K 2 Z V
22. (E) V 9 N 4 P 8 2 T
23. (E) 8 2 9 P 6 G Z V
24. (D) P 9 3 7 Z 3 G N
25. (A) 3 7 2 N 9 L Z V
26. (E) 3 4 N V K 7 P 2
27. (A) Z 8 L 9 K 5 V 7
28. (B) 3 K 9 Z G V 5 7
29. (B) 3 K 7 5 V 9 L Z
30. (A) T 8 K L V 2 9 7

REVIEWING THE KEY STRATEGIES

Remember to:

1. Practice a technique and become comfortable with it.

2. Only one suggested answer will be correct for each question.

3. A choice may be used more than once within a five-question set.

CHAPTER 6

Three Clerical Abilities Model Tests
with Answer Explanations

This chapter contains three complete full-length model tests with answers and explanations. The purpose of this chapter is to help you master the techniques for working quickly under time pressure. After correcting each model test, assess your strengths and weaknesses and return to the specific review section for additional review.

The model tests should be taken under strict test conditions. This means:

— no scratch paper permitted

— any scratch work must be done on test booklet

— answers must be marked on answer sheet

— use #2 pencils with erasers

— follow time limits exactly. (Use an alarm clock.) Fifteen minutes for each test. You may not proceed to test #2 until 15 minutes are up for test #1. Then you may not return to test #1.

— no interruptions allowed

— no aids permitted (such as dictionary, calculator, etc.)

NOTE: Sample questions are usually distributed with the announcement and if so may not be given in the official examinations.

Remember to tear out your answer sheet preceding each model test.

ANSWER SHEET

SIGNATURE: _____

(Please Sign)

EXAMINATION TITLE: _____

PLACE OF EXAMINATION: _____

City _____ State _____

TODAY'S DATE: _____

SAMPLE Ⓐ ● Ⓒ Ⓓ Ⓔ

DIRECTIONS FOR MARKING ANSWER SHEET

Use only a **No. 2 (or softer) lead pencil.** Darken completely the circle corresponding to your answer. **You must keep** your mark within the circle. Stray marks may be counted as errors. Erase **completely** all marks except your answer.

1. In the boxes below, **PRINT** your name. Print only as many letters as will fit within the areas for the last name, first initial (F.I.), and middle initial (M.I.). Below each box, darken the circle containing the same letter. SEE SAMPLE NAME GRID

SAMPLE NAME GRID

LAST NAME | F.I. | M.I.

2. In the boxes below, enter your 9-digit Social Security Number. Below each box, darken the circle in each column corresponding to the number you have entered.

SOCIAL SECURITY NUMBER

3. OCCUPATIONAL GROUP NUMBER

LAST NAME | F.I. | M.I.

SECTION 1

Make no marks or entries in the columns to the right until you receive instructions from the administrator.

PART · TEST SERIES · TEST NUMBER

1 Ⓐ Ⓑ Ⓒ Ⓓ Ⓔ	11 Ⓐ Ⓑ Ⓒ Ⓓ Ⓔ	31 Ⓐ Ⓑ Ⓒ Ⓓ Ⓔ	51 Ⓐ Ⓑ Ⓒ Ⓓ Ⓔ	71 Ⓐ Ⓑ Ⓒ Ⓓ Ⓔ	91 Ⓐ Ⓑ Ⓒ Ⓓ Ⓔ	111 Ⓐ Ⓑ Ⓒ Ⓓ Ⓔ
2 Ⓐ Ⓑ Ⓒ Ⓓ Ⓔ	12 Ⓐ Ⓑ Ⓒ Ⓓ Ⓔ	32 Ⓐ Ⓑ Ⓒ Ⓓ Ⓔ	52 Ⓐ Ⓑ Ⓒ Ⓓ Ⓔ	72 Ⓐ Ⓑ Ⓒ Ⓓ Ⓔ	92 Ⓐ Ⓑ Ⓒ Ⓓ Ⓔ	112 Ⓐ Ⓑ Ⓒ Ⓓ Ⓔ
3 Ⓐ Ⓑ Ⓒ Ⓓ Ⓔ	13 Ⓐ Ⓑ Ⓒ Ⓓ Ⓔ	33 Ⓐ Ⓑ Ⓒ Ⓓ Ⓔ	53 Ⓐ Ⓑ Ⓒ Ⓓ Ⓔ	73 Ⓐ Ⓑ Ⓒ Ⓓ Ⓔ	93 Ⓐ Ⓑ Ⓒ Ⓓ Ⓔ	113 Ⓐ Ⓑ Ⓒ Ⓓ Ⓔ
4 Ⓐ Ⓑ Ⓒ Ⓓ Ⓔ	14 Ⓐ Ⓑ Ⓒ Ⓓ Ⓔ	34 Ⓐ Ⓑ Ⓒ Ⓓ Ⓔ	54 Ⓐ Ⓑ Ⓒ Ⓓ Ⓔ	74 Ⓐ Ⓑ Ⓒ Ⓓ Ⓔ	94 Ⓐ Ⓑ Ⓒ Ⓓ Ⓔ	114 Ⓐ Ⓑ Ⓒ Ⓓ Ⓔ
5 Ⓐ Ⓑ Ⓒ Ⓓ Ⓔ	15 Ⓐ Ⓑ Ⓒ Ⓓ Ⓔ	35 Ⓐ Ⓑ Ⓒ Ⓓ Ⓔ	55 Ⓐ Ⓑ Ⓒ Ⓓ Ⓔ	75 Ⓐ Ⓑ Ⓒ Ⓓ Ⓔ	95 Ⓐ Ⓑ Ⓒ Ⓓ Ⓔ	115 Ⓐ Ⓑ Ⓒ Ⓓ Ⓔ
6 Ⓐ Ⓑ Ⓒ Ⓓ Ⓔ	16 Ⓐ Ⓑ Ⓒ Ⓓ Ⓔ	36 Ⓐ Ⓑ Ⓒ Ⓓ Ⓔ	56 Ⓐ Ⓑ Ⓒ Ⓓ Ⓔ	76 Ⓐ Ⓑ Ⓒ Ⓓ Ⓔ	96 Ⓐ Ⓑ Ⓒ Ⓓ Ⓔ	116 Ⓐ Ⓑ Ⓒ Ⓓ Ⓔ
7 Ⓐ Ⓑ Ⓒ Ⓓ Ⓔ	17 Ⓐ Ⓑ Ⓒ Ⓓ Ⓔ	37 Ⓐ Ⓑ Ⓒ Ⓓ Ⓔ	57 Ⓐ Ⓑ Ⓒ Ⓓ Ⓔ	77 Ⓐ Ⓑ Ⓒ Ⓓ Ⓔ	97 Ⓐ Ⓑ Ⓒ Ⓓ Ⓔ	117 Ⓐ Ⓑ Ⓒ Ⓓ Ⓔ
8 Ⓐ Ⓑ Ⓒ Ⓓ Ⓔ	18 Ⓐ Ⓑ Ⓒ Ⓓ Ⓔ	38 Ⓐ Ⓑ Ⓒ Ⓓ Ⓔ	58 Ⓐ Ⓑ Ⓒ Ⓓ Ⓔ	78 Ⓐ Ⓑ Ⓒ Ⓓ Ⓔ	98 Ⓐ Ⓑ Ⓒ Ⓓ Ⓔ	118 Ⓐ Ⓑ Ⓒ Ⓓ Ⓔ
9 Ⓐ Ⓑ Ⓒ Ⓓ Ⓔ	19 Ⓐ Ⓑ Ⓒ Ⓓ Ⓔ	39 Ⓐ Ⓑ Ⓒ Ⓓ Ⓔ	59 Ⓐ Ⓑ Ⓒ Ⓓ Ⓔ	79 Ⓐ Ⓑ Ⓒ Ⓓ Ⓔ	99 Ⓐ Ⓑ Ⓒ Ⓓ Ⓔ	119 Ⓐ Ⓑ Ⓒ Ⓓ Ⓔ
10 Ⓐ Ⓑ Ⓒ Ⓓ Ⓔ	20 Ⓐ Ⓑ Ⓒ Ⓓ Ⓔ	40 Ⓐ Ⓑ Ⓒ Ⓓ Ⓔ	60 Ⓐ Ⓑ Ⓒ Ⓓ Ⓔ	80 Ⓐ Ⓑ Ⓒ Ⓓ Ⓔ	100 Ⓐ Ⓑ Ⓒ Ⓓ Ⓔ	120 Ⓐ Ⓑ Ⓒ Ⓓ Ⓔ
	21 Ⓐ Ⓑ Ⓒ Ⓓ Ⓔ	41 Ⓐ Ⓑ Ⓒ Ⓓ Ⓔ	61 Ⓐ Ⓑ Ⓒ Ⓓ Ⓔ	81 Ⓐ Ⓑ Ⓒ Ⓓ Ⓔ	101 Ⓐ Ⓑ Ⓒ Ⓓ Ⓔ	121 Ⓐ Ⓑ Ⓒ Ⓓ Ⓔ
	22 Ⓐ Ⓑ Ⓒ Ⓓ Ⓔ	42 Ⓐ Ⓑ Ⓒ Ⓓ Ⓔ	62 Ⓐ Ⓑ Ⓒ Ⓓ Ⓔ	82 Ⓐ Ⓑ Ⓒ Ⓓ Ⓔ	102 Ⓐ Ⓑ Ⓒ Ⓓ Ⓔ	122 Ⓐ Ⓑ Ⓒ Ⓓ Ⓔ
	23 Ⓐ Ⓑ Ⓒ Ⓓ Ⓔ	43 Ⓐ Ⓑ Ⓒ Ⓓ Ⓔ	63 Ⓐ Ⓑ Ⓒ Ⓓ Ⓔ	83 Ⓐ Ⓑ Ⓒ Ⓓ Ⓔ	103 Ⓐ Ⓑ Ⓒ Ⓓ Ⓔ	123 Ⓐ Ⓑ Ⓒ Ⓓ Ⓔ
	24 Ⓐ Ⓑ Ⓒ Ⓓ Ⓔ	44 Ⓐ Ⓑ Ⓒ Ⓓ Ⓔ	64 Ⓐ Ⓑ Ⓒ Ⓓ Ⓔ	84 Ⓐ Ⓑ Ⓒ Ⓓ Ⓔ	104 Ⓐ Ⓑ Ⓒ Ⓓ Ⓔ	124 Ⓐ Ⓑ Ⓒ Ⓓ Ⓔ
	25 Ⓐ Ⓑ Ⓒ Ⓓ Ⓔ	45 Ⓐ Ⓑ Ⓒ Ⓓ Ⓔ	65 Ⓐ Ⓑ Ⓒ Ⓓ Ⓔ	85 Ⓐ Ⓑ Ⓒ Ⓓ Ⓔ	105 Ⓐ Ⓑ Ⓒ Ⓓ Ⓔ	125 Ⓐ Ⓑ Ⓒ Ⓓ Ⓔ
	26 Ⓐ Ⓑ Ⓒ Ⓓ Ⓔ	46 Ⓐ Ⓑ Ⓒ Ⓓ Ⓔ	66 Ⓐ Ⓑ Ⓒ Ⓓ Ⓔ	86 Ⓐ Ⓑ Ⓒ Ⓓ Ⓔ	106 Ⓐ Ⓑ Ⓒ Ⓓ Ⓔ	126 Ⓐ Ⓑ Ⓒ Ⓓ Ⓔ
	27 Ⓐ Ⓑ Ⓒ Ⓓ Ⓔ	47 Ⓐ Ⓑ Ⓒ Ⓓ Ⓔ	67 Ⓐ Ⓑ Ⓒ Ⓓ Ⓔ	87 Ⓐ Ⓑ Ⓒ Ⓓ Ⓔ	107 Ⓐ Ⓑ Ⓒ Ⓓ Ⓔ	127 Ⓐ Ⓑ Ⓒ Ⓓ Ⓔ
	28 Ⓐ Ⓑ Ⓒ Ⓓ Ⓔ	48 Ⓐ Ⓑ Ⓒ Ⓓ Ⓔ	68 Ⓐ Ⓑ Ⓒ Ⓓ Ⓔ	88 Ⓐ Ⓑ Ⓒ Ⓓ Ⓔ	108 Ⓐ Ⓑ Ⓒ Ⓓ Ⓔ	128 Ⓐ Ⓑ Ⓒ Ⓓ Ⓔ
	29 Ⓐ Ⓑ Ⓒ Ⓓ Ⓔ	49 Ⓐ Ⓑ Ⓒ Ⓓ Ⓔ	69 Ⓐ Ⓑ Ⓒ Ⓓ Ⓔ	89 Ⓐ Ⓑ Ⓒ Ⓓ Ⓔ	109 Ⓐ Ⓑ Ⓒ Ⓓ Ⓔ	129 Ⓐ Ⓑ Ⓒ Ⓓ Ⓔ
	30 Ⓐ Ⓑ Ⓒ Ⓓ Ⓔ	50 Ⓐ Ⓑ Ⓒ Ⓓ Ⓔ	70 Ⓐ Ⓑ Ⓒ Ⓓ Ⓔ	90 Ⓐ Ⓑ Ⓒ Ⓓ Ⓔ	110 Ⓐ Ⓑ Ⓒ Ⓓ Ⓔ	130 Ⓐ Ⓑ Ⓒ Ⓓ Ⓔ

MODEL TEST 1

Time allotted—15 minutes

Directions

Each question has five suggested answers. Decide which one is the best answer. Find the question number on the Answer Sheet. Show your answer to the question by darkening completely the space corresponding to the letter that is the same as the letter of your answer. Keep your mark within the space. If you have to erase a mark, be sure to erase it completely. Mark only one answer for each question.

In questions 1 through 5, compare the three names or numbers, and mark the answer—
A if ALL THREE names or numbers are exactly ALIKE
B if only the FIRST and SECOND names or numbers are exactly ALIKE
C if only the FIRST and THIRD names or numbers are exactly ALIKE
D if only the SECOND and THIRD names or numbers are exactly ALIKE
E · if ALL THREE names or numbers are DIFFERENT

1.	4826489	4824689	4826489
2.	3825431	3825431	3825431
3.	4763901	4769301	4769301
4.	Worthington Pistle	Worthington Pistel	Worthington Pistle
5.	Merriam Riwonla	Merriam Riwonia	Merriam Riwonia

In questions 6 through 10, find the correct place for the name in the box.

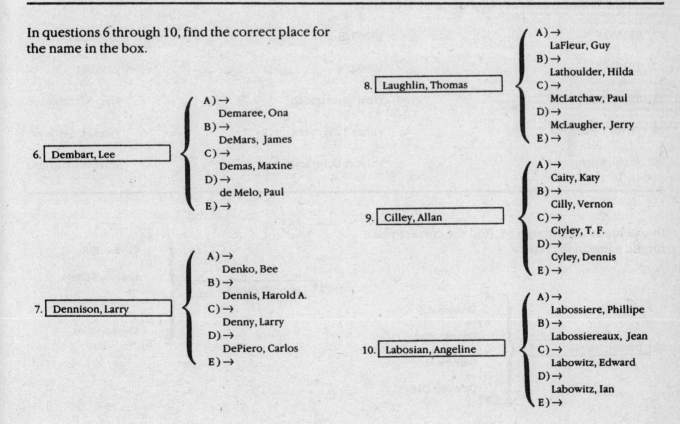

6. Dembart, Lee
   A) →
      Demaree, Ona
   B) →
      DeMars, James
   C) →
      Demas, Maxine
   D) →
      de Melo, Paul
   E) →

7. Dennison, Larry
   A) →
      Denko, Bee
   B) →
      Dennis, Harold A.
   C) →
      Denny, Larry
   D) →
      DePiero, Carlos
   E) →

8. Laughlin, Thomas
   A) →
      LaFleur, Guy
   B) →
      Lathoulder, Hilda
   C) →
      McLatchaw, Paul
   D) →
      McLaugher, Jerry
   E) →

9. Cilley, Allan
   A) →
      Caity, Katy
   B) →
      Cilly, Vernon
   C) →
      Ciyley, T. F.
   D) →
      Cyley, Dennis
   E) →

10. Labosian, Angeline
   A) →
      Labossiere, Phillipe
   B) →
      Labossiereaux, Jean
   C) →
      Labowitz, Edward
   D) →
      Labowitz, Ian
   E) →

11. Add:
58
+ 17

Answers
A) 73   B) 75
C) 78   D) 85
E) none of these

12. Subtract:
98
− 51

A) 47   B) 50
C) 53   D) 57
E) none of these

13. Multiply:
12
× 7

A) 64   B) 74
C) 84   D) 94
E) none of these

14. Divide:
3) 189

A) 60   B) 63
C) 65   D) 68
E) none of these

15. Add:
23
+ 71

A) 84   B) 87
C) 92   D) 97
E) none of these

In questions 16 through 20, find which one of the suggested answers appears in that question.

16. 3 P U 4 M T 7 9

17. T 4 2 R 9 Y 6 U

18. R 2 M U 6 4 3 P

19. 6 U 4 7 9 M R Y

20. R P 2 6 3 U T 4

Suggested Answers
{
A = 2, 4, M, U
B = 3, 4, T, R
C = 9, 2, U, R
D = 9, 3, M, T
E = none of these
}

In questions 21 through 25, compare the three names or numbers, and mark the answer—
A if ALL THREE names or numbers are exactly ALIKE
B if only the FIRST and SECOND names or numbers are exactly ALIKE
C if only the FIRST and THIRD names or numbers are exactly ALIKE
D if only the SECOND and THIRD names or numbers are exactly ALIKE
E if ALL THREE names or numbers are DIFFERENT

21.	3926528	3926528	3925628
22.	1930283	1930823	1930283
23.	Sima Serrafzadeh	Sima Serrafzadah	Sima Serrafzadeh
24.	Victor I. Sarquez	Victor T. Sarquez	Victor I. Sarquez
25.	Shizuyi Uchiyama	Shizuyi Uchiyama	Shizuyi Uchiyama

In questions 26, through 30, find the correct place for the name in the box.

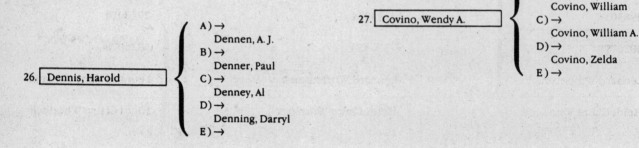

26. Dennis, Harold
{
A) →
   Dennen, A. J.
B) →
   Denner, Paul
C) →
   Denney, Al
D) →
   Denning, Darryl
E) →
}

27. Covino, Wendy A.
{
A) →
   Covino, Bill
B) →
   Covino, William
C) →
   Covino, William A.
D) →
   Covino, Zelda
E) →
}

28. DeVore, Cinthia
- A) →
  Deveren, Billy
- B) →
  Devereu, Ernest
- C) →
  Devoreaux, Robert
- D) →
  Devoreu, Carol
- E) →

29. Afitson, Roger
- A) →
  Afif, Sharon
- B) →
  Afifi, Gevorik
- C) →
  Afilador, Phillip
- D) →
  Afiniyev, Rudolf
- E) →

30. Adams, L. L.
- A) →
  Adams, Larry
- B) →
  Adams, Leroy
- C) →
  Adams, Lindy
- D) →
  Adams, Louis R.
- E) →

31. Subtract:
72
− 14

Answers
A) 58   B) 62
C) 64   D) 68
E) none of these

32. Multiply:
32
× 5

A) 150   B) 160
C) 170   D) 180
E) none of these

33. Divide:
9⟌819

A) 81   B) 91
C) 93   D) 97
E) none of these

34. Add:
18
+ 14

A) 22   B) 24
C) 28   D) 32
E) none of these

35. Subtract:
35
− 8

A) 17   B) 19
C) 29   D) 37
E) none of these

In questions 36 through 40, find which one of the suggested answers appears in that question.

36. T K 4 8 5 N Z 6

37. 8 N 6 9 3 V T P

38. T 4 V N 8 6 5 K

39. Z 6 4 T 3 P 8 N

40. 5 K N 6 V Z 9 3

Suggested Answers
A = 4, 6, V, N
B = 5, 6, Z, T
C = 3, 4, N, T
D = 3, 5, V, Z
E = none of these

In questions 41 through 45, compare the three names or numbers, and mark the answer—
A if ALL THREE names or numbers are exactly ALIKE
B if only the FIRST and SECOND names or numbers are exactly ALIKE
C if only the FIRST and THIRD names or numbers are exactly ALIKE
D if only the SECOND and THIRD names or numbers are exactly ALIKE
E if ALL THREE names or numbers are DIFFERENT

41.	9038717	9037217	9037218
42.	2983014	2983014	2938014
43.	3826798	3826978	3826978
44.	Leonard Wibbelsman	Leonard Wibblesman	Leonard Wibbelsmann
45.	Heidi Claire Whotlock	Heidi Claire Whotlock	Hiedi Claire Whotlock

In questions 46, through 50, find the correct place for the name in the box.

46. | Hatchikan, Cindy |
- A) →
- Hatch, Mark S.
- B) →
- Hatcher, George
- C) →
- Hatem, Carl
- D) →
- Hathaway, Carol
- E) →

47. | Ain, Juan |
- A) →
- Aiki, Terri
- B) →
- Aikido, Thomas
- C) →
- Aimone, Charles
- D) →
- Aintabulos, Phyllis
- E) →

48. | Rawkins, Bert |
- A) →
- Rawkens, Robert
- B) →
- Rawkens, Stuart
- C) →
- Rawkins, Annabel
- D) →
- Rawkins, B. A.
- E) →

49. | Hayad, Orville |
- A) →
- Hay, Harry
- B) →
- Hayak, Salem
- C) →
- Hayakama, N.
- D) →
- Hayashi, Shinro
- E) →

50. | Odom, Rick |
- A) →
- O'Davorin, Kenneth
- B) →
- O'Day, Dennis
- C) →
- O'Dell, David
- D) →
- O'Donnell, Gene
- E) →

Answers

51. Multiply:
$$\begin{array}{r} 23 \\ \times\ 4 \\ \hline \end{array}$$
- A) 82
- B) 88
- C) 96
- D) 98
- E) none of these

52. Divide:
$$2\overline{)82}$$
- A) 40
- B) 41
- C) 42
- D) 50
- E) none of these

53. Add:
$$\begin{array}{r} 93 \\ +\ 52 \\ \hline \end{array}$$
- A) 135
- B) 145
- C) 155
- D) 165
- E) none of these

54. Subtract:
$$\begin{array}{r} 87 \\ -\ 24 \\ \hline \end{array}$$
- A) 65
- B) 67
- C) 73
- D) 75
- E) none of these

55. Multiply:
$$\begin{array}{r} 17 \\ \times\ 8 \\ \hline \end{array}$$
- A) 106
- B) 116
- C) 126
- D) 136
- E) none of these

In questions 56 through 60, find which one of the suggested answers appears in that question.

56. 6 M J 7 Q Y 2 4

57. Y 7 5 S 4 H 9 J

58. S 5 Q J 9 7 6 M

59. 9 J 7 2 4 Q S H

60. S M 5 9 6 J Y 7

Suggested Answers
- A = 5, 7, Q, J
- B = 6, 7, Y, S
- C = 4, 5, J, S
- D = 4, 6, Q, Y
- E = none of these

In questions 61 through 65, compare the three names or numbers, and mark the answer—
  A if ALL THREE names or numbers are exactly ALIKE
  B if only the FIRST and SECOND names or numbers are exactly ALIKE
  C if only the FIRST and THIRD names or numbers are exactly ALIKE
  D if only the SECOND and THIRD names or numbers are exactly ALIKE
  E if ALL THREE names or numbers are DIFFERENT

61. 8372918	8372981	8372981
62. 2837192	2837912	2837192
63. Sigemin Ziegler	Sigemin Zeigler	Sigemin Ziegler
64. Fern Frederics	Fern Fredricks	Fern Fredericks
65. J. Michael Zigovras	J. Michael Zigovras	J. Michael Zigorvas

---

In questions 66 through 70, find the correct place for the name in the box.

66. | Hawkins, Norbert |
  A) →
    Hawkins, Lee
  B) →
    Hawkins, Lewis
  C) →
    Hawkins, N. M.
  D) →
    Hawkins, Wm. S.
  E) →

67. | Gutierrez, Beth |
  A) →
    Gutana, Edmund
  B) →
    Gutenberg, Bessie
  C) →
    Gutentag, Chas.
  D) →
    Guthrie, Bob
  E) →

68. | Ole, Bente |
  A) →
    O'Lares, Enid
  B) →
    O'Leary, Tim
  C) →
    Oleas, Patrick
  D) →
    Olender, Missy
  E) →

69. | Pott, Gregory |
  A) →
    Potvin, Pam
  B) →
    Potvist, Tilly
  C) →
    Potwin, Allan
  D) →
    Potwort, Freda
  E) →

70. | Gunther, Edward |
  A) →
    Gunn, Elliot
  B) →
    Gunnell, S. F.
  C) →
    Gura, Franklin
  D) →
    Guralt, Luke
  E) →

Answers

71. Divide:
$$7\overline{)357}$$
A) 45   B) 50
C) 51   D) 53
E) none of these

72. Add:
  29
+ 37
A) 56   B) 65
C) 66   D) 76
E) none of these

73. Subtract:
  91
− 19
A) 72   B) 78
C) 82   D) 83
E) none of these

74. Multiply:
  24
× 3
A) 66   B) 68
C) 72   D) 74
E) none of these

75. Divide:
$$9\overline{)837}$$
A) 91   B) 92
C) 93   D) 97
E) none of these

In questions 76 through 80, find which one of the suggested answers appears in that question.

76. M Q 3 7 4 Z X 5

77. 7 Z 5 8 2 F M W

78. M 3 F Z 7 5 4 Q

79. X 5 3 M 2 W 7 Z

80. 4 Q Z 5 F X 8 2

Suggested Answers

A = 3, 5, F, Z
B = 4, 5, X, M
C = 2, 3, Z, M
D = 2, 4, F, X
E = none of these

In questions 81 through 85, compare the three names or numbers, and mark the answer—
A if ALL THREE names or numbers are exactly ALIKE
B if only the FIRST and SECOND names or numbers are exactly ALIKE
C if only the FIRST and THIRD names or numbers are exactly ALIKE
D if only the SECOND and THIRD names or numbers are exactly ALIKE
E if ALL THREE names or numbers are DIFFERENT

81. 4819287	4819287	3891287
82. 3782619	3782619	3782619
83. 2736510	2735610	2736510
84. Judith A. Streigel	Judith A. Streigel	Judith A. Striegel
85. Nicholas Strimling	Nicholas Strimler	Nichlas Strimling

In questions 86 through 90, find the correct place for the name in the box.

86. Groener, Tim

A) →
Groobin, J.
B) →
Groom, James
C) →
Groot, Roger
D) →
Gropman, Paula
E) →

87. Grzchbien, Solly

A) →
Gruzzi, Maria
B) →
Grzanka, Stanley
C) →
Grzebien, Gary W.
D) →
Grzibiewski, John
E) →

88. Cicci, Thomas

A) →
Cinader, Alice
B) →
Cinciarelli, John
C) →
Cinco, Josepfina
D) →
Cinecoe, Robt.
E) →

89. Haack, Martin

A) →
Ha, Young Soon
B) →
Haack, Ernest
C) →
Haan, Patricia
D) →
Haase, Sherie
E) →

90. Amore, Joseph

A) →
Amo, Efrin
B) →
Amor, Bartolo
C) →
Amorde, Todd
D) →
Amores, Mercedes
E) →

91. Add:
    92
    + 37

Answers
A) 139   B) 142
C) 149   D) 152
E) none of these

92. Subtract:
    132
    − 45

A) 77   B) 78
C) 97   D) 94
E) none of these

93. Multiply:
    19
    × 8

A) 152   B) 157
C) 158   D) 164
E) none of these

94. Divide:
    6) 372

A) 16   B) 61
C) 62   D) 67
E) none of these

95. Add:
    18
    + 82

A) 90   B) 100
C) 110   D) 120
E) none of these

In questions 96 through 100, find which one of the suggested answers appears in that question.

96. 7 Q H 8 W Z 3 5

97. Z 8 6 F 5 J 2 H

98. F 6 W H 2 8 7 Q

99. 2 H 8 3 5 W F J

100. F Q 6 2 7 H Z 8

Suggested Answers
A = 6, 8, W, H
B = 7, 8, Z, F
C = 5, 6, H, F
D = 5, 7, W, Z
E = none of these

In questions 101 through 105, compare the three names or numbers, and mark the answer—

A if ALL THREE names or numbers are exactly ALIKE
B if only the FIRST and SECOND names or numbers are exactly ALIKE
C if only the FIRST and THIRD names or numbers are exactly ALIKE
D if only the SECOND and THIRD names or numbers are exactly ALIKE
E if ALL THREE names or numbers are DIFFERENT

101. 3921038	3912038	3923038
102. 2710935	2701935	2701935
103. Neilson Saemaidahr	Neilson Saemaidhar	Neilson Saemaidahr
104. Stephanie R. Sharron	Stephanie R. Sharon	Stephanie R. Sharon
105. Jefferey Paige Sacks	Jefferey Paige Sachs	Jeffrey Paige Sachs

In questions 106 through 110, find the correct place for the name in the box.

106. | Andeson, Louis |

A) →
Anderson, L. P.
B) →
Anderson, Peter
C) →
Andersonian, Frank
D) →
Andino, Vincent
E) →

107. | Rupolo, Victor |

A) →
Ruonala, Kenneth
B) →
Rupe, Arthur
C) →
Rupen, Osgood
D) →
Rupert, Corinne
E) →

108. American Filmathon

- A) →
  American Business Supply
- B) →
  American Cinema Editors
- C) →
  American Film Institute
- D) →
  American Foreign Services
- E) →

109. Ryan, J. Patrick

- A) →
  Ryan, Ernest
- B) →
  Ryan, John
- C) →
  Ryan, Kerry
- D) →
  Ryan, Larry
- E) →

110. Sabersky, Stephen

- A) →
  Saber, Ron
- B) →
  Sabrinsky, Judith
- C) →
  Sabur, Zena
- D) →
  Sabzinsky, Jonathan
- E) →

Suggested Answers

$$\begin{cases} A = 9, \ 3, \ H, \ X \\ B = 2, \ 3, \ Z, \ Y \\ C = 8, \ 9, \ X, \ Y \\ D = 8, \ 2, \ H, \ Z \\ E = \text{none of these} \end{cases}$$

IF YOU FINISH BEFORE THE TIME IS UP, YOU MAY GO BACK AND CHECK YOUR ANSWERS.

ANSWER KEY FOR MODEL TEST 1

Alike or Different

1. C	21. B	41. E	61. D	81. B	101. E
2. A	22. C	42. B	62. C	82. A	102. D
3. D	23. C	43. D	63. C	83. C	103. C
4. C	24. C	44. E	64. E	84. B	104. D
5. D	25. A	45. B	65. B	85. E	105. E

Alphabetizing

6. D	26. E	46. C	66. D	86. A	106. D
7. C	27. B	47. D	67. E	87. C	107. E
8. C	28. C	48. E	68. B	88. A	108. D
9. B	29. E	49. B	69. A	89. C	109. B
10. A	30. A	50. D	70. C	90. D	110. B

Arithmetic

11. B	31. A	51. E	71. C	91. E	111. B
12. A	32. B	52. B	72. C	92. E	112. C
13. C	33. B	53. B	73. A	93. A	113. C
14. B	34. D	54. E	74. C	94. C	114. B
15. E	35. E	55. D	75. C	95. B	115. A

Letters and Numbers

16. D	36. B	56. D	76. B	96. D	116. B
17. C	37. E	57. C	77. E	97. C	117. E
18. A	38. A	58. A	78. A	98. A	118. A
19. E	39. C	59. E	79. C	99. E	119. C
20. B	40. D	60. B	80. D	100. B	120. D

Answers

111. Subtract:
121
− 84

A) 35 B) 37
C) 47 D) 49
E) none of these

112. Multiply:
19
× 4

A) 72 B) 74
C) 76 D) 78
E) none of these

113. Divide:
9)810

A) 9 B) 19
C) 90 D) 91
E) none of these

114. Add:
98
+ 37

A) 125 B) 135
C) 137 D) 139
E) none of these

115. Subtract:
88
− 31

A) 57 B) 63
C) 67 D) 77
E) none of these

In questions 116 through 120, find which one of the suggested answers appears in that question.

116. Y R 9 5 2 X Z 3

117. 5 X 3 6 8 H Y M

118. Y 9 H X 5 3 2 R

119. Z 3 9 Y 8 M 5 X

120. 2 R X 3 H Z 6 8

ANALYSIS CHART FOR MODEL TEST 1

Now that you've corrected your exam, use the following chart to carefully analyze your results and spot your strengths and weaknesses. This analysis should help you focus your study and review efforts.

Section	Total Number of Questions	Number Correct	Number Incorrect	Number Unanswered*
Alike or Different	30			
Alphabetizing	30			
Arithmetic	30			
Letters and Numbers	30			
TOTAL	120			

*Since there is a small penalty for incorrect answers on the Clerical Abilities Test, you should not guess "blindly." Try to eliminate one or more of the choices before you take your educated guess.

ANSWER EXPLANATIONS FOR MODEL TEST 1

1. (C) 4826489   4824689   4826489
2. (A) 3825431   3825431   3825431
3. (D) 4763901   4769301   4769301
4. (C) Worthington Pistle   Worthington Pistel   Worthington Pistle
5. (D) Merriam Riwonla   Merriam Riwonia   Merriam Riwonia
6. (D) Demas, Maxine
    Dembart, Lee
    de Melo, Paul
7. (C) Dennis, Harold A.
    Dennison, Larry
    Denny, Larry
8. (C) Lathoulder, Hilda
    Laughlin, Thomas
    McLatchaw, Paul
9. (B) Caity, Katy
    Cilley, Allan
    Cilly, Vernon
10. (A) Labosian, Angeline
    Labossiere, Phillipe
11. (B) 75
12. (A) 47
13. (C) 84
14. (B) 63
15. (E) Correct answer: 94.
16. (D) 3 P U 4 M T 7 9
17. (C) T 4 2 R 9 Y 6 U
18. (A) R 2 M U 6 4 3 P
19. (E) 6 U 4 7 9 M R Y
20. (B) R P 2 6 3 U T 4
21. (B) 3926528   3926528
22. (C) 1930283   1930823
23. (C) Sima Serrafzadeh   Sima Serrafzadah
24. (C) Victor I. Sarquez   Victor T. Sarquez
25. (A) Shizuyi Uchiyama   Shizuyi Uchiyama
26. (E) Denning, Darryl
    Dennis, Harold
27. (B) Covino, Bill
    Covino, Wendy A.
    Covino, William
28. (C) Devereu, Ernest
    DeVore, Cinthia
    Devoreaux, Robert

29. (E) Afiniyev, Rudolf
    Afitson, Roger
30. (A) Adams, L. L.
    Adams, Larry
31. (A) 58
32. (B) 160
33. (B) 91
34. (D) 32
35. (E) Correct answer: 27.
36. (B) T K 4 8 5 N Z 6
37. (E) 8 N 6 9 3 V T P
38. (A) T 4 V N 8 6 5 K
39. (C) Z 6 4 T 3 P 8 N
40. (D) 5 K N 6 V Z 9 3
41. (E) 9037217   9037218
42. (B) 2983014   2938014
43. (D) 3826798   3826978
44. (E) Leonard Wibbelsman   Leonard Wibbelsmann
45. (B) Heidi Claire Whotlock   Hiedi Claire Whotlock
46. (C) Hatcher, George
    Hatchikan, Cindy
    Hatem, Carl
47. (D) Aimone, Charles
    Ain, Juan
    Aintabulos, Phyllis
48. (E) Rawkins, B. A.
    Rawkins, Bert
49. (B) Hay, Harry
    Hayad, Orville
    Hayak, Salem
50. (D) O'Dell, David
    Odom, Rick
    O'Donnell, Gene
51. (E) Correct answer: 92.
52. (B) 41
53. (B) 145
54. (E) Correct answer: 63.
55. (D) 136
56. (D) 6 M J 7 Q Y 2 4
57. (C) Y 7 5 S 4 H 9 J
58. (A) S 5 Q J 9 7 6 M
59. (E) 9 J 7 2 4 Q S H
60. (B) S M 5 9 6 J Y 7

61. (D) 8372918   8372981   8372981
62. (C) 2837192   2837912   2837192
63. (C) Sigemin Ziegler   Sigemin Ziegler   Sigemin Zeigler
64. (E) Fern Frederics   Fern Fredricks   Fern Fredericks
65. (B) J. Michael Zigovras   J. Michael Zigovras   J. Michael Zigorvas
66. (D) Hawkins, N. M.
    Hawkins, Norbert
    Hawkins, Wm. S.
67. (E) Guthrie, Bob
    Gutierrez, Beth
68. (B) O'Lares, Enid
    Ole, Bente
    O'Leary, Tim
69. (A) Pott, Gregory
    Potvin, Pam
70. (C) Gunnell, S. F.
    Gunther, Edward
    Gura, Franklin
71. (C) 51
72. (C) 66
73. (A) 72
74. (C) 72
75. (C) 93
76. (B) M Q 3 7 4 Z X 5
77. (E) 7 Z 5 8 2 F M W
78. (A) M 3 F Z 7 5 4 Q
79. (C) X 5 3 M 2 W 7 Z
80. (D) 4 Q Z 5 F X 8 2
81. (B) 4819287   4819287   4891287
82. (A) 3782619   3782619   3782619
83. (C) 2736510   2735610   2736510
84. (B) Judith A. Streigel   Judith A. Streigel   Judith A. Striegel
85. (E) Nicholas Strimling   Nicholas Strimler   Nichlas Strimling
86. (A) Groener, Tim
    Groobin, J.
87. (C) Grzanka, Stanley
    Grzcbbien, Solly
    Grzebien, Gary W.
88. (A) Cicci, Thomas
    Cinader, Alice
89. (C) Haack, Ernest
    Haack, Martin
    Haan, Patricia

90. (D) Amorde, Todd
    Amore, Joseph
    Amores, Mercedes
91. (E) Correct answer: 129.
92. (E) Correct answer: 87.
93. (A) 152
94. (C) 62
95. (B) 100
96. (D) 7 Q H 8 W Z 3 5
97. (C) Z 8 6 F 5 J 2 H
98. (A) F 6 W H 2 8 7 Q
99. (E) 2 H 8 3 5 W F J
100. (B) F Q 6 2 7 H Z 8
101. (E) 3921038   3912038   3923038
102. (D) 2710935   2710935   2701935
103. (C) Neilson Saemaidahr   Neilson Saemaidahr   Neilson Saemaidahr
104. (D) Stephanie R. Sharron   Stephanie R. Sharron   Stephanie R. Sharon
105. (E) Jefferey Paige Sacks   Jefferey Paige Sacks   Jeffrey Paige Sachs
106. (D) Andersonian, Frank
    Andeson, Louis
    Andino, Vincent
107. (E) Rupert, Corinne
    Rupolo, Victor
108. (D) American Film Institute
    American Filmation
    American Foreign Services
109. (B) Ryan, Ernest
    Ryan, J. Patrick
    Ryan, John
110. (B) Saber, Ron
    Sabersky, Stephen
    Sabrinsky, Judith
111. (B) 37
112. (C) 76
113. (C) 90
114. (B) 135
115. (A) 57
116. (B) Y R 9 5 2 X Z 3
117. (E) 5 X 3 6 8 H Y M
118. (A) Y 9 H X 5 3 2 R
119. (C) Z 3 9 Y 8 M 5 X
120. (D) 2 R X 3 H Z 6 8

ANSWER SHEET

SIGNATURE: _____
(Please Sign)

EXAMINATION TITLE: _____

PLACE OF EXAMINATION: _____
City _____ State _____

TODAY'S DATE: _____

SAMPLE Ⓐ ● Ⓒ Ⓓ Ⓔ

DIRECTIONS FOR MARKING ANSWER SHEET

Use only a **No. 2 (or softer) lead pencil.** Darken completely the circle corresponding to your answer. You **must** keep your mark within the circle. Stray marks may be counted as errors. Erase **completely** all marks except your answer.

SAMPLE NAME GRID

1. In the boxes below, **PRINT** your name. Print only as many letters as will fit within the areas for the last name, first initial (F.I.), and middle initial (M.I.) Below each box, darken the circle containing the same letter. SEE SAMPLE NAME GRID

LAST NAME

2. In the boxes below, enter your 9-digit Social Security Number. Below each box, darken the circle in each column corresponding to the number you have entered.

SOCIAL SECURITY NUMBER

3. OCCUPATIONAL GROUP NUMBER

SECTION 1

Make no marks or entries in the columns to the right until you receive instructions from the administrator.

TEST NUMBER   TEST SERIES   P A R T

1 Ⓐ Ⓑ Ⓒ Ⓓ Ⓔ
2 Ⓐ Ⓑ Ⓒ Ⓓ Ⓔ
3 Ⓐ Ⓑ Ⓒ Ⓓ Ⓔ
4 Ⓐ Ⓑ Ⓒ Ⓓ Ⓔ
5 Ⓐ Ⓑ Ⓒ Ⓓ Ⓔ
6 Ⓐ Ⓑ Ⓒ Ⓓ Ⓔ
7 Ⓐ Ⓑ Ⓒ Ⓓ Ⓔ
8 Ⓐ Ⓑ Ⓒ Ⓓ Ⓔ
9 Ⓐ Ⓑ Ⓒ Ⓓ Ⓔ
10 Ⓐ Ⓑ Ⓒ Ⓓ Ⓔ

11 Ⓐ Ⓑ Ⓒ Ⓓ Ⓔ
12 Ⓐ Ⓑ Ⓒ Ⓓ Ⓔ
13 Ⓐ Ⓑ Ⓒ Ⓓ Ⓔ
14 Ⓐ Ⓑ Ⓒ Ⓓ Ⓔ
15 Ⓐ Ⓑ Ⓒ Ⓓ Ⓔ
16 Ⓐ Ⓑ Ⓒ Ⓓ Ⓔ
17 Ⓐ Ⓑ Ⓒ Ⓓ Ⓔ
18 Ⓐ Ⓑ Ⓒ Ⓓ Ⓔ
19 Ⓐ Ⓑ Ⓒ Ⓓ Ⓔ
20 Ⓐ Ⓑ Ⓒ Ⓓ Ⓔ

21 Ⓐ Ⓑ Ⓒ Ⓓ Ⓔ
22 Ⓐ Ⓑ Ⓒ Ⓓ Ⓔ
23 Ⓐ Ⓑ Ⓒ Ⓓ Ⓔ
24 Ⓐ Ⓑ Ⓒ Ⓓ Ⓔ
25 Ⓐ Ⓑ Ⓒ Ⓓ Ⓔ
26 Ⓐ Ⓑ Ⓒ Ⓓ Ⓔ
27 Ⓐ Ⓑ Ⓒ Ⓓ Ⓔ
28 Ⓐ Ⓑ Ⓒ Ⓓ Ⓔ
29 Ⓐ Ⓑ Ⓒ Ⓓ Ⓔ
30 Ⓐ Ⓑ Ⓒ Ⓓ Ⓔ

31 Ⓐ Ⓑ Ⓒ Ⓓ Ⓔ
32 Ⓐ Ⓑ Ⓒ Ⓓ Ⓔ
33 Ⓐ Ⓑ Ⓒ Ⓓ Ⓔ
34 Ⓐ Ⓑ Ⓒ Ⓓ Ⓔ
35 Ⓐ Ⓑ Ⓒ Ⓓ Ⓔ
36 Ⓐ Ⓑ Ⓒ Ⓓ Ⓔ
37 Ⓐ Ⓑ Ⓒ Ⓓ Ⓔ
38 Ⓐ Ⓑ Ⓒ Ⓓ Ⓔ
39 Ⓐ Ⓑ Ⓒ Ⓓ Ⓔ
40 Ⓐ Ⓑ Ⓒ Ⓓ Ⓔ

41 Ⓐ Ⓑ Ⓒ Ⓓ Ⓔ
42 Ⓐ Ⓑ Ⓒ Ⓓ Ⓔ
43 Ⓐ Ⓑ Ⓒ Ⓓ Ⓔ
44 Ⓐ Ⓑ Ⓒ Ⓓ Ⓔ
45 Ⓐ Ⓑ Ⓒ Ⓓ Ⓔ
46 Ⓐ Ⓑ Ⓒ Ⓓ Ⓔ
47 Ⓐ Ⓑ Ⓒ Ⓓ Ⓔ
48 Ⓐ Ⓑ Ⓒ Ⓓ Ⓔ
49 Ⓐ Ⓑ Ⓒ Ⓓ Ⓔ
50 Ⓐ Ⓑ Ⓒ Ⓓ Ⓔ

51 Ⓐ Ⓑ Ⓒ Ⓓ Ⓔ
52 Ⓐ Ⓑ Ⓒ Ⓓ Ⓔ
53 Ⓐ Ⓑ Ⓒ Ⓓ Ⓔ
54 Ⓐ Ⓑ Ⓒ Ⓓ Ⓔ
55 Ⓐ Ⓑ Ⓒ Ⓓ Ⓔ
56 Ⓐ Ⓑ Ⓒ Ⓓ Ⓔ
57 Ⓐ Ⓑ Ⓒ Ⓓ Ⓔ
58 Ⓐ Ⓑ Ⓒ Ⓓ Ⓔ
59 Ⓐ Ⓑ Ⓒ Ⓓ Ⓔ
60 Ⓐ Ⓑ Ⓒ Ⓓ Ⓔ

61 Ⓐ Ⓑ Ⓒ Ⓓ Ⓔ
62 Ⓐ Ⓑ Ⓒ Ⓓ Ⓔ
63 Ⓐ Ⓑ Ⓒ Ⓓ Ⓔ
64 Ⓐ Ⓑ Ⓒ Ⓓ Ⓔ
65 Ⓐ Ⓑ Ⓒ Ⓓ Ⓔ
66 Ⓐ Ⓑ Ⓒ Ⓓ Ⓔ
67 Ⓐ Ⓑ Ⓒ Ⓓ Ⓔ
68 Ⓐ Ⓑ Ⓒ Ⓓ Ⓔ
69 Ⓐ Ⓑ Ⓒ Ⓓ Ⓔ
70 Ⓐ Ⓑ Ⓒ Ⓓ Ⓔ

71 Ⓐ Ⓑ Ⓒ Ⓓ Ⓔ
72 Ⓐ Ⓑ Ⓒ Ⓓ Ⓔ
73 Ⓐ Ⓑ Ⓒ Ⓓ Ⓔ
74 Ⓐ Ⓑ Ⓒ Ⓓ Ⓔ
75 Ⓐ Ⓑ Ⓒ Ⓓ Ⓔ
76 Ⓐ Ⓑ Ⓒ Ⓓ Ⓔ
77 Ⓐ Ⓑ Ⓒ Ⓓ Ⓔ
78 Ⓐ Ⓑ Ⓒ Ⓓ Ⓔ
79 Ⓐ Ⓑ Ⓒ Ⓓ Ⓔ
80 Ⓐ Ⓑ Ⓒ Ⓓ Ⓔ

81 Ⓐ Ⓑ Ⓒ Ⓓ Ⓔ
82 Ⓐ Ⓑ Ⓒ Ⓓ Ⓔ
83 Ⓐ Ⓑ Ⓒ Ⓓ Ⓔ
84 Ⓐ Ⓑ Ⓒ Ⓓ Ⓔ
85 Ⓐ Ⓑ Ⓒ Ⓓ Ⓔ
86 Ⓐ Ⓑ Ⓒ Ⓓ Ⓔ
87 Ⓐ Ⓑ Ⓒ Ⓓ Ⓔ
88 Ⓐ Ⓑ Ⓒ Ⓓ Ⓔ
89 Ⓐ Ⓑ Ⓒ Ⓓ Ⓔ
90 Ⓐ Ⓑ Ⓒ Ⓓ Ⓔ

91 Ⓐ Ⓑ Ⓒ Ⓓ Ⓔ
92 Ⓐ Ⓑ Ⓒ Ⓓ Ⓔ
93 Ⓐ Ⓑ Ⓒ Ⓓ Ⓔ
94 Ⓐ Ⓑ Ⓒ Ⓓ Ⓔ
95 Ⓐ Ⓑ Ⓒ Ⓓ Ⓔ
96 Ⓐ Ⓑ Ⓒ Ⓓ Ⓔ
97 Ⓐ Ⓑ Ⓒ Ⓓ Ⓔ
98 Ⓐ Ⓑ Ⓒ Ⓓ Ⓔ
99 Ⓐ Ⓑ Ⓒ Ⓓ Ⓔ
100 Ⓐ Ⓑ Ⓒ Ⓓ Ⓔ

111 Ⓐ Ⓑ Ⓒ Ⓓ Ⓔ
112 Ⓐ Ⓑ Ⓒ Ⓓ Ⓔ
113 Ⓐ Ⓑ Ⓒ Ⓓ Ⓔ
114 Ⓐ Ⓑ Ⓒ Ⓓ Ⓔ
115 Ⓐ Ⓑ Ⓒ Ⓓ Ⓔ
116 Ⓐ Ⓑ Ⓒ Ⓓ Ⓔ
117 Ⓐ Ⓑ Ⓒ Ⓓ Ⓔ
118 Ⓐ Ⓑ Ⓒ Ⓓ Ⓔ
119 Ⓐ Ⓑ Ⓒ Ⓓ Ⓔ
120 Ⓐ Ⓑ Ⓒ Ⓓ Ⓔ

101 Ⓐ Ⓑ Ⓒ Ⓓ Ⓔ
102 Ⓐ Ⓑ Ⓒ Ⓓ Ⓔ
103 Ⓐ Ⓑ Ⓒ Ⓓ Ⓔ
104 Ⓐ Ⓑ Ⓒ Ⓓ Ⓔ
105 Ⓐ Ⓑ Ⓒ Ⓓ Ⓔ
106 Ⓐ Ⓑ Ⓒ Ⓓ Ⓔ
107 Ⓐ Ⓑ Ⓒ Ⓓ Ⓔ
108 Ⓐ Ⓑ Ⓒ Ⓓ Ⓔ
109 Ⓐ Ⓑ Ⓒ Ⓓ Ⓔ
110 Ⓐ Ⓑ Ⓒ Ⓓ Ⓔ

121 Ⓐ Ⓑ Ⓒ Ⓓ Ⓔ
122 Ⓐ Ⓑ Ⓒ Ⓓ Ⓔ
123 Ⓐ Ⓑ Ⓒ Ⓓ Ⓔ
124 Ⓐ Ⓑ Ⓒ Ⓓ Ⓔ
125 Ⓐ Ⓑ Ⓒ Ⓓ Ⓔ
126 Ⓐ Ⓑ Ⓒ Ⓓ Ⓔ
127 Ⓐ Ⓑ Ⓒ Ⓓ Ⓔ
128 Ⓐ Ⓑ Ⓒ Ⓓ Ⓔ
129 Ⓐ Ⓑ Ⓒ Ⓓ Ⓔ
130 Ⓐ Ⓑ Ⓒ Ⓓ Ⓔ

MODEL TEST 2

Time allotted—15 minutes

Directions

Each question has five suggested answers. Decide which one is the best answer. Find the question number on the Answer Sheet. Show your answer to the question by darkening completely the space corresponding to the letter that is the same as the letter of your answer. Keep your mark within the space. If you have to erase a mark, be sure to erase it completely. Mark only one answer for each question.

In questions 1 through 5, compare the three names or numbers, and mark the answer—
A if ALL THREE names or numbers are exactly ALIKE
B if only the FIRST and SECOND names or numbers are exactly ALIKE
C if only the FIRST and THIRD names or numbers are exactly ALIKE
D if only the SECOND and THIRD names or numbers are exactly ALIKE
E if ALL THREE names or numbers are DIFFERENT

1. 3870936   3879036   3870963

2. 3827092   3827902   3827902

3. 3701234   3702324   3701234

4. Arno Wojecieski   Arno Wojeceiski   Arno Wojecieski

5. Laurence Zwisen   Laurence Zwisen   Lawrence Zwisen

In questions 6 through 10, find the correct place for the name in the box.

6. Melody, Rogers
A) →
    Melodee, Wilson
B) →
    Melodie, Merry
C) →
    Meloeny, Vincent
D) →
    Melore, Joseph P.
E) →

7. Sachs, George
A) →
    Sack, Uthbert
B) →
    Sacker, Peter Z.
C) →
    Sackett, Bennett
D) →
    Sackley, Daniel
E) →

8. Laidler, Clovis
A) →
    Lai, Christine
B) →
    Laib, Robin
C) →
    Laine, Bob
D) →
    Laird, P. J.
E) →

9. Mentzel, Donald
A) →
    Mensor, Albert
B) →
    Menzies, Peter
C) →
    Menzilla, Arnold
D) →
    Meono, Miguel
E) →

10. Deluccio, D. M.
A) →
    De Luna, Ronald
B) →
    Delva, Rex
C) →
    Del Valle, Antonio
D) →
    Delvecchio, Alex
E) →

11. Multiply:
    18
    × 7

Answers
A) 122   B) 124
C) 132   D) 134
E) none of these

12. Divide:

    8) 696

A) 78   B) 83
C) 87   D) 89
E) none of these

13. Add:
    92
    + 35

A) 117   B) 127
C) 137   D) 139
E) none of these

14. Subtract:
    108
    − 42

A) 56   B) 64
C) 76   D) 78
E) none of these

15. Multiply:
    92
    × 5

A) 440   B) 450
C) 460   D) 550
E) none of these

In questions 16 through 20, find which one of the suggested answers appears in that question.

16. R 6 7 4 F M 8 Q

17. 3 6 8 X V 9 Q R

18. 4 9 6 R 2 M V X

19. 2 3 V 9 6 Q M X

20. Q 5 6 X 2 8 Z R

Suggested Answers
A = 8, 3, M, R
B = 6, 3, R, X
C = 8, 2, X, Q
D = 6, 2, M, Q
E = none of these

In questions 21 through 25, compare the three names or numbers, and mark the answer—
A if ALL THREE names or numbers are exactly ALIKE
B if only the FIRST and SECOND names or numbers are exactly ALIKE
C if only the FIRST and THIRD names or numbers are exactly ALIKE
D if only the SECOND and THIRD names or numbers are exactly ALIKE
E if ALL THREE names or numbers are DIFFERENT

21. 2873012   2870312   2873012

22. 2870283   2870283   2870283

23. 2983121   2981231   2981231

24. Magdalena Koltunik   Madalena Koltunik   Magdalina Koltunik

25. Gavrilo Romendicth   Gavrilo Romendicth   Gavrilo Romenditch

In questions 26 through 30, find the correct place for the name in the box.

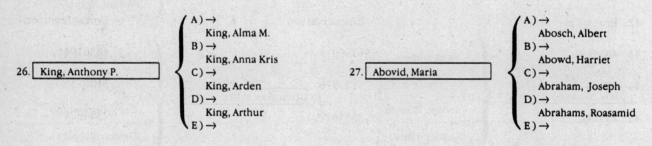

26. [King, Anthony P.]
A) →
    King, Alma M.
B) →
    King, Anna Kris
C) →
    King, Arden
D) →
    King, Arthur
E) →

27. [Abovid, Maria]
A) →
    Abosch, Albert
B) →
    Abowd, Harriet
C) →
    Abraham, Joseph
D) →
    Abrahams, Roasamid
E) →

28. Addison, Tracey

A) →
   Addams, Dick
B) →
   Adderly, D. J.
C) →
   Addotta, Cosimo
D) →
   Adduman, Nikolas
E) →

29. Mouton, N. G.

A) →
   Mouton, Betty
B) →
   Mouton, Carla
C) →
   Mouton, Lee
D) →
   Mouton, Nellie
E) →

30. Moya, Antonio

A) →
   Moy, Richard
B) →
   Moy, Toon
C) →
   Moya, Adelaide
D) →
   Moya, Armando
E) →

Answers

31. Divide:

5) 195

A) 40   B) 41
C) 44   D) 49
E) none of these

32. Add:
    35
  + 46

A) 71   B) 75
C) 79   D) 83
E) none of these

Answers

33. Subtract:
    81
  − 36

A) 35   B) 38
C) 45   D) 55
E) none of these

34. Multiply:
    72
  × 6

A) 422   B) 432
C) 442   D) 452
E) none of these

35. Divide:

3) 921

A) 37   B) 39
C) 307   D) 370
E) none of these

In questions 36 through 40, find which one of the suggested answers appears in that question.

36. 5 9 6 M 7 Z F Y

37. V 7 4 9 F 5 X M

38. 8 6 7 V 2 X F Y

39. Y 7 M 4 V 8 6 Q

40. 7 M 9 2 R 6 F Y

Suggested Answers

A = 7, 6, M, F
B = 7, 4, Y, M
C = 9, 6, Y, V
D = 9, 4, V, F
E = none of these

In questions 41 through 45, compare the three names or numbers, and mark the answer—
   A if ALL THREE names or numbers are exactly ALIKE
   B if only the FIRST and SECOND names or numbers are exactly ALIKE
   C if only the FIRST and THIRD names or numbers are exactly ALIKE
   D if only the SECOND and THIRD names or numbers are exactly ALIKE
   E if ALL THREE names or numbers are DIFFERENT

41. Ronald T. Kullaway	Ronald T. Kullaway	Ronald F. Kullaway
42. Ernest Teversen	Ernest Iversen	Ernest Ieversen
43. 4836194	4836914	4836194
44. 3129378	3123978	3129738
45. 2356421	2354621	2354621

In questions 46 through 50, find the correct place for the name in the box.

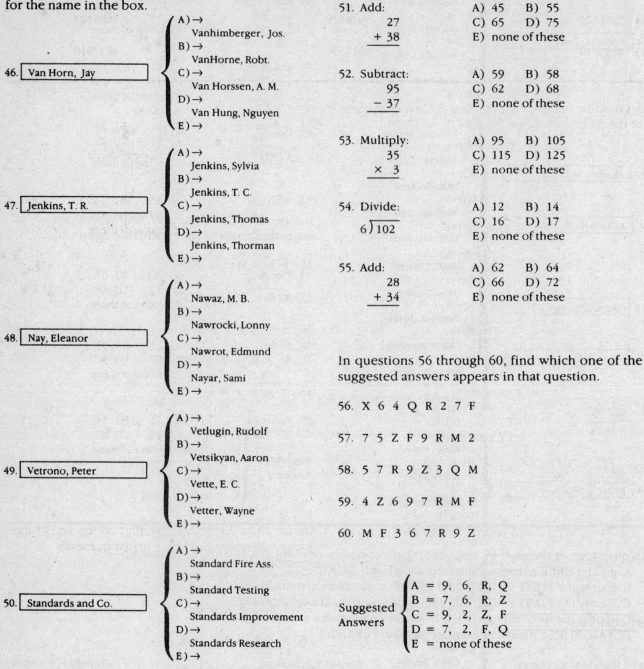

46. Van Horn, Jay
A) →
  Vanhimberger, Jos.
B) →
  VanHorne, Robt.
C) →
  Van Horssen, A. M.
D) →
  Van Hung, Nguyen
E) →

47. Jenkins, T. R.
A) →
  Jenkins, Sylvia
B) →
  Jenkins, T. C.
C) →
  Jenkins, Thomas
D) →
  Jenkins, Thorman
E) →

48. Nay, Eleanor
A) →
  Nawaz, M. B.
B) →
  Nawrocki, Lonny
C) →
  Nawrot, Edmund
D) →
  Nayar, Sami
E) →

49. Vetrono, Peter
A) →
  Vetlugin, Rudolf
B) →
  Vetsikyan, Aaron
C) →
  Vette, E. C.
D) →
  Vetter, Wayne
E) →

50. Standards and Co.
A) →
  Standard Fire Ass.
B) →
  Standard Testing
C) →
  Standards Improvement
D) →
  Standards Research
E) →

Answers

51. Add:
    27
  + 38

A) 45   B) 55
C) 65   D) 75
E) none of these

52. Subtract:
    95
  − 37

A) 59   B) 58
C) 62   D) 68
E) none of these

53. Multiply:
    35
  × 3

A) 95   B) 105
C) 115 D) 125
E) none of these

54. Divide:
  6) 102

A) 12   B) 14
C) 16   D) 17
E) none of these

55. Add:
    28
  + 34

A) 62   B) 64
C) 66   D) 72
E) none of these

In questions 56 through 60, find which one of the suggested answers appears in that question.

56. X 6 4 Q R 2 7 F

57. 7 5 Z F 9 R M 2

58. 5 7 R 9 Z 3 Q M

59. 4 Z 6 9 7 R M F

60. M F 3 6 7 R 9 Z

Suggested Answers
A = 9, 6, R, Q
B = 7, 6, R, Z
C = 9, 2, Z, F
D = 7, 2, F, Q
E = none of these

In questions 61 through 65, compare the three names or numbers, and mark the answer—
  A if ALL THREE names or numbers are exactly ALIKE
  B if only the FIRST and SECOND names or numbers are exactly ALIKE
  C if only the FIRST and THIRD names or numbers are exactly ALIKE
  D if only the SECOND and THIRD names or numbers are exactly ALIKE
  E if ALL THREE names or numbers are DIFFERENT

61. Lorraine Timbershun   Lorraine Timbershun   Loraine Timbershun

62. Michele R. Spencer   Michelle R. Spencer   Michele R. Spenser

63.	Jake Lazarwitz	Jake Lazarwits	Jake Lazarwitz
64.	3826129	3826129	3826127
65.	4837910	4837910	4837910

In questions 66 through 70, find the correct place for the name in the box.

66. | Andravillo, Frank |

A) →
   Andrade, Fred
B) →
   Andrades, Lee
C) →
   Andranik, Sami
D) →
   Andravin, Paul
E) →

67. | Saary, Armand |

A) →
   Saarinen, Eric
B) →
   Saarinter, Lois
C) →
   Saasnow, Allyn
D) →
   Saavedra, Jake William
E) →

68. | Ryder, R. Thomas |

A) →
   Rider, Robert
B) →
   Ryder, Rob
C) →
   Ryder, Robert
D) →
   Ryder, Russell
E) →

69. | Chan, Jinny |

A) →
   Chan, Cyrus A.
B) →
   Chan, James C.
C) →
   Chan, Jimmie R.
D) →
   Chan, Jin Ho
E) →

70. | Chanler, Egan |

A) →
   Chandler, Katherine
B) →
   Chandler, Lilly
C) →
   Chanler, Doris
D) →
   Chanler, Ralph
E) →

Answers

71. Subtract:
   38
  − 19

   A) 9   B) 11
   C) 19 D) 29
   E) none of these

72. Multiply:
   46
  × 4

   A) 164 B) 168
   C) 174 D) 178
   E) none of these

73. Divide:
   8$\overline{)648}$

   A) 80   B) 81
   C) 82   D) 88
   E) none of these

74. Add:
   15
  + 82

   A) 73   B) 93
   C) 87   D) 97
   E) none of these

75. Subtract:
   48
  − 31

   A) 11   B) 13
   C) 21   D) 27
   E) none of these

In questions 76 through 80, find which one of the suggested answers appears in that question.

76. 5 Q F R 3 4 7 X

77. X 4 3 5 R 6 Z V

78. R 4 Z X 3 7 9 V

79. 4 3 Y 7 8 X V F

80. 7 3 Y 9 F R 5 V

Suggested Answers
A = 9, 4, V, R
B = 9, 3, F, X
C = 5, 3, V, F
D = 5, 4, R, X
E = none of these

In questions 81 through 85, compare the three names or numbers, and mark the answer—
  A if ALL THREE names or numbers are exactly ALIKE
  B if only the FIRST and SECOND names or numbers are exactly ALIKE
  C if only the FIRST and THIRD names or numbers are exactly ALIKE
  D if only the SECOND and THIRD names or numbers are exactly ALIKE
  E if ALL THREE names or numbers are DIFFERENT

81. 9810236   9810236   9870236

82. 3784615   3786415   3786415

83. 3892767   3892767   3892767

84. Kelley Millie Laykin   Kelley Millie Layken   Kelley Millie Layken

85. Alexander Mueller   Alexandra Mueller   Alexandra Meuller

---

In questions 86 through 90, find the correct place for the name in the box.

86. Chambers, Robin
  A) →
      Chalmbers, Allen
  B) →
      Chalmburs, Pero
  C) →
      Chambers, Roberta
  D) →
      Chambers, T. Maria
  E) →

87. O'Brian, Ernest
  A) →
      O'Brien, Daniel
  B) →
      O'Brien, David
  C) →
      O'Brien, Eloise
  D) →
      O'Brien, Francis
  E) →

88. Rupprecht, Alice
  A) →
      Rupp, Dwane
  B) →
      Ruppert, MacNee
  C) →
      Ruppolo, Rupert
  D) →
      Rusch, Daniel
  E) →

89. Maii, Helen
  A) →
      Maier, Jeri
  B) →
      Maio, John
  C) →
      Maison, Renee R.
  D) →
      Maizels, Danielle
  E) →

90. Fox, Sidney N.
  A) →
      Fox, Simba
  B) →
      Fox, Sonny
  C) →
      Fox, Stephen
  D) →
      Fox, Sydney
  E) →

Answers

91. Multiply: A) 66   B) 69
        23   C) 89   D) 96
      × 3   E) none of these

92. Divide: A) 13   B) 17
      5⟌135   C) 19   D) 27
                        E) none of these

93. Add: A) 129   B) 139
        48   C) 149   D) 157
      + 81   E) none of these

94. Subtract: A) 67   B) 77
        92   C) 79   D) 87
      − 15   E) none of these

95. Multiply: A) 148   B) 164
        24   C) 168   D) 186
      × 7   E) none of these

In questions 96 through 100, find which one of the
suggested answers appears in that question.

96. Q 8 R Z Y 6 7 9

97. 5 R 9 3 Y 7 Z F

98. 5 R 7 F X Y 3 9

99. F 8 Z 7 R 3 Y 9

100. 5 4 M Y R 9 V 6

Suggested Answers
$\begin{cases} A = 9, & 8, & Y, & R \\ B = 9, & 5, & R, & F \\ C = 8, & 7, & Y, & M \\ D = 7, & 5, & M, & F \\ E = \text{none of these} \end{cases}$

In questions 101 through 105, compare the three names or numbers, and mark the answer—
A if ALL THREE names or numbers are exactly ALIKE
B if only the FIRST and SECOND names or numbers are exactly ALIKE
C if only the FIRST and THIRD names or numbers are exactly ALIKE
D if only the SECOND and THIRD names or numbers are exactly ALIKE
E if ALL THREE names or numbers are DIFFERENT

101.	3829742	3829742	3829742
102.	3783465	3738465	3783465
103.	L. M. Pisarkiewicz	L. M. Pisarkiewicz	M. L. Pisarkiewicz
104.	Francis Pivrnec	Frances Pivrnec	Francis Pivnrec
105.	Lloyd J. Pfitzer	Lloyd J. Pfitzer	Lloyd J. Pfitzer

In questions 106 through 110, find the correct place
for the name in the box.

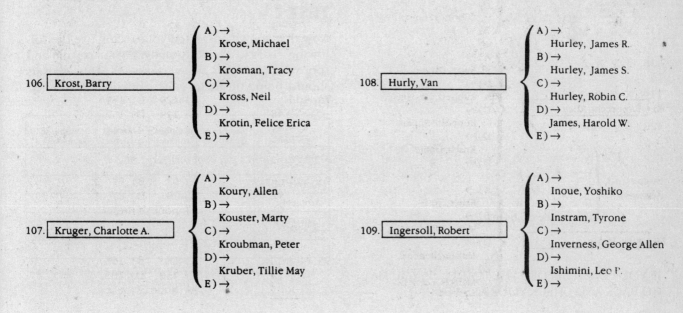

106. Krost, Barry
$\begin{cases} A) \rightarrow \\ \quad \text{Krose, Michael} \\ B) \rightarrow \\ \quad \text{Krosman, Tracy} \\ C) \rightarrow \\ \quad \text{Kross, Neil} \\ D) \rightarrow \\ \quad \text{Krotin, Felice Erica} \\ E) \rightarrow \end{cases}$

108. Hurly, Van
$\begin{cases} A) \rightarrow \\ \quad \text{Hurley, James R.} \\ B) \rightarrow \\ \quad \text{Hurley, James S.} \\ C) \rightarrow \\ \quad \text{Hurley, Robin C.} \\ D) \rightarrow \\ \quad \text{James, Harold W.} \\ E) \rightarrow \end{cases}$

107. Kruger, Charlotte A.
$\begin{cases} A) \rightarrow \\ \quad \text{Koury, Allen} \\ B) \rightarrow \\ \quad \text{Kouster, Marty} \\ C) \rightarrow \\ \quad \text{Kroubman, Peter} \\ D) \rightarrow \\ \quad \text{Kruber, Tillie May} \\ E) \rightarrow \end{cases}$

109. Ingersoll, Robert
$\begin{cases} A) \rightarrow \\ \quad \text{Inoue, Yoshiko} \\ B) \rightarrow \\ \quad \text{Instram, Tyrone} \\ C) \rightarrow \\ \quad \text{Inverness, George Allen} \\ D) \rightarrow \\ \quad \text{Ishimini, Leo P.} \\ E) \rightarrow \end{cases}$

110. Sullivan, John L.

A) →
  Sullivan, Jack
B) →
  Sullivan, Jim
C) →
  Sullivan, John
D) →
  Sullivan, Jon
E) →

Answers

111. Divide:

$7 \overline{)217}$

A) 30   B) 31
C) 32   D) 37
E) none of these

112. Add:

29
+ 51

A) 70   B) 78
C) 80   D) 90
E) none of these

113. Subtract:

89
− 18

A) 71   B) 73
C) 79   D) 81
E) none of these

114. Multiply:

52
× 9

A) 452   B) 458
C) 462   D) 466
E) none of these

115. Divide:

$6 \overline{)384}$

A) 62   B) 64
C) 66   D) 68
E) none of these

In questions 116 through 120, find which one of the suggested answers appears in that question.

116. 2 Y Q 8 V 7 5 R

117. V 6 R M 7 8 2 X

118. 3 9 X Z 2 V Q 6

119. X Z 2 Q 6 V 3 4

120. 6 F 3 R 9 2 X V

Suggested Answers

A = 7, 2, V, X
B = 7, 6, R, Q
C = 6, 3, V, Q
D = 3, 2, R, X
E = none of these

IF YOU FINISH BEFORE THE TIME IS UP, YOU MAY GO BACK AND CHECK YOUR ANSWERS.

ANSWER KEY FOR MODEL TEST 2

Alike or Different

1. E	21. C	41. B	61. B	81. B	101. A
2. D	22. A	42. E	62. E	82. D	102. C
3. C	23. D	43. C	63. C	83. A	103. B
4. C	24. E	44. E	64. B	84. D	104. E
5. B	25. B	45. D	65. A	85. E	105. A

Alphabetizing

6. C	26. C	46. B	66. D	86. D	106. D
7. A	27. B	47. C	67. C	87. A	107. E
8. C	28. C	48. D	68. B	88. D	108. D
9. B	29. D	49. B	69. E	89. B	109. A
10. A	30. D	50. C	70. D	90. A	110. D

Arithmetic

11. E	31. E	51. C	71. C	91. B	111. B
12. C	32. E	52. B	72. E	92. D	112. C
13. B	33. C	53. B	73. B	93. A	113. A
14. E	34. B	54. D	74. D	94. B	114. E
15. C	35. C	55. A	75. E	95. C	115. B

Letters and Numbers

16. E	36. A	56. D	76. D	96. A	116. E
17. B	37. D	57. C	77. D	97. B	117. A
18. E	38. E	58. E	78. A	98. B	118. C
19. D	39. B	59. B	79. E	99. A	119. C
20. C	40. A	60. B	80. C	100. E	120. D

ANALYSIS CHART FOR MODEL TEST 2

Now that you've corrected your exam, use the following chart to carefully analyze your results and spot your strengths and weaknesses. This analysis should help you focus your study and review efforts.

Section	Total Number of Questions	Number Correct	Number Incorrect	Number Unanswered*
Alike or Different	30			
Alphabetizing	30			
Arithmetic	30			
Letters and Numbers	30			
TOTAL	120			

*Since there is a small penalty for incorrect answers on the Clerical Abilities Test, you should not guess "blindly." Try to eliminate one or more of the choices before you take your educated guess.

ANSWER EXPLANATIONS FOR MODEL TEST 2

1. (E) 3870936 — 3879036 — 3870963
2. (D) 3827092 — 3827902 — 3827902
3. (C) 3701234 — 3702324 — 3701234
4. (C) Arno Wojecieski — Arno Wojeceiski — Arno Wojecieski
5. (B) Laurence Zwisen — Laurence Zwisen — Lawrence Zwisen
6. (C) Melodie, Merry — Melody, Rogers — Meloeny, Vincent
7. (A) Sachs, George — Sack, Uthbert
8. (C) Laib, Robin — Laidler, Clovis — Laine, Bob
9. (B) Mensor, Albert — Mentzel, Donald — Menzies, Peter
10. (A) Deluccio, D. M. — De Luna, Ronald
11. (E) Correct answer: 126.
12. (C) 87
13. (B) 127
14. (E) Correct answer: 66.
15. (C) 460
16. (E) R 6 7 4 F M 8 Q
17. (B) 3 6 8 X V 9 Q R
18. (E) 4 9 6 R 2 M V X
19. (D) 2 3 V 9 6 Q M X
20. (C) Q 5 6 X 2 8 Z R
21. (C) 2873012 — 2870312
22. (A) 2870283 — 2870283
23. (D) 2983121 — 2981231
24. (E) Magdalena Koltunik — Magdalena Koltunik
25. (B) Gavrilo Romendicth — Gavrilo Romendicth
26. (C) King, Anna Kris — King, Anthony P. — King, Arden
27. (B) Abosch, Albert — Abovid, Maria — Abowd, Harriet
28. (C) Adderly, D. J. — Addison, Tracey — Addotta, Cosimo
29. (D) Mouton, Lee — Mouton, N. G. — Mouton, Nellie
30. (D) Moya, Adelaide — Moya, Antonio — Moya, Armando
31. (E) Correct answer: 39.
32. (E) Correct answer: 81.
33. (C) 45
34. (B) 432
35. (C) 307
36. (A) 5 9 6 M 7 Z F Y
37. (D) V 7 4 9 F 5 X M
38. (E) 8 6 7 V 2 X F Y
39. (B) Y 7 M 4 V 8 6 Q
40. (A) 7 M 9 2 R 6 F Y
41. (B) Ronald T. Kullaway — Ronald T. Kullaway — Ronald F. Kullaway
42. (E) Ernest Teversen — Ernest Iversen — Ernest Iversen
43. (C) 4836194 — 4836914 — 4836194
44. (E) 3129378 — 3123978 — 3129738
45. (D) 2356421 — 2354621 — 2354621
46. (B) Vanhimberger, Jos. — Van Horn, Jay — VanHorne, Robt.
47. (C) Jenkins, T. C. — Jenkins, T. R. — Jenkins, Thomas
48. (D) Nawrot, Edmund — Nay, Eleanor — Nayar, Sami
49. (B) Vetlugin, Rudolf — Vetrono, Peter — Vetsikyan, Aaron
50. (C) Standard Testing — Standards and Co. — Standards Improvement
51. (C) 65
52. (B) 58
53. (B) 105
54. (D) 17
55. (A) 62
56. (D) X 6 4 Q R 2 7 F
57. (C) 7 5 Z F 9 R M 2
58. (E) 5 7 R 9 Z 3 Q M

59. **(B)** 4 Z 6 9 7 R M F
60. **(B)** M F 3 6 7 R 9 Z
61. **(B)** Lorraine Timbershun   Lorraine Timbershun   Lorraine Timbershun
62. **(E)** Michelle R. Spencer   Michelle R. Spencer   Michelle R. Spencer
63. **(C)** Jake Lazarwitz   Jake Lazarwits   Jake Lazarwitz
64. **(B)** 3826129   3826129   3826127
65. **(A)** 4837910   4837910   4837910
66. **(D)** Andranik, Sami / *Andravillo, Frank* / Andravin, Paul
67. **(C)** Saarinter, Lois / *Saary, Armand* / Saasnow, Allyn
68. **(B)** Rider, Robert / *Ryder, R. Thomas* / Ryder, Rob
69. **(E)** Chan, Jin Ho / *Cban, Jinny*
70. **(D)** Chanler, Doris / *Cbanler, Egan* / Chanler, Ralph
71. **(C)** 19
72. **(E)** Correct answer: 184.
73. **(B)** 81
74. **(D)** 97
75. **(E)** Correct answer: 17.
76. **(D)** 5 Q F R 3 4 7 X
77. **(D)** X 4 3 5 R 6 Z V
78. **(A)** R 4 Z X 3 7 9 V
79. **(E)** 4 3 Y 7 8 X V F
80. **(C)** 7 3 Y 9 F R 5 V
81. **(B)** 9810236   9810236   9870236
82. **(D)** 3784615   3786415   3786415
83. **(A)** 3892767   3892767   3892767
84. **(D)** Kelley Millie Laykin   Kelley Millie Layken   Kelley Millie Layken
85. **(E)** Alexander Mueller   Alexandra Mueller   Alexandra Meuller
86. **(D)** Chambers, Roberta / *Cbambers, Robin* / Chambers, T. Maria
87. **(A)** *O'Brian, Ernest* / O'Brien, Daniel
88. **(D)** Ruppolo, Rupert / *Rupprecbt, Alice* / Rusch, Daniel

89. **(B)** Maier, Jeri / *Maii, Helen* / Maio, John
90. **(A)** *Fox, Sidney N.* / Fox, Simba
91. **(B)** 69
92. **(D)** 27
93. **(A)** 129
94. **(B)** 77
95. **(C)** 168
96. **(A)** Q 8 R Z Y 6 7 9
97. **(B)** 5 R 9 3 Y 7 Z F
98. **(B)** 5 R 7 F X Y 3 9
99. **(A)** F 8 Z 7 R 3 Y 9
100. **(E)** 5 4 M Y R 9 V 6
101. **(A)** 3829742   3829742   3829742
102. **(C)** 3783465   3738465   3783465
103. **(B)** L. M. Pisarkiewicz   L. M. Pisarkiewicz   M. L. Pisarkiewicz
104. **(E)** Francis Pivrnec   Frances Pivrnec   Francis Pivnrec
105. **(A)** Lloyd J. Pfitzer   Lloyd J. Pfitzer   Lloyd J. Pfitzer
106. **(D)** Kross, Neil / *Krost, Barry* / Krotin, Felice Erica
107. **(E)** Kruber, Tillie May / *Kruger, Charlotte A.*
108. **(D)** Hurley, Robin C. / *Hurly, Van* / James, Harold W.
109. **(A)** *Ingersoll, Robert* / Inoue, Yoshiko
110. **(D)** Sullivan, John / *Sullivan, John L.* / Sullivan, Jon
111. **(B)** 31
112. **(C)** 80
113. **(A)** 71
114. **(E)** Correct answer: 468.
115. **(B)** 64
116. **(E)** 2 Y Q 8 V 7 5 R
117. **(A)** V 6 R M 7 8 2 X
118. **(C)** 3 9 X Z 2 V Q 6
119. **(C)** X Z 2 Q 6 V 3 4
120. **(D)** 6 F 3 R 9 2 X V

ANSWER SHEET

SIGNATURE: _____
(Please Sign)

EXAMINATION TITLE: _____

PLACE OF EXAMINATION: _____
City _____ State _____

TODAY'S DATE: _____

SAMPLE (A) ● (C) (D) (E)

DIRECTIONS FOR MARKING ANSWER SHEET

Use only a **No. 2 (or softer) lead pencil.** Darken completely the circle corresponding to your answer. You **must** keep your mark within the circle. Stray marks may be counted as errors. Erase **completely** all marks except your answer.

SAMPLE NAME GRID

LAST NAME	F.I.	M.I.
M C C A B E	C	A

1. In the boxes below, **PRINT** your name. Print only as many letters as will fit within the areas for the last name, first initial (F.I.), and middle initial (M.I.) Below each box, darken the circle containing the same letter. SEE SAMPLE NAME GRID

LAST NAME | F.I. | M.I.

2. In the boxes below, enter your 9-digit Social Security Number. Below each box, darken the circle in each column corresponding to the number you have entered

SOCIAL SECURITY NUMBER

3. OCCUPATIONAL GROUP NUMBER

SECTION 1

PART

TEST SERIES

TEST NUMBER

Make no marks or entries in the columns to the right until you receive instructions from the administrator.

1 (A)(B)(C)(D)(E)	11 (A)(B)(C)(D)(E)	31 (A)(B)(C)(D)(E)	51 (A)(B)(C)(D)(E)	71 (A)(B)(C)(D)(E)	91 (A)(B)(C)(D)(E)	111 (A)(B)(C)(D)(E)
2 (A)(B)(C)(D)(E)	12 (A)(B)(C)(D)(E)	32 (A)(B)(C)(D)(E)	52 (A)(B)(C)(D)(E)	72 (A)(B)(C)(D)(E)	92 (A)(B)(C)(D)(E)	112 (A)(B)(C)(D)(E)
3 (A)(B)(C)(D)(E)	13 (A)(B)(C)(D)(E)	33 (A)(B)(C)(D)(E)	53 (A)(B)(C)(D)(E)	73 (A)(B)(C)(D)(E)	93 (A)(B)(C)(D)(E)	113 (A)(B)(C)(D)(E)
4 (A)(B)(C)(D)(E)	14 (A)(B)(C)(D)(E)	34 (A)(B)(C)(D)(E)	54 (A)(B)(C)(D)(E)	74 (A)(B)(C)(D)(E)	94 (A)(B)(C)(D)(E)	114 (A)(B)(C)(D)(E)
5 (A)(B)(C)(D)(E)	15 (A)(B)(C)(D)(E)	35 (A)(B)(C)(D)(E)	55 (A)(B)(C)(D)(E)	75 (A)(B)(C)(D)(E)	95 (A)(B)(C)(D)(E)	115 (A)(B)(C)(D)(E)
6 (A)(B)(C)(D)(E)	16 (A)(B)(C)(D)(E)	36 (A)(B)(C)(D)(E)	56 (A)(B)(C)(D)(E)	76 (A)(B)(C)(D)(E)	96 (A)(B)(C)(D)(E)	116 (A)(B)(C)(D)(E)
7 (A)(B)(C)(D)(E)	17 (A)(B)(C)(D)(E)	37 (A)(B)(C)(D)(E)	57 (A)(B)(C)(D)(E)	77 (A)(B)(C)(D)(E)	97 (A)(B)(C)(D)(E)	117 (A)(B)(C)(D)(E)
8 (A)(B)(C)(D)(E)	18 (A)(B)(C)(D)(E)	38 (A)(B)(C)(D)(E)	58 (A)(B)(C)(D)(E)	78 (A)(B)(C)(D)(E)	98 (A)(B)(C)(D)(E)	118 (A)(B)(C)(D)(E)
9 (A)(B)(C)(D)(E)	19 (A)(B)(C)(D)(E)	39 (A)(B)(C)(D)(E)	59 (A)(B)(C)(D)(E)	79 (A)(B)(C)(D)(E)	99 (A)(B)(C)(D)(E)	119 (A)(B)(C)(D)(E)
10 (A)(B)(C)(D)(E)	20 (A)(B)(C)(D)(E)	40 (A)(B)(C)(D)(E)	60 (A)(B)(C)(D)(E)	80 (A)(B)(C)(D)(E)	100 (A)(B)(C)(D)(E)	120 (A)(B)(C)(D)(E)
	21 (A)(B)(C)(D)(E)	41 (A)(B)(C)(D)(E)	61 (A)(B)(C)(D)(E)	81 (A)(B)(C)(D)(E)	101 (A)(B)(C)(D)(E)	121 (A)(B)(C)(D)(E)
	22 (A)(B)(C)(D)(E)	42 (A)(B)(C)(D)(E)	62 (A)(B)(C)(D)(E)	82 (A)(B)(C)(D)(E)	102 (A)(B)(C)(D)(E)	122 (A)(B)(C)(D)(E)
	23 (A)(B)(C)(D)(E)	43 (A)(B)(C)(D)(E)	63 (A)(B)(C)(D)(E)	83 (A)(B)(C)(D)(E)	103 (A)(B)(C)(D)(E)	123 (A)(B)(C)(D)(E)
	24 (A)(B)(C)(D)(E)	44 (A)(B)(C)(D)(E)	64 (A)(B)(C)(D)(E)	84 (A)(B)(C)(D)(E)	104 (A)(B)(C)(D)(E)	124 (A)(B)(C)(D)(E)
	25 (A)(B)(C)(D)(E)	45 (A)(B)(C)(D)(E)	65 (A)(B)(C)(D)(E)	85 (A)(B)(C)(D)(E)	105 (A)(B)(C)(D)(E)	125 (A)(B)(C)(D)(E)
	26 (A)(B)(C)(D)(E)	46 (A)(B)(C)(D)(E)	66 (A)(B)(C)(D)(E)	86 (A)(B)(C)(D)(E)	106 (A)(B)(C)(D)(E)	126 (A)(B)(C)(D)(E)
	27 (A)(B)(C)(D)(E)	47 (A)(B)(C)(D)(E)	67 (A)(B)(C)(D)(E)	87 (A)(B)(C)(D)(E)	107 (A)(B)(C)(D)(E)	127 (A)(B)(C)(D)(E)
	28 (A)(B)(C)(D)(E)	48 (A)(B)(C)(D)(E)	68 (A)(B)(C)(D)(E)	88 (A)(B)(C)(D)(E)	108 (A)(B)(C)(D)(E)	128 (A)(B)(C)(D)(E)
	29 (A)(B)(C)(D)(E)	49 (A)(B)(C)(D)(E)	69 (A)(B)(C)(D)(E)	89 (A)(B)(C)(D)(E)	109 (A)(B)(C)(D)(E)	129 (A)(B)(C)(D)(E)
	30 (A)(B)(C)(D)(E)	50 (A)(B)(C)(D)(E)	70 (A)(B)(C)(D)(E)	90 (A)(B)(C)(D)(E)	110 (A)(B)(C)(D)(E)	130 (A)(B)(C)(D)(E)

MODEL TEST 3

Time allotted—15 minutes

Directions

Each question has five suggested answers. Decide which one is the best answer. Find the question number on the Answer Sheet. Show your answer to the question by darkening completely the space corresponding to the letter that is the same as the letter of your answer. Keep your mark within the space. If you have to erase a mark, be sure to erase it completely. Mark only one answer for each question.

In questions 1 through 5, compare the names or numbers, and mark the answer—
   A if ALL THREE names or numbers are exactly ALIKE
   B if only the FIRST and SECOND names or numbers are exactly ALIKE
   C if only the FIRST and THIRD names or numbers are exactly ALIKE
   D if only the SECOND and THIRD names or numbers are exactly ALIKE
   E if ALL THREE names or numbers are DIFFERENT

1. Willie MacCovey	Willie McCovey	Willie MacCovey
2. Antony Frennsdorff	Anthony Frennsdorf	Anthony Frensdorff
3. Frederick Kurt	Fredrick Kurt	Frederic Kurt
4. Terrence Garrity	Terrence Garrity	Terence Garrity
5. 4930752	4930572	4930572

In questions 6 through 10, find the correct place for the name in the box.

6. Kordakis, Peter
   A) →
   Koran, J.
   B) →
   Korda, Jerome
   C) →
   Kordes, Dennis
   D) →
   Kordosh, Stacey
   E) →

7. Thompson, L.W.
   A) →
   Thompson, Johnny
   B) →
   Thompson, Larry
   C) →
   Thompson, Lawrence
   D) →
   Thompson, Linda
   E) →

8. Wang, Wm.
   A) →
   Wang, Carl
   B) →
   Wang, Mei Hua
   C) →
   Wang, Paul
   D) →
   Wang, Peter
   E) →

9. Dana Computer
   A) →
   Dana Distributors
   B) →
   Dana, Jim
   C) →
   Danaman Corporation
   D) →
   Dance Express
   E) →

10. Taylor, Glenn
    A) →
    Taylor, Glenn R.
    B) →
    Taylor, Greg
    C) →
    Taylor, Haddie
    D) →
    Taylor, Irvine
    E) →

11. Multiply:
    32
   × 6

Answers
A) 182 B) 192
C) 196 D) 202
E) none of these

12. Divide:
  7)217

A) 30 B) 31
C) 33 D) 37
E) none of these

13. Add:
    58
  + 63

A) 101 B) 105
C) 111 D) 118
E) none of these

14. Subtract:
    93
  − 78

A) 15 B) 17
C) 23 D) 25
E) none of these

15. Multiply:
    26
  × 4

A) 84 B) 94
C) 104 D) 114
E) none of these

In questions 16 through 20, find which one of the suggested answers appears in that question.

16. 7 U 5 4 P 8 T M

17. M 7 U 2 Y 6 8 R

18. 6 8 7 Y 4 X T M

19. Y 7 2 5 T 9 X U

20. 9 5 8 U 7 Q T M

Suggested Answers
A = 7, 8, U, T
B = 7, 2, M, U
C = 5, 8, M, Y
D = 5, 2, Y, T
E = none of these

In questions 21 through 25, compare the three names or numbers, and mark the answer—
A if ALL THREE names or numbers are exactly ALIKE
B if only the FIRST and SECOND names or numbers are exactly ALIKE
C if only the FIRST and THIRD names or numbers are exactly ALIKE
D if only the SECOND and THIRD names or numbers are exactly ALIKE
E if ALL THREE names or numbers are DIFFERENT

21. 7428961   7428961   7428961

22. 2796231   2769231   2769231

23. Jackie M. Firstbee   Jackie N. Firstbee   Jackey M. Firsbee

24. Matthew Highland   Mathew Highland   Mathew Highland

25. Guenther Steffens   Guenther Steffens   Gunther Steffens

In questions 26 through 30, find the correct place for the name in the box.

26. Swallow, Ron
A) →
  Swaim, Flora
B) →
  Swain, J.E.
C) →
  Swainson, Ralph
D) →
  Swainvick, Patsy
E) →

27. Miller, Gayle
A) →
  Miller, Gary
B) →
  Miller, Greg
C) →
  Miller, Gregory
D) →
  Miller, Gregory P.
E) →

28. Sanders, Michael Jas.

A) →
    Sanders, Michael
B) →
    Sanders, Michael J.
C) →
    Sanders, Nicholas
D) →
    Sanders, Sandra
E) →

29. Baskin, Mark

A) →
    Basket World
B) →
    Baslow, Brigitte
C) →
    Bassett, Robert
D) →
    Bastean, Richard
E) →

30. Grella, Christa

A) →
    Gaston, M.P.
B) →
    Greenhaulgh, Vera
C) →
    Greenleaf, Douglas
D) →
    Greenlee, Kitty
E) →

31. Divide:

$9)\overline{828}$

Answers
A) 19   B) 91
C) 92   D) 99
E) none of these

32. Add:
   74
$+\ 29$

A) 83   B) 93
C) 95   D) 103
E) none of these

33. Subtract:
   82
$-\ 56$

A) 26   B) 28
C) 32   D) 36
E) none of these

34. Multiply:
   71
$\times\ \ 5$

A) 350   B) 365
C) 375   D) 385
E) none of these

35. Divide:

$7)\overline{714}$

A) 12   B) 102
C) 120   D) 122
E) none of these

In questions 36 through 40, find which one of the suggested answers appears in that question.

36. 8 T 3 P 5 4 X Y

37. X Q 4 R 8 Y 3 2

38. 3 5 X Q 4 Y R 8

39. Y 8 P U 7 6 4 X

40. 4 M R 6 Y 7 9 P

Suggested Answers

A = 7, 4, Y, X
B = 7, 8, P, R
C = 8, 3, Y, R
D = 3, 4, P, X
E = none of these

In questions 41 through 45, compare the three names or numbers, and mark the answer—
  A if ALL THREE names or numbers are exactly ALIKE
  B if only the FIRST and SECOND names or numbers are exactly ALIKE
  C if only the FIRST and THIRD names or numbers are exactly ALIKE
  D if only the SECOND and THIRD names or numbers are exactly ALIKE
  E if ALL THREE names or numbers are DIFFERENT

41. William Parkherst	William Parkhurst	William Parkhurst
42. Alan Wyzandowsky	Alan Wyzandosky	Allan Wyzandowsky
43. Bente Larsen	Bente Larsen	Bente Larson
44. John Lesczyznski	John Lesczyznski	John Lesczyznski
45. 7396932	7369632	7369632

In questions 46 through 50, find the correct place for the name in the box.

50. | Sam's Auto |
- A) →
  - Sampson, Steven
- B) →
  - Samsel, Ozzie
- C) →
  - Samuel, Tomas
- D) →
  - Sanchez, Joe
- E) →

46. | Sandberg, Kate |
- A) →
  - Sandefur, Harold
- B) →
  - Sanders, Marvine
- C) →
  - Sandor, Dominick
- D) →
  - Sands, Janice
- E) →

Answers

51. Add:
    97
    + 82
A) 155 B) 169
C) 179 D) 197
E) none of these

52. Subtract:
    81
    − 14
A) 57 B) 67
C) 75 D) 77
E) none of these

47. | Orloff, Bradford Lee |
- A) →
  - Orlean, Glenna
- B) →
  - Orlowski, Floyd
- C) →
  - Orme, Gaylord
- D) →
  - Orr, Fred
- E) →

53. Multiply:
    39
    × 3
A) 97 B) 99
C) 107 D) 117
E) none of these

54. Divide:
    3)159
A) 35 B) 53
C) 59 D) 63
E) none of these

55. Add:
    39
    + 74
A) 103 B) 105
C) 113 D) 115
E) none of these

In questions 56 through 60, find which one of the suggested answers appears in that question.

48. | Otis, Graphics |
- A) →
  - Otis, G.
- B) →
  - Otis, Lance N.
- C) →
  - Otis, T.
- D) →
  - Otis, Wm. L.
- E) →

56. R 9 8 X 4 6 Q P

57. 4 3 Y 5 8 R U X

58. 2 5 8 P 4 U Y X

59. 3 8 6 X Y 5 R P

60. P 8 7 2 T U 6 R

49. | Green, M.L. |
- A) →
  - Green, Jean
- B) →
  - Green, Krisy
- C) →
  - Green, M.
- D) →
  - Greene, Patricia
- E) →

Suggested Answers
- A = 6, 3, U, P
- B = 8, 3, P, X
- C = 6, 4, X, R
- D = 8, 4, U, R
- E = none of these

In questions 61 through 65, compare the three names or numbers, and mark the answer—
  A if ALL THREE names or numbers are exactly ALIKE
  B if only the FIRST and SECOND names or numbers are exactly ALIKE
  C if only the FIRST and THIRD names or numbers are exactly ALIKE
  D if only the SECOND and THIRD names or numbers are exactly ALIKE
  E if ALL THREE names or numbers are DIFFERENT

61.	8646808	8648608	8646808
62.	4583201	4583021	4538021
63.	6854238	6845238	6854238
64.	9324685	9324685	9324685
65.	Marion L. Woodside	Marion L. Woodside	Marion L. Woodside

In questions 66 through 70, find the correct place for the name in the box.

66. Del Faro, J.
  A) →
    DeFina, Bobby
  B) →
    DeGemaro, Dan
  C) →
    Dehbod, Christine
  D) →
    Dekreek, Dirk
  E) →

67. Haase, Seajay
  A) →
    Hase, Rudolph
  B) →
    Haase, Sergio
  C) →
    Hasselman, Peter
  D) →
    Hasselmann, Laurie
  E) →

68. Thornton, Leonard
  A) →
    Thousan, David
  B) →
    Thousand Oaks Storage
  C) →
    Thrift Rent-a-Car
  D) →
    Thundborg, Donald
  E) →

69. Golus, M.
  A) →
    Golson, Tim
  B) →
    Gomberg, Carl
  C) →
    Gomez, Salvador
  D) →
    Gonzales, Teoni
  E) →

70. Oviedo, Oscar
  A) →
    Overton, Patricia
  B) →
    Ovrid, Stephen
  C) →
    Ow, Steven
  D) →
    Owen, L.P.
  E) →

Answers

71. Subtract:
      93
    − 18

A) 75   B) 77
C) 85   D) 111
E) none of these

72. Multiply:
      17
    × 6

A) 62   B) 72
C) 92   D) 104
E) none of these

73. Divide:

    7)308

A) 41   B) 42
C) 43   D) 44
E) none of these

74. Add: A) 50   B) 60
     29   C) 70   D) 80
   + 31   E) none of these

75. Subtract: A) 55   B) 58
     92   C) 63   D) 65
   − 37   E) none of these

77. 2 3 M 7 6 X Y T

78. P 2 Q X 3 7 5 Y

79. X 2 3 9 P 8 Q Y

80. 9 R T P 3 2 7 X

In questions 76 through 80, find which one of the suggested answers appears in that question.

Suggested Answers

A = 5, 2, Y, P
B = 5, 3, T, X
C = 9, 3, Y, T
D = 9, 2, P, X
E = none of these

76. 7 3 M 5 T P 9 Y

In questions 81 through 85, compare the three names or numbers, and mark the answer—
  A if ALL THREE names or numbers are exactly ALIKE
  B if only the FIRST and SECOND names or numbers are exactly ALIKE
  C if only the FIRST and THIRD names or numbers are exactly ALIKE
  D if only the SECOND and THIRD names or numbers are exactly ALIKE
  E if ALL THREE names or numbers are DIFFERENT

81. Smiley Yarnell   Smiley Yarnel   Smily Yarnell

82. Lee P. Wangerrine   Lee P. Wangerrine   Lee P. Wangerine

83. Douglas Watkins   Douglas Watkins   Douglass Watkins

84. Tricia Connelley   Trishia Connelley   Trishia Connelly

85. Jeffrey Armantos   Jeffrey Armantos   Jeffrey Armontos

In questions 86 through 90, find the correct place for the name in the box.

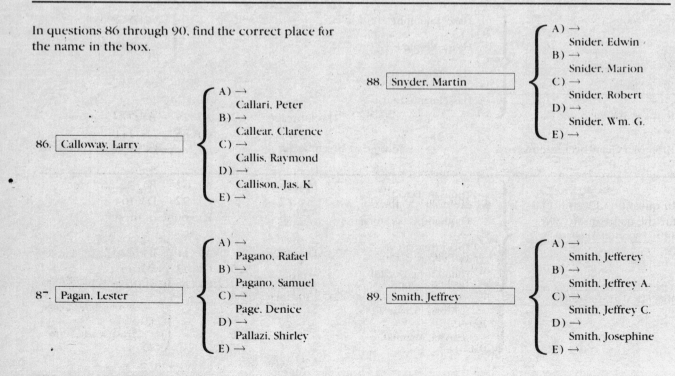

86. Calloway, Larry
  A) →
     Callari, Peter
  B) →
     Callear, Clarence
  C) →
     Callis, Raymond
  D) →
     Callison, Jas. K.
  E) →

88. Snyder, Martin
  A) →
     Snider, Edwin
  B) →
     Snider, Marion
  C) →
     Snider, Robert
  D) →
     Snider, Wm. G.
  E) →

87. Pagan, Lester
  A) →
     Pagano, Rafael
  B) →
     Pagano, Samuel
  C) →
     Page, Denice
  D) →
     Pallazi, Shirley
  E) →

89. Smith, Jeffrey
  A) →
     Smith, Jefferey
  B) →
     Smith, Jeffrey A.
  C) →
     Smith, Jeffrey C.
  D) →
     Smith, Josephine
  E) →

90. | Laitner, Phyllis |
{
A) →
   Lakadner, Brian
B) →
   Lake, Donald
C) →
   Laker, Christene
D) →
   Lemon, Craig G.
E) →
}

Answers

91. Multiply: A) 268 B) 278
          72   C) 288 D) 308
        × 4   E) none of these

92. Divide: A) 47   B) 48
                   C) 49   D) 58
        8)376   E) none of these

93. Add: A) 78   B) 94
          91   C) 104 D) 114
        + 13   E) none of these

94. Subtract: A) 37   B) 47
          72   C) 57   D) 67
        − 15   E) none of these

95. Multiply: A) 355 B) 425
          51   C) 428 D) 435
        × 7   E) none of these

In questions 96 through 100, find which one of the suggested answers appears in that question.

96. U T 3 8 7 P 5 Q

97. 2 Q 8 5 7 P U T

98. 9 7 P 5 Q 3 R U

99. 7 9 Q T 5 P U 4

100. X 8 2 R P 4 7 T

Suggested Answers
{
A = 5, 8, P, R
B = 7, 8, P, Q
C = 5, 4, Q, T
D = 7, 4, T, R
E = none of these
}

In questions 101 through 105, compare the three names or numbers, and mark the answer—
A if ALL THREE names or numbers are exactly ALIKE
B if only the FIRST and SECOND names or numbers are exactly ALIKE
C if only the FIRST and THIRD names or numbers are exactly ALIKE
D if only the SECOND and THIRD names or numbers are exactly ALIKE
E if ALL THREE names or numbers are DIFFERENT

101. 5892542   5829542   5829542

102. 7483984   7483984   7483984

103. 3869457   3869457   3869547

104. 2749572   2794572   2749572

105. Maryjean Bremmeuth   Maryjean Bremmeuth   Maryjean Bremmueth

In questions 106 through 110, find the correct place for the name in the box.

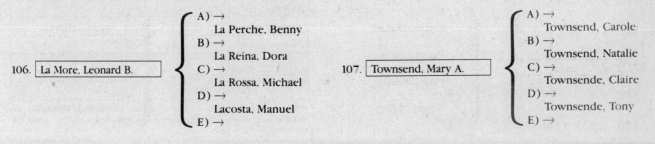

106. | La More, Leonard B. |
{
A) →
   La Perche, Benny
B) →
   La Reina, Dora
C) →
   La Rossa, Michael
D) →
   Lacosta, Manuel
E) →
}

107. | Townsend, Mary A. |
{
A) →
   Townsend, Carole
B) →
   Townsend, Natalie
C) →
   Townsende, Claire
D) →
   Townsende, Tony
E) →
}

108. Hunt, Randall G.
A) →
Hunt, A. Raymond
B) →
Hunt, Rosalie
C) →
Hunt, Thomas
D) →
Hunt, Victoria
E) →

109. Bole, Stacey
A) →
Bogush, Joann
B) →
Bolduc, Rick
C) →
Bolgna, Vincent
D) →
Bolin, Buford
E) →

110. Printmasters, Inc.
A) →
Post Time Printing Co.
B) →
Print Able, Inc.
C) →
Quick Print
D) →
Randolph Printers, Inc.
E) →

Suggested Answers
$\begin{cases} A = 5, \ 6, \ M, \ P \\ B = 5, \ 9, \ P, \ T \\ C = 6, \ 7, \ M, \ U \\ D = 7, \ 9, \ U, \ T \\ E = \text{none of these} \end{cases}$

IF YOU FINISH BEFORE THE TIME IS UP, YOU MAY GO BACK AND CHECK YOUR ANSWERS.

Answers

111. Divide:

6)384

A) 62 B) 64
C) 68 D) 72
E) none of these

112. Add:

29
+ 39

A) 58 B) 68
C) 78 D) 88
E) none of these

113. Subtract:

174
− 32

A) 140 B) 142
C) 144 D) 148
E) none of these

114. Multiply:

92
× 3

A) 267 B) 273
C) 276 D) 296
E) none of these

115. Divide:

7)707

A) 11   B) 110
C) 111 D) 112
E) none of these

In questions 116 through 120, find which one of the suggested answers appears in that question.

116. 9 2 U M P 5 Y 8

117. T 6 Q 7 P 3 M 5

118. 9 P 7 T X M 3 5

119. 9 P 5 3 M 7 Q T

120. R 6 P Q M 8 7 5

ANSWER KEY FOR MODEL TEST 3

Alike or Different

1. C	21. A	41. D	61. C	81. E	101. D
2. E	22. D	42. E	62. E	82. B	102. A
3. E	23. E	43. B	63. C	83. B	103. B
4. B	24. D	44. A	64. A	84. E	104. C
5. D	25. B	45. D	65. A	85. B	105. B

Alphabetizing

6. C	26. E	46. A	66. E	86. E	106. A
7. B	27. B	47. B	67. A	87. A	107. B
8. E	28. C	48. B	68. A	88. E	108. B
9. A	29. B	49. D	69. B	89. B	109. C
10. A	30. E	50. B	70. B	90. A	110. C

Arithmetic

11. B	31. C	51. C	71. A	91. C	111. B
12. B	32. D	52. B	72. E	92. A	112. B
13. E	33. A	53. D	73. D	93. C	113. B
14. A	34. E	54. B	74. B	94. C	114. C
15. C	35. B	55. C	75. A	95. E	115. E

Letters and Numbers

16. A	36. D	56. C	76. C	96. B	116. E
17. B	37. C	57. D	77. E	97. B	117. A
18. E	38. C	58. E	78. A	98. E	118. B
19. D	39. A	59. B	79. D	99. C	119. B
20. A	40. E	60. E	80. D	100. D	120. A

ANALYSIS CHART FOR MODEL TEST 3

Now that you've corrected your exam, use the following chart to carefully analyze your results and spot your strengths and weaknesses. This analysis should help you focus your study and review efforts.

Section	Total Number of Questions	Number Correct	Number Incorrect	Number Unanswered*
Alike or Different	30			
Alphabetizing	30			
Arithmetic	30			
Letters and Numbers	30			
TOTAL	120			

*Since there is a small penalty for incorrect answers on the Clerical Abilities Test, you should not guess "blindly." Try to eliminate one or more of the choices before you take your educated guess.

ANSWER EXPLANATIONS FOR MODEL TEST 3

1. (C) Willie MacCovey | Willie McCovey | Willie MacCovey
2. (E) Antony Frennsdorff | Anthony Frennsdorf | Anthony Frennsdorff
3. (E) Frederick Kurt | Fredrick Kurt | Frederic Kurt
4. (B) Terrence Garrity | Terrence Garrity | Terence Garrity
5. (D) 4930752 | 4930572 | 4930572
6. (C) Korda, Jerome
   Kordakis, Peter
   Kordes, Dennis
7. (B) Thompson, Johnny
   Thompson, L.W.
   Thompson, Larry
8. (E) Wang, Peter
   Wang, Wm.
9. (A) Dana Computer
   Dana Distributors
10. (A) Taylor, Glenn —
    Taylor, Glenn R.
11. (B) 192
12. (B) 31
13. (E) Correct answer: 121.
14. (A) 15
15. (C) 104
16. (A) Z U 5 4 P 8 T M
17. (B) M Z U 2 Y 6 8 R
18. (E) 6 8 7 Y 4 X T M
19. (D) Y 7 2 5 T 9 X U
20. (A) 9 5 8 U Z Q T M
21. (A) 7428961 | 7428961
22. (D) 2796231 | 2769231
23. (E) Jackie M. Firstbee | Jackie N. Firstbee
24. (D) Matthew Highland | Mathew Highland
25. (B) Guenther Steffens | Guenther Steffens
26. (E) Swainvick, Patsy
    Swalton; Ron
27. (B) Miller, Gary
    Miller, Gayle
    Miller, Greg
28. (C) Sanders, Michael J.
    Sanders, Michael Jas.
    Sanders, Nicholas

29. (B) Basket World
    Baskin, Mark
    Baslow, Brigitte
30. (E) Greenlee, Kitty
    Grella, Christa
31. (C) 92
32. (D) 103
33. (A) 26
34. (E) Correct answer: 355.
35. (B) 102
36. (D) 8 T 3 P 5 4 X Y
37. (C) X Q 4 R 8 Y 3 2
38. (C) 3 5 X Q 4 Y R 8
39. (A) Y 8 P U 7 6 4 X
40. (E) 4 M R 6 Y 7 9 P
41. (D) William Parkherst | William Parkhurst | William Parkhurst
42. (E) Alan Wyzandowsky | Alan Wyzandosky | Allan Wyzandowsky
43. (B) Bente Larsen | Bente Larsen | Bente Larson
44. (A) John Lesczyznski | John Lesczynski | John Lesczyznski
45. (D) 7369632 | 7369632 | 7369632
46. (A) Sandberg, Kate
    Sandefur, Harold
47. (B) Orlean, Glenna
    Orloff, Bradford Lee
    Orlowski, Floyd
48. (B) Otis, G
    Otis, Graphics
    Otis, T
49. (D) Green, M.
    Green, M.I.
    Greene, Patricia
50. (B) Sampson, Steven
    Sam's Auto
    Samsel, Ozzie
51. (C) 179
52. (B) 67
53. (D) 117
54. (B) 53
55. (C) 113
56. (C) R 9 8 X 4 6 Q P
57. (D) 4 3 Y 5 8 R U X
58. (E) 2 5 8 P 4 U Y X
59. (B) 3 8 6 X Y 5 R P
60. (E) P 8 7 2 T U 6 R

8646808 8646808
4583201 4538021
6854238 6845238
9324685 9324685
Marion L. Woodside Marion L. Woodside

61. (C) 8646808
62. (E) 4583201
63. (C) 6854238
64. (A) 9324685
65. (A) Marion L. Woodside
66. (E) Dekreek, Dirk
        Del Faro, J.
67. (A) Haase, Seajay
        Hase, Rudolph
68. (A) Thornton, Leonard
        Thousan, David
69. (B) Golson, Tim
        Gotus, M.
        Gomberg, Carl
70. (B) Overton, Patricia
        Oviedo, Oscar
        Ovrid, Stephen
71. (A) 75
72. (E) Correct answer: 102.
73. (D) 44
74. (B) 60
75. (A) 55
76. (C) 7 3 M 5 T P 9 Y
77. (E) 2 3 M 7 6 X Y T
78. (A) P 2 Q X 3 7 5 Y
79. (D) X 2 3 9 P 8 Q Y
80. (D) 9 R T P 3 2 7 X

Smiley Yarnel
Lee P. Wangerrine
Douglas Watkins
Trishia Connelley
Jeffrey Armantos

81. (E) Smiley Yarnell
82. (B) Lee P. Wangerrine
83. (B) Douglas Watkins
84. (E) Tricia Connelley
85. (B) Jeffrey Armantos
86. (E) Callison, Jas. K.
        Calloway, Larry
87. (A) Pagan, Lester
        Pagano, Rafael
88. (E) Snider, Wm. G.
        Snyder, Martin
89. (B) Smith, Jefferey
        Smith, Jeffrey
        Smith, Jeffrey A.

5829542
7483984
3869547
2749572

90. (A) Laitner, Phyllis
        Lakadner, Brian
91. (C) 288
92. (A) 47
93. (C) 104
94. (C) 57
95. (E) Correct answer: 357.
96. (B) U T 3 8 7 P 5 Q
97. (B) 2 Q 8 5 7 P U T
98. (E) 9 7 P 5 Q 3 R U
99. (C) 7 9 Q T 5 P U 4
100. (D) X 8 2 R P 4 Z T
101. (D) 5892542   5829542
102. (A) 7483984   7483984
103. (B) 3869457   3869457
104. (C) 2749572   2794572
105. (B) Maryjean Bremmeuth Maryjean Bremmeuth Maryjean Bremmueth
106. (A) La More, Leonard B.
        La Perche, Benny
107. (B) Townsend, Carole
        Townsend, Mary A.
        Townsend, Natalie
108. (B) Hunt, A. Raymond
        Hunt, Randall G.
        Hunt, Rosalie
109. (C) Bolduc, Rick
        Bole, Stacey
        Bolgna, Vincent
110. (C) Print Able, Inc.
        Printmasters, Inc.
        Quick Print
111. (B) 64
112. (B) 68
113. (B) 142
114. (C) 276
115. (E) Correct answer: 101.
116. (E) 9 2 U M P 5 Y 8
117. (A) T 6 Q 7 P 3 M 5
118. (B) 9 P 7 T X M 3 5
119. (B) 9 P 5 3 M 7 Q T
120. (A) R 6 P Q M 8 7 5

PART THREE

The Typing Test

CHAPTER 7

Introduction
A Diagnostic Test
Analysis

THE TYPING TEST—COPYING FROM PLAIN COPY

In this test, which is part of the Stenographer-Typist Examination, the applicant meets a single task, that of copying material exactly as it is presented. The candidate must demonstrate how rapidly he or she can do so and with what accuracy.

HOW THE TEST IS GIVEN

In the usual examination procedure, each competitor is given a copy of the test and two sheets of typewriter paper. About 15 minutes is needed for the complete typing test.

Three minutes are allowed for reading the instructions on the face of the test and 3 minutes for the practice typing. The practice exercise consists of typing instructions as to spacing, capitalization, etc., and contains a warning that any erasures will be penalized. The practice typing helps make sure that the typewriter is functioning properly.

After the 3 minutes' practice typing, the competitors put fresh paper in their machines, and turn the test page over and read the test for 2 minutes. After the 2 minutes, they are instructed to start typing the test. Five minutes are allowed for the test proper.

HOW THE TEST IS RATED

The exercise must have been typed about once to meet the speed requirement of 40 words a minute. If this speed is not attained, the test is not scored for accuracy. As shown in Example A, which follows the Diagnostic Test, a test paper that contains 17 lines meets the minimum speed requirement. Applicants have been instructed to begin and end each line precisely as in the printed test copy. From Example A it can be quickly determined whether a typing test is to be rated for accuracy and, if so, the greatest number of errors permitted for the lines typed.

The next step is to compare the test paper with the printed test exercise and to mark and charge errors. The basic principles in charging typing errors are as follows:

Charge 1 for each—
WORD or PUNCTUATION MARK incorrectly typed or in which there is an erasure. (An error in spacing which follows an incorrect word or punctuation mark is not further charged.)
SERIES of consecutive words omitted, repeated, inserted, transposed, or erased. Charge for errors within such series, but the total charge cannot exceed the number of words.
LINE or part of line typed over other material, typed with all capitals, or apparently typed with the fingers on the wrong keys.
Change from the MARGIN where most lines are begun by the applicant or from the PARAGRAPH INDENTION most frequently used by the applicant.

The typing score used in the official examination reflects both speed and accuracy, with accuracy weighted twice as heavily as speed. Other methods of rating typing often used in schools are based on gross words per minute or net words per minute (usually with not more than a fixed number of errors). Using Example B, teachers and applicants can calculate typing proficiency in terms of gross words per minute and errors, and can determine whether that proficiency meets the minimum standards of eligibility required in the regular Civil Service examination.

Example B, following the Diagnostic Test, gives the maximum number of errors permitted at various typing speeds. For example, at the minimum acceptable speed of 17 lines, or 40 gross words per minute, 3 errors are permitted for eligibility.

DIAGNOSTIC TEST

The purpose of this diagnostic test and analysis is to familiarize you with the Typing Test and to help you assess your typing skills.

Chapter 8 will give you eight full-length practice sets.

TYPING TEST—COPYING FROM PLAIN COPY

Directions

A practice exercise appears at the bottom of this page and the test exercise itself is on the next page. First study these directions. Then, when the signal is given, begin to practice by typing the practice exercise below on the paper that has been given you. The examiner will tell you when to stop typing the practice exercise.

In both the practice and the test exercises, *space, paragraph, spell, punctuate, capitalize, and begin and end each line* precisely as shown in the exercises.

The examiner will tell you the exact time you will have to make repeated copies of the test exercise. Each time you complete the exercise, simply double space and begin again. If you fill up one side of the paper, turn it over and continue typing on the other side. Keep on typing until told to stop.

Keep in mind that you must meet minimum standards in both speed and accuracy and that, above these standards, accuracy is twice as important as speed. Make no erasures, insertions, or other corrections in this plain-copy test. Since errors are penalized whether or not they are erased or otherwise "corrected," it is best to keep on typing even though you detect an error.

Practice Exercise

```
        This practice exercise is similar in form and in diffi-
culty to the one that you will be required to typewrite for
the plain-copy test.  You are to space, capitalize, punctu-
ate, spell, and begin and end each line precisely as in the
copy.  Make no erasures, insertions, or other changes in
this test because errors will be penalized even if they are
erased or otherwise corrected.  Practice typewriting this
material on scratch paper until the examiner tells you to stop,
remembering that for this examination it is more important
for you to typewrite accurately than to typewrite rapidly.
```

DO NOT TURN TO THE TEST UNTIL TOLD TO DO SO BY THE EXAMINER.

Test Exercise

Because they have often learned to know types of architecture by decoration, casual observers sometimes fail to realize that the significant part of a structure is not the ornamentation but the body itself. Architecture, because of its close contact with human lives, is peculiarly and intimately governed by climate. For instance, a home built for comfort in the cold and snow of the northern areas of this country would be unbearably warm in a country with weather such as that of Cuba. A Cuban house, with its open court, would prove impossible to heat in a northern winter.

Since the purpose of architecture is the construction of shelters in which human beings may carry on their numerous activities, the designer must consider not only climatic conditions but also the function of a building. Thus, although the climate of a certain locality requires that an auditorium and a hospital have several features in common, the purposes for which they will be used demand some difference in structure. For centuries builders have first complied with these two requirements and later added whatever ornamentation they wished. Logically, we should see as mere additions, not as basic parts, the details by which we identify architecture.

EACH TIME YOU REACH THIS POINT, DOUBLE SPACE AND BEGIN AGAIN.

Example A—Line Key for Typing Test

(LINE KEY FOR 5 MINUTE TYPING TEST SHOWING MAXIMUM NUMBER OF ERRORS PERMISSIBLE FOR VARIOUS TYPING SPEEDS, AT GRADES GS–2 TYPIST AND GS–3 STENOGRAPHER)

Speed.—In the following example, more than 16 lines must have been typed for any speed rating. This sample key is constructed on the premise that if the competitor made the first stroke in the final line (even if it was an error), he or she is given credit for that line in determining the gross words per minute.

Accuracy.—The gross words per minute typed, at any line, is the number *outside* the parentheses opposite that line. The numbers *in* the parentheses show the maximum number of errors permitted for that number of gross words per minute typed. The number of errors permitted increases with the speed. If the number of strokes per line were different, this table would have to be altered accordingly.

	Maximum Number of Errors Per Gross Words Per Minute Typed	
	1st typing of exercise	2d typing of exercise
Because they have often learned to know types of architecture by decoration, casual observers sometimes fail to realize that the significant part of a structure is not the ornamentation but the body itself. Architecture, because of its close contact with human lives, is peculiarly and intimately governed by climate. For instance, a home built for comfort in the cold and snow of the northern areas of this country would be unbearably warm in a country with weather such as that of Cuba. A Cuban house, with its open court, would prove impossible to heat in a northern winter.	——— ——— ——— ——— ——— ——— ——— ——— ——— ———	52(7) 54(7) 56(8) 59(8) 61(9) 64(9) 66(10) 68(10) 71(11) 73(11)
Since the purpose of architecture is the construction of shelters in which human beings may carry on their numerous activities, the designer must consider not only climatic conditions, but also the function of a building. Thus, although the climate of a certain locality requires that an auditorium and a hospital have several features in common, the purposes for which they will be used demand some difference in structure. For centuries builders have first complied with these two requirements and later added whatever ornamentation they wished. Logically, we should see as mere additions, not as basic parts, the details by which we identify architecture.	——— ——— ——— ——— ——— ——— 40(3)[1] 42(4) 44(5) 47(6) 49(6)	76(12) 78(12) 80(12)[2] ——— ——— ——— ——— ——— ——— ——— ———

[1]The minimum rated speed is 40 gross words per minute for typing from printed copy.

[2]Any material typed after 80 gross words per minute (which is considered 100 in speed) is *not* rated for accuracy.

Note: The number of errors shown above must be proportionately increased for tests which are longer than 5 minutes.

Table 5
Example B—Errors Permitted at Various Typing Speeds

(MAXIMUM NUMBER OF ERRORS PERMITTED ON 5-MINUTE TESTS AT VARIOUS SPEEDS FOR TYPING SCORES REQUIRED FOR TYPIST AND STENOGRAPHER POSITIONS)

Speed	Maximum Number of Errors Permitted
Gross Words Per Minute	*GS–2, GS–3, GS–4 Clerk-Typist* *GS–3, GS–4, GS–5 Clerk-Stenographer*
Under 40	Ineligible
40	3
41–42	4
43–44	5
45–47	6
48–49	6
50–52	7
53–54	7
55–56	8
57–59	8
60–61	9
62–64	9
65–66	10
67–68	10
69–71	11
72–73	11
74–76	12
77–78	12
79–80	12

NOTE: THE NUMBER OF ERRORS SHOWN ABOVE MUST BE PROPORTIONATELY INCREASED FOR TESTS WHICH ARE LONGER THAN 5 MINUTES.

Some Common Errors to Watch For
Practice, Practice, Practice

(NOTE: Each practice set should be taken as a 5-minute timed writing. Gross words a minute are listed next to each line.)

Common Typing Errors to Watch For

As you practice, beware of the following most common typing errors:

1. *Striking one letter for another.* The most common examples of this are hitting "r" for "t," or "t" for "r"; hitting "i" for "o," or "o" for "i"; hitting "a" for "s," or "s" for "a"; hitting "i" for "e," or "e" for "i"; and hitting "m" for "n," or "n" for "m." As you look over your practice typing watch for these errors.

2. *Transposing letters.* Some common examples of typing letters in reverse order are: "re" instead of "er"; "op" instead of "po"; "ew" instead of "we"; "oi" instead of "io"; and "to" instead of "ot." If you find these in your work, practice hitting those letters in the correct order.

3. *Omitted letter errors.* Incorrect hand alignment, weakness in the smaller fingers, and reading too far ahead may cause omitted-letter errors. If you find letters missing in your words, you may wish to practice improving in this area.

PRACTICE SET 1

Type the following exercise, being careful to space, paragraph, spell, punctuate, capitalize, and begin and end each line precisely as shown. Each time you complete the exercise, double space and begin again. If you fill up one side of the paper, turn it over and continue typing on the other side. Keep typing until the time is up. Make no erasures, insertions, or other corrections.

	wpm: 5
Most people want to make sure their own welfare is being taken	3
care of properly. This need will embrace such items as job security,	6
fringe benefits, and final retirement. There are dozens of other items	8
that could be grouped under personal welfare; but, people can cope with	11
these other items if the basic three are covered. For most people, per-	14
sonal welfare means more than acquiring the mere basics of life—food,	17
clothing, and shelter; they want to be able to afford a few luxuries.	20
Job security, to some, is recognized as the single most critical	22
category of these items. If you do not possess good job security, you	25
may not have adequate fringe benefits and a good retirement program. If	28
you are like most people, you expect a job that is pleasant and finan-	31
cially rewarding as well; however, a good environment is ofttimes of more	34

importance than wages to some people. Your whole outlook on life can be   37
more positive when there is no significant concern about your job security.   40
The next category that is of big concern to most workers is fringe   42
benefits. Some of the most common fringe benefits that we now tend to   45
expect are health and major medical insurance, sick leave, retirement   48
paid for by the employer, and adequate vacation and holidays. Even   51
though wages are often the center of concern for most people, the single   54
largest item of controversy between workers and employers is the size of   57
the fringe benefits package that will be paid for by the firm.   59

Retirement should be a major item of concern to all individuals.   62
Today, more than ever, the need for well-planned and well-financed   64
retirement programs is essential. Most of us can expect to spend many   67
years in retirement; hence, we should begin planning for retirement the   70
day we begin our very first job. After we have arranged the financial   73
part of our retirement, we must be just as eager to organize the kinds   76
of activities in which we can participate when we finally quit working.   79

PRACTICE SET 2

Type the following exercise, being careful to space, paragraph, spell, punctuate, capitalize, and begin and end each line precisely as shown. Each time you complete the exercise, double space and begin again. If you fill up one side of the paper, turn it over and continue typing on the other side. Keep typing until the time is up. Make no erasures, insertions, or other corrections.

wpm: 5

On display at several of the offices in our city is a small sign   3
showing what is surely a very important message. The sign says quite   .5
simply "Think." Busy workers and customers hastily look at the sign,   8
and it is interesting to conjecture that maybe the message says some-   11
thing a little bit different to every one who reads it. To some, for   14
example, it might portend that they should exercise greater caution in   17
their work; to others, it could offer encouragement to attack a pressing   19
problem that needs solving; while a third group might interpret it to be   22
a note of stimulation toward expanded creativity. That a five-letter   25
word printed on a sign should, like a tiny, mystical beacon, flash an   28
individualized message to those who read it, is itself thought provoking.   31

Every person can think. In the kingdom of animals, anthropologists   34
tell us, the power to reason is a distinctive characteristic of humans.   37
Although there appears to be little unanimity about why people can think,   40
it seems evident that we do our best job of it when faced with the pos-   42
sibility of making a mistake. At such times, we feel quite forced to   45
"act wisely," to "make a basic decision," to "use good judgment"—in   48
other words, to "think." The ability to think, therefore, is a valuable   51
prize to us; and, we will, ideally speaking, take advantage of any chance   54
to improve our capacity for it if in so doing we can develop our abil-   57
ity to avoid dangerous and expensive errors that could affect our family,   59
our friends, our city, our employer—and us.   61

PRACTICE SET 3

Type the following exercise, being careful to space, paragraph, spell, punctuate, capitalize, and begin and end each line precisely as shown. Each time you complete the exercise, double space and begin again. If you fill up one side of the paper, turn it over and continue typing on the other side. Keep typing until the time is up. Make no erasures, insertions, or other corrections.

	wpm: 5
You can safely consider that poor stroking habits are generally the	3
cause of failure to achieve high typing speeds and are the major reasons	5
for plateaus; but you can find material especially designed to help de-	8
velop quick, easy stroking. Use a part of the drill period each day to	11
work on these special drill exercises. You may not notice an immediate	14
change, but it will come if you work for it and if you analyze your	18
stroking habits very carefully. Among other specific ideas to keep before	21
you is the advice that all drills must be practiced with a definite goal in	24
mind. Unless you know what you are trying to attain, you can't hope to	26
achieve any particular degree of success. It is useless to pound away at	30
the keyboard day after day, hoping that practice will make your typing	32
perfect. Your drills should be done with very specific objectives in mind.	35
Ask your self about your objectives to determine if your exercises are	38
right for you.	38
A good course has long-term goals, or at least desired outcomes,	41
for all of its students. In order to reach these goals, each student	43
must decide upon the daily practice objectives that are appropriate to	46
his or her immediate requirements. There should be a specific objective	49
for a specific need. At times, a student will need to increase speed;	52
at other times, a student will require a reduction in speed in order to	55
eliminate error. At still other times, the goal may be to improve a	58
vital technique: keystroking, spacing, shifting, and the like.	60

PRACTICE SET 4

Type the following exercise, being careful to space, paragraph, spell, punctuate, capitalize, and begin and end each line precisely as shown. Each time you complete the exercise, double space and begin again. If you fill up one side of the paper, turn it over and continue typing on the other side. Keep typing until the time is up. Make no erasures, insertions, or other corrections.

	wpm: 5
A business firm may use one of many letter formats that are in	3
use today; but, most companies are using one of the following styles:	6
block, modified block, and modified block with paragraphs indented.	8
Some companies have now decided to use a letter style that helps them	11
to avoid sex bias in their letter writing. That style is a simplified	14
letter style, which does not include a salutation, and, therefore,	17
does not show the bias against women that was found in the usual salu-	19

tations of the past. The block style and the simplified style are quite easy   23
to type because all parts of both styles begin at the left margin. The major   26
difference between the block style and the simplified style is that the   28
salutation and the complimentary close are included in the block style but   31
are excluded from the simplified format. In addition, the simplified letter   34
style always has a subject line; the block style may or may not include one.   37
According to one study, the block style is used in about a fourth of business   40
firms. The simplified style, however, enjoys only limited use.   43

    The modified block style differs from the block and the simplified   46
styles in that the date and the closing lines in the former begin at   49
the horizontal center of the paper rather than at the left margin.   51
The modified block style—which may use paragraph indention, but more   54
often does not—is the most generally used letter style. It results in   57
a well-balanced, attractive letter with only a limited amount of time   60
spent in operating the tab control to indent the date and closing lines.   63

PRACTICE SET 5

Type the following exercise, being careful to space, paragraph, spell, punctuate, capitalize, and begin and end each line precisely as shown. Each time you complete the exercise, double space and begin again. If you fill up one side of the paper, turn it over and continue typing on the other side. Keep typing until the time is up. Make no erasures, insertions, or other corrections.

wpm: 5

    A typist for an accounting firm is expected to be one who can type   3
a great quantity of numbers and symbols quickly and accurately. Some-   6
times the job is almost entirely quantitative, which means that the   8
typist must be alert to see that no errors are allowed to remain uncor-   11
rected. A wrong number or symbol can't be recognized like a misspelled   14
word, so a typist must make sure that the number or symbol has been   17
typed correctly. Accuracy is very important. The preparation of charts and   19
tables will just naturally become a considerable part of the work-load   21
arrangement when you become a typist in an accounting office. Since so   24
much accounting work is quantitative, it stands to reason that some parts   27
of longer reports can be presented best in graphic or tabulated form, such   30
as charts or tables. It is not unusual for a longer report to have, perhaps, as   33
many as a dozen displays in its appendix.   36

    A typist in an accounting office may not journalize but will type   39
many letters and memorandums. When a change in procedure is to be ef-   42
fected, a memo is typed and sent to all concerned. A typist will need   45
to know the exact number of copies to make before starting to type. This   48
ensures that all people affected will be sure to receive the notice of   51
change. Most internal communication queries between the accounting of-   53
fice and other locations within the business are done by memo.   56

PRACTICE SET 6

Type the following exercise, being careful to space, paragraph, spell, punctuate, capitalize, and begin and end each line precisely as shown. Each time you complete the exercise, double space and begin again. If you fill up one side of the paper, turn it over and continue typing on the other side. Keep typing until the time is up. Make no erasures, insertions, or other corrections.

	wpm: 5
Telephone etiquette demands that a person should follow specific	3
rules when answering a telephone call. First, answer quickly; no one	5
likes a delay. If at all possible, the telephone should be picked up	8
on the first ring. Second, identify yourself properly; give your com-	11
pany's name, then your own name. Third, screen an incoming call; tell	14
why your boss cannot talk now, and then mention some other way in which	17
you may aid the caller. Fourth, give only essential information; you	20
must be very careful not to give any information that your employer may	22
not want you to provide. Fifth, get the necessary information from the	25
person; be polite, but try to determine who is calling and why he or	28
she is calling. And sixth, take messages accurately; have a pencil and	31
pad by your phone on which to jot down messages. If you will abide by	34
these simple rules, you will avoid many problems.	36
When placing a telephone call, be sure to follow the advice given	38
by the experts. First, be sure you have the correct number; a wrong	41
area code may cause a delay and embarrassment. Second, know the name of	44
the person you are calling; even a short hesitation may cause difficul-	47
ties with the person to whom you are speaking. Third, plan your con-	50
versation prior to making the call; respect the other person and don't	53
waste time. Fourth, give the person you are calling time to answer the	55
telephone; a rule of thumb is to allow the phone to ring a minimum of	58
ten times. Fifth, identify yourself properly and give the reason for	61
the call; avoid embarrassment and delays—the person you are calling	64
may not recognize your voice. And sixth, terminate your call promptly	67
and thank the individual you called for helping you.	69

PRACTICE SET 7

Type the following exercise, being careful to space, paragraph, spell, punctuate, capitalize, and begin and end each line precisely as shown. Each time you complete the exercise, double space and begin again. If you fill up one side of the paper, turn it over and continue typing on the other side. Keep typing until the time is up. Make no erasures, insertions, or other corrections.

	wpm: 5
What factors determine if an employee will be a success? The three	3
basic factors of success on the job are: good technical skills, good	6
human relations skills, and a good work attitude. A person must be able	8
to exhibit the required technical skills in order to perform in an ade-	11
quate manner. Also, the need to get along with other people is equal	14
in importance to technical skills. And, even if a person builds good	17
technical skills and good human relations skills, a positive feeling	20
about the job is still essential in order to be a success. Cognizance	22
of these factors plays an important part in attaining success; if any	25
one of them is not realized, an employee may feel unsuccessful.	28
A person needs to prepare adequately in order to succeed on a job.	31
Preparation for a job must start long before the first day at work. A	33

part of this preparation is building a job entry-level skill. Also, an   36
employee must learn to develop a good, positive interpersonal relation-   39
ship with others. This ability to get along well with others is not an   42
instinct—much time and effort must be devoted to achieving good human   45
relations skills. Finally, an employee should look forward to work with   48
pleasure; therefore, a positive attitude towards work must be developed   51
if the job is to be rewarding. Remember, anyone can learn to succeed as   54
an employee; all it takes is a real desire and work.   56

PRACTICE SET 8

Type the following exercise, being careful to space, paragraph, spell, punctuate, capitalize, and begin and end each line precisely as shown. Each time you complete the exercise, double space and begin again. If you fill up one side of the paper, turn it over and continue typing on the other side. Keep typing until the time is up. Make no erasures, insertions, or other corrections.

                                                                     wpm: 5

The development and expanded use of the computer has not caused the   3
large number of jobs to be lost that so many people expected about twenty- 6
five years ago. In fact, the total number of people in the work force   8
has increased during the past twenty-five years, and the computer has   11
had the effect of creating many of the new jobs. While it is indeed   14
true that the development of the computer has made many of the routine, 17
less-skilled jobs unnecessary, it has also created many other highly   20
skilled jobs which call for employees who are trained for such fields   22
as data-entry and computer operations, programing, and system analysis. 25
In short, the occupations that call for specialized training, judgment, 28
and knowledge have increased in number; and thus, the computer has, in   31
fact, helped to create even more jobs and, in turn, to increase wages.   34
There are many people who insist that the computer has not had a   37
positive effect on the worker. They assert that many firms are more   39
concerned with net profit than they are with satisfied workers. In   42
many firms, the telephone calls, the invoices, the letters, and the   45
reports can all be done with the aid of a computer. Some firms are now   48
to the point where they can see how negative the impact of technology is 51
on their employees, and these firms are beginning job enrichment pro-   53
grams that will help their employees gain greater personal satisfaction 56
from their jobs. Perhaps the development of the computer may, in the   59
end, force firms to do what should have been done earlier—create pleas- 62
ant and satisfying jobs for all workers.   64

REVIEWING THE KEY STRATEGIES

Watch out for common errors:

— striking one letter for another

— transposing letters

— omitted letter errors

PART FOUR

The Dictation Test

CHAPTER 9

Introduction
A Diagnostic Test
with Answers

THE DICTATION TEST

The dictation test, which is a part of the Stenographer-Typist Examination, includes a practice dictation and a test exercise, each consisting of 240 words. The rate of dictation is 80 words a minute.

The dictation passages are nontechnical subject matter that might be given a stenographer in a Government office. Sentence structure is not complicated and sentences are not extremely long or short. The words average 1.5 syllables in length.

As shown in Example C, Practice Dictation, each dictation passage is printed with spacing to show the point that the dictator should reach at the end of each 10 seconds in order to maintain an even dictation rate of 80 words a minute. This indication of timing is one device for assisting all examiners to conform to the intended dictation rate. All examiners are also sent instructions for dictating and a sample passage to be used in practicing dictating before the day of the test. By using these devices for securing uniform dictating and by providing alternate dictation passages that are as nearly equal as possible, the U. S. Office of Personnel Management can give each applicant a test that is neither harder nor easier than those given others competing for the same jobs.

The test differs from the conventional dictation test in the method of transcribing the notes. The applicant is not required to type a transcript of the notes, but follows a procedure that permits machine scoring of the test. When typewritten transcripts were still required, examiners rated the test by comparing every word of a competitor's paper with the material dictated and by charging errors. Fairness to those competing for employment required that comparable errors be penalized equally. Because of the variety of errors and combinations of errors that can be made in transcripts, the scoring of typewritten transcripts required considerable training and consumed much time—many months for large nationwide examinations. After years of experimentation, a transcript booklet procedure was devised that simplified and speeded the scoring procedure.

HOW THE TRANSCRIPT BOOKLET WORKS

The transcript booklet (see Example D, Diagnostic Test) gives the stenographer parts of the dictated passage, but leaves blank spaces where many of the words belong. With adequate shorthand notes, the stenographer can readily fit the correct words into the blank spaces, which are numbered 1 through 125. At the left of the printed partial transcript is a list of words, each word with a capital letter A, B, C, or D beside it. Knowing from the notes what word belongs in a blank space, the competitor looks for it among the words in the list. The letter beside the word or phrase in the list is the answer to be marked in the space on the transcript. In the list there are other words that a competitor with inadequate notes might guess belong in that space, but the capital letter beside these words would be an incorrect answer. (*Some persons find it helpful to write the word or the shorthand symbol in the blank space before looking for it in the word list. There is no objection to doing this.*)

Look, for example, at the Practice Dictation Transcript Sheet, Example D, question 10. The word dictated is "physical"; it is in the word list with a capital "D." In the transcript, blank number 10 should be answered "D."

None of the words in the list is marked "E," because the answer "E" is reserved for any question when the word dictated for that spot does not appear in the list. Every transcript booklet has spots for which the list does not include the correct words. This provision reduces the possibility that competitors may guess correct answers.

After the stenographer has written the letter of the missing word or phrase in each numbered blank of the transcript, he or she transfers the answers to the proper spaces on the answer sheet. Directions for marking the separate answer sheet are given on page 1 of Example E, Diagnostic Test.

HOW THE TEST IS ADMINISTERED

Each competitor is given a copy of the Practice Dictation Transcript Sheet (Example D), a copy of the Transcript Booklet (Example C), and an answer sheet. These are distributed at the times indicated below.

First, the Practice Dictation (see Example C) is dictated at the rate indicated by the 10-second divisions in which it is printed. This will be at the rate of 80 words a minute, for a total of 3 minutes. Then each competitor is given a copy of the Practice Dictation Transcript Sheet and allowed 7 minutes to study the instructions and to transcribe part of the practice dictation.

The test exercise (reverse side—here, page 238—of Example C) is also dictated at the rate of 80 words a minute, for 3 minutes. Then each competitor is given a Transcript Booklet and an answer sheet, and is told that he or she will have 3 minutes to read the directions on the face page, followed by 30 minutes to write the answers in the blank spaces, and then 10 minutes to transfer the answers to the answer sheet. These time limits have been found ample.

HOW THE ANSWER SHEET IS SCORED

In some rare instances where the typewritten transcript is still used, the passing standard on the total transcript is 24 or fewer errors for GS–3 Clerk-Stenographer and GS–4. Comparable standards on the parts of the dictation measured by the machine-scored method of transcription are 14 or fewer errors for GS–3 and GS–4 positions.

A stenographer who can take dictation at 80 words a minute with this degree of accuracy is considered fully qualified. Positions such as Reporting Stenographer and Shorthand Reporter require ability to take dictation at much higher speeds. The test for Reporting Stenographer is dictated at 120 words a minute. Two rates of dictation, 160 and 175 words a minute, are used for the Shorthand Reporter tests for different grade levels.

A DIAGNOSTIC TEST WITH ANSWERS

The purpose of this diagnostic exam is to familiarize you with the Dictation Test and to help you focus your practice.

Chapter 8 will give you five practice sets to help build strengths and reduce weaknesses.

ANSWER SHEET

SIGNATURE: _____
(Please Sign)

EXAMINATION TITLE: _____

PLACE OF EXAMINATION: _____
City _____ State _____

TODAY'S DATE: _____

SAMPLE Ⓐ ● Ⓒ Ⓓ Ⓔ

DIRECTIONS FOR MARKING ANSWER SHEET

Use only a **No. 2 (or softer) lead pencil.** Darken completely the circle corresponding to your answer. You **must** keep your mark within the circle. Stray marks may be counted as errors. Erase **completely** all marks except your answer.

SAMPLE NAME GRID

LAST NAME							F.I.	M.I.
M	C	C	A	B	E		C	A

1. In the boxes below, **PRINT** your name. Print only as many letters as will fit within the areas for the last name, first initial (F.I.), and middle initial (M.I.) Below each box, darken the circle containing the same letter. SEE SAMPLE NAME GRID

LAST NAME														F.I.	M.I.

2. In the boxes below, enter your 9-digit Social Security Number. Below each box, darken the circle in each column corresponding to the number you have entered.

SOCIAL SECURITY NUMBER

3. OCCUPATIONAL GROUP NUMBER

SECTION 1

			P A R T	

TEST NUMBER

TEST SERIES

Make no marks or entries in the columns to the right until you receive instructions from the administrator.

1 Ⓐ Ⓑ Ⓒ Ⓓ Ⓔ
2 Ⓐ Ⓑ Ⓒ Ⓓ Ⓔ
3 Ⓐ Ⓑ Ⓒ Ⓓ Ⓔ
4 Ⓐ Ⓑ Ⓒ Ⓓ Ⓔ
5 Ⓐ Ⓑ Ⓒ Ⓓ Ⓔ
6 Ⓐ Ⓑ Ⓒ Ⓓ Ⓔ
7 Ⓐ Ⓑ Ⓒ Ⓓ Ⓔ
8 Ⓐ Ⓑ Ⓒ Ⓓ Ⓔ
9 Ⓐ Ⓑ Ⓒ Ⓓ Ⓔ
10 Ⓐ Ⓑ Ⓒ Ⓓ Ⓔ

11 Ⓐ Ⓑ Ⓒ Ⓓ Ⓔ
12 Ⓐ Ⓑ Ⓒ Ⓓ Ⓔ
13 Ⓐ Ⓑ Ⓒ Ⓓ Ⓔ
14 Ⓐ Ⓑ Ⓒ Ⓓ Ⓔ
15 Ⓐ Ⓑ Ⓒ Ⓓ Ⓔ
16 Ⓐ Ⓑ Ⓒ Ⓓ Ⓔ
17 Ⓐ Ⓑ Ⓒ Ⓓ Ⓔ
18 Ⓐ Ⓑ Ⓒ Ⓓ Ⓔ
19 Ⓐ Ⓑ Ⓒ Ⓓ Ⓔ
20 Ⓐ Ⓑ Ⓒ Ⓓ Ⓔ

21 Ⓐ Ⓑ Ⓒ Ⓓ Ⓔ
22 Ⓐ Ⓑ Ⓒ Ⓓ Ⓔ
23 Ⓐ Ⓑ Ⓒ Ⓓ Ⓔ
24 Ⓐ Ⓑ Ⓒ Ⓓ Ⓔ
25 Ⓐ Ⓑ Ⓒ Ⓓ Ⓔ
26 Ⓐ Ⓑ Ⓒ Ⓓ Ⓔ
27 Ⓐ Ⓑ Ⓒ Ⓓ Ⓔ
28 Ⓐ Ⓑ Ⓒ Ⓓ Ⓔ
29 Ⓐ Ⓑ Ⓒ Ⓓ Ⓔ
30 Ⓐ Ⓑ Ⓒ Ⓓ Ⓔ

31 Ⓐ Ⓑ Ⓒ Ⓓ Ⓔ
32 Ⓐ Ⓑ Ⓒ Ⓓ Ⓔ
33 Ⓐ Ⓑ Ⓒ Ⓓ Ⓔ
34 Ⓐ Ⓑ Ⓒ Ⓓ Ⓔ
35 Ⓐ Ⓑ Ⓒ Ⓓ Ⓔ
36 Ⓐ Ⓑ Ⓒ Ⓓ Ⓔ
37 Ⓐ Ⓑ Ⓒ Ⓓ Ⓔ
38 Ⓐ Ⓑ Ⓒ Ⓓ Ⓔ
39 Ⓐ Ⓑ Ⓒ Ⓓ Ⓔ
40 Ⓐ Ⓑ Ⓒ Ⓓ Ⓔ

51 Ⓐ Ⓑ Ⓒ Ⓓ Ⓔ
52 Ⓐ Ⓑ Ⓒ Ⓓ Ⓔ
53 Ⓐ Ⓑ Ⓒ Ⓓ Ⓔ
54 Ⓐ Ⓑ Ⓒ Ⓓ Ⓔ
55 Ⓐ Ⓑ Ⓒ Ⓓ Ⓔ
56 Ⓐ Ⓑ Ⓒ Ⓓ Ⓔ
57 Ⓐ Ⓑ Ⓒ Ⓓ Ⓔ
58 Ⓐ Ⓑ Ⓒ Ⓓ Ⓔ
59 Ⓐ Ⓑ Ⓒ Ⓓ Ⓔ
60 Ⓐ Ⓑ Ⓒ Ⓓ Ⓔ

61 Ⓐ Ⓑ Ⓒ Ⓓ Ⓔ
62 Ⓐ Ⓑ Ⓒ Ⓓ Ⓔ
63 Ⓐ Ⓑ Ⓒ Ⓓ Ⓔ
64 Ⓐ Ⓑ Ⓒ Ⓓ Ⓔ
65 Ⓐ Ⓑ Ⓒ Ⓓ Ⓔ
66 Ⓐ Ⓑ Ⓒ Ⓓ Ⓔ
67 Ⓐ Ⓑ Ⓒ Ⓓ Ⓔ
68 Ⓐ Ⓑ Ⓒ Ⓓ Ⓔ
69 Ⓐ Ⓑ Ⓒ Ⓓ Ⓔ
70 Ⓐ Ⓑ Ⓒ Ⓓ Ⓔ

71 Ⓐ Ⓑ Ⓒ Ⓓ Ⓔ
72 Ⓐ Ⓑ Ⓒ Ⓓ Ⓔ
73 Ⓐ Ⓑ Ⓒ Ⓓ Ⓔ
74 Ⓐ Ⓑ Ⓒ Ⓓ Ⓔ
75 Ⓐ Ⓑ Ⓒ Ⓓ Ⓔ
76 Ⓐ Ⓑ Ⓒ Ⓓ Ⓔ
77 Ⓐ Ⓑ Ⓒ Ⓓ Ⓔ
78 Ⓐ Ⓑ Ⓒ Ⓓ Ⓔ
79 Ⓐ Ⓑ Ⓒ Ⓓ Ⓔ
80 Ⓐ Ⓑ Ⓒ Ⓓ Ⓔ

81 Ⓐ Ⓑ Ⓒ Ⓓ Ⓔ
82 Ⓐ Ⓑ Ⓒ Ⓓ Ⓔ
83 Ⓐ Ⓑ Ⓒ Ⓓ Ⓔ
84 Ⓐ Ⓑ Ⓒ Ⓓ Ⓔ
85 Ⓐ Ⓑ Ⓒ Ⓓ Ⓔ
86 Ⓐ Ⓑ Ⓒ Ⓓ Ⓔ
87 Ⓐ Ⓑ Ⓒ Ⓓ Ⓔ
88 Ⓐ Ⓑ Ⓒ Ⓓ Ⓔ
89 Ⓐ Ⓑ Ⓒ Ⓓ Ⓔ
90 Ⓐ Ⓑ Ⓒ Ⓓ Ⓔ

91 Ⓐ Ⓑ Ⓒ Ⓓ Ⓔ
92 Ⓐ Ⓑ Ⓒ Ⓓ Ⓔ
93 Ⓐ Ⓑ Ⓒ Ⓓ Ⓔ
94 Ⓐ Ⓑ Ⓒ Ⓓ Ⓔ
95 Ⓐ Ⓑ Ⓒ Ⓓ Ⓔ
96 Ⓐ Ⓑ Ⓒ Ⓓ Ⓔ
97 Ⓐ Ⓑ Ⓒ Ⓓ Ⓔ
98 Ⓐ Ⓑ Ⓒ Ⓓ Ⓔ
99 Ⓐ Ⓑ Ⓒ Ⓓ Ⓔ
100 Ⓐ Ⓑ Ⓒ Ⓓ Ⓔ

101 Ⓐ Ⓑ Ⓒ Ⓓ Ⓔ
102 Ⓐ Ⓑ Ⓒ Ⓓ Ⓔ
103 Ⓐ Ⓑ Ⓒ Ⓓ Ⓔ
104 Ⓐ Ⓑ Ⓒ Ⓓ Ⓔ
105 Ⓐ Ⓑ Ⓒ Ⓓ Ⓔ
106 Ⓐ Ⓑ Ⓒ Ⓓ Ⓔ
107 Ⓐ Ⓑ Ⓒ Ⓓ Ⓔ
108 Ⓐ Ⓑ Ⓒ Ⓓ Ⓔ
109 Ⓐ Ⓑ Ⓒ Ⓓ Ⓔ
110 Ⓐ Ⓑ Ⓒ Ⓓ Ⓔ

111 Ⓐ Ⓑ Ⓒ Ⓓ Ⓔ
112 Ⓐ Ⓑ Ⓒ Ⓓ Ⓔ
113 Ⓐ Ⓑ Ⓒ Ⓓ Ⓔ
114 Ⓐ Ⓑ Ⓒ Ⓓ Ⓔ
115 Ⓐ Ⓑ Ⓒ Ⓓ Ⓔ
116 Ⓐ Ⓑ Ⓒ Ⓓ Ⓔ
117 Ⓐ Ⓑ Ⓒ Ⓓ Ⓔ
118 Ⓐ Ⓑ Ⓒ Ⓓ Ⓔ
119 Ⓐ Ⓑ Ⓒ Ⓓ Ⓔ
120 Ⓐ Ⓑ Ⓒ Ⓓ Ⓔ

121 Ⓐ Ⓑ Ⓒ Ⓓ Ⓔ
122 Ⓐ Ⓑ Ⓒ Ⓓ Ⓔ
123 Ⓐ Ⓑ Ⓒ Ⓓ Ⓔ
124 Ⓐ Ⓑ Ⓒ Ⓓ Ⓔ
125 Ⓐ Ⓑ Ⓒ Ⓓ Ⓔ
126 Ⓐ Ⓑ Ⓒ Ⓓ Ⓔ
127 Ⓐ Ⓑ Ⓒ Ⓓ Ⓔ
128 Ⓐ Ⓑ Ⓒ Ⓓ Ⓔ
129 Ⓐ Ⓑ Ⓒ Ⓓ Ⓔ
130 Ⓐ Ⓑ Ⓒ Ⓓ Ⓔ

Example C—Practice Dictation

INSTRUCTIONS TO THE EXAMINER: This Practice Dictation and one exercise will be dictated at the rate of 80 words a minute. Do not dictate the punctuation except for periods, but dictate with the expression that the punctuation indicates. Use a watch with a second hand to enable you to read the exercises at the proper speed.

Exactly on a minute, start dictating.

Finish reading each two lines at the number of seconds indicated below

I realize that this practice dictation is not a part of the examination	10
proper and is not to be scored. (Period) The work of preventing and correcting	20
physical defects in children is becoming more effective as a result of a change	30
in the attitude of many parents. (Period) In order to bring about this change,	40
mothers have been invited to visit the schools when their children are being examined	50
and to discuss the treatment necessary for the correction of defects. (Period)	1 min.
There is a distinct value in having a mother see that her child is not the	10
only one who needs attention. (Period) Otherwise a few parents might feel that they	20
were being criticized by having the defects of their children singled out for medical	30
treatment. (Period) The special classes that have been set up have shown the value of	40
the scientific knowledge that has been applied in the treatment of children. (Period)	50
In these classes the children have been taught to exercise by a trained teacher	2 min.
under medical supervision. (Period) The hours of the school day have been divided	10
between school work and physical activity that helps not only to correct their defects	20
but also to improve their general physical condition. (Period) This method of treatment	30
has been found to be very effective except for those who have severe medical	40
defects. (Period) Most parents now see how desirable it is to have these classes	50
that have been set up in the regular school system to meet special needs. (Period)	3 min.

After dictating the practice, pause for 15 seconds to permit competitors to complete their notes. Then continue in accordance with the directions for conducting the examination.

After the Practice Dictation Transcript has been completed, dictate the test from the next page.

THE TEST

Finish reading
each two lines
at the number
of seconds in-
dicated below

The number enrolled in shorthand classes in the
high schools has shown a marked increase. (Period)   10

Today this subject is one of the most
popular offered in the field of   20

business education. (Period) When shorthand was
first taught, educators claimed that it was of   30

value mainly in sharpening the powers
of observation and discrimination. (Period)   40

However, with the growth of business and
the increased demand for office workers,   50

educators have come to realize the
importance of stenography as a vocational   1 min.

tool. (Period) With the differences
in the aims of instruction came changes in   10

the grade placement of the subject. (Period)
The prevailing thought has always been that it   20

should be offered in high school. (Period)
When the junior high school first came into   30

being, shorthand was moved down to that level
with little change in the manner in which   40

the subject was taught. (Period) It was soon
realized that shorthand had no place there   50

because the training had lost its vocational
utility by the time the student could   2 min.

graduate. (Period) Moreover, surveys
of those with education only through junior   10

high school seldom found them at work as
stenographers. (Period) For this reason, shorthand   20

was returned to the high school level and is
offered as near as possible to the time   30

of graduation so that the skill will be
retained when the student takes a job. (Period)   40

Because the age at which students enter
office jobs has advanced, there is now   50

a tendency to upgrade business education
into the junior college. (Period)   3 min.

After completing the dictation, pause for 15 seconds.
Give a Transcript to each competitor.

Example D—Practice Dictation Transcript Sheet

The TRANSCRIPT below is part of the material that was dictated to you for practice, except that many of the words have been left out. From your notes, you are to tell what the missing words are. Proceed as follows:

Compare your notes with the TRANSCRIPT and, when you come to a blank in the TRANSCRIPT, decide what word or words belong there. For example, you will find that the word "practice" belongs in blank number 1. Look at the WORD LIST to see whether you can find the same word there. Notice what letter (A, B, C, or D) is printed beside it, and write that letter in the blank. For example, the word "practice" is listed, followed by the letter "B." We have already written "B" in blank number 1 to show you how you are to record your choice. Now decide what belongs in each of the other blanks. (You may also write the word or words, or the shorthand for them, if you wish.) The same word may belong in more than one blank. If the exact answer is not listed, write "E" in the blank.

ALPHABETIC WORD LIST

about—B
against—C
attitude—A

being—D

childhood—B
children—A
correcting—C

doctors—B

effective—D
efficient—A
examination—A
examining—C

for—B

health—B

mothers—C

never—C
not—D

paper—B
parents—B
part—C
physical—D
portion—D
practical—A
practice—B
preliminary—D
preventing—B
procedure—A
proper—C

reason for—A
result—B
result of—C

schools—C

to be—C
to prevent—A

TRANSCRIPT

I realize that this **B** dictation is ____
                        1   2

a ____ of the ____ ____ and is ____ ____
    3   4   5   6   7
scored.

The work of ____ and ____ ____ defects in
               8   9   10

____ is becoming more ____ as a ____ a change
11   12   13

in the ____ of many ____ ....
         14   15

Each numbered blank in the TRANSCRIPT is a question. You will be given a separate answer sheet like the sample here, to which you will transfer your answers. The answer sheet has a numbered row of boxes for each question. The answer for blank number 1 is "B." We have already transferred this to number 1 in the Sample Answer Sheet, by darkening the box under "B."

Now transfer your answer for each of questions 2 through 15 to the answer sheet. That is, beside each number on the answer sheet find the letter that is the same as the letter you wrote in the blank with the the same number in the TRANSCRIPT, and darken the box below that letter.

After you have marked 15, continue with blank number 16 on the next page WITHOUT WAITING FOR A SIGNAL.

SAMPLE ANSWER SHEET

1 Ⓐ Ⓑ Ⓒ Ⓓ Ⓔ
2 Ⓐ Ⓑ Ⓒ Ⓓ Ⓔ
3 Ⓐ Ⓑ Ⓒ Ⓓ Ⓔ
4 Ⓐ Ⓑ Ⓒ Ⓓ Ⓔ
5 Ⓐ Ⓑ Ⓒ Ⓓ Ⓔ
6 Ⓐ Ⓑ Ⓒ Ⓓ Ⓔ
7 Ⓐ Ⓑ Ⓒ Ⓓ Ⓔ
8 Ⓐ Ⓑ Ⓒ Ⓓ Ⓔ

SAMPLE ANSWER SHEET (CONTINUED)

9 Ⓐ Ⓑ Ⓒ Ⓓ Ⓔ
10 Ⓐ Ⓑ Ⓒ Ⓓ Ⓔ
11 Ⓐ Ⓑ Ⓒ Ⓓ Ⓔ
12 Ⓐ Ⓑ Ⓒ Ⓓ Ⓔ
13 Ⓐ Ⓑ Ⓒ Ⓓ Ⓔ
14 Ⓐ Ⓑ Ⓒ Ⓓ Ⓔ
15 Ⓐ Ⓑ Ⓒ Ⓓ Ⓔ

Example D—continued.

ALPHABETIC WORD LIST

all—A	know—A	to discover—A
at—C	knows—D	to discuss—D
		to endorse—C
bring—A	needed—B	to visit—B
collection—B	promote—B	treatments—A
correction—C		
	recognizing—D	understand—D
discuss—C		undertake—B
during—D	reducing—A	
		virtue—D
friend—A	satisfied—D	visit—A
	say—C	volume—B
indicated—C	see—B	
insisted—D	soon—C	young—C
is—B		
is not—A	their—D	

TRANSCRIPT (continued)

In order to _____ _____ this change, mothers

(16) (17)

have been invited _____ the schools when _____

(18) (19)

children are being examined and _____ the _____

(20) (21)

necessary for the _____ of defects. There is a

(22)

distinct _____ in having a mother _____ that her

(23) (24)

child _____ the only one who needs attention. . . .

(25)

(The rest of the practice dictation is not transcribed here.)

Your notes should show that the word "bring" goes in blank 16, and "about" in blank 17. But "about" is *not in the list;* so "E" should be your answer for question 17.

The two words, "to visit—B," are needed for 18, and the one word "visit—A," would be an incorrect answer.

Compare your answers with the correct answers. If one of your answers does not agree with the correct answer, again compare your notes with the samples and make certain you understand the instructions. The correct answers for 16 through 25 are as follows: 16 A; 17 E; 18 B; 19 D; 20 D; 21 E; 22 C; 23 E; 24 B; and 25 A.

For the actual test you will use a separate answer sheet. As scoring will be done by an electronic scoring machine, it is important that you follow directions carefully. Use a medium No. 2 pencil. You must keep your mark for a question within the box. If you have to erase a mark, be sure to erase it completely. Mark only one answer for each question.

SAMPLE ANSWER SHEET

16 Ⓐ Ⓑ Ⓒ Ⓓ Ⓔ
17 Ⓐ Ⓑ Ⓒ Ⓓ Ⓔ
18 Ⓐ Ⓑ Ⓒ Ⓓ Ⓔ
19 Ⓐ Ⓑ Ⓒ Ⓓ Ⓔ
20 Ⓐ Ⓑ Ⓒ Ⓓ Ⓔ
21 Ⓐ Ⓑ Ⓒ Ⓓ Ⓔ
22 Ⓐ Ⓑ Ⓒ Ⓓ Ⓔ
23 Ⓐ Ⓑ Ⓒ Ⓓ Ⓔ
24 Ⓐ Ⓑ Ⓒ Ⓓ Ⓔ
25 Ⓐ Ⓑ Ⓒ Ⓓ Ⓔ

CORRECT ANSWERS TO SAMPLE QUESTIONS 1 THROUGH 8

1 Ⓐ ● Ⓒ Ⓓ Ⓔ
2 Ⓐ Ⓑ Ⓒ ● Ⓔ
3 Ⓐ Ⓑ ● Ⓓ Ⓔ
4 ● Ⓑ Ⓒ Ⓓ Ⓔ
5 Ⓐ Ⓑ ● Ⓓ Ⓔ
6 Ⓐ Ⓑ Ⓒ ● Ⓔ
7 Ⓐ Ⓑ ● Ⓓ Ⓔ
8 Ⓐ ● Ⓒ Ⓓ Ⓔ

For any stenographer who missed the practice dictation, part of it is given below:

"I realize that this practice dictation is not a part of the examination proper and is not to be scored.

"The work of preventing and correcting physical defects in children is becoming more effective as a result of a change in the attitude of many parents. In order to bring about this change, mothers have been invited to visit the schools when their children are being examined and to discuss the treatment necessary for the correction of defects. There is a distinct value in having a mother see that her child is not the only one who needs attention. . . ."

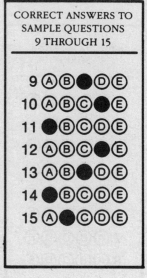

CORRECT ANSWERS TO SAMPLE QUESTIONS 9 THROUGH 15

9 Ⓐ Ⓑ ● Ⓓ Ⓔ
10 Ⓐ Ⓑ Ⓒ ● Ⓔ
11 ● Ⓑ Ⓒ Ⓓ Ⓔ
12 Ⓐ Ⓑ Ⓒ ● Ⓔ
13 Ⓐ Ⓑ ● Ⓓ Ⓔ
14 ● Ⓑ Ⓒ Ⓓ Ⓔ
15 Ⓐ ● Ⓒ Ⓓ Ⓔ

(Page 2 of Example D)

Example E—
Dictation Test Transcript Booklet

Directions for Completing the Transcript

A TRANSCRIPT of the dictation you have just taken is given on the following pages. As in the TRANSCRIPT for the practice dictation, there are numbered blank spaces for many of the words that were dictated. You are to compare your notes with the TRANSCRIPT and, when you come to a blank, decide what word or words belong there. For most of the blanks the words are included in the list beside the TRANSCRIPT; each is followed by a letter, A, B, C, or D. To show that you know which word or words belong in each blank space, you are to *write the letter* in the blank. You are to write E if the exact answer is NOT listed. (In addition you may write the word or words, or the shorthand for them, if you wish.) The same choice may belong in more than one blank.

After you have compared your notes with the TRANSCRIPT and have chosen the answer for each blank space, you will be given additional time to transfer your answers to a separate answer sheet.

— —

Directions for Marking the Separate Answer Sheet

On the answer sheet, each question number stands for the blank with the same number in the TRANSCRIPT. For each number, you are to darken the box below the letter that is the same as the letter you wrote in the TRANSCRIPT. (The answers in this booklet will not be rated.) Be sure to use your pencil and record your answers on the separate answer sheet. You must keep your mark within the box. If you have to erase a mark, be sure to erase it completely. Make only one mark for each question.

Work quickly so that you will be able to finish in the time allowed. First you should darken the boxes on the answer sheet for the blanks you have lettered. You may continue to use your notes if you have not finished writing letters in the blanks in the TRANSCRIPT, or if you wish to make sure you have lettered them correctly.

DO NOT OPEN THIS BOOKLET UNTIL TOLD TO DO SO.

WORD LIST

Write E if the answer is NOT listed.

administration—C
along the—B
area—A
at first—A

claimed—C
classes—B
concluded—D
could be—D
courses—C

decrease—D
discriminating—C
discrimination—D

education—B
enrolled—D
entering—A

field—D
first—D

given—B
great—C

increase—A
in the—D

known—D

line—C

mainly—B
marked—B
mostly—D

observation—B
observing—A
offered—C
of value—C
open—A

popular—B
power—B
powers—D
practical—A

shaping—A
sharpen—B

shorthand—D
shown—C
stenography—B
study—C
subject—A

taught—D
that—C
the—D
these—B
this—A
thought—B
to be—A
training—D

valuable—A
vast—A

TRANSCRIPT

The number _____ in shorthand _____ _____ high
     1   2   3

schools has _____ a _____ _____. Today _____ _____
       4   5   6   7   8

is one of the most _____ _____ _____ _____ of
               9   10   11   12

business _____. When _____ _____ _____ _____
    13   14   15   16   17

educators _____ that it _____ _____ _____ in _____
      18   19   20   21   22

_____ _____ of _____ and _____. . . .
23   24   25   26

WORD LIST

Write E if the answer is NOT listed.

a change—D
administration—C
aims—A
always been—A

begun—D
businesses—A

came—D
changes—B
come—C

defects—B
demand—B
differences—D

education—B
educators—D

for—D

given—B
grade—C
grading—B

has—C
had—B
have come—A
high school—B

increased—D
increasing—C
institutions—D
instruction—C
it—B

offered—C
office—A
official—C
often been—B
ought to be—B

place—B
placement—D
prevailing—B

rule—D

schools—D
shorthand—D
should be—A
significance—C
stenography—B
study—C
subject—A

thinking—C
this—A
thought—B
tool—B
to realize—B
to recognize—B

valuable—A
vocational—C

when the—D
with—A
without—C
workers—C

TRANSCRIPT (continued)

. . . However, _____ the growth of _____ and the
              27   28

_____ _____ for _____ _____, _____ have _____
29   30   31   32   33   34

_____ the _____ of _____ _____ a _____ _____.
35   36   37   38   39   40

With the _____ in the _____ of _____ _____ _____
        41   42   43   44   45

in the _____ _____ of the _____. The _____
      46   47   48   49

_____ _____ _____ that _____ _____ _____ in
50   51   52   53   54   55

_____. . . .
56

CONTINUE ON THE NEXT PAGE WITHOUT WAITING FOR A SIGNAL.

(Page 2 of Example C)

WORD LIST

Write *E* if the answer is NOT listed.

became—B	junior high—D	study—C
because—B		subject—A
	less—B	
came—D	lessened—C	taught—D
change—A	level—C	that—C
changed—C	little—A	the—D
could—C	lost—D	their—B
could be—D		there—B
	manner—B	this—A
date—D	method—C	time—B
	moved—C	training—D
first—D	moved down—B	
		usefulness—B
graduate—D	occupational—B	utility—C
graduated—B		
	recognized—A	vocational—C
had little—C		
had no—A	shorthand—D	which—A
here—D	since—C	
high—C	soon—C	
	stenography—B	
into being—A	student—A	
into business—C	students—C	

TRANSCRIPT (continued)

... When the _____ school _____ _____ _____ , _____
    57   58   59   60   61
was _____ to _____ _____ with _____ _____ in _____
    62   63   64   65   66   67
_____ _____ the _____ was _____ . It was _____ _____
68   69   70   71   72   73
that _____ _____ place _____ _____ the _____ had
     74   75   76   77   78
_____ _____ _____ _____ by the _____ the _____
79   80   81   82   83   84
_____ _____ . . . .
85   86

WORD LIST

Write *E* if the answer is NOT listed.

advanced—A	job—B	showed—A
age—A	junior high—D	so—A
as far as—C		stenographers—C
at which—D	level—C	studies—B
at work—A		surveys—A
	may be—C	
be—B		takes—A
	near as—A	taught—D
date—D	nearly as—C	tendency—B
		that—C
education—B	offered—C	there—B
enter—D	often—B	this—A
	only—B	through—D
found—D		time—B
	possible—D	training—D
graduating—A		
graduation—C	rarely—D	undertake—A
	reason—B	until—A
	reasons—D	upgrade—D
has—C	retained—B	
high school—B		when—C
	school—A	which—A
in—A	secretaries—D	will—B
in order—D	secures—D	would—D
increased—D	seldom—C	working—B
into—B		

TRANSCRIPT (continued)

...Moreover, _____ of _____ with _____ _____ _____
           87   88   89   90   91
_____ school _____ _____ them _____ as _____ . For
92   93   94   95   96
_____ _____ , shorthand was _____ to the _____
97   98   99   100
_____ and is _____ as _____ _____ to the _____ of
101   102   103   104   105
_____ _____ _____ _____ the skill _____ _____ _____
106   107   108   109   109 110   111
_____ the student _____ a _____ . Because the _____
112   113   114   115
_____ students _____ office _____ _____ _____ ,
116   117   118   119   120
there is _____ a _____ to _____ _____ education
        121   122   123   124
_____ the junior college.
125

(Page 3 of Example C)

ANSWER KEY

1.	D	26.	D	51.	C	76.	B	101.	C
2.	B	27.	A	52.	A	77.	B	102.	C
3.	D	28.	E	53.	B	78.	D	103.	A
4.	C	29.	D	54.	A	79.	D	104.	D
5.	B	30.	B	55.	C	80.	E	105.	B
6.	A	31.	A	56.	B	81.	C	106.	C
7.	A	32.	C	57.	D	82.	C	107.	A
8.	A	33.	D	58.	D	83.	B	108.	C
9.	B	34.	C	59.	D	84.	A	109.	B
10.	C	35.	B	60.	A	85.	C	110.	B
11.	D	36.	E	61.	D	86.	D	111.	B
12.	D	37.	E	62.	B	87.	A	112.	C
13.	B	38.	E	63.	C	88.	E	113.	A
14.	D	39.	C	64.	C	89.	B	114.	B
15.	E	40.	B	65.	A	90.	B	115.	A
16.	D	41.	D	66.	A	91.	D	116.	D
17.	D	42.	A	67.	D	92.	D	117.	D
18.	C	43.	C	68.	B	93.	C	118.	E
19.	E	44.	D	69.	E	94.	D	119.	C
20.	C	45.	B	70.	A	95.	A	120.	A
21.	B	46.	C	71.	D	96.	C	121.	E
22.	E	47.	D	72.	C	97.	A	122.	B
23.	D	48.	A	73.	E	98.	B	123.	D
24.	D	49.	B	74.	D	99.	E	124.	E
25.	B	50.	B	75.	A	100.	B	125.	B

CHAPTER 10

Practice, Practice, Practice

(NOTE: You will need another person to dictate each practice exercise. Allow 30 minutes to finish the transcript and mark your answers.)

PRACTICE SET 1

The Dictation

Finish reading each two lines at the number of seconds indicated below

To be able to express your ideas	
simply and clearly, it is necessary	10
that you have a good command of the	
language. (Period) The greater your vocabulary,	20
the more interesting and effective your	
conversation. (Period) Dr. Eliot, former	30
president of Harvard, said, "I recognize	
but one mental acquisition that	40
is an essential part of the education	
of a lady or a gentleman; namely,	50
an accurate and refined use of the	
mother tongue." (Period) Fortunately, this	1 min.
is an acquisition within the reach	
of everyone. (Period) Only two things	10
are necessary: a good dictionary	
and a desire to speak well. (Period)	20
Add to these the association	
with educated, intelligent people	30
and ready access to a public	
library, and there is no reason	40
in the world why you cannot	
acquire a rich and colorful	50
vocabulary. (Period) When you hear	
a new word or read it in	2 min.
a book, learn its meaning and	
pronunciation. (Period) Until you are	10
wholly familiar with the word	
and are able to use it in	20
your conversation, it is not	
a part of your vocabulary. (Period) It	30
is not enough to know how to	
pronounce a word and to have a general	40
idea of its meaning; you	
must know how to use it correctly in	50
your speech. (Period) Remember that there	
is always a right word for every purpose. (Period)	3 min.

Reprinted with permission from Gregg Shorthand Simplified for Colleges, *Leslie, Zoubeck, and Hosler, 1958, Gregg Publishing Division, McGraw-Hill Book Co., Inc.*

The Transcript

Compare your notes with the transcript. Then select the correct word for each blank space and write the letter of your choice in the space.

WORD LIST

Write E if the answer is NOT listed.

ability—B	goal—B	one—D
able—C	great—C	only—B
accurate—D	greater—B	our—D
acquire—D	greatest—D	
acquisition—B		part—A
acquisitive—C	Harvard—C	partial—C
actual—C		present—D
	ideal—B	president—A
capable—D	ideas—A	
clear—C	interest—B	realize—D
clearly—B	interesting—A	refined—D
command—C		remind—C
conservation—B	ladies—A	
conversation—B	lady—B	sensual—B
converse—C	language—A	simple—D
	length—B	
educate—C		to exist—C
effect—C	many—B	to express—B
effecting—B	mature—D	tongue—C
effective—D	medical—C	
essence—D	mental—A	use—A
essential—C	more—C	used—B
	mortal—D	
formal—C	most—A	woman—C
former—A		won—C
	natural—C	
gentleman—A	necessary—D	your—C
gentlemen—C	needed—C	

TRANSCRIPT

To be ___ ___ ___ ___ ___ and
       1   2   3   4   5

___, it is ___ that you have a ___
6   7   8

___ of the ___. The ___ your ___, the
9   10   11   12

___ ___ and ___ your ___.
13   14   15   16

Dr. Eliot, ___ ___ of ___, said, "I ___
          17   18   19   20

but ___ ___ ___ that is an ___
    21   22   23   24

___ of the ___ of a ___ or a ___;
25   26   27   28

namely, an ___ and ___ ___ of the
             29   30   31

___ ___." . . .
32   33

WORD LIST

Write E if the answer is NOT listed.

acquaint—D	intellect—B	their—A
acquire—C	intelligent—A	there—D
acquired—B		these—A
acquisition—A	liberty—D	they're—B
association—B		this—B
assumption—D	necessary—D	those—B
	needed—A	to—B
can—B	no—A	to say—B
cannot—A	now—C	to speak—C
colored—D		too—D
colorful—B	people—C	two—A
	persons—B	
desire—A	public—B	vocality—C
dream—D		
	rare—B	well—B
educated—D	rationale—B	when—C
education—C	reach—C	where—A
everybody—C	reading—A	why—D
everyone—B	realm—B	will—D
	reason—C	within—D
grand—B	republic—C	without—C
great—D	rich—C	

TRANSCRIPT (continued)

. . . Fortunately, ___ is an ___ ___ the ___ of
               34   35   36   37

___. Only ___ ___ are ___: a ___
38   39   40   41   42   43

and a ___ ___ ___. Add to ___ the ___
       44   45   46   47   48

with ___, ___ ___ and ___ ___ to a ___
     49   50   51   52   53   54

___, and ___ is ___ ___ in the ___ ___
55   56   57   58   59   60

you ___ ___ a ___ and ___ ___. . . .
    61   62   63   64   65

WORD LIST

Write *E* if the answer is NOT listed.

a—C   is—B   the—A
able—A   it—A   these—B
air—D   its—C   this—C
also—D   to abuse—D
an—B   know—C   to lose—B
and—B   to use—C
as—A   lean—A
   learn—D   vocabulary—B
book—B   learned—C   vocality—D
buck—D
   meaning—B   which—B
conservation—C   means—C   whole—D
conversation—A   mental—D   wholly—B
converse—B   moaning—A   within—A
      word—B
familiar—D   new—D   world—D
family—C   now—B
      you—B
hear—C   our—B   your—D
heard—D
here—B   part—D
holy—C   partial—B
   pronounced—C
in—C
into—D   red—C

TRANSCRIPT (continued)

. . . When ＿＿ ＿＿ a ＿＿ ＿＿ or ＿＿ ＿＿
     66   67   68   69   70   71

＿＿ a ＿＿, ＿＿ ＿＿ ＿＿ and ＿＿. Until
72   73   74   75   76   77

you ＿＿ ＿＿ ＿＿ ＿＿ ＿＿ word ＿＿
       78   79   80   81   82   83

are ＿＿ ＿＿ it in ＿＿ ＿＿, it ＿＿ ＿＿
    84   85   86   87   88   89

＿＿ ＿＿ ＿＿ your ＿＿ . . . .
90   91   92   93

WORD LIST

Write *E* if the answer is NOT listed.

all—C   into—B   there—A
alright—B   is—D   to abuse—A
an—A   it—C   to have—C
as—A   its—B   to hold—B
      to know—A
correct—B   meaning—C   to pronounce—B
correction—C   morning—B   to propose—D
correctly—D   most—D   to say—C
   must—B   to use—B
every—D   to utilize—C
everyone—B   not—B   tonight—B
   now—C
for—C   us—C
four—A   our—C
      warn—C
general—A   propose—A   who—C
gentle—C   word—A
   speak—D   work—B
how—D   speech—A   write—C
idea—D
ideal—B   than—C   your—B
in—A   that—D
inside—C   their—B

TRANSCRIPT (continued)

. . . It ＿＿ ＿＿ ＿＿ ＿＿ ＿＿ ＿＿ a ＿＿
     94   95   96   97   98   99   100

＿＿ ＿＿ a ＿＿ ＿＿ of ＿＿ ＿＿ ;
101   102   103   104   105   106

you ＿＿ know ＿＿ ＿＿ it ＿＿ ＿＿ ＿＿
     107   108   109   110   111   112

＿＿ .
113

Remember ＿＿ ＿＿ is ＿＿ a ＿＿ word
         114   115   116   117

＿＿ ＿＿ ＿＿ .
118   119   120

ANSWERS FOR PRACTICE SET 1

1. C	25. A	49. D	73. B	97. A
2. B	26. E	50. A	74. D	98. C
3. C	27. B	51. C	75. C	99. B
4. A	28. A	52. E	76. B	100. A
5. E	29. D	53. E	77. E	101. E
6. B	30. D	54. B	78. C	102. C
7. D	31. A	55. E	79. B	103. A
8. E	32. E	56. D	80. D	104. D
9. C	33. C	57. A	81. E	105. B
10. A	34. B	58. C	82. A	106. C
11. B	35. A	59. B	83. B	107. B
12. E	36. D	60. D	84. A	108. D
13. C	37. C	61. A	85. C	109. B
14. A	38. B	62. C	86. D	110. D
15. D	39. A	63. C	87. A	111. A
16. B	40. E	64. B	88. B	112. B
17. A	41. D	65. E	89. E	113. A
18. A	42. E	66. B	90. C	114. D
19. C	43. E	67. C	91. D	115. A
20. E	44. A	68. D	92. E	116. E
21. D	45. C	69. B	93. B	117. E
22. A	46. B	70. E	94. D	118. C
23. B	47. A	71. A	95. B	119. D
24. C	48. B	72. C	96. E	120. E

PRACTICE SET 2

The Dictation

Finish reading
each two lines
at the number
of seconds in-
dicated below

Each year you, with millions of other Americans, spend an agonizing	10
period of indecision considering the pros and cons of the various trips presented	20
in the travel folders you have accumulated. (Period) The fact that your	30
budget may be definitely limited does not detract from the enjoyment you	40
derive from reading of the far-off places so attractively described and	50
pictured in the literature of the various bus, railroad, steamship, and	1 min.
airlines. (Period) The annual search for something different to do during the	10
vacation period adds to the zest of the vacation itself. (Period) The extensive	20
airline services now available make it possible for one to consider trips that	30
previously were impossible because of time limitations. (Period) High among	40
the trips that might appeal to you is travel in Europe. (Period) You can relax	50
in the scenic splendor of the Old World and revel in its art masterpieces,	2 min.
its colorful native pageants, and its quaint customs and costumes. (Period)	10
Flying the Atlantic to Europe will save you precious days of that	20
all-too-short vacation period. (Period) You will have more time to spend	30
in visiting each country. (Period) It will be possible for you to become better	40
acquainted with the people and their everyday pursuits. (Period) You can	50
see some of the byways that the average tourist so frequently misses. (Period)	3 min.

Reprinted with permission from Gregg Shorthand Simplified for Colleges, *Leslie, Zoubeck, and Hosler, 1958, Gregg Publishing Division, McGraw-Hill Book Co., Inc.*

The Transcript

Compare your notes with the transcript. Then select the correct word for each blank space and write the letter of your choice in the space.

WORD LIST

Write E if the answer is NOT listed.

accumulated—A enjoyable—D   present—C
accustomed—C   enjoyment—B   presented—D
airlines—C   pros—D
airplanes—D   faced—D   prose—A
airways—B   fact—C
Americas—D   fat—B   railroad—B
Americans—A   folders—B   railway—C
another—B   folds—D   reading—A
attraction—D   reads—B
attractively—C indecision—A
               indigestion—B   spend—D
budding—A   spent—B
budget—B   limitation—B   steamer—A
bus—A   literate—D   steamship—D
bussed—B   literature—B
                                trail—C
cans—C   million—C   travel—A
cons—B   millions—D   traveled—B
considerate—C   tricks—A
               organizing—A
defined—C   other—C   varied—D
definitely—D   various—C
derailed—D   period—C   very—B
derived—C   picture—A
describe—C   pictured—D   year—B
detract—A   pitcher—C   your—C
distract—C   placed—B
disturbed—B   places—A

TRANSCRIPT

Each _____ you, with _____ of _____ _____, _____
      1   2   3   4   5

an _____ _____ of _____ _____ the _____ and _____
    6   7   8   9   10   11

of the _____ _____ _____ in the _____ _____ you
        12   13   14   15   16

have _____. The _____ that your _____ may be _____
     17   18   19   20

_____ does not _____ from the _____ you _____
21   22   23   24

from _____ of the far-off _____ so _____ _____ and
     25   26   27   28

_____ in the _____ of the _____ _____, _____, _____,
29   30   31 32   33   34

and _____. . . .
    35

WORD LIST

Write E if the answer is NOT listed.

aids—C   limitations—D   siege—B
airplane—B   limitless—A   someone—A
annual—B   limits—C
annul—C   time—B
are—B   made—A   to conclude—C
available—B   make—D   to conduct—A
availed—D   mate—C   to dew—D
                                to do—B
because—A   new—D   to due—A
become—C   now—C   tricks—D
                                trips—A
different—C   one—B
diverse—D   vacation—A
during—C   period—D   vocation—B
               possible—A
expensive—A   predated—D   wear—A
extensive—D   previously—B   were—C
               probable—C   won—D
improbable—B
its—C   search—A   zeal—B
itself—B   seek—D   zest—C
               servants—D
just—D   services—A

TRANSCRIPT (continued)

. . . The _____ _____ for _____ _____ _____ _____ the
        36   37   38   39   40   41

_____ _____ _____ to the _____ of the vacation
42   43   44   45

_____ .
46

The _____ _____ _____ _____ _____ _____ it _____
    47   48   49   50   51   52   53

for _____ _____ _____ that _____ _____ _____ _____
    54   55   56   57   58   59   60

of _____ _____. . . .
   61   62

WORD LIST

Write _E_ if the answer is NOT listed.

able—A	masterworks—B	scene—C
aged—D	may—A	scenery—A
amid—D	might—D	scenic—B
among—B		splendid—C
appear—C	native—A	
arch—C	natural—B	than—B
art—A	nature—D	that—C
	night—B	travail—D
can—D		travel—C
can't—C	old—C	tricks—C
colored—A		trips—A
colorful—C	pageants—A	
costumes—B	pages—B	world—A
customs—D		
	quaint—C	you—B
England—B	queer—D	your—A
Europe—A	quick—A	
globe—B	rebel—C	
	relapse—B	
it's—A	relax—D	
its—D	revel—B	

TRANSCRIPT (continued)

...High _____ the _____ _____ _____ _____ to
　　　　　63　　　64　　65　　66　　67

_____ is _____ in _____. You _____ _____ in the
68　　69　　　70　　　　　　71　　72

_____ _____ of the _____ _____ and _____ in
73　　74　　　　　75　　76　　　77

_____ _____ _____, its _____ _____ _____, and its
78　79　　80　　　　81　　82　　83

_____ _____ and _____ ....
84　　85　　　86

- -

WORD LIST

Write _E_ if the answer is NOT listed.

acquainted—A	misses—A	than—B
acquitted—D	misuse—C	their—C
Atlanta—B	more—C	there—B
Atlantic—B	most—D	to become—A
avarice—D	Mrs.—B	to begin—B
average—C	much—A	to share—B
		to spend—A
be—B	often—D	tourism—D
best—B	overage—B	tourist—A
better—C		twist—C
bylaws—A	passable—C	
byways—B	people—D	Utopia—A
	period—C	
can—B	person—C	vacation—A
could—D	possible—D	visited—B
country—A	possibility—A	visiting—C
county—B	precious—B	visitor—A
	precocious—D	vocation—C
day—B	pursues—B	
days—C	pursuits—C	will—D
daze—A		would—C
	safe—C	
every—C	save—A	
everyday—A	sea—A	
everyone—D	see—D	
	shall—A	
had—A	some—A	
have—B	sum—C	

TRANSCRIPT (continued)

...Flying the _____ to _____ will _____ you _____
　　　　　　87　　　88　　　　89　　　　　90

_____ of _____ all-too-short _____ _____. You _____
91　　　92　　　　　　　　　93　　94　　　　95

_____ _____ _____ _____ in _____ _____ _____. It
96　　97　　98　　99　　　100　101　102

_____ _____ _____ for you _____ _____ _____
103　104　105　　　　　　106　107　108

with the _____ and _____ _____ _____. You _____
　　　　109　　　110　111　112　　　　113

_____ _____ of the _____ that the _____ _____
114　115　　　　116　　　　　　117　118

so _____ _____.
　119　120

ANSWERS FOR PRACTICE SET 2

1. B	25. A	49. A	73. B	97. C
2. D	26. A	50. C	74. E	98. E
3. C	27. C	51. B	75. C	99. A
4. A	28. E	52. D	76. A	100. C
5. D	29. D	53. A	77. B	101. E
6. E	30. B	54. B	78. D	102. A
7. C	31. C	55. D	79. A	103. D
8. A	32. A	56. A	80. E	104. B
9. E	33. B	57. B	81. C	105. D
10. D	34. D	58. C	82. A	106. A
11. B	35. C	59. E	83. A	107. C
12. C	36. B	60. A	84. C	108. A
13. E	37. A	61. B	85. D	109. D
14. D	38. E	62. D	86. B	110. C
15. A	39. C	63. B	87. C	111. A
16. B	40. B	64. A	88. E	112. C
17. A	41. C	65. C	89. A	113. B
18. C	42. A	66. D	90. B	114. D
19. B	43. D	67. E	91. C	115. A
20. D	44. E	68. B	92. E	116. B
21. E	45. C	69. C	93. A	117. C
22. A	46. B	70. A	94. C	118. A
23. B	47. D	71. D	95. D	119. E
24. C	48. E	72. D	96. B	120. A

PRACTICE SET 3

The Dictation

Finish reading
each two lines
at the number
of seconds in-
dicated below

The boy was ten years old, and he had a passion for machinery. (Period) He	10
tinkered with all the clocks in the old white farmhouse until they kept time	20
properly. (Period) One Sunday morning after church a neighbor took out his big gold	30
huntingcase watch. (Period) He said, "Henry, can you fix my old turnip?" (Question mark) The	40
boy found that a jewel was loose in the works. (Period) He put it back into place and	50
the watch ran. (Period) The neighbors around Dearborn began to bring their ailing old	1 min.
timepieces. (Period) So young Henry Ford set up shop on a shelf in his bedroom, working	10
nights after chores. (Period) In the winter he kept warm with an oil lantern	20
between his feet. (Period) He ground a shingle nail down into a tiny screwdriver and made	30
files from knitting needles. (Period) All his life he tinkered with watches and	40
never had to use a jeweler's eyeglass. (Period) He could almost see with his long, thin,	50
steel-spring fingers: the fingers of the hands that put the nation on wheels. (Period)	2 min.
His passion for machinery became an idea, and the power of that idea has	10
rolled on through the years. (Period) He learned how to run, repair, and make every	20
kind of machine there was. (Period) Then he began on the machine that wasn't—	30
a horseless carriage. (Period) In 1896, seven years before the founding of the	40
Ford Motor Company, he trundled his first little two-passenger machine out	50
into one of the alleys of Detroit and ran it around the block. (Period)	3 min.

*Reprinted with permission from Gregg Shorthand Simplified for Colleges, Leslie,
Zoubeck, and Hosler, 1958, Gregg Publishing Division, McGraw-Hill Book Co., Inc.*

The Transcript

Compare your notes with the transcript. Then select the correct word for each blank space and write the letter of your choice in the space.

WORD LIST

Write _E_ if the answer is NOT listed.

all—C	large—B	till—B
		time—A
big—B	machine—C	timed—B
bigger—D	machinery—B	tinker—A
boat—D	meaning—C	tinkered—D
boy—A	morning—A	took—D
		turned—A
can—D	neighbor—B	turnip—B
can't—C	neighbors—C	
charge—B		until—D
church—C	oil—D	
clock—A	our—D	watch—B
		water—A
farm—A	passion—A	while—B
farmhouse—C	position—C	white—A
fix—A	proper—D	
fixed—C	properly—C	years—C
fox—B	property—A	yours—A
gold—C	take—A	
good—D	taken—B	
	ten—D	
keep—C	then—C	
kept—B	tied—C	

TRANSCRIPT

The _____ was _____ _____ _____, and he had a
    1   2   3   4

_____ for _____ . He _____ with _____ the _____ in
 5   6   7   8   9

the _____ _____ _____ _____ they _____ _____
    10   11   12   13   14   15

_____ .
 16

One _____ _____ _____ _____ a _____ _____
    17   18   19   20   21   22

_____ his _____ _____ huntingcase _____ . He said,
 23   24   25   26

"Henry, _____ you _____ my _____ _____ ?" . . .
         27   28   29   30

WORD LIST

Write _E_ if the answer is NOT listed.

abound—C	in—A	sat—A
ailed—B	into—B	self—D
ailing—C		sharp—A
around—A	jewel—B	shelf—C
	jeweler—D	ship—B
back—C		shop—D
backed—B	keep—D	sit—D
bedroom--B	lecture—B	
begin—A	loose—C	their—D
between—C	lose—D	there—C
bog—C		timepieces—A
book—D	neighborhood—D	timers—D
bottom—D	neighborhoods—A	to bring—B
brought—C	night—D	
	nights—C	under—C
chores—B	oil—A	
	old—D	warm—B
feel—C		warn—C
feet—D	pat—C	water—A
find—B	please—C	winner—C
foot—B	put—D	winter—D
found—D		work—B
	ran—D	worked—D
him—B	run—C	works—A
his—A		

TRANSCRIPT (continued)

. . . The _____ _____ that a _____ was _____ in the
        31   32   33   34

_____ . He _____ it _____ _____ _____ and the _____
 35   36   37   38   39   40

_____ .
 41

The _____ _____ Dearborn _____ _____ _____
    42   43   44   45   46

_____ _____ _____ . So _____ Henry Ford _____
 47   48   49   50   51

_____ _____ on a _____ in his _____ , _____ _____
 52   53   54   55   56   57

after _____ . In the _____ he _____ _____ with an
      58   59   60   61

_____ _____ _____ his _____ . . . .
 62   63   64   65

WORD LIST

Write E if the answer is NOT listed.

almost—B	knitted—C	puts—D
always—C	knitting—B	
	knotting—A	saw—C
can—D		see—D
could—C	life—C	seen—A
	live—B	single—C
down—B	long—B	
	lung—A	than—C
eyeball—B		then—D
eyeglass—A	made—A	thin—A
	maid—B	tinny—C
file—D	make—A	tiny—D
filed—A		
files—C	nail—D	us—B
fingered—A	nailed—B	used—A
fingers—B	nation—C	
	national—A	watched—D
grind—B	needled—A	watches—A
ground—A	needles—D	wheeled—B
	noodles—C	wheels—D
had—D	null—A	
hard—C		
	pat—B	
jewels—C	put—A	

TRANSCRIPT (continued)

...He _____ a _____ _____ _____ into a _____
      66   67   68   69   70

_____ and _____ _____ from _____ _____. All his
71   72   73   74   75

_____ he tinkered with _____ and _____ _____ to
76   77   78   79

_____ a _____ _____.
80   81   82

He _____ _____ _____ with his _____, _____, steel-
     83   84   85   86   87

spring _____: the fingers of the _____ that _____
        88   89   90

the _____ on _____....
    91   92

WORD LIST

Write E if the answer is NOT listed.

all—A	foremost—C	power—A
alleys—B	founded—D	powerful—D
allied—D	founding—C	
allies—C		ran—A
	horse sense—A	repaint—C
became—D		repair—A
become—A	ideal—C	roll—C
began—C		rolled—B
begin—D	kin—B	run—B
black—A	kind—A	
blacked—C		seven—B
blocked—D	learn—A	small—B
	learned—C	
carriage—A	little—D	threw—A
carried—C		through—D
	machine—D	to rule—B
earned—D	made—D	to run—D
every—C	make—B	trampled—A
everything—D		trundled—D
	passion—C	
finding—B	pasture—A	year—A
first—A	patient—D	yours—B

TRANSCRIPT (continued)

...His _____ for _____ _____ an _____, and the
      93   94   95   96

_____ of that idea has _____ on _____ the _____.
97   98   99   100

He _____ _____ _____, _____, and _____ _____
    101   102   103   104   105 106

_____ of _____ there was. Then he _____ on the
107   108   109

machine that wasn't—a _____ _____.
               110   111

In 1896, _____ _____ before the _____ of the
         112   113   114

Ford Motor Company, he _____ his _____ _____
                 115   116 117

two-passenger machine out into one of the _____ of
                           118

Detroit and _____ it around the _____.
       119   120

ANSWERS FOR PRACTICE SET 3

1. A	25. C	49. A	73. C	97. A
2. D	26. B	50. B	74. B	98. B
3. C	27. D	51. E	75. D	99. D
4. E	28. A	52. E	76. C	100. A
5. A	29. E	53. D	77. A	101. C
6. B	30. B	54. C	78. B	102. E
7. D	31. E	55. B	79. D	103. D
8. C	32. D	56. E	80. E	104. A
9. E	33. B	57. C	81. E	105. B
10. E	34. C	58. B	82. A	106. C
11. A	35. A	59. D	83. C	107. A
12. C	36. D	60. E	84. B	108. D
13. D	37. C	61. B	85. D	109. C
14. B	38. B	62. A	86. B	110. E
15. A	39. E	63. E	87. A	111. A
16. C	40. E	64. C	88. B	112. B
17. E	41. D	65. D	89. E	113. A
18. A	42. E	66. A	90. A	114. C
19. E	43. A	67. E	91. C	115. D
20. C	44. E	68. D	92. D	116. A
21. B	45. B	69. B	93. C	117. D
22. D	46. D	70. C	94. B	118. B
23. E	47. C	71. E	95. D	119. A
24. A	48. D	72. A	96. E	120. C

PRACTICE SET 4

The Dictation

The retail salesperson who plays such a vital part in the process of distribution	10
may well be considered one of the most important spark plugs of our economy. (Period)	20
He makes our free-enterprise system work. (Period) He persuades us to exchange	30
our money for the things that make for better and more enjoyable living. (Period)	40
By keeping the cash registers of America ringing, he also keeps our factories	50
humming. (Period) The high-pressure salesperson of yesterday, who misrepresented	1 min.
merchandise, is as obsolete today as the Model T and the patent-medicine man. (Period)	10
In the buyer's market of today, the good salesperson is the one who induces the	20
customer to purchase by showing him how he will benefit. (Period) The retail salesperson	30
should not only make people want what he has to sell, but he should also make them want to	40
but it from him. (Period) What a challenge! (Exclamation Point) What he does in the place of business in which	50
he serves reflects upon the firm, and the firm's reputation reflects upon	2 min.
him. (Period) The successful salesperson is more interested in keeping the customer's	10
good will than in turning a quick sale. (Period) Good will is an intangible	20
asset that is not visible except as it is reflected in the faces of satisfied	30
customers. (Period) However, it is the most valuable asset that any business can possess. (Period)	40
It is indeed more valuable than the building, the merchandise, or the equipment. (Period) Every	50
salesperson holds the good will of the establishment in his hands. (Period)	3 min.

Reprinted with permission from Gregg Shorthand Simplified for Colleges, *Leslie, Zoubeck, and Hosler, 1958, Gregg Publishing Division, McGraw-Hill Book Co., Inc.*

The Transcript

Compare your notes with the transcript. Then select the correct word for each blank space and write the letter of your choice in the space.

WORD LIST

Write E if the answer is NOT listed.

allow—A	improved—C	retail—C
American—A	items—B	role—A
business—B	key—D	salesman—B
		salesperson—A
can—C	life—C	seller—C
cash—D	living—D	such—C
considered—C		system—A
considering—A	make—B	systems—C
convinces—D	may—D	
	money—C	takes—C
demonstrates—A	most—D	the—C
distribution—A	much—A	things—D
		thought of—D
economy—B	our—D	to exchange—A
enjoyable—A		to trade—C
enjoyed—B	part—B	
essential—D	perhaps—A	very—C
	persuades—B	
goods—A	plays—D	way—B
	plug—D	well—B
happen—C	plugs—C	wholesale—A
	procedure—C	work—D
important—B	process—A	worthwhile—D

TRANSCRIPT

The ___(1)___ ___(2)___ who ___(3)___ ___(4)___ a ___(5)___ ___(6)___ in the ___(7)___ of ___(8)___ ___(9)___ ___(10)___ be ___(11)___ one of the ___(12)___ ___(13)___ ___(14)___ ___(15)___ of our ___(16)___. He makes ___(17)___ ___(18)___ ___(19)___ ___(20)___. He ___(21)___ us ___(22)___ our ___(23)___ for the ___(24)___ that ___(25)___ for ___(26)___ and more ___(27)___ ___(28)___....

WORD LIST

Write E if the answer is NOT listed.

allowing—B	industries—C	past—B
America—A	introduces—C	pressure—A
benefitting—B	keeping—C	registers—B
buyer—C	keeps—A	represented—B
buyer's—A		
	machines—C	show—B
cash—D	making—A	showing—C
coin—C	man—B	
consumer—C	market—D	to buy—D
continues—C	marketing—C	to peruse—B
customer—B	medical—D	to purchase—A
	medicinal—B	today—C
factories—D	medicine—C	
	mercantile—B	when—D
	merchandise—A	where—C
going—A	merchant—B	who—C
good—B	mistaken—C	whom—A
goods—A	Model T—B	why—D
		working—B
high—C	now—B	
how—A		yesterday—D
humming—B	obsolete—D	yesteryear—C
	opposite—C	
induces—A		

TRANSCRIPT (continued)

...By ___(29)___ the ___(30)___ ___(31)___ of ___(32)___ ___(33)___, he also ___(34)___ our ___(35)___ ___(36)___. The ___(37)___ - ___(38)___ salesperson of ___(39)___, ___(40)___ ___(41)___ ___(42)___, is as ___(43)___ ___(44)___ as the ___(45)___ and the patent-___(46)___ ___(47)___. In the ___(48)___ ___(49)___ of today, the ___(50)___ salesperson is the ___(51)___ who ___(52)___ the ___(53)___ ___(54)___ by ___(55)___ him ___(56)___ he will ___(57)___....

WORD LIST

Write *E* if the answer is NOT listed.

business—D	make—D	sold—C
buying—A	may—C	success—C
	might—A	successful—A
challenge—A		
could—C	office—B	than—B
customer—D	one—C	them—A
customer's—A	only—A	then—D
	over—D	they—C
do—D		to bring—D
	people—D	to buy—B
faith—B	persons—A	to say—B
firm—D	place—A	to sell—A
from—C	placed—C	turning—C
goes—B	quiet—b	up—C
good—C		upon—B
	reflected—A	
he—B	reflects—B	want—D
her—A	reputation—A	wanted—C
	reputed—C	which—A
interest—B	retail—B	will—A
interested—D		with—B
	sale—A	
keep—C	serve—D	
keeping—B	serves—C	

TRANSCRIPT (continued)

. . . The _____ salesperson _____ not _____ make
58   59   60

_____ _____what he has _____, but _____ _____ also
61   62   63   64   65

_____ _____ want _____ it _____ him. What a
66   67   68   69

_____! What he _____ in the _____ of _____
70   71   72   73

in _____ he _____ _____ _____ the _____, and the
74   75   76   77   78

firm's _____ reflects _____ _____. The _____
79   80   81   82

salesperson is more _____ in _____ the _____
83   84   85

_____ _____ _____ in _____ a _____ _____ . . . .
86   87   88   89   90   91

WORD LIST

Write *E* if the answer is NOT listed.

accept—D	helps—A	possess—B
am—B	his—D	possessed—C
any—A	holds—B	possession—D
are—D	honor—C	
assist—D	hour—A	reflect—B
		reflected—A
built—A	indeed—A	reflects—C
business—C	indication—C	
busy—B	intangible—D	satisfaction—C
	invisible—C	satisfying—B
can—A	is—A	
can't—B	it—C	than—D
could—D	its—B	the—B
		then—C
established—B	many—A	
establishment—A	merchandise—A	valuable—A
except—A	merchant—B	value—D
exception—B	more—B	valued—B
	most—D	viable—A
faced—D	much—C	visible—B
faces—B		
	or—C	was—D
hands—A	our—B	will—C
has—C		won't—B

TRANSCRIPT (continued)

. . . Good _____ _____ an _____ _____ that is not
92   93   94   95

_____ _____ as _____ is _____ in the _____ of
96   97   98   99   100

_____ customers.
101

However, it is the _____ _____ _____ that _____
102   103   104   105

_____ _____ _____ It is _____ _____ valuable
106   107   108   109   110

_____ the _____, the _____ , _____ the _____ .
111   112   113   114   115

Every _____ _____ the good will of the _____ in
116   117   118

_____ _____ .
119   120

ANSWERS FOR PRACTICE SET 4

1. C	25. B	49. D	73. D	97. A
2. A	26. E	50. B	74. A	98. C
3. D	27. A	51. E	75. C	99. A
4. C	28. D	52. A	76. B	100. B
5. E	29. C	53. B	77. B	101. E
6. B	30. D	54. A	78. D	102. D
7. A	31. B	55. C	79. A	103. A
8. A	32. A	56. A	80. B	104. E
9. D	33. E	57. E	81. E	105. A
10. B	34. A	58. B	82. A	106. C
11. C	35. D	59. E	83. D	107. A
12. D	36. B	60. A	84. B	108. B
13. B	37. C	61. D	85. A	109. A
14. E	38. A	62. D	86. C	110. B
15. C	39. D	63. A	87. A	111. D
16. B	40. C	64. B	88. B	112. E
17. D	41. E	65. E	89. C	113. A
18. E	42. A	66. D	90. E	114. C
19. A	43. D	67. A	91. A	115. E
20. D	44. C	68. B	92. C	116. E
21. B	45. B	69. C	93. A	117. B
22. A	46. C	70. A	94. D	118. A
23. C	47. B	71. E	95. E	119. D
24. D	48. A	72. A	96. B	120. A

PRACTICE SET 5

The Dictation

Finish reading each two lines at the number of seconds indicated below

We say that Father keeps the house running. (Period) Father says that the house	10
keeps him running. (Period) Probably both statements are true. (Period) Let us look	20
at it in the most favorable light— the light of a lovely summer evening. (Period)	30
Father has come home from the office, has had his dinner, and has arbitrated	40
all the children's quarrels. (Period) He has settled down in his favorite chair	50
on the porch to relax and enjoy the summer evening. (Period) Right away we know	1 min.
that Father is either new to country living or that he is an incurable	10
optimist. (Period) Every beautiful summer evening he sits in that same chair to	20
relax, and every beautiful summer evening something drags him out of the chair. (Period)	30
This evening perhaps the telephone bell rings. (Period) Almost immediately Father hears	40
Mother say, "Of course, he will be delighted." (Period) Then Mother	50
comes out and breaks the news to Father that Mrs. Jones, their neighbor,	2 min.
has offered to give her some plants if Father will get them	10
now. (Period) So, Father climbs into the car and drives over to get the	20
plants and drives back, only to find, naturally, that he is to plant	30
the plants for Mother and that they are very delicate plants	40
that must be planted immediately. (Period) By this time the beautiful	50
summer evening has faded and the mosquitoes have come out. (Period)	3 min.

Reprinted with permission from Gregg Shorthand Simplified for Colleges, *Leslie, Zoubeck, and Hosler, 1958, Gregg Publishing Division, McGraw-Hill Book Co., Inc.*

The Transcript

Compare your notes with the transcript. Then select the correct word for each blank space and write the letter of your choice in the space.

WORD LIST

Write *E* if the answer is NOT listed.

arbiter—B	hard—D	of—B
arbitrated—A	he's—B	office—C
are—B	hid—B	often—A
as—C	him—C	orbited—C
	his—D	our—D
boat—B	home—B	
both—A	horse—C	pair—C
	house—A	
came—B	hut—D	quakes—C
children's—C		quarrels—B
child's—B	if—D	
come—D	it—A	racing—B
	it's—D	running—D
dined—C	keep—D	
	keeps—B	said—D
even—C		say—C
evening—A	light—A	simmer—D
every—D	lit—C	stated—A
	lively—A	summer—A
	look—C	
farther—B	lovely—C	true—A
favorable—D	luck—B	truth—B
favorite—B		
fro—C	many—C	
from—A	most—B	us—D
	much—A	

TRANSCRIPT

We _____ that _____ _____ the _____ _____. Father
   1   2   3   4   5

_____ that the house keeps _____ running. Probably
6   7

_____ _____ _____ _____.
8   9   10   11

Let _____ _____ at _____ in the _____ _____
    12   13   14   15   16   17

— the light _____ a _____ _____ _____. Father has
           18   19   20   21

_____ _____ _____ the _____, has _____ his _____,
22   23   24   25   26   27

and has _____ _____ the _____ _____. . . .
        28   29   30   31

- -

WORD LIST

Write *E* if the answer is NOT listed.

always—C	he—B	relapse—A
	him—D	relax—C
beautiful—D		
beauty—C	incubate—B	saddled—C
bountiful—A	incurable—C	same—C
	injure—A	sat—B
continent—D		sets—C
	knew—C	settled—B
done—A	know—B	share—B
down—D	known—D	sits—A
drag—C		some—D
drugs—A	life—B	someone—C
	live—C	something—B
either—A	living—A	
enjoy—D		than—C
ether—C	new—B	that—D
even—C		to relapse—D
evening—A	optometrist—A	to relax—B
ever—C	our—D	
every—D	out—B	us—A
farther—B	porch—A	we—C
Father—D	pouch—C	when—D
favorable—D		
favored—B		

TRANSCRIPT (continued)

. . . He has _____ _____ in his _____ chair on the
          32   33   34

_____ _____ and _____ the _____ _____. Right
35   36   37   38   39

_____ _____ _____ that _____ is _____ _____ to
40   41   42   43   44   45

_____ _____ or _____ he is an _____ _____. Every
46   47   48   49   50

_____ summer evening _____ _____ in that _____
51   52   53   54

_____ to _____, and _____ _____ summer
55   56   57   58

evening _____ _____ _____ _____ of
          59   60   61   62

the _____. . . .
   63

WORD LIST

Write *E* if the answer is NOT listed.

be—C
being—D
bell—C
bowl—A
bricks—A
bride—B

came—C
come—B
comes—A

delighted—B
deluded—D

even—B
evening—A

get—C
got—D

hear—A
heard—C
hears—D
her—C

hers—A
herself—D

if—A
immediate—C
immediately—B

James—D
Jones—C

knew—A

Miss—B
mom—B
Mrs.—A

neighbor—A
new—D
news—D
night—C
now—A

of—C
offered—D

offhand—B
our—A
out—C

perchance—C
perhaps—D
plans—D
plants—B
purchase—A

ring—D
rings—A

said—D
says—A
sum—C

telegraph—D
telephone—B
their—B
them—B
they're—A
those—A

TRANSCRIPT (continued)

... This _____ _____ the _____ _____ _____. Almost
            64   65   66   67   68
_____ Father _____ _____ _____, "Of course, he will
   69   70   71   72
_____ _____." Then Mother _____ _____ and _____
  73   74   75   76   77
the _____ to Father that _____ _____, _____ _____,
       78   79   80   81   82
has _____ _____ _____ _____ _____ _____ Father
     83   84   85   86   87   88
will _____ _____ _____ ....
      89   90   91

WORD LIST

Write *E* if the answer is NOT listed.

above—B
and—A
are—A

back—D
bake—B
barge—D
bargain—B
beautiful—D
begin—A
bountiful—C

came—B
car—A
cart—D
climbs—C
climbed—D
come—C

delicate—D
delicious—A
driven—C
drives—D
drove—D
dug—A

even—B
evening—C
ever—C
every—C

faded—B
faith—C
Father—E
feted—D
found—A

immaterially—C
immediately—A
into—B
is—E

masked—A
most—B
must—C

naturally—C
neutral—A

one—A
only—C

our—D
over—C

part—A
partial—C
planted—B
plants—B

solely—D
soon—D

than—C
that—D
them—B
they—A
time—B
to find—B
to get—C
to have—B
to plant—D

very—B

TRANSCRIPT (continued)

So, _____ _____ _____ the _____ and _____ _____
      92   93   94   95   96   97
_____ the _____ _____ _____ _____ , only to
  98   99   100   101   102
find, _____ , that he _____ _____ the plants for
       103   104   105
Mother and _____ _____ _____ _____ _____ plants
             106   107   108   109   110
that _____ be _____ _____ . By this _____ the
      111   112   113   114
_____ _____ _____ has _____ and the _____
 115   116   117   118   119
have _____ out.
      120

ANSWERS FOR PRACTICE SET 5

1. C	25. C	49. C	73. C	97. C
2. E	26. E	50. E	74. B	98. C
3. B	27. E	51. D	75. A	99. B
4. A	28. A	52. B	76. C	100. A
5. D	29. E	53. A	77. E	101. D
6. B	30. C	54. C	78. D	102. D
7. C	31. B	55. E	79. A	103. C
8. A	32. B	56. C	80. C	104. E
9. E	33. D	57. D	81. B	105. D
10. B	34. E	58. D	82. A	106. D
11. A	35. A	59. B	83. D	107. A
12. D	36. B	60. E	84. E	108. A
13. C	37. D	61. D	85. C	109. B
14. A	38. E	62. B	86. E	110. D
15. B	39. A	63. E	87. B	111. C
16. D	40. E	64. A	88. A	112. B
17. A	41. C	65. D	89. C	113. A
18. B	42. B	66. B	90. B	114. B
19. C	43. D	67. C	91. A	115. D
20. A	44. A	68. A	92. E	116. E
21. A	45. C	69. B	93. C	117. C
22. D	46. E	70. D	94. B	118. B
23. B	47. A	71. E	95. A	119. E
24. A	48. D	72. E	96. D	120. C

The Office Machine Operator Special Tests— Simplified Typing Test/Letter Series Test

CHAPTER 11

Introduction to the Simplified Typing Test A Diagnostic Test

THE SIMPLIFIED TYPING TEST

Special tests are added when Office Machine Operator positions are covered by the examination. If the Office Assistant examination has not included a typing test, then a Simplified Typing Test is given for positions such as Data Transcriber, which may require knowledge of a typewriter-style keyboard. Applicants for Electric Accounting Machine Operator (Tabulating Machine Operator) and Cryptographic Equipment Operator are required to take a reasoning test in the form of Letter Series (see Chapter 13).

If the examination for Office Machine Operator positions is announced separately, verbal abilities and clerical tests are given with the appropriate special tests. All applicants for Office Machine Operator positions are required to pass the Verbal Abilities Test and the Clerical Abilities Test.

NATURE OF THE TEST

Persons who have passed the Clerk-Typist examination may be appointed as Cold-Type Composing Machine Operators. Otherwise, applicants for positions requiring knowledge of the typewriter-style keyboard must pass the 10-minute Simplified Typing Test. Ths test does not include any punctuation, and the interchangeable use of capital or small letters is permitted since the machines that appointees will operate have no shift key.

HOW THE TEST IS ADMINISTERED AND SCORED

The Simplified Typing Test is administered in the same manner as the Typing Test. Each competitor will need a copy of the test and two sheets of typewriter paper. About 25 minutes will be needed for the Simplified Typing Test.

Five minutes will be allowed for reading the instructions on the face of the test. Ten minutes will be allowed for the practice exercise. After the practice typing, competitors put fresh paper in their machines, and turn the test page over and begin the test. Ten minutes are allowed for the test proper. As the test is scored by the number of correct lines, no erasures or corrections are allowed.

HOW TO DETERMINE THE TEST SCORE

For the Simplified Typing Test, the minimum passing score for GS–2 is 25 correct lines.

A DIAGNOSTIC TEST

The purpose of this diagnostic exam is to familiarize you with the Simplified Typing Test. This unique exam type requires a great deal of practice. Chapter 12 will give you seven full-length practice sets.

Directions

This is a test of your knowledge of the typewriter keyboard.

Type each line precisely as it is in the exercise.

Double space between lines; *single space* between words; use all *capitals.*

Type *one column down the center* of the sheet.

Leave about a 2½-inch *margin* on the left.

If you notice that you made an error, double space and begin the same line again. *Do not make any erasures or any other kinds of corrections.*

If you finish before time is called, begin typing the exercise again.

If you were copying from a list like the practice exercise at the bottom of this page and you abandoned incorrect lines, you would be credited for having the first three lines of the exercise correctly typed if your paper looked like this —

NESBIT ED ELECTRICIAN TRANSIT BELMONT

FOLEY, DA

FOLEY DAVID SURVV

FOLEY DAVID SURVEYOR BAY COMPANY AVON

LEWIS DAN LINEMAN HYDROPOWER B

LEWIS DAN LINEMAN HYDRO POWER BEDFORD

Now copy the ten lines of the practice exercise below, in one column. If you finish before time is called, begin copying the exercise a second time. You will not be rated on this practice. The purpose of this practice is to let you exercise your fingers and to see that your machine is working properly.

Practice List

NESBIT ED ELECTRICIAN TRANSIT BELMONT

FOLEY DAVID SURVEYOR BAY COMPANY AVON

LEWIS DAN LINEMAN HYDRO POWER BEDFORD

BURKERT KARL MINER PENN COLLIERY GARY

NESBITT GUY WELDER UNITED STEEL AKRON

PRICE IRA DRYCLEANING SERVICE MANAGER

ADAM FRED ASSEMBLER AND BENCH GRINDER

BROWN MAX AUTOMOBILE MECHANIC SKILLED

WEST CORA DEMONSTRATOR OFFICE DEVICES

LOMAN LEO CALCULATING MACHINE REPAIRS

THE TEST

Time allotted—10 minutes

Type as many of these lines as you can in the time allowed. Double space. Type them in one column down the center of your sheet.

If you notice that you have made an error, double space and begin the same line again. Do NOT make any ERASURES or other corrections.

BABB FRIEDA AMESBURY MD BILTMORE BLVD

BACKUS EARL PONTIAC OREG RADCLIF APTS

BERRY ELMER CLAYTONA MINN ROSLYN ARMS

BEAUMONT WM SHERWOOD ILL GUNTHER CORP

BOWMAN LOIS GREENVILLE ALA HILL HOUSE

BUTCHER BOB BARPORT MISS ROSWELL STRT

CAPARELLO A GRANTLAND WIS FOREST LANE

DONAHUE EDW PORTLAND MO WHITELAW AVEN

ESSEX LOUIS HANOVER KANS HUNTERS APTS

FOWLER JOHN LOGANPORT LA ST PIERRE CT

HARTLEY GEO SUNCLIFFE LA CHESTER STRT

ISERMAN JOE HUNTSVILLE WY MARINE CLUB

JACOBS FRED FAIRPORT ILL GRENADA DRIV

KEMPER SAML PERDUE IND BEVERIDGE BLDG

KENNEDY LEO SEWARDS WASH TARBORO PARK

LAWRENSON W GASTONIA CONN SOCONY BLVD

LINDERMAN F LEWISTOWN IND SEWELL AVEN

LONG GERALD GALESBURG KY NICHOLS REST

MARTIN BRAD SHAMROCK TEX FEDERAL BLDG

MORTON CHAS MEMPHIS GA CARSTAIRS VIEW

NAYLOR PAUL MANHATTAN TENN WOODY REST

NATHANSON L CLARENDON VT SEAVIEW PKWY

OBERG CAREY KNOXVILLE VA WINSTON HALL

PARKER HUGH GLENLEY WASH HOOVERS LANE

PINCKERTS M BLYFIELD ALA BURKARD BROS

POTTER ROBT WASHINGTON FLA CITRUS WAY

SKUPCEK JAS PULLMAN ME STOCKERLY BLDG

SNYDER WILL BLUERIDGE MINN OAKEN YARD

TREADWELL R GRISSBY MASS PIRATES PIKE

WALKER CARL KITTANING PA JOHNSON CORP

CONTINUE WITH NEXT COLUMN.

ACME ELECTRIC INC ADAIRSVILLE AERIALS

ARTHURS DRUG CORP EAST WILTON POWDERS

A SIMPSON TOOL CO RICHARDSTON HAMMERS

BRIGHTWOOD AND CO WALLA WALLA BASKETS

BROOKE PAINTS INC SIOUX FALLS SIZINGS

CARLTON AND BLOCK WINTON CITY GASKETS

CROWN TOOL CO INC MITCHELBURG SHOVELS

CRUCIBLE STEEL CO E SANDERTON ROLLERS

DANIEL V GENTZ CO WHITNYVILLE KETTLES

DUNN AND SONS INC BELLINGSHAM BOILERS

ELI WYNN AND BROS YELLOWSTONE CUTTERS

E WYLAND AND SONS NORFORDTOWN HANDLES

EXPERT IRON WORKS CALLENSBURG ENGINES

F A GREGORY STORE STEUBENVINE CHISELS

FARMERS SUPPLY CO GREAT RIVER HALTERS

FREY GAS LIGHT CO FREYCHESTER BURNERS

GRECIAN MARBLE CO FAIRDEALING STATUES

HAMDEN MUSIC MART GREENCASTLE VIOLINS

I MASON TOOL SHOP CORTANNINGS GIMLETS

JOHN WEST AND SON HENSONVILLE SPRINGS

JOHN W WILLIS INC GEORGESBURG BEAKERS

LA BANTA PRODUCTS GRAY ISLAND MATCHES

LEIGH IMPORTS INC LANDISVILLE WOOLENS

L PARKER GLASS CO SHREVESTOWN BOTTLES

MURRAY OPTICAL CO MILLERVILLE GLASSES

NEW YORK BAR CORP BARTHOLOMEW LANCETS

OFFICE SUPPLY INC NUTTALLBURG LEDGERS

PAPER PRODUCTS CO PAXTONVILLE TISSUES

P FRY ELECTRIC CO MONTGOMEREY MAGNETS

REO VARIETY STORE RUTERSVILLE LADDERS

R J HOWARDS MILLS HYATTSVILLE TROWELS

S TODT AND COOPER SPRINGFIELD RIPSAWS

TREIK BROS AND CO LOGANSVILLE REAMERS

UTAH SUPPLY STORE CEDAR WOODS TRIPODS

V G CORNELL SHOPS FREEMANPORT WINCHES

IF YOU FINISH BEFORE TIME IS CALLED, BEGIN COPYING THE LIST THE SECOND TIME.

CHAPTER 12

Practice, Practice, Practice

This chapter gives you seven full-length practice tests, which should be taken under strict timed conditions. Allow only 10 minutes for each practice set.

Because this method of testing your knowledge of the typewriter keyboard is unique and probably unfamiliar to you, it is essential that you do additional practice. Repeating the practice sets can be helpful.

Remember, this test is scored by the number of *correct* lines; therefore, you must not erase or correct any errors.

PRACTICE SET 1

Type as many of these lines as you can in the time allowed. Double space. Type them in one column down the center of your sheet.

If you notice that you have made an error, double space and begin the same line again. Do NOT make any ERASURES or other corrections.

ANGEL GRACE BRINKLEY AR SURFSIDE WALK

BERRY ALICE BRIGHTON AL TAMARIND LANE

MATTHEWS WM CULLMAN IL ROWLAND CIRCLE

MORELAND ED DAYVILLE CT VENTURA HOUSE

MULLIN MARK CORSSWELL MI VICTORIA AVE

OSTER HELEN CARBONDALE PA MOLINA CORP

PARISH KIRK CARROLLTON GA MANVIEW AVE

POPE MARCIA CEDARVILLE OH MANOR DRIVE

QUINN KELLY CHALMETTE LA COLOARDO WAY

RADER EDWIN BOULDER CO EASTLAKE HOUSE

REAGAN PAUL BUCHANAN MI DURANGO COURT

REID GEORGE MIDDLEBURY VT DOROTHY AVE

RUSSELL JAS TAMASQUA PA MANSFIELD STR

SANDERSON I WOODVILLE MS ISABEL DRIVE

SAVAGE CARL SYRACUSE NY MICHELLE PKWY

SHAPIRO BEA SWEETWATER ND MILLER CORP

SINCLAIR WM SYCAMORE IL RICHVIEW ARMS

SLATER CHAS TOWNSEND MT REDCLIFF LANE

SMALL STEVE TORRINGTON WY LINCOLN AVE

SPENCER JOE ZANESVILLE OH LOMBARD WAY

STOKES GARY WOODBINE IA LILLIAN HOUSE

TAYLOR STAN ONEONTA NY HEATHER CIRCLE

TOMLINSON P YERINGTON NV HUTCHINS CIR

TUCKER ENID OWENSBORO KY HAYWORTH WAY

VALDEZ PAUL MARINETTE WI HIGHLAND AVE

VAZQUEZ LON PROVIDENCE RI HAYFORD APT

WADE NORMAN MEDFIELD MA CLARIDGE LANE

WARREN LYNN DUCHESS UT COGSWELL HOUSE

WOODS DIANE DULUTH MN COHASSETT DRIVE

YOUNG VINCE BRADDOCK PA CENTINELA STR

CONTINUE WITH NEXT COLUMN.

ALARM SUPPLIES CO TAYLORVILLE BURGLAR

AMERICAN TILE INC E ROSSVILLE CERAMIC

B AND D AVIATIONS LOS ANGELES CHARTER

COMER AND FUENTES PUTNAM CITY CANDLES

DEWEY PLUMBING CO SANTA CLARA SHOWERS

FORTSONS WORD PRO MT PROSPECT RESUMES

GANTERS LUMBER CO EAGLE RIVER ROOFING

HAMILTON BROTHERS GREENCASTLE HAMMERS

JOANS UNIFORMS CO SHELBYVILLE CLOTHES

JOYCE AND MARTINI JOHNSONBURG LAWYERS

KIDS R US SERVICE TUNKHANNOCK CLOTHES

MAIN DISTRIBUTING MONROE PARK STATUES

MARINAS BIKE SHOP FOREST HILL BICYCLE

MEYERS AND DURHAM STURGIS BAY ROOFING

NAKAHARA BROTHERS GREAT FALLS ROOFING

PACIFIC BLINDS CO UPPER MILLS AWNINGS

PEDRINO WINDOW CO SANTA MARIA FRAMING

QMC SERVICES CORP MADISONBURG IMPORTS

ROSS AVIATION INC GRAND BANKS AIRLINE

SECURITY GATES CO EAST SEWARD CLOSERS

STONEWALL SHOE CO JOPLIN CITY BOOTERY

SUNRISE GIFT SHOP LENOIR CITY FLOWERS

TAUB AND THORNTON OLIVER HILL LAWYERS

THOMPSONS FABRICS HOLDENVILLE BATTING

TRIANGLE CLEANERS SPRINGFIELD LAUNDRY

VALLEY PORCELAINS LIVINGSTONE BATHTUB

WLM AIR CARGO INC MOUNT OLIVE FREIGHT

XENOS REFINISHING LITTLE ROCK SANDERS

YODERS FISHING CO MONDOVI BAY NETTING

ZIMMERMANS PHOTOS PORT ARTHUR CAMERAS

IF YOU FINISH BEFORE TIME IS CALLED, BEGIN COPYING THE LIST THE SECOND TIME.

PRACTICE SET 2

Type as many of these lines as you can in the time allowed. Double space. Type them in one column down the center of your sheet.

If you notice that you have made an error, double space and begin the same line again. Do NOT make any ERASURES or other corrections.

ABEL HORACE TAYLORVILLE IL JACKMAN ST

ARMSTRONG N TILLAMOOK OR IRONDALE AVE

AUSTIN DOUG WILTON ND PICKERING DRIVE

AYERS FRANK SHELBYVILLE IN JALAPAN WY

BARTON ROBT SHERIDAN OR PEARTREE BLVD

CADMAN THOS IOWA FALLS IA VANOWEN WAY

DIAMOND BEN JEFFERSON GA VERONICA AVE

FLOYD OSCAR GABRIEL TX MONTEZUMA GLEN

GAINES MARY PAYNESVILLE MN HERALD HWY

GRIMES BERT PASADENA CA MOUNTAIN ROAD

HARRISON WM FREDONIA KS LIBERTY HOUSE

HUELSMANN S FORT MEADE FL LOOKOUT AVE

ISHIKAWA LE BUSHNELL IL OAKLAWN COURT

MENDOZA MAX BYESVILLE OH NOVELDA CORP

METKOVICH R COATESVILLE PA WEBSTER ST

MYERS LARRY CODY WY CARMELITA LANE NE

OGONOWSKI A FRANKLIN LA BONSALLO LANE

POTTER FRED SCOTT CITY KS CALGROVE PL

PURCELL JAS PROVIDENCE RI BENFIELD ST

QUICK CRAIG ROSSVILLE GA HUNSAKER WAY

QUINN STEVE ST GEORGE UT BENJAMIN HWY

RADA HAROLD MARSHFIELD MO LIGGETT CTY

RAMIREZ TED DES MOINES IA LEADWELL CT

RASMUSSEN N EAST MEDFORD OK SHARON ST

RAY WILLARD MAYSVILLE KY BERMUDA ROAD

ROYAL SUSAN SAN BENITO CA GUNNISON ST

RUSCH KEVIN OSGOOD IN HALLWOOD LANE S

TAYLOR LEON OVERLAND MO PARK OAK ROAD

WHEATLEY ED ZEELAND MI QUEENSIDE CLUB

WISE ARTHUR SANTA MONICA CA PURDUE ST

CONTINUE WITH NEXT COLUMN.

ADRA SERVICES INC FORESTVILLE MAILING

AVALON MAILING CO BRIDGEVILLE PRINTER

AVION AIR FREIGHT BUNKER HILL EXPRESS

BOBS LOCK AND KEY WEST AUBURN LOCKERS

CHILDRENS BOOK CO EAGLE GROVE RECORDS

CREATIVE HAIR INC MILLERSBURG BARBERS

CROWNS APPLIANCES EATONE PARK FREEZER

DANAN ADVERTISING MT PLEASANT CONCERT

EMPIRE PROPERTIES NEW HOLLAND ESCROWS

FENNELL INSURANCE PORT HERALD LEASING

GROSSMAN AND HALL ITHACA CITY LAWYERS

HERTWOOD ANTIQUES MORAN BLUFF GALLERY

HUGHES TERMITE CO NORTH PEASE CONTROL

HUNTERS BOOKS INC JERSEYVILLE RECORDS

INFO MGMT SYSTEMS BRACEBRIDGE COPYING

JONES PLUMBING CO BEDSIN HILL HEATING

KESON CAMERA SHOP CARLINVILLE LEDGERS

LAWNDALE BLOCK CO KENTON CITY CENTERS

MASTER TATTAN INC AYDEN RIVER BASKETS

NIPPON EXPRESS CO FREDERICTON FREIGHT

ORVAL ENTERPRISES MORNINGSIDE MAGNETS

PARAMOUNT RV CORP POWELL CITY CAMPERS

RAND MUFFLER CORP CENTERSBURG SPRINGS

RICKERTS CABINETS BUENA VISTA HANDLES

ROCKYS SANDWICHES GUNTERVILLE LUNCHES

SECURITY AVIATION CEDAR FALLS ENGINES

SMITH AND STAKINS AMBERG CITY LAWYERS

TRI CITY TITLE CO MOUNDSVILLE ESCROWS

UNIVERSAL FORWARD NORTH OGDEN FREIGHT

V L DECORATING CO ALCOVE CITY FIXTURE

WESTWOODS LEASING BELLA VISTA RENTALS

WIDE AREA PAGINGS ALMAN RIVER MESSAGE

IF YOU FINISH BEFORE TIME IS CALLED, BEGIN COPYING THE LIST THE SECOND TIME.

PRACTICE SET 3

Type as many of these lines as you can in the time allowed. Double space. Type them in one column down the center of your sheet.

If you notice that you have made an error, double space and begin the same line again. Do NOT make any ERASURES or other corrections.

ADCOCK MAYE AUSTIN TX SUNFLOWER DRIVE

BABB ANDREW INDEPENDENCE MO WILCOX CT

BEYER JAMES KNOXVILLE TN COUNTRY VIEW

CAIN SHARON CALVERTON NY ANNETTE APTS

DAVIS LARRY ALEXANDRIA VA WATSON REST

GRAY EDWINA PHOENIX AZ SOUTHERN DRIVE

JACKSON JAS FAIRBANKS AL DOUGLAS REST

KAUFMAN RON ASHDOWN AR VALENCIA DRIVE

KLEIN LYNNE SHAWNEE OK ROSECRANS APTS

LAMMERS SUE MARYVILLE MO CRESTVIEW CT

LAPIN FRANK PITTSBURGH PA CRESCENT ST

LOGAN HARRY DEARBORN MI HYACINTH CLUB

MELNICK VAL WINNFIELD LA MAYBROOK WAY

NEWMAN ALAN LAWRENCEVILLE GA PALM AVE

PEREZ GLENN NASHVILLE TN SIERRA HOUSE

PEYTONS VAL BELLEVILLE IL ZELZAH LANE

PLINER JEFF ROCHESTER NY ABBOTT DRIVE

RAMAGE LISA GREENSBORO NC GUNDRY VIEW

REEVES DAVE SHENANDOAH IA YUKON DRIVE

ROLFE SALLY JACKSONVILLE FL HALSEY CT

SHIBATA JAS WATERTOWN WI CENTRAL BLDG

SILVERMAN M MANCHESTER NH CHESTER STR

SINGLETON L WATERBURY CT CAMPUS DRIVE

SMITH PETER ELLENVILLE NY CANAL HOUSE

STANEK ROSE PORTLAND ME CAMPBELL APTS

TESDAHL RAY LANCASTER NY ADDISON CORP

THORPE JOHN LUNENBURG MD BLAKELY BLDG

VARNUM MIKE WILMINGTON PA BEVERLY WAY

WEBER ROBIN CARRIZOZO NM VIVIAN HOUSE

WILLIAMS ED COLDWATER KS WILLIAMS STR

CONTINUE WITH NEXT COLUMN.

A TO Z LEGAL SRVS LOS ANGELES LAWYERS

ALS WAVE MATE INC IMPERIALCTY CONSULT

BARRYS BAR SUPPLY GREEN RIVER BURNERS

BATEMAN PEST CORP MIDDLERIDGE TERMITE

CALIFORNIA FINISH HADDONFIELD WINDOWS

CAREER SERVICE CO WILLOWBROOK RESUMES

CHRIS PIZZA STOPS EAGLE RIDGE PARTIES

DIANES AND ROCKYS HAPPY TRAIL LUNCHES

DIRECT A PAGE INC NORTH CLIFF BEEPERS

EVANS BABY SHOPPE KINGS RIDGE CLOTHES

FURMANTI AND SONS MAPLE WOODS LAWYERS

HONEYCUTT ASPHALT PARKWESTERN PATCHES

J OCEAN CLOTHIERS OCEAN RIDGE DRESSES

JAYS POODLE SALON HALLEYVILLE KENNELS

KELL PICTURES INC SIGNAL HILL FRAMING

LINNS CARD SHOPPE MULBERRY PK LEDGERS

LONGS ELECTRONICS GRAND LAKES RECORDS

MARKS WORKCLOTHES TRIDENT CTY CLOTHES

MORRISON ALUMINUM WAGON TRAIL PATCHES

NYLANDERS STUDIOS CULVER CITY PASTELS

PHILS ENTERPRISES BELLINGBURG LAWYERS

QUINN AND SON INC N HOLLYWOOD CONSULT

ROLFE ROLFE ROLFE SPRINGSTEIN CHISELS

ROSE POOL AND SPA GRAHAM CITY HEATERS

ROYS POOL SERVICE GOLDENFIELD FILTERS

S TOOM AND LINDEN LOGANSVILLE REAMERS

SLUMBER BABY SHOP EMERY LAKES CLOTHES

TIMOTHY BERG CORP PARKWESTERN STYLING

UTAH SUPPLIES INC NORTH WILEN KETTLES

VARGAS AND SON CO LOS ANGELES AERIALS

ZIPPERS AND STUFF WESTERN WAY FABRICS

ZOO ANIMALS TO GO LARRYSVILLE ANIMALS

IF YOU FINISH BEFORE TIME IS CALLED, BEGIN COPYING THE LIST THE SECOND TIME.

PRACTICE SET 4

Type as many of these lines as you can in the time allowed. Double space. Type them in one column down the center of your sheet.

If you notice that you have made an error, double space and begin the same line again. Do NOT make any ERASURES or other corrections.

ADLER DAVID CINCINNATI OH SUPERIOR CT

ATKINSON JO ROANOKE VA CAVALIER HOUSE

BAIRD MYRON PONTIAC MI BILTMORE HOUSE

BLACK DIANE SEATTLE WA RICHMOND DRIVE

ESSIE LOWEN ABERDEEN SD SHOEMAKER AVE

FOX ROBERT OGALLALA NE LOWEMONT ARMS

FREEMAN JIM CHEYENNE WY ASHWORTH BLVD

GARNER KENT LOVELAND CO HIGHDALE LANE

GASS DANIEL WATERLOO IA WHITAKER CORP

JOHNSON BOB SACRAMENTO CA WESTERN WAY

KLOOSTER ED MINNEAPOLIS MN CENTURY CT

LINN RANDAL PELLA IA PARAMOUNT COURTS

LITTLE ANDY BUFFALO NY IRONWOOD DRIVE

LONG ARTHUR BROWNSVILLE TX PARADE AVE

MARASCO EVE LOUISVILLE KY JAVELIN WAY

MARIS LOUIS CHICAGO IL FLORENCE HOUSE

MCPHERSON E OMAHA NE MANCHESTER HOUSE

MORTON DANE SAN DIEGO CA CARROLL LANE

MURPHY DEAN BRANCHVILLE SC PALERMO CT

NEAL GERALD HONOLULU HI PROSPECT APTS

ORTEGA RYAN LOGAN UT MORNINGSIDE PKWY

OSTERHOLT A AMARILLO TX GILBERT HOUSE

PARKER LYNN DALLAS TX QUEENSLAND BLVD

PATTERSON J BROOKHAVEN MI SIMMONS STR

RUSTAD JOHN MEMPHIS TN HOLLYWOOD CLUB

SHERLOCK WM DAYTON IA WESTCHESTER AVE

SIDMAN GREG SCRANTON PA HAWTHORNE AVE

VARGAS EARL PORTLAND OR WEBSTER HOUSE

WASSON JEFF INGLEWOOD CA OVERLAND AVE

YOUNG COREY FT DODGE WI GARDENIA BLVD

CONTINUE WITH NEXT COLUMN.

A TO Z SOUND CORP W GREENBELT PAGINGS

AGENCY RENT A CAR GLOVERTOWNE LEASING

AMERICAN PLUMBING MONTMORENCY HEATERS

AMY LAMINATING CO GLENS FALLS PLASTIC

ASHLEY ART CENTER CULVER CITY FRAMING

BURNS TYPESETTING SANTAFE SPG GRAPHIC

C AND L TOWING CO CERISE CITY CARRIER

DIAL ONE PEST INC SOUTH HILLS TERMITE

EAGLE AUDIO VIDEO GREEN HILLS REPAIRS

GORDON INDUSTRIES MARLBOROUGH BEEPERS

HILL PET GROOMING HALLETTBURG KITTENS

JETTONS GALLERIES STUDIO CITY FRAMING

KENTWOOD CLEANERS FORESTVILLE LAUNDRY

KITCHENS AND MORE SAXTON CITY BASKETS

LAWRENCE JEWELERS MORRISVILLE WATCHES

LYNNES AUTOMOTIVE SHREVESPORT REPAIRS

M WILSON GLASS CO HAMLIN CITY BOTTLES

MARIES INDUSTRIES W HOLLYWOOD PILLOWS

MEDICAL ARTS LABS FOREST HILL TESTING

MILLER TELEVISION GRAND HAVEN REPAIRS

MURPHY STUDIO INC SIGNAL HILL PASTELS

NEW WATCH REPAIRS FRIEDLANDER JEWELRY

ORIGINAL PIZZA CO CANOGA PARK PARTIES

PIONEER VIDEO INC LOS ANGELES RENTALS

PROFESSIONAL WORD DAYTON CITY RESUMES

RANDALLS PHARMACY KINGS CREST POWDERS

SPARKLING LAUNDRY GAITHERBURG CLEANER

SUZANNES KITCHENS MAPLE GROVE BASKETS

TIDELINE IMPORTER SIOUX FALLS BOTTLES

VILLAGE DRUGS INC HIDDEN PINE POWDERS

WESTSIDE CAB CORP HEARTSHORNE TAXICAB

YOUNG AUTO REPAIR JACKSONBURG REPAIRS

IF YOU FINISH BEFORE TIME IS CALLED, BEGIN COPYING THE LIST THE SECOND TIME.

PRACTICE SET 5

Type as many of these lines as you can in the time allowed. Double space. Type them in one column down the center of your sheet.

If you notice that you have made an error, double space and begin the same line again. Do NOT make any ERASURES or other corrections.

BOOTH KELLY REEDSPORT OR RINDGE HOUSE

BROWN NORMA PENDLETON OR RAYMOND PKWY

CAMPBELL WM COOPERSTOWN ND SHAVER WAY

CARTER ALAN FARMINGTON UT GOTHIC REST

CLARRIDGE T SEWARD NH SEPULVEDA PLACE

COOK RODNEY CHAMPAIGN IL SEADLER BROS

CURREY FRED DARLINGTON WI TRAVIS PARK

DONALDSON C LORDSBURG NM THOMAS PLACE

GARCIA BILL GOLDFIELD NV TELFAIR YARD

GARDNER ROY MORNINGSIDE IA SWEET LANE

HANDEL SAML POCATELLO ID SERRANO BLVD

HODSON KENT ENGLEWOOD CO TRENTON PKWY

JOSEPH JOHN WATERLOO IA FRANKLIN ARMS

KAPLAN CARL SHELBY NC UNIVERSITY BLVD

KATZ DANIEL HUMBOLDT IA VALINDA DRIVE

LANDON BART OCEANSIDE CA SHADOW PLACE

LAWSON JACK PLACERVILLE CA UNION ROAD

MADISON ANN ROSEVILLE MN ARMY POST RD

MARTINEZ WM RUSSELL KS ALVERSTONE WAY

MOORE AARON APPLETON MN TYBURNE HOUSE

NASH GORDON OKANOGAN WA E VALLEY VIEW

OWEN DONALD LIVINGSTON MT MAYFAIR AVE

PATTON JUDY HURRICANE UT UPLAND PLACE

PETERSON ED MONTAGUE MI TUSCANY HOUSE

POWERS ANNE MOUNT AYR IA DELGANY CLUB

PULIDO ADAM COLUMBIA KY WATKINS DRIVE

RICE DENNIS REPUBLIC WA RELIANCE LANE

ROSE ARTHUR SPRINGFIELD IL HARVEY WAY

SULLIVAN ED MUSKEGON MI TRUXTON DRIVE

THOMAS ERIC MONTPELIER ID SEVILLE WAY

CONTINUE WITH NEXT COLUMN.

ALARM SYSTEMS INC BLUE ISLAND PATROLS

ARMANS VACUUM INC WERNERVILLE VACUUMS

BELLOTTO AUTO INC GRAND RIVER LININGS

BEST AND SONS INC PORTERVILLE SHOVELS

BILLS CAMERA SHOP LOS ANGELES PICTURE

CRES CLINICAL LAB FOREST CITY TESTING

DELIAN MUSIC CORP NORTONSBURG VIOLINS

DIAMONDS PLUMBING MONTEREY PK HEATERS

GOODS SHEET METAL VIKING CITY WELDING

HEALTH HABIT CLUB WEST OAKMAN WORKOUT

JAY OF CALIFORNIA N TARRYTOWN COPYING

MAGIC FIGURE CLUB PARTONVILLE WORKOUT

MCPHERSON AND SON GRANDEVILLE WOOLENS

MURPHY STUDIO INC VISTA FALLS PICTURE

NATIONAL TRAILERS DANTONSPORT RENTALS

NATIONWIDE CREDIT OTTERSVILLE FINANCE

RESTER INDUSTRIES GREENCASTLE PAGINGS

ROYS POOL SERVICE GOLDENFIELD FILTERS

RUSSELLS JEWELERS FRANKLIN PK WATCHES

SELF STORAGE CORP MINNEAPOLIS STORAGE

SMILEY ASSOCIATES GRAND FORKS PUMPERS

SPECIALTY WELDING HANSONVILLE SIZINGS

TUCKWOOD MUSIC CO E PARAMOUNT GUITARS

UNITED LEASING CO GREAT BLUFF LEASING

V A LAMINATING CO GLOVERVILLE PLASTIC

VIDEO FILMEX CORP CEDAR FALLS RENTALS

WESTERN MOVING CO N URBANDALE STORAGE

WESTSIDER LAUNDRY GALLATIN PK CLEANER

WHITMORE CLEANERS GAINESVILLE LAUNDRY

YALE MUSIC STUDIO MILTONVILLE VIOLINS

YOUNG SHAVER SHOP N URBANDALE SHAVERS

YUKON AVE NURSERY WESTCHESTER GARDENS

IF YOU FINISH BEFORE TIME IS CALLED, BEGIN COPYING THE LIST THE SECOND TIME.

PRACTICE SET 6

Type as many of these lines as you can in the time allowed. Double space. Type them in one column down the center of your sheet.

If you notice that you have made an error, double space and begin the same line again. Do NOT make any ERASURES or other corrections.

ADAMS MARIA KENNEWICK WA NATHENE CORP

ASHE MARTIN WHEATLAND WY NEWCOMB ARMS

BEATTY CHAD LENNOX CA NATHANSON CREST

BRYANT MARY STEVENSVILLE MT MEAD HALL

CARROLL JOE WELLSVILLE UT MAYNARD WAY

GREENE OWEN MIDVILLE NY HUBBARD COURT

HALEY KAREN HAMILTON VA BREMAND HOUSE

HALL THOMAS VILLISCA IA BRANDON HILLS

HARTMAN DON WARREN IN MACDONNELL APTS

JONES FRANK WATERVILLE WA STEWART AVE

JOSEPH JOHN WATERLOO IA FRANKLIN ARMS

KAPLAN JOAN SHELBY AK UNIVERSITY BLVD

LARSEN LYLE SIKESTON MO MADISON COURT

QUINN DAVID MONDOVI WI LONGTON SQUARE

REAVES DALE MORRISON IL HARVARD COURT

RUSSELL GUY MOUNT PLEASANT SC LUND ST

SAKAI ALVIN MADISON FL NORTH ILLINOIS

SCHULTZ RON GARRISON ND JASMINE HOUSE

SIMON JAMES GENEVA NY JEFFERSON COURT

STROCK GARY GILLETTE WY WASHINGTON WY

TAYLOR LYLE DENISON TX SOUTH JENNINGS

TURNER NINA DODGE CITY KS BEVERLY WAY

VANCE BRUCE DUBUQUE IA STANFORD CLUBS

WAKEFIELD S DUCKTOWN TN MARYLAND CORP

WARD EUGENE BOLLINGTON MT EUCLID BLVD

WELCH MARIA BOONTON NJ WELLESLEY LANE

WHITE JAMES BLOOMFIELD NE SEAFIELD ST

WILSON ANDY HARTWELL GA SHERBOURNE CT

WOOD JANICE HARTFORD CT NEARSIDE LANE

WYMAN SUSAN HAMILTON MO NEWBROOK APTS

CONTINUE WITH NEXT COLUMN.

ACE FREIGHT LINES ORANGEVILLE SENDERS

ADEC LABORATORIES E WATERTOWN POWDERS

AIRPORT STATIONER WESTCHESTER PENCILS

ALPHA DATA SYSTEM SPRINGSTEIN RIBBONS

AMERICAN PRODUCTS CHILLICOTHE MATCHES

BAY OFFICE SUPPLY OLMOSE PARK COPYING

BRITE RUGS CO INC CARTERVILLE CARPETS

CARAVAN MOTEL INC GROTON CITY ROOMING

COMPUTERS R US CO MOUNT PEALE RIBBONS

FABRICS AND STUFF MONTE VISTA FABRICS

FLAME CUTTERS INC BLUE ISLAND GRINDER

G AND L ENGINEERS GREAT FALLS HAMMERS

GARDEN SPOT HOTEL GREENEWOODS ROOMING

GOLD STAR NURSERY WESTCHESTER GARDENS

GRAND CHARTER INC W KERRVILLE CRUISES

H FRONER CONCRETE BRIDGEVILLE CEMENTS

HAIR IS US SHOPPE MURRYSVILLE STYLING

HOUSE OF STYLINGS ALBUQUERQUE SHAMPOO

JOHNSON AND ALROD EAST DAYTON LAWYERS

LANDSCAPE ARTISTS N COACHELLA FLOWERS

LEWIS ELECTRIC CO WEST SAMSON WIRINGS

LINDSEYS LIMOSINE N KNOXVILLE DRIVERS

RALFS PHOTOGRAPHY VENTUR CITY PICTURE

SANCTION SECURITY RICHARDTOWN PATROLS

SHERIDAN HARDWARE GREAT RIVER HAMMERS

SQUIRE TUXEDO INC CEDAR WOODS RENTALS

STEVES JANITORIAL BROWNSVILLE CLEANER

SUPREME GARDENING NEWTONVILLE SHOVELS

WESTWOOD BUILDING SANTA CLARA SIZINGS

WORLD TRAVEL CORP OVAR ISLAND CRUISES

YOUNG BROS MOVING FLOWER CITY STORAGE

YALE MUSIC STUDIO MILTONVILLE VIOLINS

IF YOU FINISH BEFORE TIME IS CALLED, BEGIN COPYING THE LIST THE SECOND TIME.

PRACTICE SET 7

Type as many of these lines as you can in the time allowed. Double space. Type them in one column down the center of your sheet.

If you notice that you have made an error, double space and begin the same line again. Do NOT make any ERASURES or other corrections.

ADKINS KATY HAMMONTON NJ HYPERION WAY

BALDWIN PAT LYNDONVILLE VT JACKSON CT

BECKER GENE LUMBERTON MS IMPERIAL AVE

BERG WALTER LOUISVILLE KY CRESTWAY ST

CHAN SANDRA MACKENZIE OR CROCKER ROAD

CLARK ALLEN MIDDLESBORO KY LOMITA WAY

COBB HAROLD NIOBRARA NE LINDBLADE AVE

CURTIS RUTH NORMAN OK MARAVILLA DRIVE

DECKER RICK NOBLETON IN MARIMBA COURT

DOUGLAS DEE OGDENSBURG NY MARKTON CIR

EDWARDS ART OAKDALE LA MULHOLLAND HWY

EVANS ALICE NORWICH CT MOONRIDGE ROAD

FELIX PETER RICE LAKE WI LINDLEY WALK

FONTANA ANN ROGERS CITY MI OAKLAWN DR

GELLER EARL SAN ANTONIO TX NORMAN WAY

GOODE CLARA SANDERSVILLE GA OAKLEY ST

GRAY GEORGE SANDPOINT ID REXFORD CLUB

GRIGGS PAUL SYLVANIA GA RINALDI DRIVE

HARRIS JOHN FULLERTON LA RAYMOND ARMS

HAYES CRAIG GIBSON CITY IL WAVERLY ST

HOLM DONALD FAIRVIEW OK WALGROVE BLVD

HUNTLEY BOB EVANSTON WY YARNELL COURT

JOHNSON JAN ESSEXVILLE MI HUSTON LANE

KING THOMAS ENTERPRISE AL ISABEL PKWY

KNIGHT DALE FAYETTEVILLE NC CLOVIS PK

KAMACHI SAM FALCONER NY CLIFTON VISTA

LOUFF BRIAN DES MOINES IA COLFAX ARMS

MANNING LEE DODGEVILLE WI AVALON BLVD

MATHIS DOUG DOUGLAS TN ATLANTIC DRIVE

MATSUMOTO F CUMBERLAND MD MORGAN ROAD

CONTINUE WITH NEXT COLUMN.

ANDRE BEAUTY MART E INGLEWOOD STYLING

ANNS CATERING INC W BIG SANDY LUNCHES

ASTROS CAR FINISH YELLOWSTONE WAXINGS

BELL HOTEL CO INC W GREYCOURT ROOMING

BROWN CORNELL LTD W KITTANING BEAKERS

COASTAL CLEANINGS WALLA WALLA CARPETS

CONN AND SONS INC E PRINCETON ENGINES

CURRY AND PICKARD GRANBY CITY LAWYERS

EXPOS TRAVEL SRVS PAINESVILLE CRUISES

FLOWERS BY ANDREW E MANHATTAN FLOWERS

JAMES AND BENNETT N SUMMERTON CUTTERS

JOES ITALIAN DELI WARRENSBURG LUNCHES

KENT AND SONS INC LEVERSVILLE SPRINGS

LEIGH FENCING INC MONROEVILLE STATUES

LINCOLN INTERIORS CAMPBELLTON CARPETS

MARK I CUTLER INC MORRISVILLE GASKETS

MAYOR BROS TRAVEL MOUNDSVILLE CRUISES

N E TIME PLUMBING S CLARINDON PLUMBER

OFFICE SUPPLY INC CLEARFIELDS LEDGERS

OPTICAL DISCOUNTS CIRCLE CITY GLASSES

PHILLIPS GLASS CO BISHOPVILLE BOTTLES

QUALITY WORK CORP NORTHBRIDGE BOTTLES

RAINBOW CARPET CO W LEXINGTON CARPETS

RELIABLE IRON INC NORTHBRIDGE ENGINES

RIVIERA FINANCIAL NEW HAMPTON LENDERS

ROBERTS BEAUTY CO LOS ANGELES SHAMPOO

ROYALTY TUX SHOPS SIOUX FALLS RENTALS

SILK SCREEN ASSOC W STOCKHOLM ROLLERS

SUNSET LUMBER INC MOUNDSVILLE SIZINGS

THE MESSENGER INC WALLINGFORD SENDERS

TITAN TOOL CO INC SHELBYVILLE SHOVELS

ZAIN TRADING CORP GRAND FALLS WOOLENS

IF YOU FINISH BEFORE TIME IS CALLED, BEGIN COPYING THE LIST THE SECOND TIME.

CHAPTER 13

Introduction to the Letter Series Test
Diagnostic Test
with Answer Explanations

THE LETTER SERIES TEST

The Letter Series Test is *no longer used* on the Federal Civil Service Examinations. We have not deleted this chapter because some state and local agencies may still use the Letter Series type question on their exams.

NATURE OF THE TEST

The Letter Series Test consists of 30 sets of letters which follow a definite order determined by a rule. The applicant must study each set of letters to discover the rule governing the order and then apply the rule in selecting the next two letters from the suggested answers that will continue the set of letters in the same order.

HOW THE TEST IS ADMINISTERED AND SCORED

For the Letter Series Test, students or applicants are allowed up to 2 minutes for each sample question and a total of 20 minutes for the 30 questions. The sample questions are explained in detail before the test itself is begun. For the first sample question, the following statement is read to students or applicants. "The order in this series of letters is the letter x alternating with letters in alphabetical order starting with c so that if the series were continued for two more letters it would read x c x d x e x f x, and f x are the two letters you would look for. In your sample, the set f x is labeled 'A.' This is the answer for this question."

The other sample questions are based on the fol-

lowing rules. The order in the second sample question is pairs of letters starting with u u and going backward through the alphabet. The order in the third sample question is the letter a alternating with letters in alphabetical order. The order in the fourth sample question is two consecutive letters; the next letter is skipped; then come the next two consecutive letters. The last sample question has two alternating groups of letters: the first group consists of every second letter, a c e g, skipping a letter each time; the second group consists of letters in consecutive order, beginning r s t.

The score for the Letter Series Test is the number of correct answers.

HOW TO DETERMINE THE TEST SCORE

Since the Letter Series test is no longer used on the Federal Examination, state or local agencies may have their own scoring system. Check with the local agency for the requirements.

THE LETTER SERIES DIAGNOSTIC TEST

The purpose of this diagnostic test is to familiarize you with the Letter Series Test and offer you some insight into the reasoning process.

Chapter 14 will give you five full-length practice sets with explanations.

Now tear out the answer sheet on the next page, and read the samples that follow.

ANSWER SHEET

SIGNATURE: _____
(Please Sign)

EXAMINATION TITLE: _____

PLACE OF EXAMINATION: _____

TODAY'S DATE: _____

City _____ State _____

SAMPLE Ⓐ ● Ⓒ Ⓓ Ⓔ

DIRECTIONS FOR MARKING ANSWER SHEET

Use only a **No. 2 (or softer) lead pencil.** Darken completely the circle corresponding to your answer. You **must keep** your mark within the circle. Stray marks may be counted as errors. Erase **completely** all marks except your answer.

SAMPLE NAME GRID

LAST NAME

F.I.	M.I.
C	A

1. In the boxes below, **PRINT** your name. Print only as many letters as will fit within the areas for the last name, first initial (F.I.), and middle initial (M.I.) Below each box, darken the circle containing the same letter. SEE SAMPLE NAME GRID

2. In the boxes below, enter your 9-digit Social Security Number. Below each box, darken the circle in each column corresponding to the number you have entered.

LAST NAME

F.I.   M.I.

3. OCCUPATIONAL GROUP NUMBER

SOCIAL SECURITY NUMBER

SECTION 1

Make no marks or entries in the columns to the right until you receive instructions from the administrator.

PART

TEST SERIES

TEST NUMBER

1 Ⓐ Ⓑ Ⓒ Ⓓ Ⓔ	11 Ⓐ Ⓑ Ⓒ Ⓓ Ⓔ	21 Ⓐ Ⓑ Ⓒ Ⓓ Ⓔ	31 Ⓐ Ⓑ Ⓒ Ⓓ Ⓔ	41 Ⓐ Ⓑ Ⓒ Ⓓ Ⓔ	51 Ⓐ Ⓑ Ⓒ Ⓓ Ⓔ	61 Ⓐ Ⓑ Ⓒ Ⓓ Ⓔ	71 Ⓐ Ⓑ Ⓒ Ⓓ Ⓔ	81 Ⓐ Ⓑ Ⓒ Ⓓ Ⓔ	91 Ⓐ Ⓑ Ⓒ Ⓓ Ⓔ	101 Ⓐ Ⓑ Ⓒ Ⓓ Ⓔ	111 Ⓐ Ⓑ Ⓒ Ⓓ Ⓔ	121 Ⓐ Ⓑ Ⓒ Ⓓ Ⓔ
2 Ⓐ Ⓑ Ⓒ Ⓓ Ⓔ	12 Ⓐ Ⓑ Ⓒ Ⓓ Ⓔ	22 Ⓐ Ⓑ Ⓒ Ⓓ Ⓔ	32 Ⓐ Ⓑ Ⓒ Ⓓ Ⓔ	42 Ⓐ Ⓑ Ⓒ Ⓓ Ⓔ	52 Ⓐ Ⓑ Ⓒ Ⓓ Ⓔ	62 Ⓐ Ⓑ Ⓒ Ⓓ Ⓔ	72 Ⓐ Ⓑ Ⓒ Ⓓ Ⓔ	82 Ⓐ Ⓑ Ⓒ Ⓓ Ⓔ	92 Ⓐ Ⓑ Ⓒ Ⓓ Ⓔ	102 Ⓐ Ⓑ Ⓒ Ⓓ Ⓔ	112 Ⓐ Ⓑ Ⓒ Ⓓ Ⓔ	122 Ⓐ Ⓑ Ⓒ Ⓓ Ⓔ
3 Ⓐ Ⓑ Ⓒ Ⓓ Ⓔ	13 Ⓐ Ⓑ Ⓒ Ⓓ Ⓔ	23 Ⓐ Ⓑ Ⓒ Ⓓ Ⓔ	33 Ⓐ Ⓑ Ⓒ Ⓓ Ⓔ	43 Ⓐ Ⓑ Ⓒ Ⓓ Ⓔ	53 Ⓐ Ⓑ Ⓒ Ⓓ Ⓔ	63 Ⓐ Ⓑ Ⓒ Ⓓ Ⓔ	73 Ⓐ Ⓑ Ⓒ Ⓓ Ⓔ	83 Ⓐ Ⓑ Ⓒ Ⓓ Ⓔ	93 Ⓐ Ⓑ Ⓒ Ⓓ Ⓔ	103 Ⓐ Ⓑ Ⓒ Ⓓ Ⓔ	113 Ⓐ Ⓑ Ⓒ Ⓓ Ⓔ	123 Ⓐ Ⓑ Ⓒ Ⓓ Ⓔ
4 Ⓐ Ⓑ Ⓒ Ⓓ Ⓔ	14 Ⓐ Ⓑ Ⓒ Ⓓ Ⓔ	24 Ⓐ Ⓑ Ⓒ Ⓓ Ⓔ	34 Ⓐ Ⓑ Ⓒ Ⓓ Ⓔ	44 Ⓐ Ⓑ Ⓒ Ⓓ Ⓔ	54 Ⓐ Ⓑ Ⓒ Ⓓ Ⓔ	64 Ⓐ Ⓑ Ⓒ Ⓓ Ⓔ	74 Ⓐ Ⓑ Ⓒ Ⓓ Ⓔ	84 Ⓐ Ⓑ Ⓒ Ⓓ Ⓔ	94 Ⓐ Ⓑ Ⓒ Ⓓ Ⓔ	104 Ⓐ Ⓑ Ⓒ Ⓓ Ⓔ	114 Ⓐ Ⓑ Ⓒ Ⓓ Ⓔ	124 Ⓐ Ⓑ Ⓒ Ⓓ Ⓔ
5 Ⓐ Ⓑ Ⓒ Ⓓ Ⓔ	15 Ⓐ Ⓑ Ⓒ Ⓓ Ⓔ	25 Ⓐ Ⓑ Ⓒ Ⓓ Ⓔ	35 Ⓐ Ⓑ Ⓒ Ⓓ Ⓔ	45 Ⓐ Ⓑ Ⓒ Ⓓ Ⓔ	55 Ⓐ Ⓑ Ⓒ Ⓓ Ⓔ	65 Ⓐ Ⓑ Ⓒ Ⓓ Ⓔ	75 Ⓐ Ⓑ Ⓒ Ⓓ Ⓔ	85 Ⓐ Ⓑ Ⓒ Ⓓ Ⓔ	95 Ⓐ Ⓑ Ⓒ Ⓓ Ⓔ	105 Ⓐ Ⓑ Ⓒ Ⓓ Ⓔ	115 Ⓐ Ⓑ Ⓒ Ⓓ Ⓔ	125 Ⓐ Ⓑ Ⓒ Ⓓ Ⓔ
6 Ⓐ Ⓑ Ⓒ Ⓓ Ⓔ	16 Ⓐ Ⓑ Ⓒ Ⓓ Ⓔ	26 Ⓐ Ⓑ Ⓒ Ⓓ Ⓔ	36 Ⓐ Ⓑ Ⓒ Ⓓ Ⓔ	46 Ⓐ Ⓑ Ⓒ Ⓓ Ⓔ	56 Ⓐ Ⓑ Ⓒ Ⓓ Ⓔ	66 Ⓐ Ⓑ Ⓒ Ⓓ Ⓔ	76 Ⓐ Ⓑ Ⓒ Ⓓ Ⓔ	86 Ⓐ Ⓑ Ⓒ Ⓓ Ⓔ	96 Ⓐ Ⓑ Ⓒ Ⓓ Ⓔ	106 Ⓐ Ⓑ Ⓒ Ⓓ Ⓔ	116 Ⓐ Ⓑ Ⓒ Ⓓ Ⓔ	126 Ⓐ Ⓑ Ⓒ Ⓓ Ⓔ
7 Ⓐ Ⓑ Ⓒ Ⓓ Ⓔ	17 Ⓐ Ⓑ Ⓒ Ⓓ Ⓔ	27 Ⓐ Ⓑ Ⓒ Ⓓ Ⓔ	37 Ⓐ Ⓑ Ⓒ Ⓓ Ⓔ	47 Ⓐ Ⓑ Ⓒ Ⓓ Ⓔ	57 Ⓐ Ⓑ Ⓒ Ⓓ Ⓔ	67 Ⓐ Ⓑ Ⓒ Ⓓ Ⓔ	77 Ⓐ Ⓑ Ⓒ Ⓓ Ⓔ	87 Ⓐ Ⓑ Ⓒ Ⓓ Ⓔ	97 Ⓐ Ⓑ Ⓒ Ⓓ Ⓔ	107 Ⓐ Ⓑ Ⓒ Ⓓ Ⓔ	117 Ⓐ Ⓑ Ⓒ Ⓓ Ⓔ	127 Ⓐ Ⓑ Ⓒ Ⓓ Ⓔ
8 Ⓐ Ⓑ Ⓒ Ⓓ Ⓔ	18 Ⓐ Ⓑ Ⓒ Ⓓ Ⓔ	28 Ⓐ Ⓑ Ⓒ Ⓓ Ⓔ	38 Ⓐ Ⓑ Ⓒ Ⓓ Ⓔ	48 Ⓐ Ⓑ Ⓒ Ⓓ Ⓔ	58 Ⓐ Ⓑ Ⓒ Ⓓ Ⓔ	68 Ⓐ Ⓑ Ⓒ Ⓓ Ⓔ	78 Ⓐ Ⓑ Ⓒ Ⓓ Ⓔ	88 Ⓐ Ⓑ Ⓒ Ⓓ Ⓔ	98 Ⓐ Ⓑ Ⓒ Ⓓ Ⓔ	108 Ⓐ Ⓑ Ⓒ Ⓓ Ⓔ	118 Ⓐ Ⓑ Ⓒ Ⓓ Ⓔ	128 Ⓐ Ⓑ Ⓒ Ⓓ Ⓔ
9 Ⓐ Ⓑ Ⓒ Ⓓ Ⓔ	19 Ⓐ Ⓑ Ⓒ Ⓓ Ⓔ	29 Ⓐ Ⓑ Ⓒ Ⓓ Ⓔ	39 Ⓐ Ⓑ Ⓒ Ⓓ Ⓔ	49 Ⓐ Ⓑ Ⓒ Ⓓ Ⓔ	59 Ⓐ Ⓑ Ⓒ Ⓓ Ⓔ	69 Ⓐ Ⓑ Ⓒ Ⓓ Ⓔ	79 Ⓐ Ⓑ Ⓒ Ⓓ Ⓔ	89 Ⓐ Ⓑ Ⓒ Ⓓ Ⓔ	99 Ⓐ Ⓑ Ⓒ Ⓓ Ⓔ	109 Ⓐ Ⓑ Ⓒ Ⓓ Ⓔ	119 Ⓐ Ⓑ Ⓒ Ⓓ Ⓔ	129 Ⓐ Ⓑ Ⓒ Ⓓ Ⓔ
10 Ⓐ Ⓑ Ⓒ Ⓓ Ⓔ	20 Ⓐ Ⓑ Ⓒ Ⓓ Ⓔ	30 Ⓐ Ⓑ Ⓒ Ⓓ Ⓔ	40 Ⓐ Ⓑ Ⓒ Ⓓ Ⓔ	50 Ⓐ Ⓑ Ⓒ Ⓓ Ⓔ	60 Ⓐ Ⓑ Ⓒ Ⓓ Ⓔ	70 Ⓐ Ⓑ Ⓒ Ⓓ Ⓔ	80 Ⓐ Ⓑ Ⓒ Ⓓ Ⓔ	90 Ⓐ Ⓑ Ⓒ Ⓓ Ⓔ	100 Ⓐ Ⓑ Ⓒ Ⓓ Ⓔ	110 Ⓐ Ⓑ Ⓒ Ⓓ Ⓔ	120 Ⓐ Ⓑ Ⓒ Ⓓ Ⓔ	130 Ⓐ Ⓑ Ⓒ Ⓓ Ⓔ

Directions

In each question in this test, there is at the left a series of letters which follow some definite order, and, at the right, five sets of two letters each.

Look at the letters in the series at the left and find out what order they follow. Now decide what the next two letters in that series would be if the order were continued. Then find that set in one of the five suggested answers at the right and darken completely the space on your answer sheet which has the same letter as the correct answer.

Sample questions 1, 2, 3, 4, and 5 are given below. Mark the answer to each on your answer sheet in spaces 1 through 5.

1. x c x d x e x .... A) f x   B) f g   C) x f   D) e f   E) x g

The order in this series is the letter *x* alternating with letters in alphabetical order starting with *c* so that if the series were continued for two more letters, it would read: x c x d x e x f x and *f x* are those two letters you would look for.

In the five sets of letters on the right, in question 1, the set *f x* is labeled A. Therefore, you should mark space A on your answer sheet for sample question 1. Do it now.

2. u u t t s s r .... A) r r   B) r q   C) q r   D) q q   E) r s

The order in this series is pairs of letters starting with *u u* and going *backward* through the alphabet so that if the series were continued for two more letters, it would read: u u t t s s r r q and *r q* are those two letters you would look for.

In the five sets of letters on the right in question 2, the set *r q* is labeled B. Therefore, you should mark space B on your answer sheet for sample question 2. Do it now.

3. a v a w a x a .... A) z a   B) y z   C) y a   D) a z   E) a y

If you discover the order in this series, you will see that the next two letters should be *y a*. In the five sets of letters on the right, the set *y a* is labeled C. Therefore, you should mark space C on your answer sheet for sample question 3. Do it now.

Now work sample questions 4 and 5 and mark the answers on the answer sheet.

4. a b d e g h j .... A) k l   B) l n   C) j m   D) l m   E) k m

5. a r c s e t g .... A) h i   B) h u   C) u j   D) u i   E) i v

If you worked the sample questions correctly, you should have marked space E for question 4 and space D for question 5.

You will have 20 minutes to answer the test questions. The first question is number 6, so be sure to start with space 6 on your answer sheet.

DO NOT TURN THIS PAGE UNTIL TOLD TO DO SO.

THE TEST

In each series of letters below determine what the order of the letters is and decide what the next two letters should be. From the suggested answers at the right choose the one that gives the next two letters in the series and darken the corresponding space on your answer sheet.

abcdefghijklmnopqrstuvwxyz

6. mnomnom .... A) mn   B) no   C) nm   D) on   E) om

7. eeaeebe .... A) ee   B) ef   C) ce   D) fe   E) ec

8. fggfhhf .... A) ff   B) fi   C) ii   D) if   E) jj

9. ppqrrst .... A) tt   B) uv   C) uu   D) tu   E) tv

10. lcdlefl .... A) lg   B) gh   C) le   D) fg   E) gg

11. gnvhowi .... A) pj   B) xj   C) ip   D) px   E) xq

12. rlsmtnu .... A) ov   B) uv   C) vw   D) ow   E) vo

13. shriqjp .... A) ko   B) kl   C) ok   D) pk   E) on

14. abzcdye .... A) xg   B) xw   C) fw   D) fx   E) fg

15. eegiikm .... A) mn   B) oo   C) oq   D) mo   E) nm

16. jhnlrpv .... A) tx   B) sz   C) tz   D) sy   E) zt

17. qgriskt .... A) ul   B) mu   C) lu   D) mn   E) lm

18. ehifijg .... A) hi   B) jk   C) ik   D) hj   E) ij

19. tghuefv .... A) dc   B) dw   C) de   D) cd   E) cw

20. hgfkjin .... A) ml   B) po   C) lm   D) op   E) mo

21. rpnljhf .... A) ec   B) dc   C) eb   D) db   E) ed

22. egthjtk .... A) lt   B) mt   C) lm   D) tl   E) mn

23. bdcegfh .... A) gi   B) ik   C) ji   D) jl   E) hj

24. ehjmort .... A) vy   B) wz   C) vx   D) xz   E) wy

25. frhtjvl .... A) mn   B) wy   C) xn   D) nw   E) xm

26. mpnqorp .... A) sq   B) qr   C) tq   D) qs   E) sr

27. gikhjli .... A) kl   B) jk   C) jl   D) jm   E) km

28. acfhkmp .... A) sv   B) rt   C) ru   D) su   E) qr

GO ON TO THE NEXT PAGE.

abcdefghijklmnopqrstuvwxyz

29. c d f g j k m .... A) n q   B) p q   C) o p   D) n p   E) o r

30. h g l m l q r .... A) q r   B) q w   C) r w   D) q v   E) r q

31. c d f g j k o .... A) p t   B) p u   C) t x   D) t z   E) s x

32. f d h f j h l .... A) j m   B) i n   C) j n   D) k m   E) i m

33. r n p t p r v .... A) s u   B) r t   C) x z   D) z x   E) t r

34. d f h h e g i i f h j .... A) j g   B) g g   C) g i   D) j i   E) l l

35. y x v t s q o n l j i .... A) h f   B) h g   C) g e   D) f e   E) g f

If you finish before the time is up, you may go back and check your answers.

ANSWER KEY

1. A		8. C		15. D		22. B		29. A
2. B		9. D		16. C		23. C		30. D
3. C		10. B		17. B		24. E		31. B
4. E		11. D		18. B		25. C		32. C
5. D		12. A		19. D		26. A		33. B
6. B		13. A		20. A		27. E		34. A
7. E		14. D		21. D		28. C		35. C

ANSWER EXPLANATIONS

Explanations for questions 1 through 3 are given on page 281.

4. **(E)** a b d e g h j k m
   Two consecutive letters, the next letter is skipped; then two consecutive letters, the next letter is skipped; and so on.

5. **(D)** a r c s e t g u i
   Two alternating groups of letters: the first group (a, c, e, g, i) skips a letter each time; the second group is letters in consecutive order (r, s, t, u).

6. **(B)** m n o m n o m n o
   The letters m n o repeating.

7. **(E)** e e a e e b e e c
   Double e, then a; double e, then b; double e, then c; and so on.

8. **(C)** f g g f h h f i i
   f, then double g; f, then double h; f, then double i; and so on.

9. **(D)** p p q r r s t t u
   A pair of the same letter followed by the next consecutive letter once; then a pair of the next consecutive letter followed by the next consecutive letter once; and so on.

10. **(B)** l c d l e f l g h
    l followed by two consecutive letters, starting with c; then l again followed by the next two consecutive letters; repeat sequence.

11. **(D)** g n v h o w i p x
    Three alternating groups of letters: each group is in consecutive order—(g, h, i); (n, o, p); and (v, w, x). Note how a part of each group appears every third letter.

12. **(A)** r l s m t n u o v
    Two alternating groups of letters: each group is in consecutive order—(r, s, t, u, v) and (l, m, n, o).

13. **(A)** s h r i q j p k o
    Two alternating groups of letters: the first group goes backward consecutively (s, r, q, p, o); the other group is in forward consecutive order (h, i, j, k).

14. **(D)** a b z c d y e f x
    The first two letters of the alphabet, then the last letter; the next two letters after a b, followed by the next to last; the next two letters after c d, followed by the one before the next to last; and so on.

15. **(D)** e e g i i k m m o
    Double letter, then skip a letter, single letter, then skip a letter; repeat.

16. **(C)** j h n l r p v t z
Begin with j: second letter back, then sixth letter forward; second letter back, then sixth letter forward: and so on.

17. **(B)** q g r i s k t m u
Two alternating groups of letters: the first group goes forward consecutively (q, r, s, t, u); the second group goes forward skipping a letter each time (g, i, k, m).

18. **(B)** e h i f i j g j k
Three alternating groups of letters, each consecutive and interspersed: (e ⓗ i f ⓘ j g ⓙ k)

19. **(D)** t g h u e f v c d
Two alternating groups of letters: the first group is consecutive and appears every third letter (t, u, v); the other group consists of pairs of consecutive letters, each pair coming before the previous pair ($g h, e f, c d$).

20. **(A)** h g f k j i n m l
Three backward consecutive letters, followed by the next three backward consecutive letters: ($h g f, k j i, n m l$).

21. **(D)** r p n l j h f d b
Goes consecutively backward but skips every other letter: (r, skips q, then p, skips o, then n, skips m, then l, skips k, then j, skips i, then h, etc.).

22. **(B)** e g t h j t k m t
A forward pair skipping the middle letter (e, g), then t; the next consecutive pair, skipping the middle letter (h, j), then t; then the next consecutive pair (k, m), then t.

23. **(C)** b d c e g f h j i
Ahead two, back one, ahead two; ahead two, back one, ahead two; ahead two, back one, and so on.

24. **(E)** e h j m o r t w y
Ahead three, ahead two; repeat.

25. **(C)** f r h t j v l x n
Two alternating groups of letters: each group skips a letter (f, h, j, l, n, and r, t, v, x).

26. **(A)** m p n q o r p s q
Two alternating groups of letters, each consecutive: (m, n, o, p, q and p, q, r, s).

27. **(E)** g i k h j l i k m
Three letters, skipping a letter each time (g, i, k); then the next consecutive set of three skipping letters (h, j, l); followed by the next consecutive set of three skipping letters (i, k, m).

28. **(C)** a c f h k m p r u
Two ahead, then three ahead; repeat.

29. **(A)** c d f g j k m n q
A pair of consecutive letters, then skip one letter, the next pair of consecutive letters, then skip two letters; repeat.

30. **(D)** h g l m l q r g v
Back one, ahead five, ahead one; repeat.

31. **(B)** c d f g j k o p u
A pair of consecutive letters then skip one; the next pair of consecutive letters, then skip two; the next pair of consecutive letters, then skip three; and so on.

32. **(C)** f d h f j h l j n
Back two, up four; repeat.

33. **(B)** r n p t p r v r t
Back four, up two, up four; repeat.

34. **(A)** d f h h e g i i f h j j g
Each set of four letters follows the order skip one, skip one, double the last letter (d, f, h, h); then repeat this sequence starting with the next consecutive letter after the *first* from the last sequence (e, g, i, i); then (f, h, j, j); then (g, i, k, k); and so on.

35. **(C)** y x v t s q o n l j i g e
Going backward only: a pair of consecutive letters, skip one, then a single letter, skip one; repeat.

Practice, Practice, Practice

(NOTE: Allow 20 minutes for each practice set.)

PRACTICE SET 1

In each series of letters below determine what the order of the letters is and decide what the next two letters should be. From the suggested answers at the right choose the one that gives the next two letters in the series.

abcdefghijklmnopqrstuvwxyz

1. cdfgijl .... A) m n   B) m o   C) m p   D) o p   E) o q   _____

2. yxvusrp .... A) m o   B) q m   C) o n   D) o m   E) n o   _____

3. jklnopr .... A) t u   B) s t   C) s u   D) u v   E) s v   _____

4. bcfgjkn .... A) o r   B) o p   C) q r   D) p q   E) p r   _____

5. bbcddef .... A) f f   B) g g   C) g h   D) h i   E) f g   _____

6. pponnml .... A) l k   B) k l   C) k j   D) l l   E) k i   _____

7. yyxwwvu .... A) t u   B) u t   C) u v   D) t s   E) s t   _____

8. cbafedi .... A) g h   B) h g   C) g f   D) k j   E) f g   _____

9. nomljki .... A) h g   B) h i   C) h f   D) h e   E) f h   _____

10. defdefd .... A) d e   B) f d   C) e d   D) e f   E) f e   _____

11. yxwutsq .... A) p o   B) o n   C) p n   D) r p   E) o p   _____

12. ttabuuc .... A) c v   B) d e   C) d v   D) v v   E) v d   _____

13. llzkkyj .... A) x j   B) j i   C) j x   D) j l   E) v j   _____

14. efdhigk .... A) l j   B) j l   C) j m   D) m j   E) l m   _____

15. onlkihf .... A) e d   B) e c   C) e b   D) d b   E) d c   _____

16. brcsdte .... A) f g   B) u v   C) v f   D) u f   E) u g   _____

17. ewhuksn .... A) p q   B) p q   C) q q   D) q r   E) r q   _____

18. aadegij .... A) m m   B) m n   C) n m   D) l m   E) m l   _____

abcdefghijklmnopqrstuvwxyz

19. noppqrs .... A) ts   B) st   C) ut   D) tu   E) uv   _____

20. ghiijkk .... A) lm   B) mn   C) no   D) kl   E) ki   _____

21. abtcdse .... A) fg   B) fg   C) fr   D) fu   E) gf   _____

22. zaxcvet .... A) fs   B) fr   C) gs   D) gu   E) gr   _____

23. ylmwnou .... A) qs   B) ps   C) pq   D) qr   E) pr   _____

24. tssrrrq .... A) qp   B) pp   C) qq   D) op   E) oo   _____

25. jjhhffd .... A) dd   B) dc   C) db   D) da   E) de   _____

26. vuuttts .... A) rr   B) st   C) pr   D) rs   E) ss   _____

27. nspqrot .... A) sp   B) mv   C) vm   D) ps   E) uv   _____

28. ghajkbm .... A) no   B) nd   C) nc   D) oc   E) co   _____

29. vctfrip .... A) jn   B) ln   C) jm   D) lm   E) jo   _____

30. acddeghhi .... A) kk   B) ll   C) kl   D) km   E) mm   _____

ANSWER EXPLANATIONS FOR PRACTICE SET 1

1. **(B)** cdfgijlmo
   Two consecutive letters, then skip a letter; repeat.

2. **(D)** yxvusrpom
   Going backward: two consecutive letters, then skip one; repeat.

3. **(B)** jklnoprst
   Three consecutive letters, then skip one; repeat.

4. **(A)** bcfgjknor
   Two consecutive letters, then skip two; repeat.

5. **(E)** bbcddeffg
   Consecutive letters, but every other one is doubled.

6. **(A)** pponnmllk
   Consecutive letters backward, but every other one is doubled.

7. **(B)** yyxwwvuut
   Consecutive letters backward, but every other one is doubled.

8. **(B)** cbafedihg
   Continuing sets of three consecutively backward letters.

9. **(C)** nomljkihf
   One forward, two back, one back, two back; repeat. This is a difficult one.

10. **(D)** defdefdef
    The letters d e f repeating.

11. **(A)** yxwutsqpo
    Consecutive letters backward, skipping every fourth letter.

12. **(C)** ttabuucdv
    Two alternating groups of letters: the first group is repeating pairs of consecutive letters ($t\,t$, $u\,u$, $v\,v$, etc.); the second group is pairs of consecutive letters ($a\,b$, $c\,d$, $e\,f$, etc).

13. **(C)** llzkkyjjx
    Two alternating groups of letters: the first group is pairs of doubled letters backward consecutively ($l\,l$, $k\,k$, $j\,j$, etc.); the other group is single letters backward consecutively (z, y, x, w, etc.)

14. **(A)** efdhigklj
    One ahead, two back, four ahead; repeat.

15. **(B)** onlkihfec
    Consecutive letters backward, skipping every third letter.

16. **(D)** brcsdteuf
    Two alternating groups of letters, each consecutive: b, c, d, e, f and r, s, t, u.

17. **(C)** ewhuksnqq
    Two alternating groups of letters: the first group goes forward, skipping every two letters (e, h, k, n, q); the other group goes backward, skipping every other letter (w, u, s, q).

18. **(A)** aadegijmm
    Two alternating groups of letters: the first group goes forward, skipping every two letters (a, d, g, j, m); the second group goes forward, skipping every three letters (a, e, i, m).

19. **(B)** n o p p q r s s t
Consecutive letters forward, with every third letter doubled.

20. **(A)** g h i i j k k l m
Consecutive letters forward, but the third letter of a set becomes the first letter of the next set.

21. **(C)** a b t c d s e f r
Two alternating groups of letters. The first group is pairs of consecutive letters (*a b, c d, e f*); the other group is single letters, consecutively backward (*t, s, r*).

22. **(E)** z a x c v e t g r
Two alternating groups of letters: the first group goes backward, skipping every other letter (*z, x, v, t, r*); the second group goes forward, skipping every other letter (*a, c, e, g*).

23. **(C)** y l m w n o u p q
Two alternating groups of letters: the first group is single letters going backward, skipping every other letter (*y, w, u*); the second group is pairs of consecutive letters going forward (*l m, n o, p q*).

24. **(C)** t s s r r r q q q
Consecutive letters going backward, each letter increasing in number by one: one *t*, two *s*'s, three *r*'s, four *q*'s, and so on.

25. **(C)** j j h h f f d d b
Going backward: a pair of the same letters, skip the next letter; repeat (*j j, h h, f f, d d, b b*).

26. **(E)** v u u t t t s s s
Going backward: consecutive letters increasing in number by one (one *v*, two *u*'s, three *t*'s, four *s*'s, and so on).

27. **(B)** n s p q r o t m v
Two alternating groups of letters: the first group goes forward, skipping every other letter (*n, p, r, t, v*); the second group goes backward, skipping every other letter (*s, q, o, m*).

28. **(C)** g h a j k b m n c
Two alternating groups of letters: the first group is consecutive letters in pairs, skipping every third letter (*g h, j k, m n*); the other group is consecutive single letters (*a, b, c,*).

29. **(B)** v c t f r i p l n
Two alternating groups of letters: the first group goes backward, skipping every other letter (*v, t, r, p, n*); the other group goes forward, skipping every two letters (*c, f, i, l*).

30. **(C)** a c d d e g h h k l
Forward as follows: beginning with *a*, skip a letter, then double the next consecutive letter, then go to the next consecutive letter; repeat.

PRACTICE SET 2

In each series of letters below determine what the order of the letters is and decide what the next two letters should be. From the suggested answers at the right choose the one that gives the next two letters in the series.

a b c d e f g h i j k l m n o p q r s t u v w x y z

1. f g i j m n p	A) r u	B) q t	C) s t	D) r s	E) q s	_____
2. k j o p o t u	A) t u	B) u t	C) t z	D) u z	E) t y	_____
3. f g i j m n r	A) s w	B) s x	C) w a	D) w c	E) v q	_____
4. i g k i m k o	A) l p	B) m p	C) l q	D) m q	E) n p	_____
5. u q s w s u y	A) w y	B) v x	C) u w	D) a c	E) c a	_____
6. d g e h f i g	A) j h	B) k h	C) j k	D) k j	E) h k	_____
7. c y x t s o n	A) j i	B) i j	C) k j	D) l k	E) i h	_____
8. g y h x i w j	A) k x	B) x k	C) v k	D) v i	E) k v	_____
9. m n n o p p q	A) r s	B) q r	C) r r	D) s r	E) s s	_____
10. n b p z r x t	A) v v	B) v x	C) x v	D) w v	E) u w	_____
11. h g r j i r l	A) r k	B) r n	C) k r	D) m r	E) r m	_____

abcdefghijklmnopqrstuvwxyz

12. dcebfag	A) hz	B) zh	C) zi	D) ih	E) yh	_____
13. gjilknm	A) po	B) pq	C) qr	D) qp	E) on	_____
14. degjkmp	A) rt	B) qr	C) qt	D) qs	E) rs	_____
15. grjsmtp	A) ur	B) us	C) up	D) uw	E) uu	_____
16. adehilm	A) nq	B) qp	C) pq	D) op	E) rs	_____
17. jimlpo	A) nr	B) sw	C) qu	D) sr	E) nm	_____
18. dheifjg	A) kh	B) hk	C) hi	D) ij	E) kl	_____
19. nkmjli	A) gj	B) kh	C) lj	D) fh	E) kl	_____
20. eebeece	A) ee	B) aa	C) ed	D) ef	E) de	_____
21. zwyvxuw	A) tv	B) sv	C) ts	D) st	E) vs	_____
22. wevfugt	A) sf	B) fs	C) hs	D) hu	E) sh	_____
23. qpponnm	A) lk	B) ml	C) kl	D) ll	E) kk	_____
24. aefjkop	A) uv	B) tu	C) ut	D) st	E) rs	_____
25. pbndlfj	A) hf	B) jh	C) gh	D) ig	E) hh	_____
26. vwltulr	A) lp	B) sl	C) ql	D) lq	E) ls	_____
27. zaybxcw	A) vd	B) dv	C) du	D) uv	E) ev	_____
28. wturspq	A) no	B) nm	C) ml	D) mn	E) op	_____
29. bcwvdeutf	A) gt	B) th	C) gs	D) hi	E) hs	_____
30. aecgeigki	A) ik	B) mk	C) om	D) mo	E) jm	_____

ANSWER EXPLANATIONS FOR PRACTICE SET 2

1. **(B)** f g i j m n p q t
   A pair of consecutive letters, then skip one letter, the next pair of consecutive letters, then skip two letters; repeat.

2. **(E)** k j o p o t u t y
   Back one, ahead five, ahead one; repeat.

3. **(B)** f g i j m n r s x
   A pair of consecutive letters, then skip one letter; the next pair of consecutive letters, then skip two; the next pair of consecutive letters, then skip three; and so on.

4. **(D)** i g k i m k o m q
   Back two, up four; repeat.

5. **(C)** u q s w s u y u w
   Back four, up two, up four; repeat.

6. **(A)** d g e h f i g j h
   Alternating consecutive sets: (*defgh*)(*ghij*).

7. **(A)** c y x t s o n j i
   Back four, back one; repeat.

8. **(C)** g y h x i w j v k
   Two alternating groups: the first group goes forward consecutively (*g, h, i, j, k*); the second group goes backward consecutively (*y, x, w, v*).

9. **(C)** m n n o p p q r r
   A single letter, then the next consecutive letter doubled; the next consecutive single letter, then the next consecutive letter doubled; and so on.

10. **(A)** n b p z r x t v̄ v̄
Two alternating groups of letters: the first group skips one letter as it goes forward; the other group skips one letter as it goes backward.

11. **(C)** h g r j i r l k r
Consecutive backward pairs, separated by the letter *r*.

12. **(B)** d c e b f a g z h
Two alternating groups of letters: one consecutive forward; the other consecutive backward.

13. **(A)** g j i l k n m p o
Ahead three, back one; repeat.

14. **(D)** d e g j k m p q s
Beginning with *d*, the next consecutive letter, then skip one letter, then skip two letters; repeat.

15. **(B)** g r j s m t p u s
Two alternating groups of letters: the first group goes forward skipping two letters (*g, j, m, p, s*); the second group goes forward consecutively (*r, s, t, u*).

16. **(C)** a d e h i l m p q
Three ahead, then one ahead; repeat.

17. **(D)** j i m l p o s r
Back one, ahead four; repeat.

18. **(A)** d h e i f j g k h
Two alternating groups of letters, each consecutive: (*d, e, f, g, h*) and (*h, i, j, k*).

19. **(B)** n k m j l i k h
Back three, ahead two; repeat.

20. **(C)** e e b e e c e e d
Double *e*, then *b*; double *e*, then *c*; and so on.

21. **(A)** z w y v x u w t v
Working backward starting at *z*, go three back,

then two forward; three back, two forward; and so on.

22. **(C)** w e v f u g t h s
Two alternating groups: the first group goes backward consecutively (*w, v, u, t, s*); the second group goes forward consecutively (*e, f, g, h*).

23. **(D)** q p p o n n m l l
Going backward only: a single letter, then the next consecutive letter doubled; the next consecutive letter single, then the next consecutive letter doubled; and so on.

24. **(B)** a e f j k o p t u
Ahead four, ahead one; repeat.

25. **(E)** p b n d l f j h h
Two alternating groups of letters: the first group skips one letter as it goes backward; the other group skips one letter as it goes forward.

26. **(B)** v w l t u l r s l
Consecutive forward pair followed by letter *l*; then go two backward from starting letter *v* to get next consecutive forward pair (*t u*), followed by letter *l*; go two backward from *t* to get next consecutive pair (*r s*), followed by *l*.

27. **(B)** z a y b x c w d v
Two alternating groups of letters: one consecutive backward; the other consecutive forward.

28. **(A)** w t u r s p q n o
Back three, ahead one; repeat.

29. **(C)** b c w v d e u t f g s
Two alternating groups of letters: the first group, consecutive pairs going forward (*b c, d e, f g*); the second group, consecutive pairs going backward (*w v, u t, s r*).

30. **(B)** a e c g e i g k i m k
Ahead four, then back two; repeat.

PRACTICE SET 3

In each series of letters below determine what the order of the letters is and decide what the next two letters should be. From the suggested answers at the right choose the one that gives the next two letters in the series.

a b c d e f g h i j k l m n o p q r s t u v w x y z

1. a f a g a h a	A) i a	B) i j	C) a i	D) h i	E) a j
2. x x w w v v u	A) u u	B) u t	C) t u	D) t t	E) u v
3. d y d z d a d	A) c k	B) b c	C) b d	D) d c	E) d b
4. d e g h j k m	A) n o	B) o q	C) m p	D) o p	E) n p
5. d u f v h w j	A) k x	B) k l	C) x l	D) f y	E) x m
6. p q r p q r p	A) r p	B) r q	C) q p	D) q r	E) p q
7. h h d h h e h	A) h h	B) h i	C) f h	D) i h	E) h f
8. i j j i k k i	A) i i	B) l l	C) i l	D) l i	E) m m

9.	sstuuvw	A) wy	B) wx	C) xx	D) xy	E) ww	_____
10.	ofgohio	A) jj	B) ij	C) oh	D) jk	E) oj	_____
11.	jqykrzl	A) at	B) sa	C) ls	D) am	E) sm	_____
12.	uovpwqx	A) yr	B) rz	C) yz	D) xy	E) ry	_____
13.	vkultms	A) rq	B) sn	C) rn	D) no	E) nr	_____
14.	decfgbh	A) az	B) aj	C) ij	D) iz	E) ia	_____
15.	hhjllnp	A) rt	B) pr	C) rr	D) qp	E) pq	_____
16.	mkqousy	A) vc	B) wq	C) vb	D) wc	E) cw	_____
17.	tjulvnw	A) px	B) so	C) ox	D) pq	E) op	_____
18.	hklilmj	A) kl	B) ln	C) mn	D) km	E) lm	_____
19.	wjkxhiy	A) gf	B) gz	C) gh	D) fg	E) fz	_____
20.	kjinmlq	A) po	B) sr	C) op	D) rs	E) pr	_____
21.	usqomki	A) hf	B) gf	C) he	D) ge	E) hg	_____
22.	hjwkmwn	A) ow	B) pw	C) op	D) wo	E) pq	_____
23.	egfhjik	A) jl	B) ln	C) ml	D) mo	E) km	_____
24.	hkmpruw	A) yb	B) zc	C) ya	D) ac	E) zb	_____
25.	iukwmyo	A) pq	B) zb	C) aq	D) qz	E) ap	_____
26.	psqtrus	A) vt	B) tu	C) wt	D) tv	E) pu	_____
27.	jlnkmol	A) no	B) mn	C) mo	D) mp	E) np	_____
28.	dfiknps	A) vy	B) uw	C) ux	D) vx	E) tu	_____
29.	gikkhjllikm	A) mj	B) jj	C) jl	D) ml	E) oo	_____
30.	baywvtrqoml	A) ki	B) kj	C) jh	D) ih	E) ji	_____

ANSWER EXPLANATIONS FOR PRACTICE SET 3

1. **(A)** afagahaia
   The letter $\bar{a}$ alternating with letters in alphabetical order, starting with f.
2. **(B)** xxwwvvuut
   Pairs of letters, starting with $x x$ and going backward through the alphabet.
3. **(C)** dydzdadbd
   The letter d alternating with letters in alphabetical order, starting with y.
4. **(E)** deghjkmnp
   Two consecutive letters, then skip the next letter; the next two consecutive letters, then skip the next letter; and so on.

5. **(C)** d u f v h w j x l

Two alternating groups of letters: the first group (d, f, h, j) skips a letter each time; the second group consists of letters in consecutive order (u, v, w, x).

6. **(D)** p q r p q r p q r

The letters p q r repeating.

7. **(E)** h h d h h e h h f

Double h, then d; double h, then e; double h, then f; and so on.

8. **(B)** i j j i k k i l l

i, then double j; i, then double k; i, then double l; and so on.

9. **(B)** s s t u u v w w x

A pair of the same letter, then the next consecutive letter once; a pair of the next consecutive letter, then the next consecutive letter once; and so on.

10. **(D)** o f g o h i o j k

o, then, starting with f, two consecutive letters; then o again, followed by the next two consecutive letters; then o again and so on.

11. **(B)** j q y k r z l s a

Three alternating groups of letters: each group is in consecutive order (j, k, l), (q, r, s), (y, z, a).

12. **(E)** u o v p w q x r y

Two alternating groups of letters: each group is in consecutive order (u, v, w, x, y), (o, p, q, r).

13. **(E)** v k u l t m s n r

Two alternating groups of letters: the first group goes backward consecutively (v, u, t, s, r); the other group goes forward consecutively (k, l, m, n).

14. **(E)** d e c f g b h i a

The fourth and fifth letters of the alphabet, then the third letter; the next two letters (sixth and seventh), then the second; and so on.

15. **(B)** h h j l l n p p r

Double letter, then skip one letter, then single letter, then skip one letter; repeat.

16. **(D)** m k q o u s y w c

Begin with m: second letter back, then sixth letter forward; repeat.

17. **(A)** t j u l v n w p x

Two alternating groups of letters: the first group goes forward consecutively (t, u, v, w, x); the second group goes forward skipping a letter each time (j, l, n, p).

18. **(C)** h k l i l m j m n

Three alternating groups of letters, each consecutive: (h, i, j), (k, l, m), (l, m, n).

19. **(D)** w j k x h i y f g

Two alternating groups of letters: the first group is consecutive and appears every third letter (w, x, y); the other group consists of pairs of consecutive letters, each pair coming before the previous pair ($j k, h i, f g$).

20. **(A)** k j i n m l q p o

Three backward consecutive letters, followed by the next three backward consecutive letters: ($k j i, n m l, q p o$).

21. **(D)** u s q o m k i g e

Goes consecutively backward but skips every other letter: u, skips t; then s, skips r; then q, skips p; then o, skips n; then m, skips l; and so on.

22. **(B)** h j w k m w n p w

A forward pair skipping the middle letter (h, j), then w; the next consecutive pair, still skipping the middle letter (k, m), then w; the next consecutive pair (n, p), then w.

23. **(C)** e g f h j i k m l

Ahead two, back one, ahead two; ahead two, back one, ahead two; ahead two, back one, and so on.

24. **(E)** h k m p r u w z b

Ahead three, ahead two; repeat.

25. **(C)** i u k w m y o a q

Two alternating groups of letters, each group skips a letter: i, k, m, o, q and u, w, y, a.

26. **(A)** p s q t r u s v t

Two alternating groups of letters, each consecutive: p, q, r, s, t and s, t, u, v.

27. **(E)** j l n k m o l n p

Three letters, skipping a letter each time (j, l, n); then the next consecutive set of three skipping letters (k, m, o), followed by the next consecutive set of three skipping letters (l, n, p).

28. **(C)** d f i k n p s u x

Two ahead, then three ahead; repeat.

29. **(A)** g i k k h j l l i k m m j

Each set of four letters follows the order skip one, skip one, double the third letter (g, i, k, k); then the sequence is repeated, starting with the next consecutive letter after the *first* from the last sequence (h, j, l, l); and so on.

30. **(C)** b a y w v t r q o m l j h

Going backward only: a pair of consecutive letters ($b a$), skip one (z), then a single letter (y), skip one (x); a pair of consecutive letters ($w v$), skip one (y), then a single letter (t), skip one (s); and so on.

PRACTICE SET 4

In each series of letters below determine what the order of the letters is and decide what the next two letters should be. From the suggested answers at the right choose the one that gives the next two letters in the series.

abcdefghijklmnopqrstuvwxyz

1. adbecfd .... A) ge   B) he   C) gh   D) hg   E) eh   _____

2. dveuftg .... A) hu   B) uh   C) sh   D) sf   E) hs   _____

3. jkklmmn .... A) po   B) no   C) oo   D) op   E) pp   _____

4. zvuqplk .... A) gf   B) fg   C) hg   D) ih   E) fe   _____

5. kymwouq .... A) su   B) us   C) ts   D) rt   E) ss   _____

6. edogfoi .... A) ok   B) ho   C) jo   D) oj   E) oh   _____

7. azbycxd .... A) ew   B) we   C) wf   D) fe   E) ve   _____

8. zywtsqn .... A) ml   B) mj   C) lj   D) mk   E) lk   _____

9. wltkqjn .... A) il   B) ik   C) in   D) ig   E) ii   _____

10. qsmoike .... A) gc   B) ha   C) ga   D) hb   E) ag   _____

11. jtirhpg .... A) fo   B) nf   C) of   D) nm   E) on   _____

12. vsrurqt .... A) sr   B) qp   C) rp   D) wq   E) rq   _____

13. gtsfvue .... A) wx   B) wd   C) wv   D) xw   E) xd   _____

14. stupqrm .... A) no   B) kl   C) on   D) lk   E) nl   _____

15. ikmoqsu .... A) vx   B) wx   C) vy   D) wy   E) vw   _____

16. vtgsqgp .... A) og   B) ng   C) on   D) go   E) nm   _____

17. ywxvtus .... A) tr   B) rp   C) qr   D) qo   E) sq   _____

18. vsqnlig .... A) eb   B) dc   C) ec   D) ca   E) db   _____

19. uisgqeo .... A) nm   B) db   C) cm   D) nd   E) cn   _____

20. nkmjlik .... A) ji   B) hj   C) gj   D) jn   E) hi   _____

21. trpsqor .... A) po   B) qp   C) pn   D) qo   E) qn   _____

22. zxuspnk .... A) he   B) ig   C) if   D) hf   E) ji   _____

23. xwutqpn .... A) mj   B) kj   C) lk   D) mk   E) li   _____

24. stonoji .... A) ji   B) jd   C) id   D) je   E) ij   _____

abcdefghijklmnopqrstuvwxyz

25. xwutqpl .... A) kg   B) gc   C) kf   D) ga   E) hc   _____

26. uwsuqso .... A) qn   B) rm   C) pn   D) qm   E) rn   _____

27. imkgkie .... A) ig   B) hf   C) ca   D) ac   E) gi   _____

28. vvtrrpn .... A) nm   B) ll   C) lj   D) nl   E) mn   _____

29. bceghjlmoqr .... A) su   B) st   C) tv.   D) uv   E) tu   _____

30. ywuusrppn .... A) jj   B) lj   C) hf   D) mj   E) nl   _____

ANSWER EXPLANATIONS FOR PRACTICE SET 4

1. **(A)** adbecfdge
   Ahead three, back two; repeat.
2. **(C)** dveuftgsh
   Two alternating groups: the first group goes forward consecutively (*d, e, f, g, h*); the second group goes backward consecutively (*v, u, t, s*).
3. **(C)** jkklmmnoo
   A single letter, then the next consecutive letter doubled; then the next consecutive letter single, then the next consecutive letter doubled; and so on.
4. **(A)** zvuqplkgf
   Back four, back one; repeat.
5. **(E)** kymwouqss
   Two alternating groups of letters: the first group skips one letter as it goes forward; the other group skips one letter as it goes backward.
6. **(B)** edogfoiho
   Consecutive backward pairs, separated by the letter *o*.
7. **(B)** azbycxdwe
   Two alternating groups of letters: one consecutive forward, the other consecutive backward.
8. **(D)** zywtsqnmk
   Going backward from *z*: the next consecutive letter, then skip one letter, then skip two letters; repeat.
9. **(B)** wltkqjnik
   Two alternating groups of letters: the first group goes backward skipping two letters (*w, t, q, n, k*); the second group goes backward consecutively (*l, k, j, i*).
10. **(C)** qsmoikega
    Beginning with *q*: second letter forward, then sixth letter backward; repeat.
11. **(B)** jtirhpgnf
    Two alternating groups of letters: the first group goes backward consecutively (*j, i, h, g, f*); the second group goes backward skipping one letter (*t, r, p, n*).

12. **(B)** vsrurqtqp
    Three alternating groups of letters, each consecutively backward (*v, u, t*), (*s, r, q*), (*r, q, p*).
13. **(D)** gtsfvuexw
    Two alternating groups of letters: the first group goes backward consecutively and appears every third letter (*g, f, e*); the other group consists of pairs of consecutive backward letters (*t s, v u, x w*), with two letters skipped between pairs.
14. **(A)** stupqrmno
    Three consecutive letters; then three letters back from *s* to begin the next three consecutive letters (*p q r*); then three back from *p* to start the next three consecutive letters (*m n o*).
15. **(D)** ikmoqsuwy
    Goes forward but skips every other letter (*i*, skips *j*; then *k*, skips *l*; then *m*, skips *n*; etc.).
16. **(B)** vtgsqgpng
    A backward pair, skipping the middle letter (*v, t*), then *g*; followed by the next consecutive backward pair, skipping the middle letter (*s, q*), then *g*; and so on.
17. **(C)** ywxvtusqr
    Back two, ahead one, back two; back two, ahead one, back two; back two, ahead one, and so on.
18. **(E)** vsqnligdb
    Back three, back two; repeat.
19. **(C)** uisgqeocm
    Two alternating groups of letters: each group goes backward and skips a letter: *u, s, q, o, m* and *i, g, e, c*.
20. **(B)** nkmjlikhj
    Two alternating groups of letters, each consecutively backward: *n, m, l, k, j* and *k, j, i, h*.
21. **(C)** trpsqorpn
    Three letters of the alphabet in reverse order, skipping a letter each time (*t, r, p*); then the next consecutive backward set, skipping letters (*s, q, o*); followed by the next consecutive backward set, skipping letters (*r, p, n*).

22. **(C)** z x u s p n k i f
Two back, then three back; repeat.
23. **(A)** x w u t q p n m j
Going backward: pair of consecutive letters,
then skip one, the next pair of consecutive letters, then skip two; the next pair of consecutive
letters, then skip one, the next pair of consecutive letters, then skip two.
24. **(D)** s t o n o j i j e
Ahead one, back five, back one; repeat.
25. **(C)** x w u t q p l k f
Going backward: pair of consecutive letters,
then skip one; the next pair of consecutive letters, then skip two; the next pair of consecutive
letters, then skip three; and so on.

26. **(D)** u w s u q s o q m
Ahead two, back four; repeat.
27. **(A)** i m k g k i e i g
Ahead four, back two, back four; repeat.
28. **(D)** v v t r r p n n l
Going backward: double letter, then skip a letter, then a single letter, then skip a letter; repeat.
29. **(C)** b c e g h j l m o q r t v
going forward: a pair of consecutive letters,
skip 1, then a single letter, skip 1; repeat.
30. **(B)** y w u u s r p p n l j
Going backward: skip every other letter, dou-
bling the third letter of the set; then repeat.

PRACTICE SET 5

In each series of letters below determine what the order of the letters is and decide what the next two letters
should be. From the suggested answers at the right choose the one that gives the next two letters in the
series.

abcdefghijklmnopqrstuvwxyz

		A)	B)	C)	D)	E)	
1.	a b x c d x e	A) f x	B) g x	C) g h	D) j x	E) e x	_____
2.	a a b c c d e	A) e e	B) f f	C) e f	D) e g	E) g g	_____
3.	z p y p x p w	A) p v	B) v p	C) w p	D) p w	E) o p	_____
4.	r s t r s t r	A) t r	B) s t	C) r s	D) r t	E) t u	_____
5.	j l n p r t v	A) x z	B) w x	C) y z	D) r t	E) w y	_____
6.	j a k b l c m	A) e d	B) n o	C) d n	D) l c	E) n p	_____
7.	a d t e h t i	A) i j	B) l t	C) k m	D) m k	E) n p	_____
8.	z z a y y b x	A) z x	B) c c	C) c x	D) x x	E) x c	_____
9.	i i j k k l m	A) z i	B) m o	C) m n	D) m i	E) n m	_____
10.	a d e f g j k	A) l m	B) n o	C) a d	D) m n	E) o p	_____
11.	z l w m t n q	A) p o	B) o n	C) l v	D) k r	E) q r	_____
12.	f p h n j l l	A) j n	B) l m	C) m p	D) j k	E) l n	_____
13.	a g e k i o m	A) s q	B) q s	C) p r	D) n o	E) a g	_____
14.	e h g j i l k	A) l m	B) n m	C) m l	D) p o	E) e h	_____
15.	b c f g h k l	A) n m	B) p q	C) m p	D) m n	E) p n	_____
16.	a y b v c s d	A) r p	B) r q	C) e e	D) p e	E) q e	_____

abcdefghijklmnopqrstuvwxyz

17. a b d a b e a .... A) b c   B) b f   C) b a   D) a f   E) a a   _____

18. a z b y c x d .... A) w e   B) e w   C) v u   D) f t   E) u e   _____

19. a g d j g m j .... A) p m   B) r o   C) o r   D) k d   E) j o   _____

20. g d j g m j p .... A) m s   B) j l   C) j n   D) k p   E) p s   _____

21. f e t j i t n .... A) t m   B) m t   C) p o   D) o t   E) n m   _____

22. c q e o g m i .... A) o q   B) i k   C) k k   D) k m   E) k n   _____

23. a b s c d t e .... A) h i   B) f g   C) h e   D) e u   E) f u   _____

24. y h w i u j s .... A) k q   B) r q   C) q p   D) y h   E) t r   _____

25. a f b g c h d .... A) e f   B) i e   C) i j   D) j k   E) j r   _____

26. d g f i h k j .... A) m l   B) m n   C) n o   D) n m   E) l k   _____

27. a b d g h j m .... A) n o   B) n q   C) o q   D) n p ·   E) o p   _____

28. d o g p j q m .... A) r o   B) r p   C) r m   D) r t   E) r r   _____

29. b c e f h i k l n .... A) r s   B) o q   C) p t   D) o p   E) p s   _____

30. a y c w e u g s i .... A) m k   B) m n   C) q m   D) q k   E) s i   _____

ANSWER EXPLANATIONS FOR PRACTICE SET 5

1. **(A)** a b x c d x e f x
   Two consecutive letters, then the letter x, followed by the next two consecutive letters, then x, and so on.

2. **(C)** a a b c c d e e f
   A letter twice, then the next consecutive letter once; the next consecutive letter twice, then the next consecutive letter once; and so on.

3. **(A)** z p y p x p w p v
   The letter p alternating with consecutive letters going backward.

4. **(B)** r s t r s t r s t
   The letters $r s t$ repeating.

5. **(A)** j l n p r t v x z
   Consecutive letters skipping every other letter.

6. **(C)** j a k b l c m d n
   Two alternating groups of consecutive letters: $j k l m n$ and $a b c d$.

7. **(B)** a d t e h t i l t
   Beginning with a, skip two letters, then the next letter, insert a t; the next letter, skip two, then the next letter h, insert a t; and so on. This is a difficult problem.

8. **(E)** z z a y y b x x c
   Two alternating groups of letters: the first group doubles each letter and goes backward consecutively; the second group goes forward consecutively.

9. **(C)** i i j k k l m m n
   Consecutive letters forward; however, every other letter is doubled.

10. **(A)** a d e f g j k l m
    Beginning with a, skip two letters, then the next three consecutive letters; then skip two letters, then the next three consecutive letters.

11. **(B)** z l w m t n q o n
    Two alternating groups of letters: the first group goes backward skipping two letters (z, w, t, q, n); the other group goes forward consecutively (l, m, n, o).

12. **(A)** f p h n j l l j n
    Two alternating groups of letters: one group goes forward skipping every other letter (f, h, j, l, n); the other group goes backward skipping every other letter (p, n, l, j).

13. **(A)** a g e k i o m s q
    Ahead six, back two; repeat.
14. **(B)** e h g j i l k n m
    Ahead three, back one; repeat.
15. **(C)** b c f g h k l m p
    The pattern is three consecutive letters, then skip the next two, then repeat. Note that the pattern begins one letter in on the first group of three (*b c* instead of *a b c*).
16. **(D)** a y b v c s d p e
    Two alternating groups of letters: the first group is consecutive letters going forward (*a, b, c, d, e*); the second group skips two letters (*y, v, s, p*) going backward.
17. **(B)** a b d a b e a b f
    Consecutive letters beginning with *d* (*d, e, f*), each preceded by *a b*: *a b d, a b e, a b f*.
18. **(A)** a z b y c x d w e
    Two alternating groups of letters: the first group goes forward consecutively (*a, b, c, d, e*); the other group goes backward consecutively (*z, y, x, w*).
19. **(A)** a g d j g m j p m
    Two alternating groups of letters: both groups go forward skipping every two letters (*a, d, g, j, m* and *g, j, m, p*).
20. **(A)** g d j g m j p m s
    Two alternating groups of letters: both groups go forward, skipping every two letters (*g, j, m, p, s* and *d, g, j, m*).
21. **(B)** f e t j i t n m t
    Two letters backward, insert *t*, skip four letters forward; two letters backward, insert *t*, skip four letters forward; and so on.
22. **(C)** c q e o g m i k k
    Two alternating groups of letters: the first group goes forward, skipping every other letter (*c, e,*

g, i, k); the other group goes backward, skipping every other letter (*q, o, m, k*).
23. **(E)** a b s c d t e f u
    Two alternating groups of letters: the first group consists of pairs of consecutive letters (*a b, c d, e f, g h*); the other group, beginning with *s*, goes backward consecutively (*s, t, u*).
24. **(A)** y h w i u j s k q
    Two alternating groups of letters: the first group goes backward, skipping every other letter (*y, w, u, s, q*); the other group goes forward consecutively (*h, i, j, k*).
25. **(B)** a f b g c h d i e
    Two alternating groups of letters: each group goes forward consecutively (*a, b, c, d, e* and *f, g, h, i*).
26. **(A)** d g f i h k j m l
    Ahead three, back one; repeat.
27. **(D)** a b d g h j m n p
    Beginning with *a*, the next consecutive letter, then skip one letter, then skip two letters; repeat.
28. **(B)** d o g p j q m r p
    Two alternating groups of letters: the first goes forward but skips two letters (*d, g, j, m, p*); the second group goes forward consecutively (*o, p, q, r*).
29. **(B)** b c e f h i k l n o q
    Going forward: a pair of consecutive letters, then skip one letter; the next consecutive pair, then skip one letter; and so on.
30. **(D)** a y c w e u g s i q k
    Two alternating groups of letters: the first group goes forward skipping every other letter (*a, c, e, g, i, k*); the other group goes backward skipping every other letter (*y, w, u, s, q*).

Appendix A

Samples of
    Questions for the Telephone Operator Test
    Questions for the Accounting Clerk Test
    Questions for the Computation Test
    Questions for the Clerical Checking Test

The following four types of tests are *no longer used* on the Federal Civil Service Examinations. We have not deleted them from our appendix because some state and local agencies may still use one or all of these types.

THE TELEPHONE OPERATOR TEST

MEASURES SKILL IN HEARING AND REMEMBERING NUMBERS

Questions like samples 29 through 39 are to test the accuracy with which you hear numbers like telephone numbers and make correct connections for the numbers that you hear. In the test, the examiner will give you a number as the first question, then pause for you to answer the question, then give you a number as the second question, and so on. For almost every number that the examiner gives, you have that number below, together with three wrong numbers. You are to pick out the number you hear and make a check mark at the right of it. If the number is not one of the four listed for the question, check "none of these."

Part of a list such as the examiner would use in reading these sample questions is shown in the column at the right. Have someone dictate these practice numbers to you.

Just as in the actual test do not ask the examiner to repeat any number. If you miss one, try to get the next question. As you will notice, the dictation is slow at first and then becomes faster. In the first sample, the answer has been checked for you.

SAMPLE QUESTIONS

29. A) 1 3 4 4
    B) 3 1 3 4
    C) 3 1 4 4 ✓
    D) 4 1 3 3
    E) none of these

30. A) 2 6 8 7
    B) 2 7 6 8
    C) 2 8 6 7
    D) 2 8 7 6
    E) none of these

31. A) 1 0 0 9 3
    B) 1 0 9 0 3
    C) 1 9 0 0 3
    D) 1 9 3 0 0
    E) none of these

32. A) 6 2 3 7 5
    B) 6 7 2 3 5
    C) 6 7 2 5 3
    D) 7 6 2 3 5
    E) none of these

33. A) 1 5 5 9 6
    B) 5 1 1 6 9
    C) 5 1 9 9 6
    D) 5 5 1 9 6
    E) none of these

34. A) 3 2 8 9 7
    B) 3 8 2 9 7
    C) 3 8 9 2 7
    D) 8 3 2 9 7
    E) none of these

35. A) 4 1 3 6 2
    B) 4 1 6 2 3
    C) 4 1 6 3 2
    D) 4 6 1 3 2
    E) none of these

36. A) 6 6 8 1
    B) 8 1 6 6
    C) 8 8 6 1
    D) 8 0 6 6 1
    E) none of these

37. A) 5 7 6 8 5
    B) 5 7 6 8 9
    C) 5 7 8 6 9
    D) 7 5 6 8 9
    E) none of these

38. A) 4 7 2 8
    B) 4 7 8 2
    C) 4 0 7 2 8
    D) 4 7 2 0 8
    E) none of these

39. A) 3 6 2 8
    B) 3 8 2 8
    C) 3 8 2 6 8
    D) 8 3 6 2 8
    E) none of these

Sample Examiner's List

The rates at which the examiner is to read are shown by the 10-second markings at the right. He or she should read each number as rapidly as he or she would tell an operator what phone number he or she wants, and then he or she should pause before reading the next. For example, in the first 10 seconds he or she should read 3144, pause, read 2687, pause, and be ready to begin 19300. The pauses become shorter as he or she moves down the list of numbers.

3 1 4 4	
2 6 8 7	10 sec.
1 9 3 0 0	
6 7 2 3 5	20 sec.
5 1 1 9 6	
3 8 2 9 7	
4 1 6 3 2	30 sec.
8 6 6 1	
5 7 6 8 9	
4 7 2 8	
8 3 6 2 8	40 sec.

On the Sample Answer Sheet in the column at the right, you are to show the answer you have checked for each question. Do this by darkening completely the oval under the letter that is the same as the letter of the answer you checked. Be accurate because a check mark beside a correct answer in the list of questions will not do you any good unless you darken the same answer space on the answer sheet.

Sample Answer Sheet

29 A B C D E
30 A B C D E
31 A B C D E
32 A B C D E
33 A B C D E
34 A B C D E
35 A B C D E
36 A B C D E
37 A B C D E
38 A B C D E
39 A B C D E

Correct Answers to Sample Questions

29 A B ● D E
30 ● B C D E
31 A B C D ●
32 A ● C D E
33 A B C D ●
34 A ● C D E
35 A B C D ●
36 A B C D ●
37 A B ● D E
38 ● B C D E
39 A B C D ●

ACCOUNTING CLERK TEST

Questions 9 and 10 are based on the application of the regulation presented below. All information necessary to answer the questions is given in the regulation and in the paragraph of directions following the regulation.

Regulation (on which sample questions 9 and 10 are based):
Full-time employees shall earn and be credited with sick leave at the rate of 4 hours per pay period of two workweeks duration. Four work hours are equal to ½ workday.

Directions (for sample questions 9 and 10):
The following table gives the sick-leave records of two full-time employees for the current leave year. For each of these employees the workweek consists of five 8-hour days and the leave year consists of 26 pay periods. For each employee, determine the balance of accumulated sick leave to the credit of the employee at the end of the current leave year. At the right side of the table are four suggested answers designated A, B, C, and D, at the top of the columns. If one of the suggested answers is correct, darken the proper space on the Sample Answer Sheet. If the correct answer is not given under A, B, C, or D, darken the space under E on the Sample Answer Sheet.

Questions:

Em-ployee	Accumulated Sick Leave from Preceding Year	Sick Leave Used in Current Year	Balance of Accumulated Sick Leave at End of Current Year				
			A	B	C	D	E
	Days - Hours	Days Hours	Days Hours	Days Hours	Days Hours	Days Hours	Days Hours
9. No. 9	8 – 4	2 – 1	6 – 3	19 – 3	23 – 5	32 – 3	None of these
10. No. 10	60 – 0	8 – 7	51 – 3	51 – 7	64 – 3	68 – 7	these

11. A voucher contained the following items:

6 desks @ $89.20 . . . . $525.20
8 chairs @ $32.50 . . . . 260.00

Total $885.20

The terms were given on the voucher as 3%, 10 days; net, 30 days. Verify the computations, which may be incorrect, and calculate the correct amount to be paid. If payment is made within the discount period, the amount to be paid is

A) $761.64
B) $771.34
C) $795.20
D) $858.64
E) none of these

**Sample
Answer Sheet**

9   A B C D E
10 A B C D E
11 A B C D E
12 A B C D E
13 A B C D E

Questions 12 and 13 are based on the following portion of a withholding tax table:

If the payroll period with respect to an employee is MONTHLY:

And wages are —		And number of withholding exemptions claimed is				
At least	But less than	0	1	2	3	4
		The amount of income tax to be withheld shall be				
$688	$704	$125.20	$85.20	$45.20	$ 5.20	0
704	720	128.00	88.00	48.00	8.00	0
720	736	131.20	91.20	51.20	11.20	0

**Correct Answers to
Sample Questions**

9   A B C D E
10 A B C D E
11 A B C D E
12 A B C D E
13 A B C D E

12. K received a monthly wage of $705.60 the first 3 months of the year and $730.00 the remaining 9 months. He claimed 3 exemptions for the first 4 months and 4 for the remaining 8 months. What was the total income tax withheld during the year?

A) $ 0.00
B) $24.00
C) $35.20
D) $44.80
E) none of these

13. L, who has 2 exemptions, receives a monthly wage of $702.00. If no amounts other than income tax were withheld, his monthly take-home pay would be

A) $616.80
B) $656.80
C) $696.80
D) $702.00
E) none of these

COMPUTATION TEST

These sample questions show how the questions are to be recorded. Read the directions for each set of questions and then answer them. Record your answers on the Sample Answer Sheets provided on each page of this booklet. Then compare your answers with those given in the Correct Answers to Sample Questions on the same page. Solve each problem and see which of the suggested answers is correct. Darken the space on the Sample Answer Sheet corresponding to the correct answer. Some questions have four suggested answers, others have five.

Computations

1. Add:
963
257
416
____

Answers
A) 1,516
B) 1,526
C) 1,636
D) 1,726
E) none of these

2. Add:
1,725
881
40
____

Answers
A) 2,556
B) 2,546
C) 2,646
D) 2,456
E) none of these

3. Add:
245
413
____

Answers
A) 658
B) 657
C) 655
D) 656
E) none of these

4. Add:
653
972
148
____

Answers
A) 1,752
B) 1,673
C) 1,773
D) 1,653
E) none of these

5. Add:
75
6
89
____

Answers
A) 168
B) 170
C) 196
D) 171
E) none of these

6. Multiply:
45
5
____

Answers
A) 200
B) 215
C) 225
D) 235
E) none of these

7. Multiply:
70
9
____

Answers
A) 629
B) 620
C) 639
D) 640
E) none of these

8. Multiply:
952
34
____

Answers
A) 33,378
B) 31,367
C) 30,267
D) 32,368
E) none of these

9. Multiply:
280
62
____

Answers
A) 17,360
B) 17,267
C) 17,362
D) 17,260
E) none of these

10. Multiply:
346.05
.83
_____

Answers
A) 287.2225
B) 287.2015
C) 287.2215
D) 287.2205
E) none of these

Sample Answer Sheet

	A	B	C	D	E
1	○	○	○	○	○
2	○	○	○	○	○
3	○	○	○	○	○
4	○	○	○	○	○
5	○	○	○	○	○
6	○	○	○	○	○
7	○	○	○	○	○
8	○	○	○	○	○
9	○	○	○	○	○
10	○	○	○	○	○

Correct Answers to Sample Questions

	A	B	C	D	E
1	○	○	●	○	○
2	○	○	●	○	○
3	●	○	○	○	○
4	○	●	○	○	○
5	○	●	○	○	○
6	○	○	●	○	○
7	○	●	○	○	○
8	○	○	○	●	○
9	●	○	○	○	○
10	○	○	●	○	○

11. Subtract:	*Answers*	12. Subtract:	*Answers*	13. Subtract:	*Answers*
33	A) 25	685	A) 621	1,970	A) 1,110
8	B) 26	74	B) 611	858	B) 1,112
——	C) 35	——	C) 521	——	C) 1,111
	D) 36		D) 601		D) 1,100
	E) none of these		E) none of these		E) none of these

14. Subtract:	*Answers*	15. Subtract:	*Answers*	16. Divide:	*Answers*
2,973	A) 688	790	A) 509		A) 3
2,284	B) 678	281	B) 500	$40 \overline{\smash{)}1{,}208}$	B) 30
——	C) 679	——	C) 508		C) 33
	D) 689		D) 501		D) 40
	E) none of these		E) none of these		E) none of these

17. Divide:	*Answers*	18. Divide:	*Answers*	19. Divide:	*Answers*
	A) 12		A) 20		A) 2,110
$9 \overline{\smash{)}189}$	B) 20	$6 \overline{\smash{)}126}$	B) 24	$85 \overline{\smash{)}170{,}850}$	B) 2,000
	C) 22		C) 22		C) 2,010
	D) 21		D) 26		D) 2,001
	E) none of these		E) none of these		E) none of these

20. Divide:	*Answers*
	A) .0000025
	B) .000025
$.005 \overline{\smash{)}.000025}$	C) .0025
	D) .025
	E) none of these

Sample Answer Sheet

```
    A B C D E
11  ○ ○ ○ ○ ○
12  ○ ○ ○ ○ ○
13  ○ ○ ○ ○ ○
14  ○ ○ ○ ○ ○
15  ○ ○ ○ ○ ○
16  ○ ○ ○ ○ ○
17  ○ ○ ○ ○ ○
18  ○ ○ ○ ○ ○
19  ○ ○ ○ ○ ○
20  ○ ○ ○ ○ ○
```

Correct Answers to Sample Questions

```
    A B C D E
11  ● ○ ○ ○ ○
12  ○ ● ○ ○ ○
13  ○ ● ○ ○ ○
14  ○ ○ ● ○ ○
15  ● ○ ○ ○ ○
16  ○ ○ ● ○ ○
17  ○ ● ○ ○ ○
18  ○ ○ ○ ● ○
19  ○ ● ○ ○ ○
20  ○ ○ ○ ● ○
```

THE CLERICAL CHECKING TEST

This type of test has been used in the past, but is presently *no longer used* by the federal government. It is used by some companies and state and local governments.

The test takes 8 minutes total for both parts. It is scored rights minus wrongs. There are 125 proper name pairs and 125 digit span pairs. The digit pairs range from 3 digits to 9 digits.

The name pairs use proper people and corporate names. First name, middle initial, and last names; first initial, middle name, and last names; and first and middle initial and last names are all used in the pairs.

1.	Robert Levenson - Roberta Levenson
2.	E. G. Cummings - E. G. Cummings
3.	Arthur Jerome Ash - Arthur Jerome Asch
4.	William M. Smythe - William N. Smythe
5.	etc.

1.	27349801 - 17134801
2.	493 - 492
3.	58700 - 58709
4.	98001 - 98001
5.	etc.

Mark A if the two names or numbers are exactly alike.
Mark B if the two names or numbers differ in any way.

Appendix B

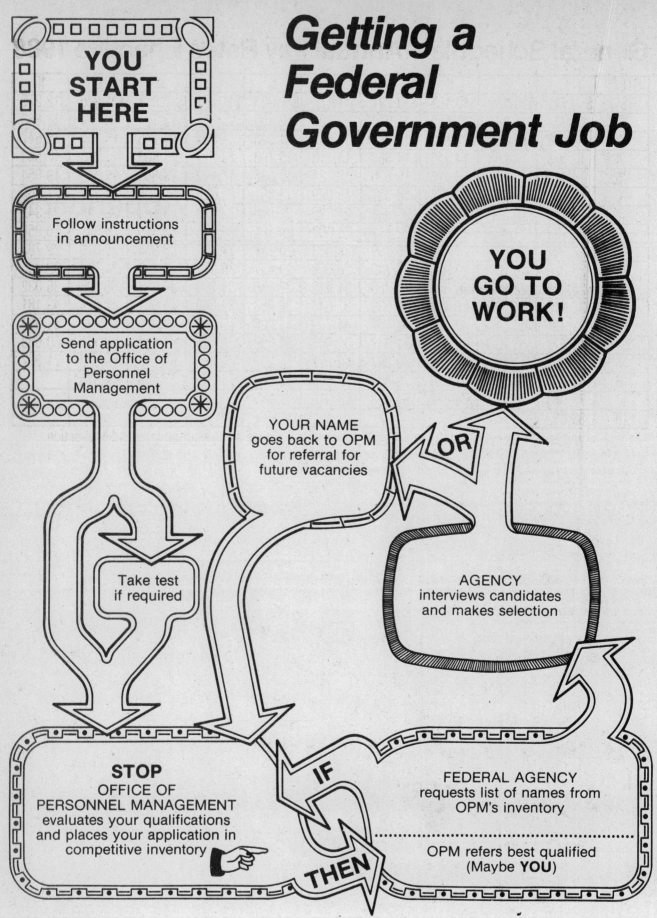

Getting a
Federal
Government Job

YOU
START
HERE

Follow instructions
in announcement

Send application
to the Office of
Personnel
Management

Take test
if required

STOP
OFFICE OF
PERSONNEL MANAGEMENT
evaluates your qualifications
and places your application in
competitive inventory

YOUR NAME
goes back to OPM
for referral for
future vacancies

YOU
GO TO
WORK!

OR

AGENCY
interviews candidates
and makes selection

IF

THEN

FEDERAL AGENCY
requests list of names from
OPM's inventory

OPM refers best qualified
(Maybe **YOU**)

General Schedule—Annual Pay Rates Effective 1988

STEPS	1	2	3	4	5	6	7	8	9	10
GS-1	$ 9,811	$10,139	$10,465	$10,791	$11,117	$11,309	$11,631	$11,955	$11,970	$12,275
2	11,032	11,294	11,659	11,970	12,103	12,459	12,815	13,171	13,527	13,883
3	12,038	12,439	12,840	13,241	13,642	14,043	14,444	14,845	15,246	15,647
4	13,513	13,963	14,413	14,863	15,313	15,763	16,213	16,663	17,113	17,563
5	15,118	15,622	16,126	16,630	17,134	17,638	18,142	18,646	19,150	19,654
6	16,851	17,413	17,975	18,537	19,099	19,661	20,223	20,785	21,347	21,909
7	18,726	19,350	19,974	20,598	21,222	21,846	22,470	23,094	23,718	24,342
8	20,739	21,430	22,121	22,812	23,503	24,194	24,885	25,576	26,267	26,958
9	22,907	23,671	24,435	25,199	25,963	26,727	27,491	28,255	29,019	29,783
10	25,226	26,067	26,908	27,749	28,590	29,431	30,272	31,113	31,954	32,795
11	27,716	28,640	29,564	30,488	31,412	32,336	33,260	34,184	35,108	36,032
12	33,218	34,325	35,432	36,539	37,646	38,753	39,860	40,967	42,074	43,181
13	39,501	40,818	42,135	43,452	44,769	46,086	47,403	48,720	50,037	51,354
14	46,679	48,235	49,791	51,347	52,903	54,459	56,015	57,571	59,127	60,683
15	54,907	56,737	58,567	60,397	62,227	64,057	65,887	67,717	69,547	71,377
16	64,397	66,544	68,691	70,838	72,500	73,660*	75,765*	77,870*	79,975*	
17	73,958*	76,423*	78,888*	81,353*	83,818*					
18	86,682*									

*Federal employees who earn more than $72,500 receive no increase as a result of congressional action.
U.S. Office of Personnel Management

QUALIFICATION STANDARDS

All of the jobs listed on the next page are covered by the Verbal Abilities Test and Clerical Abilities Test, except for Sales Store Clerical and Data Transcriber, which are covered by the Clerical Speed Test only.

Also, any *seasonal* job at the Internal Revenue Service would probably use the Clerical Speed Test only. (Seasonal jobs are jobs which exist only during the first half of a year when tax returns are being processed.)

The two tests are used at grades GS–2, GS–3, and GS–4. No test is required for GS–1, or GS–5, with one exception: the Clerk-Stenographer requires the two tests at the GS–5 level.

The typing and stenographer speeds described on the following pages are the official speeds. The length of education and experience which are qualifying are those shown here; these reflect the new standards.

QUALIFICATION STANDARDS

MINIMUM QUALIFICATION REQUIREMENTS FOR ONE-GRADE INTERVAL CLERICAL AND ADMINISTRATIVE SUPPORT POSITIONS

(p. 1)

This qualification standard is to be used for one-grade interval clerical and administrative support positions. Two-grade interval positions in any of these series are covered by the appropriate standard for two-grade interval occupations. Following is a list of occupational series covered by this standard. For a description of the work performed and of typical grade levels in these occupations, refer to the series definitions in the *Handbook of Occupational Groups and Series of Classes* and/or to individual position classification standards.

GS-072	Fingerprint Identification	GS-545	Military Pay
GS-134	Intelligence Aid and Clerk	GS-561	Budget Clerical and Assistance
GS-203	Personnel Clerical and Assistance	GS-590	Time and Leave
GS-204	Military Personnel Clerical and Technician	GS-592	Tax Examining
GS-302	Messenger*	GS-593	Insurance Accounts
GS-303	Miscellaneous Clerk and Assistant	GS-675	Medical Record Technician
GS-304	Information Receptionist	GS-679	Medical Clerk
GS-305	Mail and File	GS-963	Legal Instruments Examining
GS-309	Correspondence Clerk	GS-986	Legal Clerk and Technician
GS-312	Clerk-Stenographer and Reporter	GS-998	Claims Clerical
GS-318	Secretary	GS-1001	General Arts and Information
GS-319	Closed Microphone Reporting	GS-1046	Language Clerical
GS-322	Clerk-Typist	GS-1087	Editorial Assistance
GS-332	Computer Operation	GS-1101	General Business and Industry
GS-335	Computer Clerk and Assistant	GS-1105	Purchasing
GS-344	Management Clerical and Assistance	GS-1106	Procurement Clerical and Assistance
GS-350	Equipment Operator	GS-1107	Property Disposal Clerical and Technician
GS-351	Printing Clerical	GS-1152	Production Control
GS-356	Data Transcriber	GS-1411	Library Technician
GS-357	Coding	GS-1421	Archives Technician
GS-359	Electric Accounting Machine Operation	GS-1531	Statistical Assistant
GS-382	Telephone Operating	GS-1802	Compliance Inspection and Support
GS-385	Teletypist	GS-1897	Customs Aid
GS-388	Cryptographic Equipment Operation	GS-2005	Supply Clerical and Technician
GS-390	Communications Relay Operation	GS-2091	Sales Store Clerical
GS-392	General Communications	GS-2102	Transportation Clerk and Assistant
GS-394	Communications Clerical	GS-2131	Freight Rate
GS-503	Financial Clerical and Assistance	GS-2132	Travel
GS-525	Accounting Technician	GS-2133	Passenger Rate
GS-530	Cash Processing	GS-2134	Shipment Clerical and Assistance
GS-540	Voucher Examining	GS-2151	Dispatching
GS-544	Payroll		

---

*Under 5 U.S.C. 3310, appointment to Messenger positions is restricted to persons entitled to veteran preference as long as such persons are available.

September 1987

GS-1/6 and above: The following table shows total amounts of experience required and allowable substitutions of education for that experience.

Grade/Positions	Experience		OR	Education
	General	Specialized		
GS-1 All positions	None	None		None
GS-2 All positions	3 months	None		High school graduation or equivalent
GS-3 Clerk-Steno ——————— All other positions	6 months	None		High school graduation or equivalent ——————— 1 year above high school
GS-4 All positions	1 year	None		2 years above high school
GS-5 Clerk-Steno ——————— All other positions	2 years ——— None	None ——— 1 year equivalent to GS-4		4 years above high school (There is no educational substitution for Reporting Stenographer, Shorthand Reporter, or Closed Microphone Reporter positions.)
GS-6 and above All positions	None	1 year equivalent to next lower grade level		Generally, not applicable

Equivalent combinations of education and experience are qualifying for all grade levels and positions for which both education and experience are acceptable.

EXPERIENCE

General Experience—(All positions except Reporting Stenographer, Shorthand Reporter, and Closed Microphone Reporter): Progressively responsible clerical, office, or other work which indicates ability to acquire the particular knowledge and skills needed to perform the duties of the position to be filled. Specialized experience may be substituted for general experience.

Specialized Experience—(All positions except Reporting Stenographer, Shorthand Reporter, and Closed Microphone Reporter): Experience which is directly related to the position to be filled and which has equipped the candidate with the particular knowledge, skills, and abilities to successfully perform the duties of that position. To be creditable, specialized experience must have been at least equivalent to the next lower grade level.

Experience for Reporting Stenographer, Shorthand Reporter, and Closed Microphone Reporter—One year of experience at least equivalent to the next lower grade level using the skills and equipment appropriate to the position to be filled is required for all positions. Following is a description of qualifying experience for these positions.

Reporting Stenographer, GS-5: Experience as a clerk-stenographer, secretary, reporting stenographer, or in another position which included application of stenography and typing skills as a significant part of the work.

Reporting Stenographer, Shorthand Reporter, and Closed Microphone Reporter, GS-6: Experience as a reporting stenographer, hearing reporter, or in another position in which the primary duty was to make and transcribe manual or machine-written shorthand records of hearings, interviews, or similar proceedings.

Shorthand Reporter and Closed Microphone Reporter, GS-7 and above: Experience as a court reporter, or hearing reporter, or in another position in which the primary duty was to make verbatim records of proceedings.

Use of Selective Factors—Agencies may identify some positions in an occupation, especially at the higher grade levels, that require knowledge, skills, and abilities (KSA's) that are in addition to the minimum requirements described in this standard. The need for these special requirements can be met through the use of selective factors in both the competitive and inservice recruitment processes. Selective factors must be job related, essential for the successful performance of the position, and represent KSA's which could not be reasonably acquired on the job during the period of training customary for the position being filled.

EDUCATION

High school graduation or the equivalent may be substituted for experience at the GS-2 level for the occupations listed, except Clerk-Stenographer, where it may be substituted for experience at the GS-3 entry level.

Successfully completed education above the high school level in any field for which high school graduation or the equivalent is a prerequisite may be substituted for the experience required at grades GS-3 through GS-5 for all positions except Reporting Stenographer, GS-5. This education must have been obtained in an accredited business, secretarial or technical school, junior college, college or university. One full year of full time academic study is 30 semester hours, 45 quarter hours, or the equivalent, of college or at least 20 hours of classroom instruction per week for approximately 36 weeks in a business, secretarial, or technical school.

September 1987

CLERICAL AND ADMINISTRATIVE SUPPORT POSITIONS

As a general rule, education may not be substituted for experience above GS-5 for most positions covered by this standard; however, graduate education may be substituted for experience in those few instances where the graduate education is directly related to the work of the position.

Intensive Short-Term Training—Completion of an intensive, specialized course of study of less than 1 year (such as for computer operator) may meet in full the experience requirements for GS-3. Courses of this type normally require completion of up to 40 hours per week of instruction rather than the usual 20 hours per week and are usually of *at least* 3 months duration. Such courses may have been obtained through a variety of programs such as those offered by business or technical schools, and through military training programs. To be creditable, such a course must have been designed specifically as career preparation for the work of the position being filled and must have provided the applicant with the necessary knowledge, skills, and abilities to do the work.

COMBINING EDUCATION AND EXPERIENCE

Equivalent combinations of successfully completed post high school education and experience may be used to meet total experience requirements at grades GS-5 and below, except for Reporting Stenographer, GS-5.

For GS-3 and GS-4 level positions, determine the applicant's total qualifying experience as a percentage of the experience required for the grade level; then determine the applicant's education as a percentage of the education required for the grade level; then add the 2 percentages. The total percentage must equal at least 100 percent to qualify an applicant for that grade level.

For all GS-5 level positions (except Clerk-Stenographer, which does not require specialized experience), only education in excess of the first 60 semester hours (i.e., beyond the 2nd year) is creditable toward meeting the specialized experience requirement. One full academic year of study (30 semester hours) *beyond the 2nd year* is equivalent to 6 months of specialized experience.

The following are examples of how education and experience may be combined. They are examples only, and are not all inclusive:

• The position to be filled is a Payroll Clerk, GS-4. An applicant has 8 months of qualifying experience and 20 semester hours of college. The applicant meets 67 percent of the required experience and 33 percent of the required education. The applicant meets 100 percent of the total requirements and is qualified for the position.

• The position to be filled is a Clerk-Typist, GS-4. The applicant has 4 months of qualifying experience and 1 year of business school. The applicant meets 33 percent of the required experience and 50 percent of the required education. The applicant meets 83 percent of the total requirements and is not qualified for the position.

• The position to be filled is a Clerk-Stenographer, GS-5. An applicant has 1 year of qualifying experience and 90 semester hours of college. The applicant meets 50 percent of the required experience and 75 percent of the required education. The applicant exceeds 100 percent of the total requirements and is qualified for the position.

• The position to be filled is a Personnel Clerk, GS-5. The applicant has 9 months of specialized experience and 75 semester hours of college (15 semester hours beyond the 2nd year and the equivalent of 3 months of specialized experience). The applicant meets 75 percent of the required experience and 25 percent of the required education. The applicant meets 100 percent of the requirement for 1 year of specialized experience and is qualified for the position.

WRITTEN TEST REQUIREMENTS

No written test is required for appointment to positions at the GS-1 level.

A written test is required at grades GS-2 through GS-4 for competitive appointment to all positions covered by this standard.

A written test is required at the GS-5 level for competitive appointment to Clerk-Stenographer, GS-312, positions only. No written test is required for other positions covered by this standard at GS-5 or above.

For inservice placement action the written test is not required. If a written test is used, it may not be used on a pass/fail basis. However, typing, data transcription, and stenographic proficiency, where required, may be demonstrated for inservice actions through the appropriate performance test, proficiency certificate, or self-certification.

PROFICIENCY REQUIREMENTS

Clerk-Typist, Clerk-Stenographer, Data Transcriber and Positions with Parenthetical Titles of (Typing), (Stenography), or (Data Transcription)

In addition to meeting experience or education requirements, applicants for these positions must show possession of the following skills, as appropriate. Applicants may meet these requirements by passing the appropriate performance test, presenting a certificate of proficiency from a school or other organization authorized to issue such certificates by the Office of Personnel Management local office, or by self-certifying their proficiency. Performance test results and certificates of proficiency are acceptable for 3 years. Agencies may verify proficiency skills of self-certified applicants by administering the appropriate performance test.

> Clerk-Typist, GS-2/4 and (Typing) (any grade):
> 40 words per minute typing speed†
>
> Data Transcriber, GS-2/4 and (Data Transcription) (any grade)
> skill in operating an alphanumeric data transcribing machine
> *or* 20 words per minute typing speed† for GS-2 transcription duties
> *or* 25 words per minute typing speed† for GS-3 and GS-4 transcription duties
>
> Clerk-Stenographer, GS-3/4:
> 40 words per minute typing speed† *and*
> 80 words per minute dictation speed‡
>
> Clerk-Stenographer, GS-5:
> 40 words per minute typing speed† *and*
> 120 words per minute dictation speed‡
>
> (Stenography) (any grade):
> 40 words per minute typing speed† *and either*
> 80 words per minute dictation speed‡ for GS-3 and GS-4 stenographic duties *or*
> 120 words per minute dictation speed‡ for GS-5 stenographic duties

NOTE: The level of proficiency for stenographic and data transcribing duties required by positions with parenthetical titles is based on the grade level of those duties and not necessarily on the overall grade of the position. For example, a position classified as Secretary (Stenography), GS-318-5, may require either 80 or 120 words per minute dictation speed depending upon the level of difficulty of the stenographic duties. Or, a position classified as Payroll Clerk (Data Transcription), GS-544-4, may require either 20 or 25 words per minute depending upon the level of difficulty of the transcribing duties.

Therefore, before filling positions of this type, first determine the grade level of the duties which require the additional skill, then determine the skill level required. (For further information on this requirement, see Flysheet No. 1 to the position classification standard for the Clerk-Stenographer and Reporter Series, GS-312.)

Reporting Stenographer, Shorthand Reporter, and Closed Microphone Reporter

In addition to meeting the experience requirements, applicants for these positions must show possession of the following skills with equipment appropriate to the specific position.

> Reporting Stenographer, GS-5/6: 120 words per minute dictation speed§
>
> Shorthand Reporter and Closed Microphone Reporter, GS-6: 160 words per minute dictation speed§
>
> Shorthand Reporter and Closed Microphone Reporter, GS-7 and above: 175 words per minute dictation speed§

Applicants must also be able to produce accurate typewritten transcripts of recorded proceedings.

Applicants for competitive appointment and inservice applicants for initial assignment to these three positions at all grade levels must demonstrate the specific skill and level of proficiency required by the position to be filled. Also, inservice applicants for promotion to positions which have a higher proficiency requirement than the position previously held must demonstrate the higher level of proficiency. Applicants may demonstrate this proficiency by either passing a dictation test at the required speed or presenting a certificate of proficiency showing speed and accuracy equivalent to those used in the Office of Personnel Management's performance tests for these positions. The certificate must show that the candidate demonstrated the required proficiency, i.e., dictation speed, to a teacher of stenography, shorthand reporting, or closed microphone reporting within the past year. Applicants for these positions may not self-certify dictation proficiency.

---

†Words per minute are based on a five minute sample with three or fewer errors.

‡The maximum number of errors allowed in a dictation sample equals 10% of the required dictation speed (80 wpm or 120 wpm) multiplied by the number of minutes in the sample.

§The maximum number of errors allowed in a dictation sample for these 3 positions equals 5% of the required dictation speed multiplied by the number of minutes in the sample.

United States Office of Personnel Management

Office of Washington Examining Services
P.O. Box 14179
Washington, D.C. 20044

Announcement No. WA-8-06
November 1987
Open Continuous

Clerical Positions

Clerk-Typist, GS-2/3/4

Clerk-Stenographer, GS-3/4/5

Secretary, GS-3/4

***Messenger, GS-2/3/4**

Clerical Support Positions, GS-2/3/4

Do Not Apply Under This Announcement for Summer Jobs

Location of Jobs

Washington, D.C.; Maryland: Counties of Charles, Montgomery, and Prince Georges; **Virginia:** Cities of Alexandria, Fairfax, and Falls Church and Counties of Arlington, Fairfax, King George, Loudoun, Prince William, and Stafford; and **Overseas Atlantic.**

Salary

Federal salary rates are adjusted periodically. Current information regarding salaries may be obtained from the Federal Job Information/Testing Center in the Office of Personnel Management, 1900 E Street NW., Washington, D.C. 20415.

Occupations Covered

Clerk/Assistant	Computer Operator	Military Pay Clerk
Clerk-Stenographer	Management Clerk/Assistant	Payroll Clerk
Clerk-Typist	Medical Clerk	Tax Accounting Clerk
*Messenger	Medical Records Clerk/Technician	Time and Leave Clerk
Secretary	Information Reception Clerk	Voucher Examining Clerk
Archives Clerk/Technician	Office Equipment Operator	Fingerprint Identification Clerk
Arts and Information Clerk	Printing Clerk	Intelligence Clerk/Aid
Business Clerk	Supply Clerk/Technician	Language Clerk
Procurement Clerk/Assistant	Dispatching Clerk	Claims Clerk
Production Control Clerk	Passenger Rate Clerk	Legal Clerk/Technician
Property Disposal Clerk/Technician	Transportation Clerk/Assistant	Legal Instruments Examining Clerk
Purchasing Agent	Customs Clerk/Aid	Correspondence Clerk
Coding Clerk	Library Clerk/Technician	Mail and File Clerk
Communications Clerk	Editorial Clerk/Assistant	Personnel Clerk/Assistant
Communications Relay Operator	Electronic Accounting Machine Operator	Military Personnel Clerk/Technician
Communications Technician	Accounting Clerk/Technician	Statistical Clerk/Assistant
Cryptographic Equipment Operator	Budget Clerk/Assistant	Telephone Operator
Teletypist	Cash Processing Clerk	Freight Rate Clerk
Compliance Inspection Clerk	Financial Clerk/Assistant	Shipping Clerk/Assistant
Computer Clerk/Assistant	Insurance Accounts Clerk	Travel Clerk

This list may not be all-inclusive.

Qualification Requirements

A WRITTEN TEST IS REQUIRED FOR ALL OCCUPATIONS COVERED BY THIS ANNOUNCEMENT.
The following chart reflects the minimum qualification requirements.

GRADE/POSITIONS	EDUCATION	OR	EXPERIENCE	
			GENERAL	SPECIALIZED
GS-2—ALL POSITIONS	High school graduation or equivalent	OR	3 months	None
GS-3 Clerk-Steno	High school graduation or equivalent	OR	6 months	None
GS-3—ALL POSITIONS	1 year above high school	OR	6 months	None
GS-4—ALL POSITIONS	2 years above high school	OR	1 year	None
GS-5 Clerk-Steno	4 years above high school	OR	2 years	None

Equivalent combinations of education and experience are qualifying for all grade levels and positions for which both education and experience are acceptable.

---

* Under 5 U.S.C. 3310, appointment to Messenger positions is restricted to persons entitled to veteran preference as long as such persons are available.

For all positions requiring a qualified typist the minimum typing speed is 40 wpm with three errors or less. Clerk-Stenographer, GS-3/4, and any other occupation at the GS-3/4 level with a parenthetical title of (Stenography) must have a minimum short-hand speed of 80 wpm with 24 errors or less. Clerk-Stenographer, GS-5, must have a minimum shorthand speed of 120 wpm with 18 errors or less. You may meet these requirements at the time of appointment by indicating these skills on your *Application for Federal Employment* (SF 171), presenting a Certificate of Proficiency (OPM Form 680) or taking a performance test given by the agency.

For All Positions

"General experience" is progressively responsible clerical, office OR other work which indicates ability to acquire the particular knowledge and skills needed to perform the duties of the position to be filled.

SPECIALIZED EXPERIENCE MAY BE SUBSTITUTED FOR GENERAL EXPERIENCE. Unpaid or volunteer work will be credited on the same basis as salaried experience.

Education

Successfully completed education above the high school level in any field for which high school graduation or the equivalent is a prerequisite may be substituted for the experience required at grades GS-3 through GS-5 for all positions. This education must have been obtained in an accredited business, secretarial or technical school, junior college, college or university. One full year of full-time academic study is 30 semester hours, 45 quarter hours, or the equivalent, of college or at least 20 hours of classroom instruction per week for approximately 36 weeks in a business, secretarial, or technical school.

Intensive Short-Term Training—Completion of an intensive, specialized course of study of less than one year (such as for computer operator) may meet in full the experience requirements for GS-3. Courses of this type normally require completion of up to 40 hours per week of instruction rather than the usual 20 hours per week and are usually of *at least* three months duration. Such courses may have been obtained through a variety of programs such as those offered by business or technical schools, and through military training programs. To be creditable, such a course must have been designed specifically as career preparation for the work of the position being filled and must have provided the applicant with the necessary knowledge, skills, and abilities to do the work.

No credit will be allowed for training which has been obtained **only** or **primarily** in the basic skill of shorthand or typing refresher courses.

Certificates of Proficiency

If you wish, you may present a Certificate of Proficiency in typing and/or shorthand which meets the speed and accuracy requirements. To be acceptable, the certification must be made on OPM Form 680 or on an official form or letterhead of the testing organization and include the following information:

- The date the test was administered;
- The length of the test in minutes;
- The total number of words typed per minute on at least a 5-minute test, and the total number of errors made; and
- For stenographer, the rate of dictation in words per minute on a 3-minute test, and the total number of errors made.

We accept certificates of proficiency from the following sources:

- Public and parochial schools;
- Accredited private high schools;
- Business, commercial, and secretarial schools accredited by such accrediting organizations as the Association of Independent Colleges and Schools or the appropriate State education department;

- Junior colleges and colleges which are accredited or whose work is accepted for advance credit by the State University of the State in which they are located;
- Courses approved for training under Veterans Administration programs sponsored or approved by the U.S. Office of Education or by an appropriate State Office of Education to provide training or retraining of the handicapped or for vocational rehabilitation purposes;
- Federal, State, or other public or private agencies with programs in support of personnel utilization and economic opportunity such as the Neighborhood Youth Corps, Job Corps, Opportunities Industrialization Centers, and other agencies that provide training under provisions of the Comprehensive Employment and Training Act;
- State Employment Service Offices;
- Military hospitals or agencies and other Federal hospitals or agencies which provide training in connection with occupational therapy or vocational rehabilitation programs in typing and/or shorthand; and
- Federal agencies which provide in-service training in typing or shorthand to civilian or military personnel.

Time Limitations on Certificates of Proficiency

The test on which the certificate of proficiency is based must have been taken within one year of the date on which the certificate was issued. The certificate is good for three years from the date of issue.

How to Apply

1. Take the general written test.
2. Bring to the test room:
   A completed SF 171, *Application for Federal Employment*, if you wish assistance in your efforts to seek employment.

Information About the Test

Written Test—The general test of verbal abilities and clerical aptitude consists of 205 items, 80 of which must be correct to minimally qualify, and requires about two hours to administer to competitors. The test is given on a walk-in basis every Monday through Friday at 8:30 a.m. at the Office of Personnel Management, 1900 E Street, NW., Washington, D.C., in Room 1416. To accommodate those applicants unable to take the morning test, an afternoon test will be given on the third Friday of each month at 1:00 p.m. in Room 1416. Applicants may also take the written test at the locations listed on page 3.

Testing of Applicants With Physical Handicaps

The Blind—If you are blind, you will be required to take the test of verbal abilities but not the clerical aptitude test.

The Deaf—If you are deaf, you will be required to take the clerical aptitude test, but not the verbal abilities test.

Other—Appropriate modifications in the testing procedure may be authorized, depending on the nature of the handicap.

For testing in the Washington, D.C. area, applicants with physical handicaps may call the Office of Personnel Management (632-5528 or 653-9260) to arrange for special testing.

Minimum Age Requirement

You must meet the age requirements. The usual minimum is 18, but high school graduates may apply at 16. If you are 16 or 17 and are out of school but not a high school graduate you may be hired only if (1) you have successfully completed a formal training program preparing you for work (for example, training provided under the Comprehensive Employment and Training Act or in similar Government or private programs), or (2) you have been out of school for at least three months, not counting the summer vacation, and school authorities write a letter on their official stationery agreeing with your preference for work instead of additional schooling. Appropriate forms will be given to you by the agency that wants to hire you.

How to Get a Job

Simplified hiring procedures make it easier for persons seeking Clerical and Administrative Support Positions to be given immediate employment consideration in the Washington, D.C. metropolitan area.

In order to do this you should submit an *Application for Federal Employment* (SF 171) and a copy of your *Notice of Written Test Results* to agencies where you wish to work. **You must keep the original Notice.**

Applicants who have current eligibility for Clerk-Typist/Clerk-Stenographer may submit their *Notice of Results* together with a SF 171 to be considered for employment. These Notices will be valid indefinitely.

Job Information

The Office of Personnel Management furnishes information about Federal employment opportunities, qualification requirements, and application procedures without charge. Residents of the Washington, D.C. metropolitan area may call the Federal Job Information/Testing Center on 653-8468 for information or 254-9847 for forms listed in this announcement. Residents of other areas should check the local telephone directory under "United States Government" for the address and telephone number of the nearest Federal Job Information/Testing Center.

"Civil Service" Schools

The Office of Personnel Management has no connection with any so-called "civil service" school or private employment agency. No "civil service" school or employment agency can guarantee that you will be found qualified for a particular position or that you will rank high enough on a list of eligibles to be offered a job with the Federal Government.

Equal Employment Opportunity

All qualified applicants will receive consideration for appointment without regard to race, religion, color, national origin, sex, political affiliations, handicap, or any other non-merit factor.

Testing Locations

JUSTICE (BUREAU OF PRISONS)
320 1st St., NW., Room 412
Washington, D.C. 20534
Appointment Only (202) 272-4245

AGRICULTURE RESEARCH SERVICE
Personnel Division
Building. 003, Room 319
Beltsville, Maryland 20705
Appointment Only (301) 344-3961

DEPARTMENT OF HEALTH AND
 HUMAN SERVICES
National Institutes of Health
9000 Rockville Pike
Building 31C, Room B3C08
Bethesda, Maryland 20892
Walk-in Test Mon., Wed. and Fri. at
 8:30 a.m.; limited to 25 per test date
 (301) 496-6261

ARMY (FORT MYER)
Civilian Personnel Office
Building 469, Room 401
Fort Myer, Virginia 22211-5050
Appointment Only (202) 696-3180/3036

DEPARTMENT OF THE ARMY
Hoffman Civilian Personnel Office
Military District of Washington
200 Stovall Street
Room 1S39, Hoffman II
Alexandria, Virginia 22332-0800
Appointment Only (703) 325-8840

NAVY (CRYSTAL CITY)
1921 Jefferson Davis Hwy.
Crystal Mall Building, Building 2
S. Arlington, Virginia 20376-5006
Appointment Only (202) 692-9554

DEFENSE LOGISTICS AGENCY
DASC-KSE Cameron Station
Building 6, Room 214
Alexandria, Virginia 22304-6130
Appointment Only (202) 274-7087/88

VETERANS ADMINISTRATION
 (CENTRAL OFFICE)
810 Vermont Ave., NW., Room 115
Washington, D.C. 20420
Appointment Only (202) 233-2459

GEOLOGICAL SURVEY
12201 Sunrise Valley Drive, Room 1A315,
 MS-215
Reston, Virginia 22092
Appointment Only (703) 648-6131

DEPARTMENT OF DEFENSE
 (PENTAGON)
Directorate for Personnel and Security
Pentagon, Room 3A346
Washington, D.C. 20310-1155
Appointment Only (202) 697-1062

AGRICULTURE (HEADQUARTERS)
Room 1078, South Building
14th St. and Independence Ave., SW.
Washington, D.C. 20250
Walk-in Test Tuesday at 8:00 a.m. and
 11:30 a.m.; limited to 20 per test date
 (202) 447-5625

DEPARTMENT OF COMMERCE
Bureau of the Census
Personnel Division
Suitland, Maryland 20746
Appointment Only (301) 763-7470

BOLLING AFB
Main Entrance
Building P20, Room 240
Washington, D.C. 20332-5000
Appointment Only (202) 767-5449

INTERNAL REVENUE SERVICE
1111 Constitution Ave., NW., Room 1501
Washington, D.C. 20224
Appointment Only (202) 682-2617

OFFICE OF PERSONNEL MANAGEMENT
Office of Washington Area Examining Operations

OCCUPATIONAL DUTY SHEET

Secretary
GS-318

DUTIES OF THE POSITION: Secretaries are responsible for the performance of a variety of tasks, including telephone and receptionist duties; scheduling appointments and conferences; receiving mail and preparing replies; reviewing outgoing mail; maintaining records and files; making travel arrangements; assembling and disassembling information; transmitting staff instructions; and performing stenographic or typing services when required.

QUALIFICATION REQUIREMENTS: Applicants for these positions must have had progressively responsible experience of the length shown in the table below and of the nature described in the paragraphs following.

Grade	Total Experience
GS-3	6 months at the next lower grade level or equivalent experience.
GS-4 or 5	1 year at the next lower grade level or equivalent experience.
GS-6	6 months at the next lower grade level or equivalent experience.
GS-7 through GS-9	6 months at the next lower grade level or equivalent experience or 1 year at the second lower grade level.

QUALIFYING EXPERIENCE FOR GS-3: Candidates must have a general background in the performance of routine clerical duties which demonstrate all of the following:

- basic knowledge of office routines and functions sufficient to refer visitors and telephone calls and to route correspondence by name or functional area;

AND

- knowledge of clerical practices and procedures sufficient to file material and obtain requested information from the file;

AND

- knowledge of spelling, punctuation, and syntax sufficient to identify and correct grammatical errors.

QUALIFYING EXPERIENCE FOR GS-4: Candidates must have a background in the performance of a variety of clerical duties which demonstrates all of the following:

- working knowledge of many different office procedures such as those needed to request a variety of office equipment, supplies, publication material, and maintenance services, when each of these requires a different procedure;

AND

- ability to understand an organization and its functions sufficient to establish file systems for classifying, retrieving, and disposing of materials; refer telephone calls and visitors; distribute and control mail; maintain leave records; and provide general and non-technical information.

QUALIFYING EXPERIENCE FOR GS-5 AND ABOVE: Candidates must have a background in the performance of a variety of clerical duties which demonstrates all of the following:

- ability to organize effectively the flow of clerical processes in an office;

AND

- ability to organize and design a filing system;

AND

- ability to make arrangements for such things as travel, conferences, meetings;

AND

- ability to locate and assemble information for various reports, briefings, and conferences;

AND

- ability to compose non-technical correspondence.

SUBSTITUTION OF EDUCATION FOR EXPERIENCE: Except for any requirement for passing performance tests to demonstrate skill in shorthand and or typing (when required), the following will apply:

Grade	Education
GS-3	1 academic year of full-time business school or 1 academic year of education above the high school level.

GS-4   2 academic years of full-time business school or
                        2 academic years of education above the high
                        school level.

GS-5   4 academic years of education in an accredited
                        college or university.

There is no substitution of education for experience above the GS-5 level.
Thirty semester hours or 45 quarter hours or equivalent is considered one year
of academic study.

BASIS OF RATING: Applicants will be rated on achievements, training and information contained in their Supplemental Qualifications Statement (EWA-505) and
Personal Qualifications Statement (SF-171).

FORMS TO FILE: Standard Form 171 (Personal Qualifications Statement)
                  OPM 1203-X (Form B, Employment Availability Statement)
                  SSW-560 (Supplemental Instructions for Completing OPM Form
                         1203-X)
                  EWA-505 (Supplemental Qualifications Statement for Secretarial
                         Positions)
                  SSW-32 (Supplemental Qualifications Statement) - self-certifi-
                         cation of proficiency.

ASPIRE HIGHER WITH THE POWER... OF WORDS!

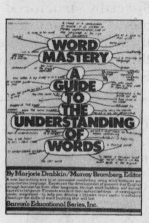

504 ABSOLUTELY ESSENTIAL WORDS
$6.95, Can. $9.95 (3702-2)
Builds practical vocabulary skills through funny stories and cartoons plus practice exercises.

BUILDING AN EFFECTIVE VOCABULARY
$7.95, Can. $10.95 (2041-3)
Covers all the methods of evaluating words to improve communication skills.

1001 PITFALLS IN ENGLISH GRAMMAR
$8.95, Can. $11.95 (3719-7)
Examines the most common errors in the English language.

1100 WORDS YOU NEED TO KNOW
$6.95, Can. $9.95 (2264-5)
This book is the way to master more than 1100 useful words and idioms taken from the mass media.

WORD MASTERY: A Guide to the Understanding of Words $6.95, Can. $9.95 (0526-0)
Enhances word use and word development through the presentation of words in such natural settings as newspapers and magazines. Practice exercises are included.

WRITE YOUR WAY INTO COLLEGE
$7.95, Can. $10.95 (2997-6)
A step-by-step guide to writing an effective college application essay. Actual student essays are included with helpful critiques.

GETTING YOUR WORDS ACROSS
$7.95, Can. $10.95 (2082-0)
The unique basic vocabulary book that uses brief articles, exercises and crossword puzzles to build word power.

HANDBOOK OF COMMONLY USED AMERICAN IDIOMS $5.95, Can. $7.95 (2816-3)
With 1500 popular idioms, this book will benefit both English-speaking people and those learning English as a second language.

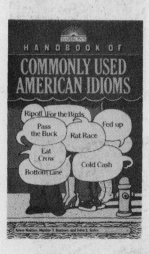

BARRON'S EDUCATIONAL SERIES
250 Wireless Boulevard
Hauppauge, New York 11788
Canada: Georgetown Book Warehouse
34 Armstrong Avenue
Georgetown, Ontario L7G 4R9

Prices subject to change without notice. Books may be purchased at your bookstore, or by mail from Barron's. Enclose check or money order for total amount plus sales tax where applicable and 10% for postage and handling (minimum charge $1.50, Can. $2.00). All books are paperback editions.

MAXIMIZE YOUR MATH SKILLS!

BARRON'S EASY WAY SERIES

Specially structured to maximize learning with a minimum of time and effort, these books promote fast skill building through lively cartoons and other fun features.

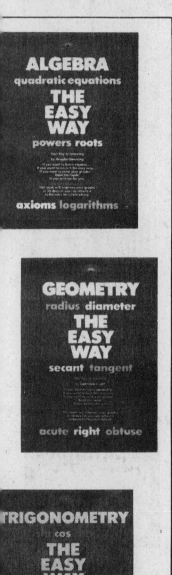

ALGEBRA THE EASY WAY
Revised Second Edition
Douglas Downing, Ph.D.
In this one-of-a-kind algebra text, all the fundamentals are covered in a delightfully illustrated adventure story. Equations, exponents, polynomials, and more are explained. 320 pp. (4194-1) $9.95, Can. $13.95

CALCULUS THE EASY WAY
Revised Second Edition
Douglas Downing, Ph.D.
Here, a journey through a fantasy land leads to calculus mastery. All principles are taught in an easy-to-follow adventure tale. Included are numerous exercises, diagrams, and cartoons which aid comprehension. 228 pp. (4078-3) $9.95, Can. $13.95

GEOMETRY THE EASY WAY
Lawrence Leff
While other geometry books simply summarize basic principles, this book focuses on the "why" of geometry: why you should approach a problem a certain way, and why the method works. Each chapter concludes with review exercises. 288 pp. (2718-3) $9.95, Can. $13.95

TRIGONOMETRY THE EASY WAY
Douglas Downing, Ph.D.
In this adventure story, the inhabitants of a faraway kingdom use trigonometry to solve their problems. Covered is all material studied in high school or first-year college classes. Practice exercises, explained answers and illustrations enhance understanding. 288 pp. (2717-5) $9.95, Can. $13.95

FM: FUNDAMENTALS OF MATHEMATICS
Cecilia Cullen and Eileen Petruzillo, editors
Volume 1 (2501-6) — Formulas; Introduction to Algebra; Metric Measurement; Geometry; Managing Money; Probability and Statistics. 384 pp. $14.95, Can. $21.00
Volume 2 (2508-3) — Solving Simple Equations; Tables, Graphs and Coordinate Geometry; Banking; Areas; Indirect Measurement and Scaling; Solid Geometry. The ideal text/workbooks for pre-algebra students and those preparing for state minimum competency exams. They conform with the New York State curriculum, and follow units recommended by the New York City Curriculum Guide. 384 pp. $12.95, Can. $17.95

SURVIVAL MATHEMATICS
Edward Williams
Presented here are refreshing, practical new math concepts for basic computational skills. Numerous practice exercises build competency skills. 416 pp., $9.95, Can. $13.95 (2012-X)

Books may be purchased at your bookstore, or by mail from Barron's. Enclose check or money order for total amount plus sales tax where applicable and 10% for postage (minimum charge $1.50, Can. $2.00). All books are paperback editions. Prices subject to change without notice.

Barron's Educational Series, Inc.
250 Wireless Boulevard
Hauppauge, New York 11788
In Canada:
Georgetown Book Warehouse
34 Armstrong Ave.
Georgetown, Ontario L7G 4R9